Nineteenth-century English

The study of the recent history of English is crucial in making connections between early and present-day English. This volume focuses on the nineteenth century, an important period of both stability and change for the English language. Through ten detailed case studies, it highlights the relationships between English, its users and nineteenth-century society, looking particularly at gender differences and variation across genres. It also discusses major structural aspects of nineteenth-century English, such as nouns, verbs and adjectives, and Germanic vs Romance vocabulary. Although the nineteenth century is often viewed as a relatively stable period in the development of the language, this volume shows the 1800s to be a time of significant change, some of which continued into the twentieth century. By making comparisons possible with both earlier and later periods, it makes an important contribution to our overall understanding of the history of the English language.

MERJA KYTÖ is Professor of English Language at Uppsala University, Sweden.

MATS RYDÉN is Professor Emeritus of English Language at Uppsala University, Sweden.

ERIK SMITTERBERG is a Post-doctoral Research Fellow in English Linguistics at Stockholm University, Sweden.

STUDIES IN ENGLISH LANGUAGE

The aim of this series is to provide a framework for original studies of English, both
present-day and past. All books are based securely on empirical research, and represent
theoretical and descriptive contributions to our knowledge of national varieties of
English, both written and spoken. The series covers a broad range of topics and
approaches, including syntax, phonology, grammar, vocabulary, discourse, pragmatics
and sociolinguistics, and is aimed at an international readership.

General editor
MERJA KYTÖ (Uppsala University)

Editorial Board
BAS AARTS (University College London), JOHN ALGEO (University of Georgia),
SUSAN FITZMAURICE (Northern Arizona University), RICHARD HOGG (University
of Manchester), CHARLES F. MEYER (University of Massachusetts)

Already published

CHRISTIAN MAIR   *Infinitival Complement Clauses in English: a Study of Syntax
in Discourse*

CHARLES F. MEYER   *Apposition in Contemporary English*

JAN FIRBAS   *Functional Sentence Perspective in Written and Spoken Communication*

IZCHAK M. SCHLESINGER   *Cognitive Space and Linguistic Case*

KATIE WALES   *Personal Pronouns in Present-day English*

LAURA WRIGHT (ed.)   *The Development of Standard English, 1300–1800: Theories,
Descriptions, Conflicts*

CHARLES F. MEYER   *English Corpus Linguistics: Theory and Practice*

STEPHEN J. NAGLE and SARA L. SANDERS (eds.)   *English in the Southern United
States*

ANNE CURZAN   *Gender Shifts in the History of English*

KINGSLEY BOLTON   *Chinese Englishes*

IRMA TAAVITSAINEN and PÄIVI PAHTA (eds.)   *Medical and Scientific Writing in
Late Medieval English*

ELIZABETH GORDON, LYLE CAMPBELL, JENNIFER HAY, MARGARET
MACLAGAN, ANDREA SUDBURY and PETER TRUDGILL   *New Zealand English:
Its Origins and Evolution*

RAYMOND HICKEY (ed.)   *Legacies of Colonial English*

Nineteenth-century English

Stability and change

Edited by

MERJA KYTÖ
Uppsala University, Sweden

MATS RYDÉN
Uppsala University, Sweden

ERIK SMITTERBERG
Stockholm University, Sweden

CAMBRIDGE UNIVERSITY PRESS

CAMBRIDGE UNIVERSITY PRESS
Cambridge, New York, Melbourne, Madrid, Cape Town, Singapore, São Paulo, Delhi

Cambridge University Press
The Edinburgh Building, Cambridge CB2 8RU, UK

Published in the United States of America by Cambridge University Press, New York

www.cambridge.org
Information on this title: www.cambridge.org/9780521117241

First published 2006
This digitally printed version 2009

A catalogue record for this publication is available from the British Library

ISBN 978-0-521-86106-9 hardback
ISBN 978-0-521-11724-1 paperback

Contents

Plates

Figures

Tables

Contributors

INGEGERD BÄCKLUND is a Docent and retired Senior Lecturer in English Linguistics at Uppsala University (Sweden). Her research interests include present-day spoken and written English syntax as well as various aspects of academic and professional writing, such as metatext.

TONY FAIRMAN is a teacher of English as a Second or Foreign Language, with experience in Britain, Germany and Africa. He has published on pedagogical matters and more recently on Late Modern English.

PETER GRUND, who is currently doing post-doctoral research at the University of Michigan, Ann Arbor, received his PhD in English Linguistics from Uppsala University in 2004. In his thesis he presented an edition of an Early Modern English alchemical text. His research interests include English historical linguistics, historical genre analysis, manuscript studies and editing.

LARISA OLDIREVA GUSTAFSSON received her PhD in English Linguistics from Uppsala University in 2002. In her thesis she investigated variation in the use of preterite and past participle forms in Early and Late Modern English. She is currently working on Late Modern English grammatical theory.

CHRISTINE JOHANSSON received her PhD in English Linguistics from Uppsala University in 1995, and is now a Senior Lecturer in English Linguistics at Uppsala University. She has published on the use and distribution of relativizers in past and Present-day English.

MARK KAUNISTO is a Post-doctoral Research Fellow at the Department of English, University of Tampere (Finland). His research interests include historical and present-day word-formation processes in English, morphology, and corpus linguistics. In his PhD thesis, he examined the variation and change in the use of English adjective pairs ending in *-ic/-ical*.

MERJA KYTÖ is Professor of English Language at Uppsala University. She specializes in historical linguistics and corpus studies. She has participated in the compilation of various historical corpora, among them the Helsinki Corpus of

English Texts. Her current research projects include work on a volume devoted to characteristics of spoken interaction of the past in collaboration with Dr Jonathan Culpeper (Lancaster University, UK).

Professor Dr CHRISTIAN MAIR holds a Chair at Albert-Ludwigs-Universität in Freiburg (Germany). He has contributed significantly to advances in modern corpus linguistics by compiling the Freiburg updates of the LOB (Lancaster-Olso/Bergen) and Brown corpora, FLOB (Freiburg-LOB) and Frown (Freiburg-Brown) and by developing corpus methodology as regards, among other things, the use of the *Oxford English Dictionary* in linguistic investigations. His current research interests include recent change in English and developments in Late Modern English.

SUZANNE ROMAINE has been Merton Professor of English Language at the University of Oxford since 1984. Her research interests lie primarily in historical linguistics and sociolinguistics, and she has published extensively in areas such as societal multilingualism, linguistic diversity, language change, language acquisition and language contact. She has conducted fieldwork in Europe as well as in the Pacific Islands region. Her other areas of interest include corpus linguistics, language and gender, literacy and bilingual/immersion education.

JUHANI RUDANKO is Professor of English at the University of Tampere. He has worked on aspects of English grammar, including the system of English predicate complementation and its development in recent centuries, and on pragmatics and the application of pragmatic theory to the study of Shakespeare; he has also published on the early history of the American Bill of Rights.

MATS RYDÉN is Professor Emeritus of English Language at Uppsala University. He has published widely on Early and Late Modern English syntax, on topics such as relative markers, the *be/have* variation with intransitives, and the progressive. His current research interests include the history of botanical terminology in English.

ERIK SMITTERBERG received his PhD in English Linguistics from Uppsala University in 2002; he is currently a Post-doctoral Research Fellow in English Linguistics at Stockholm University. His thesis topic, the progressive in nineteenth-century English, reflects his specific interest in Late Modern English syntax and corpus linguistics.

TERRY WALKER is a Senior Lecturer in English at Mid-Sweden University. She received her PhD in English Linguistics from Uppsala University in 2005; the topic of her thesis was variation and development in the use of *you* and *thou* in Early Modern English dialogues. Her research interests include historical pragmatics, sociolinguistics, variation studies and the compilation of historical corpora.

Acknowledgements

Many scholars will agree that knowledge of the past is necessary for a full understanding of the present. Nineteenth-century English, the subject of this book, is part of the linguistic past, but is also close enough to the present to give a modern impression in many respects. Partly as a consequence of this seemingly intermediate status, the English of the 1800s has received comparatively little attention from language historians. The ten case studies in the present volume aim at compensating for this relative dearth of research; they also shed light on the tension between stability and change which is shown to characterize nineteenth-century English.

In preparing this volume, we have received generous assistance from fellow scholars as well as academic institutions. It is our pleasure to acknowledge their contributions here.

We would first like to recognize the contribution of the International Conferences on the English Language in the Late Modern Period 1700–1900, held at Edinburgh in 2001 and at Vigo in 2004. These conferences have greatly increased interest in the study of Late Modern English, and helped us to come into contact with many researchers interested in the language of this period.

Financial contributions from several organizations have facilitated the completion of the present volume. We wish to thank the Department of English at Uppsala University, the Faculty of Humanities and Social Sciences at Örebro University, the Department of English at Stockholm University, and Helge Ax:son Johnsons stiftelse.

Many thanks are due to our fellow scholars who have contributed to this volume, for entrusting us with their studies and for responding to editorial suggestions in a highly co-operative spirit. We also gratefully acknowledge the valuable feedback we received on the manuscript from three anonymous readers. Finally, we thank Helen Barton, the linguistics editor at Cambridge University Press, for her kind support during the preparation of this book.

The Editors

Introduction: Exploring nineteenth-century English – past and present perspectives

MERJA KYTÖ, MATS RYDÉN AND
ERIK SMITTERBERG

1 Introduction

The structure and use of the English language has been studied, from both synchronic and diachronic perspectives, since the sixteenth century.[1] The result is that, today, English is probably the best researched language in the world. But the field is as unlimited as language itself, and therefore there will always be gaps in our knowledge of the historical development of English as well as of its time-bound, or synchronic, uses. In this respect, Late Modern English (1700–1950) has been given less scholarly attention than other periods in the history of English. This is particularly true of the nineteenth century and the first half of the twentieth century. The main reason why this period has been relatively ignored by historical linguists is presumably that at first sight it appears little different from Present-day English, resulting in the view that not much has happened in the language in the course of the last 200 years or so (for discussion, see Romaine 1998a: 7; Rydén 1979: 34; Rydén and Brorström 1987: 9). As Beal (2004: xi) points out, until the millennium the nineteenth century was also 'the last century' from a contemporary scholar's perspective. The recency of nineteenth-century developments may have added to the view that the language of this period was not an interesting topic for historical research, where the 'antiquity' of the English language has often been in focus.

However, knowledge of the immediate or recent past is often crucial for our understanding of the language of the present day. Thus it is important to connect research on earlier periods, including Late Modern English, and on Present-day English into a coherent account aiming at a synthesis of the historical development of the English language. Areas of research such as verb syntax and the enrichment of the lexicon would benefit from such a coherent treatment. Moreover, such research should cover both stability and change in language. Yet the nineteenth century 'remains largely an unexplored territory' in this context (Kytö, Rudanko and Smitterberg 2000: 85; cf. also Denison 1998: 92). However, there are a number of relevant monographs such as Arnaud (1973), Dekeyser (1975) and Smitterberg (2005). Romaine (1998b) has also contributed greatly to our

1

knowledge of nineteenth-century English, and Poutsma (1914–29) remains an important source of information. In addition, there are some recent overviews of nineteenth-century English, such as Bailey (1996) and Görlach (1998 and 1999). These studies invite rather than preclude further research, and above all, they indicate that there is a rising scholarly interest in nineteenth-century English.[2]

A few *contemporaneous* studies of nineteenth-century linguistic usage exist, such as Andersson (1892) (relative clauses), Ljunggren (1893–4) (*shall/will*), Palmgren (1896) (temporal clauses) and Western (1897) (*can/may/must*). Also worthy of mention in the context of nineteenth-century English studies are Koch's and Mätzner's grammars (first issued in the 1860s) and Sweet's *A New English Grammar* (published in 1891 and 1898), which is the first modern English grammar written by an Englishman.[3] The language of great nineteenth-century authors has also received some scholarly attention.[4] A study on metaphors like Stitt (1998), bridging the gap between linguistic and literary studies, should also be noted here.

In the form of ten specialized case studies, the present volume aims to provide an overview of some intriguing aspects of nineteenth-century English that will shed new light on the language of this period. For reasons discussed in section 2.2, the variety in focus in most of the case studies is the standard language used in nineteenth-century South-Eastern England. This Introduction addresses some central methodological issues involved, and outlines the case studies, with special reference to the ways in which they illuminate both stability and change in nineteenth-century English.

2   Corpus linguistics and nineteenth-century English

2.1   The corpus-based approach

Most of the studies included in the present volume are based on data drawn from electronic text or citation collections, which are now considered the mainstay of empirical linguistic research. For Present-day English, the compilation of the seminal Brown and LOB (Lancaster-Oslo/Bergen) corpora, representative of 1960s usage, provided an impetus for a huge upsurge in research. Their structure has since been paralleled by other corpus compilers in order to enable the study of short-term linguistic change (e.g. by comparisons with the 1990s LOB and Brown 'clones', Freiburg-LOB and Freiburg-Brown) as well as regional variation (e.g. the Kolhapur corpus and the Wellington Corpus of New Zealand English).[5] In the 1980s, the compilation of the Helsinki Corpus of English Texts, comprising c. 1.5 million words, was a landmark in the historical study of the English language, from the Old English period up until the early 1700s. Since then, there has been an ever-growing interest in the compilation of historical corpora of English. However, as yet, computerized corpora covering the 1800s (and the early 1900s) have not been many (valuable exceptions include the ARCHER Corpus (A Representative Corpus of Historical English Registers), which covers but does not specifically focus on the nineteenth century, and the Corpus of Late Modern English Prose, which covers the period 1861–1919 and centres on letters and journals).[6] This lack of interest in compiling corpora devoted to nineteenth-century English is probably a reflection of, among other things, the above-mentioned deceptive similarity to Present-day English exhibited by the language of the 1800s.

As regards Present-day English, the possibility of collecting texts representative of the language as a whole, from a linguistic as well as an extralinguistic perspective, offers new possibilities for linguistic research. As implied above, for the period following 1960 we have corpora including a wide variety of spoken as well as written genres. This availability of relevant texts enables an approach to language variation that takes medium into account as an extralinguistic parameter. Thus the researcher need not rely on genres consisting of speech recorded in writing, intended to represent speech. The immediate descriptive and pedagogical applications of corpora covering learner English and/or a wide spectrum of native-speaker Present-day English also influence corpus compilation. Moreover, compared with earlier periods, it is easy to correlate present-day linguistic data with extralinguistic factors not only on the textual level (e.g. cross-genre studies), but also on the level of the language user. This is because the characteristics of individual language users with respect to parameters such as social network structure, socioeconomic status and education are comparatively easy to ascertain and can be coded for as part of the compilation process. Most such user-related variables are more difficult to code for within a diachronic framework, gender being the main exception.[7]

2.2   The nineteenth-century perspective

In addition to the need for analysing nineteenth-century English as a link between Present-day and earlier periods of English, there are also reasons internal to the nineteenth century that justify the study of this period. Some of them are related to the comparatively rich and varied textual material available to us from this century. Owing to the spread of literacy during the 1800s, we have access to written texts produced by a greater proportion of all language users than is the case for any preceding period (however, as Tony Fairman's contribution to the present volume shows, the concept of literacy itself needs to be addressed in more detail). This is especially true as regards female language users: the nineteenth century thus offers promising possibilities of investigating the gender variable as a factor in language change (see below). In addition, research on the Brown, LOB, Frown and FLOB corpora has shown that as short a time span as thirty years may be sufficient to observe changes in linguistic usage, provided that the researcher has access to a sufficiently large corpus. The possibility of correlating short-term linguistic change in nineteenth-century English with the many important sociopolitical developments that took place during this period further adds to the potential of this approach to the study of linguistic variation.

The nineteenth century is also characterized by genres becoming more and more diverse in their linguistic make-up; for instance, the language of formal expository genres like academic writing and that of informal non-expository genres such as private letters diverge increasingly (see Biber and Finegan 1997: 272–3). In addition, the nineteenth century was crucial to the development of some genres that were to become (or remain) highly influential in the century that followed. Not only private letters, but also newspaper language, the novel and scientific discourse belong to this group of genres. These characteristics make nineteenth-century English a vital period for researchers interested in genre and cross-genre studies from a synchronic as well as a diachronic perspective.

Finally, the 1800s constitute a formative period in the development of many extraterritorial varieties of English. The nineteenth century is important with regard to the divergence of American and Canadian English from British English, and probably even more important as regards the development of Southern Hemisphere varieties of English. A full description of nineteenth-century English thus requires a broad regional scope: results valid for one regional variety of nineteenth-century English cannot safely be claimed to hold for the English language as a whole.

However, focusing on one variety may provide scholars with a useful starting-point for comparisons. Accordingly, the majority of the case studies included in the present volume are based on Standard English English, the most extensively researched variety across the centuries so far. From a diachronic perspective, they thus further our understanding of the development of Standard Englishes. At the same time, in synchronic terms, they help to establish a background against which nineteenth-century extraterritorial and non-standard varieties can be contrasted. A study such as Tony Fairman's (this volume) points to the potential of such a comparative perspective.

2.3   The CONCE project and the present volume

Given the wide range of research possibilities and the shortage of available corpora, any one corpus project must be selective in terms of attempting to capture the spectra of variation existing in nineteenth-century English. The present volume is, for the most part, a result of one such corpus project, launched at the Departments of English at Uppsala University and the University of Tampere in the mid-1990s. The aim of the project was to compile CONCE (A Corpus of Nineteenth-century English), a one-million-word corpus focusing on English English, and to produce research based on this new source of linguistic data.

Regardless of which period in the history of English researchers focus on, they are likely to take an interest in language variation and change. In investigating language change, scholars may carry out a synchronic study of a past stage of the language, such as nineteenth-century English, for comparison forwards and/or backwards in time. In this perspective, they may use CONCE as a synchronic whole and compare the results with those attested for, say, Early Modern English

Table 0.1. *Word counts for period samples in CONCE and for the whole corpus, excluding the words within reference codes and text-level codes.*

Period	Total
1 (1800–1830)	346,176
2 (1850–1870)	341,842
3 (1870–1900)	298,796
Total	986,814

or Present-day English. In the present book, this research strategy is used by, for instance, Juhani Rudanko, in his study of the pattern *in -ing* in the nineteenth and twentieth centuries.

However, scholars may also chart the development of a linguistic feature within a single historical stage of the English language. As mentioned above, recent studies based on the LOB, FLOB, Brown and Frown corpora are indicative of an increasing interest in such short-term linguistic change. Reflecting this research interest, the texts in CONCE have been stratified into three subperiods, covering, broadly speaking, the beginning, middle and end of the nineteenth century, viz. 1800–30 (period 1), 1850–70 (period 2), and 1870–1900 (period 3). This division makes it possible to study short-term developments across the 1800s.

The texts in CONCE have been coded using text-level and reference codes based on those applied to the Helsinki Corpus (see Kytö 1996b), making it possible to exclude, for instance, foreign language and headings from the counts. However, the system used for CONCE is slightly more rigorous, enabling the exclusion of passages such as stage directions in plays (see the Appendix for a full list of text-level codes). Table 0.1 presents word counts per period for the CONCE corpus.[8]

The division of the texts in CONCE into periods of several decades rather than single years, as with corpora such as LOB and FLOB, was a necessary compromise between the interests of (a) obtaining a sufficiently narrow periodization for cross-period comparisons to be reliable, and (b) including only texts that reflect authentic nineteenth-century English. In addition, important extralinguistic developments in England during the nineteenth century were taken into account. For instance, period 1 predates most of the political reforms of nineteenth-century England (e.g. the Reform Bills), while period 3 follows many of them (see Kytö, Rudanko and Smitterberg 2000: 87). Most studies in the present volume make use of this periodization in attempts to reveal diachronic variation within nineteenth-century English; for instance, Peter Grund and Terry Walker's study of the subjunctive in adverbial clauses traces the development of this verb form in relation to indicatives and modal auxiliaries across the century.

Table 0.2. *Description of the genres in CONCE.*

Genre	Characteristics
Debates	Recorded debates from the Houses of Parliament
Trials	Trial proceedings (in dialogue format)
Drama	Prose comedies including farces
Fiction	Novels
Letters	Personal letters (between relatives or close friends)
History	Historical monographs
Science	Monographs pertaining to the natural or social sciences

However, merely looking at texts from different historical periods of English may not be enough to identify the locus of the change under scrutiny, as linguistic change is frequently mediated through other extralinguistic parameters as well as time. Considering such parameters becomes even more important when relevant extralinguistic developments have taken place within and/or between the period(s) covered by the investigation. In the present volume, two extralinguistic parameters receive special attention: genre and gender.

Multi-feature/multi-dimensional analyses of both Present-day English and historical stages of the language, such as Biber (1988), Biber and Finegan (1997) and Geisler (2002, 2003), have shown that the frequency of a large number of linguistic features co-varies in texts, so that a given genre is characterized by different co-occurrence patterns along dimensions of linguistic variation. These patterns may also change across time, and Biber and Finegan's (1997) study indicates that the nineteenth century is of central importance in displaying increasing *genre diversity* in terms of linguistic make-up. The divisions between, on the one hand, oral, popular and/or non-expository genres, and, on the other hand, literate, specialized and/or expository genres are of particular relevance in this respect. In some cases, differences in the distribution of linguistic features across the genre parameter can also be used as a cross-section of linguistic change, with advanced genres representing a later stage in the development. However, accounting for this diversity requires that the researcher sample a range of genres. This requirement was one of the criteria used in the compilation of CONCE.

The original aim of the CONCE project was to provide comparative nineteenth-century follow-up material to the Helsinki Corpus of English Texts. Consequently, several genres are present in both corpora in order to increase comparability. In particular, it was deemed important to sample both speech-related and non-speech-related genres, and both formal and informal written genres, in order to enable research on how the use of nineteenth-century English varied according to the parameters of medium and formality. A brief description of the seven genres included in CONCE is given in table 0.2 (from Kytö, Rudanko and Smitterberg 2000: 88).

Table 0.3. *Word counts for period, genre and period/genre subsamples in CONCE and for the whole corpus, excluding the words within reference codes and text-level codes.*

Period	Debates	Trials	Drama	Fiction	Letters	History	Science	Total
1	19,908	62,360	31,311	42,032	121,624	30,904	38,037	346,176
2	19,385	60,570	29,543	39,045	131,116	30,504	31,679	341,842
3	19,947	67,588	29,090	30,113	90,891	30,564	30,603	298,796
Total	59,240	190,518	89,944	111,190	343,631	91,972	100,319	986,814

In addition, the fact that the texts in CONCE have been stratified with respect to both time and genre makes it possible to combine these two parameters in analyses of how linguistic change is reflected across the genre parameter. As implied above, for some changes this will result in a diversified picture with some genres being more advanced than others for each particular change. Table 0.3 (from Kytö, Rudanko and Smitterberg 2000: 89) presents word counts by period and genre for the CONCE corpus (for the full list of source texts, see the Appendix).

Reflecting the make-up of CONCE as well as the importance of the genre parameter, many of the contributions to this book focus on cross-genre variation. Among others, Christine Johansson considers three of the genres in CONCE in an analysis of the use of relative clauses in nineteenth-century English.

As regards gender, the rich textual material available from the nineteenth century makes it possible to investigate the interaction of several factors that, according to previous research, increase differences between female and male usage. Labov (2001: 292–3) claims that, on the whole, women will conform more than men to prestige norms if these norms are specified overtly; conversely, in processes of change from below, which take place below the level of normative consciousness, women tend to be leaders in linguistic change. There are several ways in which nineteenth-century English is an excellent testing ground for comparisons of these different influences on female and male usage. First, as mentioned above, the percentage of female literates increases dramatically during the 1800s (see Altick 1957: 171). Consequently, texts produced by women are more readily available in the nineteenth century than previously. Secondly, nineteenth-century attitudes to language variation embodied a largely prescriptive attitude on the part of grammarians. This attitude resulted in a number of grammars in which some lexical and morphosyntactic variants were promoted at the expense of others (see e.g. Dekeyser 1975, who compares precept and usage as regards number and case relations in nineteenth-century English, and Denison 1998: 150–8, who studies the emergence and diffusion of the progressive passive). The 1800s thus afford more data concerning

Table 0.4. *Word counts for the letters by female and male writers in CONCE, excluding the words within reference codes and text-level codes.*

Period	Female	Male
1	69,271	52,353
2	62,340	68,776
3	50,154	40,737
Total	181,765	161,866

both usage and precept than most other periods in the history of English (see section 2.2).

Reflecting the importance of gender aspects in nineteenth-century English, CONCE was compiled to enable a gender perspective on language variation and change. In an effort to include both women's and men's voices, the Letters genre has been stratified in order to include the same number of texts by female and male letter-writers. The necessity of reducing idiolectal influence on the overall figures meant that more informants were sampled for the Letters genre than for the other genres: each period includes five texts by female letter-writers and five by male letter-writers.[9] The Letters genre may be regarded as especially suitable for studying the interaction of the gender parameter, change from above and below and linguistic precept. It constitutes a written category that is influenced by spoken and/or colloquial norms; moreover, in general, private letters are not normally intended for publication. Considering these production circumstances, the texts in Letters can be expected to contain both language that has been influenced by the norms promoted in grammars, and less self-monitored language. Word counts by period and gender in Letters are given in table 0.4 (from Kytö, Rudanko and Smitterberg 2000: 90).

Strictly, the letter-writers have in fact been coded according to their biological sex rather than their socioculturally established gender identity. However, given that the differences in language use between women and men attested in the CONCE data are likely to be due to gender rather than sex, and in the interests of simplicity and consistency, we will use the term 'gender' to refer to the parameter. Many of the studies contained in this volume investigate linguistic variation with gender by comparing female and male usage; for instance, Ingegerd Bäcklund looks at how terms for women and men were modified linguistically in nineteenth-century English.

Needless to say, the parameters of genre and gender can be studied simultaneously, and several studies in the present volume combine the two. This approach has great potential, as a cross-genre comparison may reveal stylistic grading in the distribution of a linguistic feature, a finding that can then serve as the background for a study of differentiation between women's and men's language. Merja Kytö and Suzanne Romaine use this perspective in an analysis of adjective comparison in CONCE.

However, a volume such as this, which aims to provide an overview of nineteenth-century English from several angles, cannot rely solely on extant corpora. There are both linguistic and extralinguistic reasons for extending the scope of the material studied beyond that currently covered by corpora. To begin with, the study of low-frequency features may reveal results that are of great theoretical and methodological significance; but a historical corpus like CONCE does not, on its own, provide sufficient material for all such investigations. In addition, in spite of the enlargement of the franchise and the spread of literacy during the 1800s, the texts which have been sampled in electronic corpora by and large reflect the language used by the upper echelons of nineteenth-century society. In order to provide a fuller picture, it is therefore necessary to sample texts outside those available in computerized corpora. Christian Mair's and Tony Fairman's contributions reflect this need to go beyond corpora when approaching particular research questions. Basing his research on the *OED* on CD-ROM, with its vast quotation database, Mair investigates verb complementation after *remember*. Fairman has compiled his own material, which includes pauper letters written chiefly between 1800 and 1834, in order to investigate the written language of these, often barely literate, letter-writers and compare some aspects of their production with those attested in letters by more fully schooled and wealthier people.

3   Empirical evidence of nineteenth-century English: stability and change

The studies included in this volume illustrate nineteenth-century English on several levels. As discussed in section 1, nineteenth-century English is of particular interest because it displays what may be termed a deceptive similarity to present-day usage in many respects. Some features of the English language have remained stable in the past 200 years; others, however, have developed over time. Reflecting this tension between stability and change, some studies included in the present work did not reveal evidence of language change in progress, pointing rather to stability and linguistic continuity. Other studies, in contrast, unearthed new evidence of differences across time.

In diachronic studies, the focus is often on linguistic change. However, linguistic stability is also an essential object of study, as the possibility of tracing conditioning factors, both linguistic and extralinguistic, allows comparison of the situations that appear to encourage change with those which seem to promote stability (Raumolin-Brunberg 2002: 102; see also Rydén 1979: 19). Linguistic stability is not a concept exclusive to nineteenth-century English: as Raumolin-Brunberg (2002) has shown, linguistic features may exhibit stability for centuries. However, the 1800s offer linguists excellent opportunities of relating their results to extralinguistic parameters, such as sociopolitical events and stylistic judgements (as observed in style manuals, grammar books, etc.), that may promote either change or stability. Given its importance, the stability vs change parameter is taken into account in the overview (below) of the studies in this volume.

It is of course difficult to group studies as focusing on either linguistic stability or change: many diachronic investigations yield evidence of both, depending on factors such as the level of analysis chosen (e.g. subperiodization scheme, the range of genres and informants included, and the level of detail in linguistic analyses). Nevertheless, a tentative grouping of the studies can be established on this parameter, based on dominating trends in the data. Of the ten studies included in the volume, three present results that highlight stability rather than change, as against the five that emphasize change over stability. In two studies, the starting-point and/or the results do not justify a conclusive classification in this respect. These three groups of studies will be presented in that order below.

Drawing for data chiefly on the Science genre of CONCE, Larisa Oldireva Gustafsson shows that continuity rather than change characterizes the use of the passive in nineteenth-century scientific writing, although there is a great deal of variation among the authors represented. In fact, this variation is found to underlie some of the apparent changes in Gustafsson's data, such as the higher frequency of passives in simple sentences towards the end of the century (subordinate clauses constitute the most frequent locus of passives in all periods, however). Gustafsson shows that there are also considerable differences in usage between scientific texts and private letters written by the same person (Charles Darwin), as also found by Mark Kaunisto with regard to *that of/those of* constructions.

The overall frequency of the passive in the Science genre remains stable across the 1800s, despite the variation among authors mentioned above. Neither does the distribution of the passive across the parameters of tense, aspect and mood seem to change dramatically across the 1800s, small increases in the relative frequency of future passives, perfect passives and indicative passives notwithstanding: present-tense indicative passives that are unmarked for aspect dominate the distribution in all periods. There is shown to be a good deal of continuity with Present-day English regarding which main verbs are used most commonly in passives in scientific writing. The author concludes that the development of the passive as a characteristic feature of English scientific writing is most likely to have taken place before the nineteenth century. The results also imply that genre is a more important parameter than time regarding the use of the passive from 1800 onwards.

Christine Johansson analyses the use of relativizers in nineteenth-century English, and the distribution of *that* and *wh*-forms (*who, whose, whom* and *which*) in particular. She shows that at least in Trials, Science and Letters, *wh*-forms are used much more frequently than the relativizer *that*. In Present-day English, *that* has been gaining ground, but this development was still in its early stages at the end of the nineteenth century. Of special interest in her study is the attention paid to the use of relativizers across speaker roles in Trials, and the gender-based differences in Letters. The use of *that* could not be linked with speaker roles such as 'members of the legal profession' and representatives of other occupations. *That* is slightly more common in the letters written by women, but overall, it is rare in nineteenth-century correspondence. There is, however, variation in individual (female or male) writing styles, with some writers using relative clauses with *that* more frequently than other writers. Johansson also takes a closer look at typical syntactic environments of *that* and *wh*-forms (for example, sentential relative clauses, cleft sentences and pronominal antecedents).

The use of the anaphoric pronouns *that/those* in connection with a following *of*-phrase, as in 'I hope my <u>moral code</u> is nearly as good as *that of* my neighbours' (from a play by Thomas Holcroft), is investigated by Mark Kaunisto. In Present-day English these constructions are generally associated with expository writing and formal communication situations. Kaunisto shows that, in the nineteenth century, 'the use of *that of/those of* structures had already become fully established, at least as regards its relative frequency'. According to the results obtained by Kaunisto, this frequency is relatively low, and there are tangible differences between genres. The *that of/those of* constructions occur most frequently in formal discourse such as Debates, Science and History, leaving Fiction, Letters, Drama and Trials with fewer occurrences across the century.

The data also show variation in the 'anaphoric distance', i.e. the distance between the pronoun and its referent, from zero to over twenty words. Interestingly, there appears to be a degree of correspondence between the relative frequency of the *that of/those of* constructions and the anaphoric distance across the genres: in genres characterized by frequent use of the constructions above, the anaphoric distance is also greater. On average, the greatest distances are found in Debates and Science, and the shortest in Drama and Trials, suggesting an association between formality and degree of anaphoric distance.

In contrast to the three studies described above, a total of five studies, introduced below, present results which suggest that linguistic change was in progress regarding the feature studied. As was the case for the studies that pointed to stability, the parameters of genre and gender have often been found to be important conditioning factors on the variation attested.

In her analysis of modifiers of common nouns with female and male reference, such as *person, creature, woman, lady, man, gentleman, mother* and *father*, Ingegerd Bäcklund shows how the nineteenth-century use of female and male terms can, to a certain extent, be taken to mirror the separate spheres of women's and men's lives. The adjectives modifying male terms tend to refer to social status whilst those modifying female terms more often refer to women's appearance. Men thus appear as powerful individuals, active in the public sphere, whereas women appear as submissive, dependent and gentle in their domestic sphere. At the same time the results obtained may suggest, to some extent, that the changing role of women in the nineteenth century was reflected in the descriptions of women and girls.

A number of interesting differences emerged when the use of modifiers by female and male writers was investigated. Whilst both groups increasingly used modifiers across the century (female authors notably so towards the end of the century), male writers used more modifiers than female writers. There were also differences in the kind of modifiers used by female and male writers. For instance, the male writers in the material were more prone to refer to women in negative terms than were female writers; they also used negative modifiers about women more often than about men. In texts by female writers, it is female reference that dominates, whilst in men's texts men are referred to more often than women.

Linguistic change in progress can also be observed in Peter Grund and Terry Walker's study of the subjunctive in adverbial clauses in nineteenth-century English. Using data drawn from the entire CONCE corpus, Grund and Walker include subjunctive verb phrases, indicative verb phrases and verb phrases containing modal auxiliaries in their investigation in order to enable a detailed analysis of the competition between these paradigmatic options. Adopting a broad definition of semantic equivalence, and defining the subjunctive in morphosyntactic terms, they are thus able to compare the relative incidence of forms such as '. . . if the temperature *be increased*' (subjunctive), '. . . if the Queen *was deposed*' (indicative), and '. . . unless something *should occur*' (modal).

The study shows that the indicative increased at the expense of both the subjunctive and verb phrases with modal auxiliaries especially towards the end of the century, but also that the ratio of subjunctives to modal auxiliaries actually increased, suggesting that 'the indicative rather than constructions with modal auxiliaries was the preferred alternative to the subjunctive, especially in the speech-related genres'. The importance of the genre parameter is also clear from the fact that subjunctives were more common in genres characterized by informational production rather than involved production in Geisler's (2002) factor score analysis of the CONCE corpus; formal registers also seem to favour the subjunctive. Among the linguistic factors studied is the type of subjunctive verb phrase: it is shown that the frequency of the subjunctive form *be*, as well as that of subjunctive forms of verbs other than BE declined sharply over the nineteenth century, whereas the subjunctive form *were* proved more resistant.

Merja Kytö and Suzanne Romaine explore variation in adjective comparison in nineteenth-century English. This variation involves rivalry between the historically older inflectional forms (e.g. *happier/happiest*), and the periphrastic constructions (e.g. *more/most elegant*). Instances of the double forms (*more quicker*, *most delightfulest*) were very rare in the material. The analysis revealed a steady increase in the use of inflectional forms throughout the period studied. As in previous studies of adjective comparison, word structure, notably word length and the nature of word endings, was shown to constrain variation. For example, as early as in the Early Modern English period, word endings such as *-ous* (e.g. *gracious*) and *-ful* (*painful*) promoted the use of the periphrastic form in disyllabic adjectives. As regards syntactic functions and the use of comparative forms, usage in the last decades of the nineteenth century resembled that of the present day.

The analysis of some central extralinguistic factors revealed a great deal of variation across the seven genres and three subperiods. The importance of stylistic factors such as the need by speakers for emphasis and clarity was found partly to account for the anomalies in the results obtained. The gender parameter also influenced the distributions of the variants: there was variation in the ways in which male and female letter writers used inflectional and periphrastic forms. For instance, male writers commonly used *dearest* in addressing women (mostly wives, sisters or mothers), but only seldom when writing to male addressees. However, *dearest* was used by female writers to female addressees when they addressed each other as well as men (mostly husbands). Forms such as *dearest, dearest*, or *dearest dear*, or the superlative followed by title rather than first name, e.g. *My dearest Mrs. Martin*, found in the letters by women writers, pointed to the intimate nature of their discourse.

Exploiting the citation database of the *Oxford English Dictionary*, Christian Mair presents interesting evidence of continuous change in usage in the past two centuries regarding nonfinite clausal complements of the verb *remember*. The use of the construction comprising *remember* + NP + *V-ing* has been on the increase but not at the expense of the gerundial construction with the genitive/possessive subject, held to be 'correct' by prescriptivists. The *remember* + NP + *V-ing* construction emerged simultaneously with the related construction with the genitive/possessive, and was firmly established in nineteenth-century usage. Thus there is little or no foundation for the prescriptive arguments that have given historical precedence to the possessive case in gerundial constructions depending on *remember*, with regard to full noun phrases and probably also pronouns. Mair ascribes the subsequent preference for the genitive in formal written English to the victory of 'the prescriptively minded stylistic conservatives'. In overall terms, retrospective infinitival complements were not only replaced by gerunds but there was also an additional increase in the use of the gerund, probably due to a decrease in the use of finite-clause complements. Mair concludes that 'it was during the nineteenth century that the way was prepared irreversibly for the emergence of present-day usage conventions'.

In another study covering the nineteenth and twentieth centuries, Juhani Rudanko investigates the development of a narrowly defined linguistic feature, viz. *in -ing* constructions that function as complements of matrix verbs, as in 'The Titans delight *in upsetting* the odds'. He examines the occurrence of this construction in the CONCE and LOB corpora, as well as two subcorpora of the Bank of English corpus (the London *Times* newspaper segment and the spoken British English segment).

Rudanko's study shows that linguistic change has taken place regarding the *in -ing* construction. The range of matrix verbs that select the construction has broadened semantically. In both CONCE and the twentieth-century corpora, matrix verbs that belong to the semantic group 'engage in', e.g. *succeed*, predominate; however, his twentieth-century data also contain a noticeable proportion of matrix verbs belonging to the group 'be contained in', e.g. *consist*, of matrix verbs of emotion, e.g. *delight*, and of the matrix verb *believe*. The occurrence of matrix verbs belonging to the group 'be contained in' is also relevant to the interpretation of the understood subject of the *-ing* clause. With matrix verbs of the 'engage in' type, the understood subject of the *-ing* clause is interpreted as coreferential with that of the superordinate clause; when the matrix verbs belong to the 'be contained in' type, however, the interpretation of the understood subject is more context-dependent. Although Rudanko's investigation does not explicitly address cross-genre variation, the clear differences attested between the two subcorpora of the Bank of English regarding both the overall frequency of the *in -ing* construction and the matrix verbs selecting it suggest that the parameters of genre and medium are relevant to the use of the construction.

As mentioned above, there are two studies which cannot be classified as highlighting either change or stability. Focusing on less-schooled language, Tony Fairman investigates documents from English Record Offices, primarily from the early nineteenth century. Fairman considers word choice (Anglo-Saxon vs Latinate) as well as spelling in his account. He shows that many less than fully schooled writers had difficulty spelling words with a non-Germanic stress pattern, and that the percentage of Latinate words in letters varied greatly depending on whether the writer was fully or minimally schooled. Fairman also shows that the spelling of surnames varied depending on the strategy used by the person who wrote down the name of the less-schooled writer.

Fairman contextualizes his study by examining contemporaneous textbooks and syllabuses. He emphasizes the importance of examining the division between Germanic and Latinate lexis, the ways in which schooled English spread – or failed to spread – to writers of unschooled English, and the classification of less schooled English. As the empirical part of Fairman's approach is synchronic, the division between change and continuity is not immediately relevant to his study. By examining a type of language that has so far been comparatively neglected by, for example, editors, Fairman makes the present volume more representative of nineteenth-century English as a whole.

Erik Smitterberg gives evidence of both continuity and change in his study of partitive constructions consisting of a partitive noun followed by the preposition *of* and a prepositional complement, as in 'a *bit of advice*', in the CONCE corpus. He shows that the overall frequency of partitive constructions was stable across time. However, there are considerable cross-genre differences, suggesting that partitives are characteristic chiefly of texts reflecting informational rather than involved production; this impression is strengthened by an analysis of gender differences in the frequency of partitives. Similarly, a classification of the partitives into five semantic groups showed that there was little diachronic variation in the material regarding the relative frequency of these groups, while there were clear cross-genre differences. In general, expository genres tended to have a high percentage of quantitative partition, while non-expository genres presented a more varied picture, with higher percentages of partitives of quality, shape, time and intensity.

In contrast to the above, an analysis of verbal concord with partitives where the partitive noun and the complement of the preposition *of* do not agree in number showed tendencies towards linguistic change, in which the complement increasingly governed concord. However, definite conclusions are difficult to reach for two main reasons. First, partitive nouns and prepositional complements may differ as regards their tendency to control verbal concord, depending partly on semantic connections with the rest of the sentence. Secondly, a case study of partitives with the partitive noun *number* showed that there was no significant difference between nineteenth- and twentieth-century English with respect to concord, and that syntactic factors may affect concord choice.

4   Concluding remarks

The aim of the present volume is to provide an overview of nineteenth-century English by way of empirical studies of various features exhibiting both stability and change. Many of the studies included have emphasized the importance of genre and gender as extralinguistic factors conditioning language use. Moreover, the fact that most of the studies are based on the same, structured corpus increases the comparability of the results. At the same time, given the limitations of any closed corpus, it is clear that, for some research purposes, it is important to draw material from sources outside the corpus.

This volume does not claim to fill in all the gaps in our knowledge of nineteenth-century English. For instance, Fairman's study highlights the importance of considering the language of less than fully schooled people as regards nineteenth-century English as a whole. Generally speaking, non-standard varieties of English (e.g. social and regional dialects) deserve more scholarly attention, as do, for example, Scottish, Irish, and extraterritorial varieties of the language (see e.g. Beal 2004; Kortmann 2004; Hickey 2004). Beyond the nineteenth century, we need corpus-based, empirical studies of early twentieth-century English, another period as yet underexplored regarding both standard and non-standard varieties. We hope that the studies in this volume will encourage further research in these important areas.

Notes

1. Examples of early scholars include John Palsgrave (d. 1554) as 'a pioneer in vernacular language description' (see Stein 1997) and Richard Mulcaster (d. 1611) as a linguist (see Polifke 1999). Regarding interest in the systematic study of Old English texts in Elizabethan England, see Adams (1917) and Graham (2000).
2. Diachronic studies of the whole of the twentieth century are even more rare than studies of the nineteenth century. Exceptions include Övergaard (1995), Westin (2002) and Mair (2006). Brorström (1963), Lindkvist (1950) and Rydén and Brorström

(1987) cover all or part of the Modern English period, including the first half of the twentieth century. The last-mentioned work was the main outcome of a project entitled 'Late Modern English Syntax 1700–1900', which was launched by Mats Rydén at the English Department, Stockholm University, in 1983.

3. On nineteenth-century prescriptive grammars, see Görlach (1998). Interestingly, the first reasonably comprehensive book on the history of the English language, R. G. Latham's *The English Language*, was first published in 1841 (5th edn 1862). It is a combination of a grammar and a history of English (see Quirk 1961a).

4. These writers include e.g. Swinburne (Serner 1910), Carroll (Sutherland 1970), Thackeray (Phillipps 1978) and Hardy (Elliott 1984). Austen and Dickens, in particular, have attracted attention, as seen from studies by, for instance, Phillipps (1970), Page (1972), and Stokes (1991) on Austen, and Quirk (1961b and 1974), Gerson (1967), Brook (1970), and Sørensen (1985 and 1989) on Dickens.

5. In addition, corpora of spoken English have been compiled, such as the London–Lund Corpus. More recently, corpora sampled on an unprecedented scale, such as the British National Corpus, have been made available, as have various corpora of learner English.

6. The Lancaster1931 corpus, which is being compiled at Lancaster University, will be a very valuable tool for studies of early twentieth-century English.

7. However, it may be problematic even to find a sufficient number of texts produced by women for early periods in the history of English. The same largely holds for members of the lower socioeconomic ranks. A user-centred approach to language variation and change is of course also possible for earlier periods, as witnessed by studies such as Walker (2005). However, it is more difficult and time-consuming to carry out, as the data necessary both to construct a continuum such as that of socioeconomic status in for example the 1600s and to position language users of that time along this continuum are more difficult to come by.

8. If the Helsinki Corpus principles were applied to CONCE, the total word count would be 1,030,409. Some studies in the present volume draw on word counts calculated by other programs, which may lead to slight differences in the word counts applied.

9. The only exception to this sampling principle occurs in period 3, where a misleading period code necessitated the removal of one text by a female letter-writer from the corpus. In addition to Letters, Fiction also includes female novelists, and care was taken to represent female speakers as witnesses in Trials. However, in Fiction there are only three texts per period, and the speakers in Trials have not been coded for gender as part of the corpus mark-up. Thus, the Letters genre offers the best opportunities for studies of gender variation based on CONCE.

1 Modifiers describing women and men in nineteenth-century English

INGEGERD BÄCKLUND

1 Introduction

The investigation presented here concerns modifying expressions used in descriptions of real or fictional women and men by nineteenth-century female and male writers. The aim is to study whether, in these descriptions, the social changes that occurred during the century, especially in the role of women, are reflected in linguistic change, and if so, to what extent. The expressions under investigation are modifiers such as *good-natured, sallow, troublesome* and *of fortune*, and they will be studied from a qualitative as well as a quantitative perspective.

During the nineteenth century, the notion that women and men belonged to separate spheres of society very much influenced the way gender roles were formed. This notion had its roots in eighteenth-century economic, social and political conditions, and practically every aspect of life was influenced by it (Kingsley Kent 1999: 154). Powerful and respectable men operated in the public sphere of work and politics; virtuous and dependent women reigned over the domestic sphere, 'where their authority over all matters pertaining to morality and civility went uncontested' (Kingsley Kent 1999: 147).

During the century, however, women challenged this notion of separate spheres. The women's movement developed and women demanded certain civil rights, access to education and, the most radical demand of all, the right to vote (Kingsley Kent 1999: 191–3; see also section 4.7 below). In 1869, Girton, the first college for women was founded and by and by, what Kingsley Kent (1999: 229) terms 'new women' were admitted to colleges and universities. Many women who accepted the importance of home and family nevertheless opposed the idea that women should restrict themselves to being 'Queens over their own hearths' (Lewis 1991: 6). It became important for them to take an active part in life outside their homes. Leading figures 'argued strongly for women's domestic talents to be put to use in local government and in local institutions – in workhouses, hospitals and schools – as well as in the homes of the poor within the local community' (Lewis 1991: 8). Obviously, this would mean widening the sphere of women, giving them greater mobility outside the home and active involvement in public affairs.

Thus the nineteenth century was a period during which gender roles and above all women's role in society underwent considerable change. At the beginning of the century, the notion of separate social spheres for women and men was firmly established; at the end of the century, the women's suffrage movement, dominated by middle-class women, had grown strong and the stage was set for the suffragettes' battle for the franchise at the beginning of the twentieth century (Leneman 1998: 37–8).

The aforementioned aim of this study is to try to pinpoint possible linguistic changes within a restricted area, that of modifying expressions, by investigating whether changes in gender roles and in social roles are reflected in the way females and males are described in nineteenth-century drama, fiction and private letters. Linguistic effects of the drastic changes in English society during the period in question are discussed by Görlach (1999: 41–3), and he also points to 'an awareness among a great number of educated speakers of social change and its reflection in linguistic change – including measures to retain social distance'. The present study will address questions such as: Does the consciousness of the changing social role of women and of their growing claims to full citizenship and legal rights seem to affect the descriptions of females in the course of the century? Are men described in the same way at the end of the century as at the beginning? To answer these and related questions the investigation will concentrate on discovering which modifiers are used together with certain frequent nouns referring to females and males. Another question to be addressed concerns possible differences in the use of such modifiers between female and male nineteenth-century writers. Finally, certain comparisons will be made between the results of the present study concerning the use of positive, negative and neutral modifiers and corresponding findings of Wallin-Ashcroft (2000), who deals with collocations with female and male terms in eighteenth-century novels.

2   Material

The data for the present investigation are taken from three of the genres in CONCE (A Corpus of Nineteenth-century English), namely Drama, Fiction and Letters (see the Introduction to the present volume). These genres were chosen because it was believed that they would contain a high number as well as a varied sample of premodifying adjectives and postmodifying *of*-phrases used in connection with female and male referring expressions. The Letters genre covers slightly more than a third of the CONCE corpus, Fiction and Drama about a tenth each (see Kytö, Rudanko and Smitterberg 2000: 88–9). The corpus is structured into three subperiods, 1800–30, 1850–70 and 1870–1900 (see Introduction). The sub-set used for this investigation includes all texts within the three genres in question, thus covering approximately 543,000 words, which equals 55 per cent of the CONCE corpus (cf. Kytö, Rudanko and Smitterberg 2000: 89). In this

Table 1.1. *Number of words by female and male writers per period in the sub-corpus.*

Period	Female writers	Male writers	Total
1 (1800–30)	88,869 (45%)	105,493 (55%)	194,362
2 (1850–70)	89,582 (45%)	109,783 (55%)	199,365
3 (1870–1900)	60,173 (40%)	89,271 (60%)	149,444
Total	238,624 (44%)	304,547 (56%)	543,171

sub-corpus, the category of Letters constitutes 63 per cent, Fiction 20 per cent, and Drama 17 per cent of the material. Thus Letters, the written genre which is generally regarded as closest to the colloquial stratum and most sensitive to language change clearly dominates in this study. It is hoped that this fact may make it possible to discover possible changes in the description of men and women that took place over the nineteenth century.

Table 1.1 shows the amount of text written by women and men within each period and in the sub-corpus as a whole. As the table shows, in all three periods more text is written by men than by women, and the difference is greatest in the last period. These differences will be taken into account in the analysis of the results.

With a few exceptions explained below, the data consist of all instances of certain nouns referring to females and males that are premodified by an adjective or postmodified by a non-genitival *of*-phrase, as in (1).

(1) *a gentleman of condition*
     (Letters, Charles Dickens, 1850–70, p. 538)

The investigation includes fifteen nouns. These have been chosen so as to allow comparisons with the results of Wallin-Ashcroft (2000). They correspond to the most frequent terms for females and males in Wallin-Ashcroft's three largest categories. She divides her female and male terms into six main categories; the majority of her tokens fall within three of those categories, namely *central epicene terms*, that is, basic terms for human beings excluding those that define gender, *central general terms*, which are basic terms that are gender-specific, and, finally, *relational terms*, referring to a person's standing in relation to other people. The latter two categories are subdivided into female and male terms. For my investigation I have chosen the three most frequent nouns from each of the five resulting categories, disregarding Wallin-Ashcroft's distinction between adult and non-adult terms. This has resulted in the following list of nouns:

• Epicene terms: *person, creature, child*
• General female terms: *woman, lady, girl*

- General male terms: *man, gentleman, fellow*
- Relational female terms: *mother, sister, daughter*
- Relational male terms: *father, brother, husband*

Obviously, the list above will not make comparisons possible between pairs of terms such as *husband–wife, boy–girl*, but this has not been regarded as crucial since the focus here is on modification, not on the nouns themselves.[1] They were selected only because it was expected that they would be frequent in the present corpus also.

From the CONCE sub-set described above all instances of the nouns in question that are premodified by adjectives or followed by *of*-phrases have been extracted.[2] A few instances containing certain types of adjectives or *of*-phrases have been excluded from the material. According to Warren (1984: 12) there are three possible functions for adjectives modifying nouns: they are characterizing/describing, classifying or identifying/specifying. In the present study, only noun phrases containing descriptive and characterizing expressions are included. This means that expressions such as *the only person, the very man, the same girl*, with restrictive adjectives (see Quirk et al. 1985: 430) are excluded from the data. The adjective in a noun phrase such as *her eldest daughter* is also categorized as identifying/specifying, and such phrases are thus omitted, as are *of*-phrases with genitive meaning, as in (2).

(2) *the daughter of these people*
     (Fiction, Theodore Edward Hook, 1800–30, p. II, 178)

In a few instances, phrases containing descriptive adjectives have also been excluded from the data. This is the case with two types of noun phrases, namely phrases where the word *lady* is used as a title, as in (3), and a few instances where the descriptive adjective is part of a title, as in (4).

(3) I've been dancing with *old Lady Ptarmigant*.
     (Drama, T. W. Robertson, 1850–70, p. 54)

(4) This, sir, is the '*Young Lady's Best Companion*,' [. . .]
     (Drama, T. W. Robertson, 1850–70, p. 57)

Finally, opening and closing phrases in letters, such as *Dear Mother* and *Your affectionate Father* have not been included among the data, since they may be regarded as formulaic and thus do not reflect a choice on the part of the author, in the same way as other premodifying adjectives, when it comes to describing or characterizing men and women.

3   Method

The noun phrases in the material have been classified according to period, genre, gender of author, gender of referent and semantic category of the adjectives or *of*-phrases. In connection with the classification of gender of referent, a few noun phrases were found where the head is an epicene term in the plural, referring to specified individuals, female and male, as in (5), or to female and male referents in general, as in (6). Such instances have been excluded from the material, since they, obviously, do not reflect possible differences in the descriptions of female and male referents.

(5) Now I should tell you that <u>Bilderdijk and his wife</u> [. . .] took me into their house at Leiden, [. . .] But it would take a longer letter than this to contain all that I could say of *these most excellent and most remarkable persons*.
(Letters, Robert Southey, 1800–30, p. 405)

(6) 'No, my dear; clergymen don't go out hunting; or how could they teach *the poor little children?*'
(Fiction, Charlotte Mary Yonge, 1850–70, p. I, 95)

Another small group that has been excluded from the investigation consists of noun phrases with an epicene noun in the singular whose referent either is not specified by the author of the novel or the play, as in (7), or is not mentioned in the context by the writer of the novel or the letter, as in (8).

(7) [. . .] he was not going up 'grumpums' by himself in a corner, with a fat woman, *a sick child*, a fine lady, and a drunken sailor; [. . .]
(Fiction, Theodore Edward Hook, 1800–30, p. III, 317)

(8) [. . .] she went to throw herself upon *the poor Child*'s grave [. . .]
(Letters, Sara Hutchinson, 1800–30, p. 51)

As a basis for the semantic categorization of the adjectives in the material, a model used by Hene (1984) has been adopted. For her study of how girls and boys are described in books for young Swedish-speaking readers from the middle of the twentieth century, Hene (1984) has created an elaborate system of classification, where adjectives are brought together in semantic fields at various levels. A general basis for this classification is whether the adjective is 'intrapersonal' or 'interpersonal'. Intrapersonal adjectives focus on the referent as an individual (*thin, sick, angry, quick*), whereas interpersonal adjectives describe the referent as a social being (*lonely, reserved, amiable, rich*) (Hene 1984: 40). Hene's classification includes twelve intrapersonal semantic fields and three interpersonal ones, all with a number of sub-fields (Hene 1984: 39–43). This model has been simplified and adapted slightly to suit the needs of the present more restricted study, so that the classification of adjectives and *of*-phrases here includes six intrapersonal categories and four interpersonal ones, all without sub-fields. The fields or categories, listed in alphabetical order, are as follows.

Intrapersonal categories	Interpersonal categories
Ability	Address
Age	Attitude
Appearance	Situation
Mental State	Sociability
Nationality	
Physical State	

Among the intrapersonal categories Age and Nationality are self-explanatory, whereas the scope of the other categories needs some clarification. First of all, however, it should be pointed out that neither in Hene (1984: 40) nor here is a distinction made between adjectives and, in the present study, *of*-phrases that denote a temporary state, such as *happy* and those that denote a more stable quality, such as *kind-hearted*. Both types are included in the same category, in this case Mental State, because in a categorization of the present type it may sometimes be difficult to draw a line between what is stable and what is temporary (Hene 1984: 40–1), as illustrated in (9)–(10).

> (9) Honora wrote to Mrs. Charteris for permission to dismiss the *mischievous* woman, and obtained full consent, [. . .]
> (Fiction, Charlotte Mary Yonge, 1850–70, p. I, 113)
> (10) I should be the most *ungrateful* creature if I did!
> (Drama, Tom Taylor, 1850–70, p. 292)

The category of Ability comprises items that denote talents, experience and knowledge, such as *musical, skilful, of learning*. The category of Appearance includes modifiers referring to looks, bodily constitution, and clothing, such as *pretty, stout, elegant*. The intrapersonal category of Mental State embraces adjectives and *of*-phrases that refer to mental properties and states, intelligence, will-power, character and mood. Examples are *kind, brilliant, obstinate, sensible, desperate*. To the category of Physical State, finally, belong modifiers that refer to life and health (*dead, sickly*) or physiological states or needs (*wide-awake, hungry*).

The four interpersonal categories are more diverse than the intrapersonal ones. In Hene's classification (1984: 43 and 230–3) the category of Address includes adjectives occurring in phrases of address, such as *good* in (11), as well as adjectives that modify nouns without actually describing their referents, such as *dear* in (12).

> (11) [. . .] Here, take this purse, *good* fellow.
> (Drama, Thomas Morton, 1800–30, p. 71)
> (12) The master of this house is a kind *dear* old fellow: [. . .]
> (Letters, William Makepeace Thackeray, 1850–70, p. 5)

Hene (1984: 43) treats these two uses as belonging to the same category because they say something about the attitude of the speaker rather than about the person referred to. In the present study, however, it was felt that more interesting observations might be made if the two uses were kept apart. Therefore instances such as *dear* in (12) have here been given a separate category, called Attitude. In this category are adjectives like *dear, little, old* and *poor*.

Of the remaining interpersonal fields, that of Situation comprises modifiers referring to people's social situation, that is, to their family relations and to the areas of work, economy, reputation and popularity, such as *widowed, of letters, rich, illustrious* and *honourable*. The last category in the list above has been termed Sociability, following Hene (1984), and it includes adjectives and *of*-phrases denoting attitudes, manners, behaviour, as well as assessment of attitudes etc. Examples of this category are *grave, genteel, motherly, sweet, weary*.

It is important to point out that in the semantic classification of modifiers in the material, it is the contextual meaning that has been decisive. This means, for instance, that the same lexical item may be assigned to different categories depending on context. An obvious example here is the word *poor*, which is sometimes classified as Situation and sometimes as Attitude.

In addition to the semantic categorization described above, each adjective or *of*-phrase has been classified according to whether it denotes a positive quality (+), a negative quality (−) or whether it might be thought of as neutral (+/−). Obviously, this is a subjective evaluation, even more difficult owing to the fact that the material is between a hundred and two hundred years old; nevertheless it has been included, since it was felt that such a classification might yield interesting results. In this admittedly impressionistic classification, I have followed Persson (1990: 52). Persson defines his criterion for 'plus words' as the answer to the question 'Is it generally thought better to be X than not to be X?' The 'minus words' are defined by the reverse question. Modifiers in instances where it was felt that no clear answer to either question could be given were regarded as neutral. With one or two exceptions depending on context, all items in the category of Age in the present study are classified as neutral. Words like *fat* and *thin* have also been classed as neutral, since, presumably, present-day connotations might not be valid, or at least not to the same degree, for nineteenth-century speakers. Only modifiers which could be regarded as clear cases are classified as positive or negative. Nonetheless, it is important to keep in mind what Görlach (1999: 8) observes concerning '[h]ow difficult a proper evaluation of 19th-century niceties can be'. Görlach states that 'where the "meaning" was obvious to language-conscious contemporaries, minimal stylistic distinctions can be lost on later readers who do not share the cultural and sociolinguistic background'.

Returning to the principles for the present classification, it should be mentioned that the adjective *poor* is naturally classified as negative when it refers to someone's financial situation. But also when it belongs to the category of Attitude, it has been classed as a minus word, even though it expresses positive feelings of affection and pity. It was felt, nevertheless, that an expression with *poor*, as in (13), has more negative connotations than, for instance, *dear* in (14).

(13) [$Lady B.$] My *poor − poor* boy!
    (Drama, T. W. Robertson, 1850–70, p. 92)

(14) [. . .] to do yourself and me and your *dear* mother credit.
    (Letters, Samuel Taylor Coleridge, 1800–30, p. 513)

Example (13) illustrates another decision in connection with the categorization: when adjectives are repeated for emphasis, as in (13), they have been counted as one occurrence of the adjective in question. This type of repetition, as well as other means of giving emphasis to expressions in the data, such as the use of the superlative, or words like *really*, *uncommonly* and *very*, has not been included in the present analysis.

To conclude the description of the categorization of modifiers used in the present study, it should be pointed out that borderlines between categories are sometimes fuzzy (cf. Hene 1984: 43). This applies above all to the borderline between the categories of Mental State and Sociability, since mental qualities, such as kindness or generosity are naturally apparent in the manners and behaviour of the person in question. The fuzziness may be illustrated by (15)–(16).

(15) She is really an *agreable* girl, so I think I may like her, [. . .]
(Letters, Jane Austen, 1800–30, p. 65)

(16) [. . .] and I have the snuggest little lodgings conceivable with a *motherly good* woman [. . .] to wait on me.
(Letters, George Eliot, 1850–70, p. 42)

Here *agreable* and *motherly* have been assigned to the category of Sociability, because they were felt to refer mainly to manners and behaviour, whereas *good* was classed as a Mental State term, referring to the person's character. It is hoped that this potential fuzziness in connection with some modifiers will not skew the results to any considerable extent.

4   Results

The presentation of my results opens with an overview of all modifiers in the material and their reference. (The expression 'the reference of a modifier' is used henceforth as an abbreviation for 'the reference of the noun that the modifier modifies'.) The distribution of modifiers across semantic categories and their reference is then presented, with certain categories of particular interest discussed in more detail. The presentation also includes strings of modifiers and modifiers consisting of non-genitival *of*-phrases. Next, the focus shifts to the use of modifiers by female versus male writers; similarities and differences in distribution across semantic categories are discussed. Following this comes a presentation of the results of the categorization of positive, negative and neutral modifiers, both in terms of reference and gender of writer. The category of Mental State is given extensive treatment in a separate subsection. Finally, some comparisons will be made with some results from an eighteenth-century corpus (Wallin-Ashcroft 2000).[3]

4.1   Overview

The sub-corpus yielded 1,148 phrases, 511 with female reference and 637 with male reference. The preponderance of male reference (55 per cent) is not unexpected. It has been shown in several studies that men are more often talked about

Table 1.2. *Distribution of modifiers with female and male reference over time.*

Period	Female reference	Male reference	Total
1	199 (45%)	248 (55%)	447
2	203 (40%)	308 (60%)	511
3	219 (48%)	242 (52%)	461
Total	621 (44%)	798 (56%)	1,419

Table 1.3. *Number of modifiers per 1,000 words.*

Period	Words	Modifiers	Modifiers/1,000 words
1	194,362	447	2.3
2	199,365	511	2.6
3	149,444	461	3.1
Total	543,171	1,419	2.6

than women (cf. for example Romaine 1999: 109; Persson 1990: 50; Hene 1984: 248). The noun phrases extracted contain 1,419 modifiers, of which 1,336 are adjectives, either single premodifiers or members of strings of modifiers, and 82 items (6 per cent) are postmodifying *of*-phrases. The distribution of modifiers with female and male reference across the three periods is shown in table 1.2. The table shows a drop in the percentage of modifiers with female reference between periods 1 and 2 followed by an increase between periods 2 and 3 (and conversely, a decrease in the proportion of male reference in period 3), so that towards the end of the century female reference is nearly as common as male reference (48 per cent vs 52 per cent).

As regards density of modifiers, table 1.3 shows the number of occurrences per 1,000 words in the three periods and in the material as a whole. Table 1.3 reveals that there is an increase in the use of modifiers in the course of the century. Görlach (1999: 158–60) points to a development from a 'classical' prose style in many pre-1830 texts to a more elaborated 'romantic' style in later periods. This might explain the increase in the use of modifiers that is found in the present study. Phillipps (1984: 41–2) discusses a statement by Meredith (quoted in Phillipps 1984: 36) saying that English upper-class speech 'is characterized by a lavish use of vowels and adjectives'; Phillipps finds that, as far as adjectives are concerned, the same observation has been made by other writers as well: adjectives, especially 'enthusiastic epithets' are frequent. All Phillipps's quotations are from the latter half of the century and, possibly, the increase in the use of modifiers in the present material is a reflection of this characteristic of upper-class speech reported towards the end of the century. Another possible reason would

Table 1.4. *Distribution of intrapersonal vs interpersonal semantic categories over time.*

Period	Intrapersonal	Interpersonal	Total
1	242 (54%)	205 (46%)	447
2	268 (52%)	243 (48%)	511
3	295 (64%)	166 (36%)	461
Total	**805 (57%)**	614 (43%)	1,419

be that the change is a result of an increase in the frequency of nouns, at the expense of pronouns, in the texts examined. In order to get a rough indication of whether this hypothesis might be supported empirically, a search was run for the forms *he* and *she* unambiguously tagged as 'pronoun', and for the forms *him* and *her* unambiguously tagged as 'oblique pronoun' (excluding genitive functions of *her*), in a version of CONCE that has been tagged using the EngCG–2 tagger. However, the results did not seem to imply change: in the texts examined for the present study, there were 21 such forms per 1,000 words in period 1, 18 in period 2, and 20 in period 3.

4.2   Semantic categories

As mentioned above, the modifiers have been grouped into ten categories depending on their meaning in the given context. These semantic categories are of two kinds: intrapersonal, with modifiers focusing on the person as an individual, and interpersonal, with modifiers describing the individual in interplay with other people. The account of the semantic categories in the material begins with an overview of intrapersonal vs interpersonal modifiers in general and their distribution over time, followed by their distribution regarding female and male reference. An account of the distribution of semantic categories within the two groups is then given, followed by a more detailed analysis of some of the categories.

Table 1.4 shows that in all three periods intrapersonal modifiers are more common than interpersonal ones. The difference is greatest in period 3. In period 1 and period 2, there is but a slight preponderance of the intrapersonal modifiers, whereas period 3 shows a considerably larger proportion of intrapersonal modifiers; focusing on people as individuals rather than in relation to others has apparently become more important. These differences over time are statistically significant.[4]

Table 1.5a shows the distribution of modifiers with female reference between intrapersonal and interpersonal semantic categories and table 1.5b the corresponding figures for male reference. Tables 1.5a and 1.5b show that the increase in intrapersonal modifiers in period 3 occurs in descriptions of both women and

Table 1.5a. *Distribution of modifiers with female reference between intrapersonal and interpersonal semantic categories.*

Period	Intrapersonal	Interpersonal	Total
1	99 (50%)	100 (50%)	199
2	110 (54%)	93 (46%)	203
3	146 (67%)	73 (33%)	219
Total	355 (57%)	266 (43%)	621

Table 1.5b. *Distribution of modifiers with male reference between intrapersonal and interpersonal semantic categories.*

Period	Intrapersonal	Interpersonal	Total
1	143 (58%)	105 (42%)	248
2	158 (51%)	150 (49%)	308
3	149 (61%)	93 (41%)	242
Total	450 (56%)	348 (44%)	798

men. But it is also clear that the relative frequency of intrapersonal modifiers in that period is higher for modifiers with female reference than for those with male reference (67 per cent vs 61 per cent). Thus, in period 3 women and girls are described by their inherent qualities rather than by their social characteristics considerably more often than in earlier periods and also more often than men are thus described. The differences over time per category in tables 1.5a and 1.5b are statistically significant; the overall differences between female and male reference (the last rows of the tables) are not ($p > 0.05$).[5] It is above all in the category of Appearance that the relative increase in female reference occurs, as shown in table 1.6a.

Tables 1.6a and 1.6b reveal that the intrapersonal categories are very different as regards size. Owing to low expected frequencies in certain categories, significance tests have not been carried out on the data in tables 1.6a and 1.6b. The following observations might be of interest, however. With both types of reference, the largest categories are those of Age and Mental State, together covering 74 per cent of the female instances and 81 per cent of the male ones. Modifiers belonging to the categories of Ability, Nationality and Physical state, on the other hand, occur rather seldom. A comparison of the two tables, however, reveals certain differences between the categories as regards reference. For the largest category, Mental State, there is a decrease in modifiers with male reference

Table 1.6a. *Distribution of female reference across intrapersonal categories.*

Period	Ability	Age	Appearance	Nationality	Mental	Physical	Total
1	2 (2%)	34 (34%)	18 (18%)	4 (4%)	39 (39%)	2 (2%)	99
2	0 (0%)	52 (47%)	10 (9%)	3 (3%)	41 (37%)	4 (4%)	110
3	1 (1%)	47 (32%)	36 (25%)	8 (5%)	52 (36%)	2 (1%)	146
Total	3 (1%)	133 (37%)	64 (18%)	15 (4%)	132 (37%)	8 (2%)	355

Table 1.6b. *Distribution of male reference across intrapersonal categories.*

Period	Ability	Age	Appearance	Nationality	Mental	Physical	Total
1	10 (7%)	41 (29%)	12 (8%)	1 (1%)	71 (50%)	8 (6%)	143
2	13 (8%)	58 (37%)	6 (4%)	2 (1%)	72 (46%)	7 (4%)	158
3	2 (1%)	66 (44%)	18 (12%)	1 (1%)	56 (38%)	6 (4%)	149
Total	25 (6%)	165 (37%)	36 (8%)	4 (1%)	199 (44%)	21 (5%)	450

over time, whereas those with female reference are more stable. This means that mental qualities of women and girls are mentioned equally often in descriptions from all three periods, whereas for men such modifiers are less frequent in period 3, compared to earlier periods. However, it should be noted that, for all periods, modifiers denoting mental qualities are more frequent in descriptions of men than in those of women and girls. In the second largest category, that of Age, table 1.6a shows a relative decrease in female reference between period 2 and period 3, whereas table 1.6b shows a steady increase in male reference over all three periods.

The third largest category, that of Appearance, has already been mentioned as the intrapersonal category where female reference increases considerably in period 3: from 9 per cent to 25 per cent. In this category, an increase occurs also for modifiers with male reference, between period 2 and period 3, but with fewer instances; here the rise is from 4 per cent to 12 per cent. This means, generally speaking, that in descriptions of people more attention is paid to outward appearance and looks towards the end of the century than in earlier periods. However, tables 1.6a and 1.6b also show that for all three periods, it is mainly the appearance of girls and women that is referred to. Moreover, Nationality and Appearance are the only intrapersonal categories where the instances with female reference are more numerous than those with male reference. This dominance of female reference becomes even more marked when one considers that the relative frequency of female reference in the material as a whole is 44 per cent (cf. table 1.2).

Table 1.7a. *Distribution of female reference across interpersonal categories.*

Period	Address	Attitude	Situation	Sociability	Total
1	29 (29%)	27 (27%)	16 (16%)	28 (28%)	100
2	23 (25%)	32 (34%)	13 (14%)	25 (27%)	93
3	12 (16%)	20 (27%)	18 (25%)	23 (32%)	73
Total	64 (24%)	79 (30%)	47 (18%)	76 (28%)	266

Table 1.7b. *Distribution of male reference across interpersonal categories.*

Period	Address	Attitude	Situation	Sociability	Total
1	9 (9%)	34 (32%)	33 (31%)	29 (28%)	105
2	49 (33%)	36 (24%)	39 (26%)	26 (17%)	150
3	20 (22%)	29 (31%)	26 (28%)	18 (19%)	93
Total	78 (22%)	99 (28%)	98 (28%)	73 (21%)	348

If the total frequencies for each period displayed in tables 1.6a and 1.6b are considered, it is found that the intrapersonal modifiers with male reference are equally distributed over periods (no. of instances: 143, 158, 149), whereas for those with female reference, period 3 has a much larger share (no. of instances: 99, 110, 146). This means that the inherent qualities of men are mentioned equally often in all three periods, whereas towards the end of the century, women are not only referred to with modifiers relatively more often (cf. table 1.2), but they are also described more often as individuals than in relation to others. If the totals for each semantic category in tables 1.6a and 1.6b are compared, the differences between female and male reference are statistically significant.[6]

As regards the interpersonal modifiers, those which describe a person as a social being, frequencies and the distribution of reference over semantic categories are shown in tables 1.7a and 1.7b.[7] These tables reveal that the interpersonal categories are more equal in size than the intrapersonal ones (cf. tables 1.6a and 1.6b).[8] The largest interpersonal category, for both types of reference, is Attitude, reflecting the attitude of the writer towards the referent. This group is closely followed by that of Sociability in the descriptions of women and girls, and by that of Situation in the descriptions of men. For the latter category a comparison between tables 1.7a and 1.7b shows a fairly even distribution across the periods for modifiers of Situation with male reference, whereas for those with female reference there is a relative increase from 14 per cent in period 2 to 25 per cent in period 3. Thus, although men are more often than women described with modifiers referring to their social status, economy or reputation in all three periods, it appears that, towards the end of the century, the social situation of women is referred to nearly as often as is that of men. For the category of Sociability, the picture is different. Here a comparison between tables 1.7a and 1.7b shows that in period 1, modifiers of Sociability, which denote attitudes, manners and behaviour, are equally frequent with female and male reference (28 per cent). In period 3, on the other hand, these modifiers have become more frequent in descriptions of women and girls (32 per cent) and considerably less frequent in descriptions of men (19 per cent). Tables 1.7a and 1.7b also show that the category of Sociability is the only interpersonal category where there are more instances with female reference than with male reference. The difference is small but should be compared with the proportion of female reference in general, which is 44 per cent (cf. table 1.2).

To turn to the category of Address, the figures for female reference (table 1.7a) and for male reference (table 1.7b) show an uneven distribution across the periods. In period 1, modifiers are used considerably more often when the person addressed is a woman than when he is a man: 29 vs 9 per cent. In period 2, there is a sharp rise in male reference: from 9 to 33 per cent. In period 3, finally, there is a drop of about 10 percentage points with regard to both genders. These figures reflect certain differences among genres within the category of Address. In the first period, twenty-nine of the thirty-eight (29+9) instances come from Drama, and twenty-one of those have female reference, as in (17) below. In the second period, forty-two of the seventy-two instances (49+23) occur in Letters and thirty-four of the forty-two instances refer to males. With the exception of two instances, all these are found in letters from Charles Darwin, mostly to his son, and they all take the form 'My dear/est old man/fellow', as exemplified in (18). In the third period, finally, the instances are fewer and here sixteen of the thirty-two occurrences (12+20) come from Fiction. Among those, there is one instance of female reference; all the rest are of the form 'young man/gentleman', as in (19).

(17)   Nay, *my sweet young lady*, how could she act otherwise, [. . .]
       (Drama, Thomas Holcroft, 1800–30, p. 40)

(18)   Farewell *my dear old man*.
       (Letters, Charles Darwin, 1850–70, p. VII, 97; p. VIII, 466)

(19)   '*Young man*,' he said, 'you know nothing. Your ignorance is shameful.'
       (Fiction, Walter Besant, 1870–1900, p. II, 244)

Finally, the largest of the interpersonal categories in tables 1.7a and 1.7b is that of Attitude. This category is different from the others in several respects. Here, as mentioned earlier, the modifier, rather than characterizing the referent, reflects the writer's attitude towards the person in question. Another difference has to do with type/token ratio: in this category there are fewer types than in other categories and there is a marked dominance of two adjectives. Among the 178 instances (79+99) shown in tables 1.7a and 1.7b, only eleven different adjectives are represented. There are eighty-two occurrences of *poor*, sixty-six of *dear*, eighteen of *little*, and five of *good*. The remaining seven adjectives occur only once each. Regarding female and male reference among modifiers denoting Attitude, the figures in tables 1.7a and 1.7b show that modifiers expressing the attitude of the speaker/writer towards the person in question are used roughly as often about women as about men in all three periods.

To sum up: the data consist of 805 intrapersonal modifiers and 614 interpersonal ones. The preponderance of intrapersonal modifiers is most pronounced in the third period; to focus on a person as an individual rather than in relation to others thus becomes more common towards the end of the century (table 1.4). This relative increase in intrapersonal modifiers occurs in descriptions of both women and men but is most marked in the descriptions of women, so that in period 3, female reference of intrapersonal modifiers is relatively more frequent than male reference (tables 1.5a and 1.5b). The increase in female reference in the intrapersonal category occurs above all in the category of Appearance. In this category, there is a predominance of female reference in all three periods and a considerable increase in female reference in period 3 (tables 1.6a and 1.6b). The intrapersonal categories are very uneven in size: the two largest, Age and Mental state, together account for 74 per cent of the modifiers with female reference and 81 per cent of those with male reference. For the Mental State category, male reference is more frequent than female reference in all three periods, whereas for the category of Age, proportions vary slightly between the periods.

The interpersonal modifiers, that is, the modifiers that describe the referent in relation to society or other people, are less frequent than the intrapersonal ones. The four categories are fairly equal in size although the category of Attitude is the largest (tables 1.7a and 1.7b). In the category of Situation, denoting a person's social status, economy or reputation, male reference is more common in all three periods, but, in period 3, there is an increase in female reference, so that towards the end of the century, the social situation of women is referred to nearly as often that of men. For the category of Sociability, which reflects manners and behaviour, the proportions in period 1 are the same for female and male reference, whereas in periods 2 and 3, women and girls are described with such modifiers more often than men. Regarding the category of Address, the distribution of female and male reference varies with genre and period in the sub-corpus. In the period 1800–30, there is a predominance of female reference, and the instances come mostly from Drama. In the periods 1850–70 and 1870–1900, male reference is more frequent than female; in the middle period, male instances come mainly from personal letters, in the last period from Fiction. Finally, in the category of Attitude, female and male reference are more or less equally common throughout the material. This category is different from all the others in that very few types of modifiers are used, and two adjectives, *dear* and *poor*, account for 84 per cent of the instances.

Table 1.8. *Distribution of strings of modifiers with female vs male reference.*

	2 modifiers		3 modifiers		4 modifiers		5 modifiers		
Period	Female	Male	Female	Male	Female	Male	Female	Male	Total
1	19	28	3	5	–	1	–	–	56
2	25	50	4	7	–	1	–	1	88
3	23	22	4	6	–	2	–	–	57
Total	67	100	11	18	–	4	–	1	201

4.3   Strings of modifiers

In the great majority of the 1,148 phrases in the data, there is but one modifier. In 201 instances, however, the phrase consists of a noun with two or more modifiers. The length and reference of these strings of modifiers and their distribution over time is shown in table 1.8.

Table 1.8 shows that a string with two modifiers is by far the most common type: such strings comprise 83 per cent (167/201) of the total number of noun phrases with multiple modification. Strings of three modifiers occur in twenty-nine instances (14 per cent), whereas longer strings are rare. Strings of different length in the material are exemplified in (20)–(24), and (25) shows the only string consisting of five modifiers in the data.

(20)   '[. . .] I had not expected more than *a very tolerably well-looking woman of a certain age*; I did not know that I was to find *a pretty young woman* in Mrs. Weston.'
(Fiction, Jane Austen, 1800–30, p. II, 86)

(21)   He told me, too, of his connection with *a poor and humble girl*, who would shortly become the mother of his child.
(Drama, T. W. Robertson, 1850–70, p. 92)

(22)   *My dear old fellow* |Yours affect| C. Darwin
(Letters, Charles Darwin, 1850–70, p. VII, 21)

(23)   He, on the other hand, is *a well-meaning, honest, honourable person*, full of integrity and common-sense; [. . .]
(Fiction, Theodore Edward Hook, 1800–30, p. I, 241)

(24)   But I do like them so, and he is *a kind gentle dear old fellow* and sometimes he talks quite beautifully.
(Letters, Anne Thackeray Ritchie, 1870–1900, p. 176)

(25)   You *poor dear soft-headed – soft-hearted – soft-shinned creature!* What would you do without me?
(Drama, Tom Taylor, 1850–70, p. 288)

Table 1.9. *Distribution and relative frequency of* of-*phrases with female vs male reference.*

	Female reference			Male reference			Total		
Period	*of*-phr.	adj.	Total	*of*-phr.	adj.	Total	*of*-phr.	adj.	Total
1	8 (4%)	191	199	32 (13%)	216	248	40 (9%)	407	447
2	8 (4%)	195	203	19 (6%)	289	308	27 (5%)	484	511
3	4 (2%)	215	219	11 (5%)	231	242	15 (3%)	446	461
Total	20 (3%)	601	621	62 (8%)	736	798	82 (6%)	1,337	1,419

As revealed in table 1.8, male reference is even more frequent compared with female reference in noun phrases containing strings of modifiers than it is in the material as a whole (56 per cent; see table 1.2): of the 201 strings, 123, or 61 per cent, have male reference. This predominance is manifest above all in period 2, where male reference is twice as frequent as female reference (50 vs 25). This is also the period with the largest number of strings of modifiers. Both these facts have to do with the comparatively large number of strings of the type *my dear/est old man/fellow* occurring in Letters from period 2, which has already been commented on in connection with table 1.7b above.

As (20) exemplifies, some of the strings in the material contain a combination of adjectives and *of*-phrases; there are nineteen such instances, consisting of one or several adjectives and one or two *of*-phrases. The *of*-phrases in the data will be described in the next section.

4.4   Of-*phrases as modifiers*

As mentioned in 4.1, the material contains eighty-two instances of *of*-phrases as modifiers, which is 6 per cent of the total number of modifiers. Table 1.9 shows their reference and relative frequency over the periods. According to table 1.9, the non-genitival postmodifying *of*-phrase is a structure that becomes less frequent over time: 9 per cent of the modifiers in the material from period 1 are *of*-phrases and 3 per cent in period 3. Table 1.9 also shows that the distribution of reference is more uneven with regard to *of*-phrases than in the material as a whole: 76 per cent of the postmodifiers (62/82) have male reference compared to 56 per cent of all modifiers. It is above all in period 1 that male reference is more common than female reference. Here 13 per cent of all modifiers with male reference are *of*-phrases compared to 4 per cent of the modifiers with female reference. In all periods the predominance of male reference may be explained, at least partly, by the distribution of the *of*-phrases across semantic categories.

Table 1.10a. *Distribution of of-phrases with female reference across semantic categories.*

Period	Age	Appearance	Mental	Situation	Sociability	Total
1	1	–	2	5	–	8
2	1	1	2	2	2	8
3	–	–	1	3	–	4
Total	2	1	5	10	2	20

Table 1.10b. *Distribution of of-phrases with male reference across semantic categories.*

Period	Ability	Appearance	Mental	Physical	Situation	Sociability	Total
1	7	1	9	1	14	–	32
2	2	1	7	–	9	–	19
3	–	–	3	–	6	2	11
Total	9	2	19	1	29	2	62

Regarding distribution over semantic categories, the majority of instances belong to the category of Situation, as shown in tables 1.10a and 1.10b.[9] Tables 1.10a and 1.10b show that approximately every second instance of a postmodifying *of*-phrase describes the social situation of the referent, whether male or female; (26)–(28) are typical examples. A quarter of the instances with female reference and almost a third of the instances with male reference belong to the category of Mental State, exemplified by (29). Example (30) represents the category of Ability, where all instances have male reference. For this small category, which only includes 25 instances with male reference in the data as a whole (table 1.6b), it is interesting to note that nine of these consist of an *of*-phrase.

(26)   *a woman of the town*
       (Letters, George Byron, 1800–30, p. I, 203)

(27)   *the young lady of property*
       (Drama, W. S. Gilbert, 1870–1900, p. 18)

(28)   *every real man of science*
       (Letters, Charles Darwin, 1850–70, p. VII, 214)

(29)   *a man of quick impulse and energetic action*
       (Drama, W. S. Gilbert, 1870–1900, p. 18)

(30)   *a man of known musical talent*
       (Fiction, Jane Austen, 1800–30, p. II, 107)

Table 1.11. *Frequency of modifiers in texts by female and male writers.*

| Period | Female writers | | | Male writers | | |
	Words	Modifiers	Modifiers/ 1,000 words	Words	Modifiers	Modifiers/ 1,000 words
1	88,869	158	1.8	105,439	289	2.7
2	89,582	162	1.8	109,783	349	3.1
3	60,173	150	2.5	89,271	311	3.5
Total	238,624	470	2.0	304,547	949	3.1

Thus, as shown in table 1.10b, the bulk of the *of*-phrases with male reference (57/62) belong to the categories of Ability, Mental State and Situation. These are also the categories where male reference is most dominant when all modifiers are considered (cf. tables 1.6a, 1.6b, 1.7a, and 1.7b). Thus, given the fact that *of*-phrases in the material are used above all to describe a person's abilities, mental qualities or social situation, the preponderance of male reference is to be expected. The investigation now turns to possible differences in the use of modifiers between female and male writers in the sub-corpus.

4.5   Female vs male writers

As was shown in table 1.1, 44 per cent of the text in the present sub-corpus is produced by women and 56 per cent by men. The discussion now focuses on the use of modifiers with the nouns under investigation by women and men. Table 1.11 shows the total number of modifiers used by women and men, respectively, and the number of modifiers per 1,000 words. Of the 1,419 modifiers in the material, 470, which is 33 per cent, occur in texts by female writers, while male writers use modifiers of the type investigated here considerably more often than female writers, with 949 occurrences.

It is clear from table 1.11 that the increase in the use of modifiers over time, already shown in table 1.3, is present in texts by both female and male authors. In texts written by men there is a gradual increase from 2.7 modifiers/1,000 words at the beginning of the century to 3.1 in mid-century and 3.5 towards the end of the century. For women writers the increase in the use of modifiers only occurs in the last period, 1870–1900, but their texts display a greater difference in this regard in relation to the earlier periods than the men's texts in consecutive periods. The general increase in numbers of modifiers per 1,000 words towards the end of the century may be seen as a reflection of the upper-class tendency to use numerous adjectives (see 4.1). But the greater increase in modifiers in texts by women than in those by men might also indicate an adaptation on the part of the female writers to a more male style of writing.

Table 1.12a. *Frequency of intrapersonal and interpersonal modifiers used by female writers.*

Period	Intrapersonal	Interpersonal	Total
1	88 (56%)	70 (44%)	158
2	85 (52%)	77 (48%)	162
3	94 (63%)	56 (37%)	150
Total	267 (57%)	203 (43%)	470

Table 1.12b. *Frequency of intrapersonal and interpersonal modifiers used by male writers.*

Period	Intrapersonal	Interpersonal	Total
1	154 (53%)	135 (47%)	289
2	183 (52%)	166 (48%)	349
3	201 (65%)	110 (35%)	311
Total	538 (57%)	411 (43%)	949

The use of intrapersonal and interpersonal modifiers by female and male writers respectively is presented in tables 1.12a and 1.12b, which show a fairly uniform picture: in each of the three periods the proportions of intrapersonal and interpersonal modifiers are more or less the same for female and male writers. In periods 1 and 2, slightly more than half the number of modifiers are intrapersonal, whereas in period 3, there is a rise from 52 per cent to 63 per cent in texts by women and to 65 per cent in texts by men. Only the figures displayed in table 1.12b have proved statistically significant.[10] However, it is interesting to note in connection with the rise in intrapersonal modifiers that according to the figures in table 1.4, it is mainly those with female reference that become more frequent towards the end of the century. This could mean that in the period 1870–1900 writers become more interested in describing women and girls as individuals rather than describing their social status and manners. The overall distribution of reference in texts by female and male writers is shown in tables 1.13a and 1.13b.

Table 1.13a shows that, on the whole, there is a slight preference for female reference in texts by female writers, 51 per cent in period 1, 54 per cent in period 2, and 61 per cent in period 3. Even if these differences over time are not statistically significant (p > 0.05) the gradually increasing tendency among female writers to refer to women more often than to men might possibly reflect a growing wish on

Table 1.13a. *Distribution of reference in texts by women.*

Period	Female reference	Male reference	Total
1	80 (51%)	78 (49%)	158
2	88 (54%)	74 (46%)	162
3	92 (61%)	58 (39%)	150
Total	260 (55%)	210 (45%)	470

Table 1.13b. *Distribution of reference in texts by men.*

Period	Female reference	Male reference	Total
1	119 (41%)	170 (59%)	289
2	115 (33%)	234 (67%)	349
3	127 (41%)	184 (59%)	311
Total	361 (38%)	588 (62%)	949

their part to highlight the doings of women in their texts. Conversely, table 1.13b shows a predominance of male reference in texts by men. In period 2, as many as 67 per cent of the modifiers have male reference; however, that may partly be due to the high frequency of the phrase *my dear old man* and similar expressions in the letters from that period, a phenomenon that has already been mentioned in connection with the discussion of the category of Address above.[11] Nevertheless, generally speaking, the present results indicate that writers tend to refer to people of their own sex somewhat more often than they refer to the opposite sex. The differences in reference between female and male writers displayed in the totals of tables 1.13a and 1.13b are statistically significant.[12]

Another interesting question is whether the distribution of modifiers over the different semantic categories is similar or not for female and male writers: this information is presented in table 1.14.[13] It is clear from table 1.14 that women and men seem to use modifiers from the intrapersonal categories (Ability, Age, Appearance, Mental State, Nationality, and Physical State) to roughly the same extent. Among the interpersonal categories (Address, Attitude, Situation and Sociability), however, there are some differences. The difference between the use of modifiers by female and male writers is greatest in the category of Address. In the material written by women, 4 per cent of the modifiers belong to this category, whereas the corresponding figure for the men's texts is 13 per cent. In other words, when addressing people, the male writers in the sub-corpus use noun phrases with modifiers considerably more often than the female writers

Table 1.14. *Modifiers used by female vs male writers according to semantic category.*

Writer	Abil.	Age	App.	Nat.	Ment.	Phys.	Addr.	Attit.	Sit.	Soc.	Total
Female	6	94	29	14	110	14	19	75	40	69	470
	(1%)	(20%)	(6%)	(3%)	(24%)	(3%)	(4%)	(16%)	(9%)	(15%)	
Male	22	204	71	5	221	15	123	103	105	80	949
	(2%)	(21%)	(8%)	(1%)	(23%)	(2%)	(13%)	(11%)	(11%)	(8%)	
Total	28	298	100	19	331	29	142	178	145	149	1,419
	(2%)	(21%)	(7%)	(1%)	(23%)	(2%)	(10%)	(13%)	(10%)	(10%)	

do.[14] The use of modifiers in Address has already been exemplified in (17)–(19) above.

In connection with this difference in addressing people, the question of gender of the addressee is obviously interesting. Of the nineteen modifiers belonging to the category of Address and used by female writers only one has male reference, namely *kind* in (31), used in addressing the writer's husband. An example of a female writer addressing a woman is given in (32).

(31) Here is an answer by the same post as your wish will come, *my own kind husband.*
   (Letters, Elizabeth Wilson, 1850–70, p. 551)

(32) Goodnight *my dear young woman,* [. . .]
   (Letters, Anne Thackeray Ritchie, 1870–1900, p. 187)

Of the 123 modifiers used by male writers when addressing people, 48 (39 per cent) refer to women or girls and 75 to men.[15] So when the frequencies for female and male writers are compared it is clear that not only do the women in the material use this type of noun phrase with modifiers to a much lesser extent than do the men, but they also seem quite reluctant to address men in this way. The male writers, on the other hand, do not hesitate to use modifiers when addressing women as well as men. To address people in this way, as exemplified in (33)–(36), gives a somewhat condescending impression and thus might be seen as a way of signalling superiority. This would explain why nineteenth-century female writers use it to such a limited extent.

(33) [. . .] Here, take this purse, *good fellow.*
   (Drama, Thomas Holcroft, 1800–30, p. 71)

(34) I'm glad you *young ladies* are not here: [. . .]
   (Letters, William Makepeace Thackeray, 1850–70, p. 33)

(35) *My good woman,* a single word from me to those at the Deanery [. . .]
   (Drama, Arthur Pinero, 1870–1900, p. 111)

(36) This is my Property, *young gentleman*; and I come here every day to execute orders.
(Fiction, Walter Besant, 1870–1900, p. II, 248)

Returning to the interpersonal categories in table 1.14, there is one more category where usage differs considerably between female and male writers and that is Sociability, the category of modifiers describing manners and behaviour. Here there are almost as many instances by female writers as by male writers, and the category comprises 15 per cent of the total number of modifiers used by women, but only 8 per cent of the men's modifiers. Clearly, manners and behaviour is an area that interests women more than men, when it comes to describing people. As regards reference within this category, it has already been pointed out, in connection with tables 1.7a and 1.7b, that this is the only interpersonal category where there are more instances of female reference than of male (76 vs 73). The difference may seem small, but in view of the proportions of female and male reference in the other categories, it is still interesting. It would seem as if two tendencies converge here: firstly, writers in the material have been shown to refer more often to their own sex than to the opposite sex; secondly, modifiers belonging to the category of Sociability are considerably more frequent in the texts by female writers than by male writers.

Finally, the comparison of percentages in table 1.14 shows that female writers seem somewhat more inclined to use modifiers from the category of Attitude (mainly *poor* and *dear*) than are male writers: 16 per cent of the women's instances and 11 per cent of the men's fall into this category.

To sum up, the word count carried out on the texts in the sub-corpus has shown that 44 per cent of the material is written by women, 56 per cent by men. In the texts by women, the frequency of modifiers is 2.0 per 1,000 words, in those by men 3.1 per 1,000 words (table 1.11). If time periods are compared, there is a gradual increase in the number of modifiers per 1,000 words in men's texts from 2.7 to 3.5, whereas for women there is a marked increase in period 3, from 1.8 to 2.5. The difference in frequency between female and male writers is greatest in period 2, with 1.8 instances per 1,000 words for women and 3.1 for men. The proportions of intrapersonal and interpersonal modifiers are fairly similar over the time periods for female and male writers, with an increase in intrapersonal modifiers in period 3 (tables 1.12a and 1.12b). The analysis of the distribution of reference in the material showed that the writers referred somewhat more frequently to people of their own sex than to the opposite sex (tables 1.13a and 1.13b).

As regards the distribution of modifiers across the semantic categories, female and male writers used modifiers from the different intrapersonal categories to roughly the same extent (table 1.14). Among the interpersonal categories, the greatest difference between writers was found in the category of Address. The female writers used nineteen modifiers (thirteen noun phrases); the corresponding figure for male writers was 123 modifiers (103 noun phrases). As regards gender of the addressee, only one instance in the texts by women had male reference, whereas in the men's texts thirty-eight modifiers had female reference and seventy-five male reference. The difference in use might be explained in terms of signalling condescension and superiority. Other differences among the interpersonal categories concerned Sociability and Attitude. Modifiers belonging to the former category comprised 15 per cent of the instances used by female writers and 8 per cent of those by male writers. This is also the only interpersonal category where female reference is more frequent than male in the material as a whole. Regarding the category of Attitude, the proportion of such modifiers is somewhat greater in texts by female writers than by male writers. The question of general attitude or value embedded in the modifiers in the material will be discussed in the following section.

4.6   Positive, negative and neutral modifiers

As already mentioned in section 3 above, each modifier has been classified according to whether it could be considered as denoting a positive quality, a negative quality or whether it might be thought of as neutral. The admittedly subjective criteria for that classification were accounted for together with certain considerations in connection with the classification. The results of the analysis are presented in tables 1.15 and 1.16. Tables 1.15a and 1.15b give an overview of female and male reference, and in tables 1.16a and 1.16b the instances are further grouped according to gender of author.

Table 1.15a shows that in periods 1 and 3 more than half of the modifiers used about women and girls are positive and that in all periods the negative modifiers form the smallest group. In period 3 the percentage of negative modifiers falls from 18 per cent to 11 per cent of all modifiers with female reference, at the same time as the neutral modifiers also become less frequent during this time. When it comes to modifiers with male reference the picture is somewhat different. Table 1.15b shows that the proportion of negative modifiers with male reference is fairly constant over time with a slight rise in period 3, whereas there is a considerable drop in the proportion of positive modifiers between periods 2 and 3 with a corresponding rise in the proportion of neutral modifiers.

If the totals for positive, negative and neutral modifiers in tables 1.15a and 1.15b are compared it can be seen that positive modifiers in the material are somewhat more common with female reference than with male reference (50 per cent vs 46 per cent), whereas negative modifiers show a slight preponderance of male reference (15 per cent vs 18 per cent). These results are not statistically significant ($p > 0.05$) but they might still be of some interest, since they seem not to be in line with what Persson (1990: 53) found in his investigation of collocations with *girl*, *woman*, *boy* and *man* as they occur in the Brown and LOB corpora. Calculated in the same way as the present results (with female terms as one group and male terms as the other), his figures give 32 per cent negative modifiers with female reference and 28 per cent with male reference. Admittedly,

Table 1.15a. *Distribution of positive, negative and neutral modifiers with female reference.*[a]

Period	Positive	Negative	Neutral	Total
1	115 (58%)	35 (18%)	49 (24%)	199
2	82 (40%)	37 (18%)	84 (41%)	203
3	114 (52%)	24 (11%)	81 (37%)	219
Total	**311 (50%)**	**96 (15%)**	**214 (35%)**	**621**

[a] The results obtained for the use of positive, negative and neutral modifiers with female reference are statistically significant. The chi-square value is 19.607; df = 4; $p < 0.001$.

Table 1.15b. *Distribution of positive, negative and neutral modifiers with male reference.*[a]

Period	Positive	Negative	Neutral	Total
1	133 (53%)	46 (18%)	69 (29%)	248
2	161 (52%)	47 (15%)	100 (33%)	308
3	76 (31%)	48 (20%)	118 (49%)	242
Total	**370 (46%)**	**141 (18%)**	**287 (36%)**	**798**

[a] The results obtained for the use of positive, negative and neutral modifiers with male reference are statistically significant. The chi-square value is 35.220; df = 4; $p < 0.001$.

the twentieth-century corpora are different from the present sub-set of CONCE, but the difference is still interesting. Examples from the sub-corpus of negative modifiers with female and male reference are given in (37)–(39).

(37) Let me get rid of *this troublesome woman*, ma'am, [. . .]
(Drama, John Poole, 1800–30, p. 24)

(38) [$Lady P.$] You *shameless girl*! and he without a penny!
(Drama, T. W. Robertson, 1850–70, p. 72)

(39) [. . .] because she has a husband she loves – *a neglectful husband* at best, [. . .]
(Fiction, Mary Braddon, 1870–1900, p. III, 93)

It is also clear from tables 1.15a and 1.15b that neutral modifiers are equally common with female and male reference. Regarding changes between the periods, there is an increase in neutral modifiers over time in both tables, but otherwise the picture is varied.

Table 1.16a. *Distribution of positive, negative and neutral modifiers with female and male reference in texts by female writers.*

| Period | Female reference | | | | Male reference | | | | Total |
	Pos.	Neg.	Neut.	Total	Pos.	Neg.	Neut.	Total	
1	50	4	26	80	36	19	23	78	158
	(62%)	(5%)	(32%)		(46%)	(24%)	(29%)		
2	40	9	39	88	40	9	25	74	162
	(45%)	(10%)	(44%)		(54%)	(12%)	(34%)		
3	52	6	34	92	30	8	20	58	150
	(57%)	(7%)	(37%)		(52%)	(14%)	(34%)		
Total	142	19	99	260	106	36	68	210	470
	(55%)	(7%)	(38%)		(50%)	(17%)	(33%)		

Table 1.16b. *Distribution of positive, negative and neutral modifiers with female and male reference in texts by male writers.*

| Period | Female reference | | | | Male reference | | | | Total |
	Pos.	Neg.	Neut.	Total	Pos.	Neg.	Neut.	Total	
1	65	31	23	119	97	27	46	170	289
	(54%)	(26%)	(19%)		(57%)	(16%)	(27%)		
2	42	28	45	115	121	38	75	234	349
	(37%)	(24%)	(39%)		(52%)	(16%)	(32%)		
3	62	18	47	127	46	40	98	184	311
	(49%)	(14%)	(37%)		(25%)	(22%)	(53%)		
Total	169	77	115	361	264	105	219	588	949
	(47%)	(21%)	(32%)		(44%)	(17%)	(39%)		

Tables 1.16a and 1.16b give a more detailed view, where certain differences become clearer. It becomes apparent from table 1.16a that on the whole female writers use positive and neutral modifiers nearly as often with male as with female reference. Negative modifiers, on the other hand, are used considerably more often about men than about women and girls by female writers. These results are statistically significant.[16] Table 1.16a shows no significant development over time (p > 0.05). The differences between periods shown in table 1.16b, that is, the use by male writers of positive, negative and neutral modifiers, have proved significant for female as well as for male reference, however.[17] Table 1.16b shows that with both types of reference male writers use nearly twice as many neutral modifiers in period 3 as in period 1. They also seem more inclined to use positive modifiers about men than about women and girls in period 2. In period 3

positive modifiers are more frequent when the person mentioned is a woman or a girl than when the referent is a man. There are also more negative modifiers about men and fewer about women and girls in period 3 than in earlier periods.

Tables 1.16a and 1.16b show that the female writers use negative modifiers with female reference in 7 per cent of their instances, whereas the corresponding figure for male writers is 21 per cent.[18] Thus it seems that the male authors are considerably more inclined to use negative modifiers about women and girls than the female authors are. The predominance of terms with negative connotations referring to women that is observed in several studies (see, for example, Romaine 1999: 92–5 and Persson 1990: 50–7) should perhaps be interpreted as primarily mirroring male attitudes to the opposite sex.[19] But at the same time it should be pointed out that the decrease in negative modifiers with female reference shown in table 1.15a occurs in texts written by men. Another conclusion that may be drawn from tables 1.16a and 1.16b is that modifiers with negative connotations used with reference to men are equally frequent in texts by female and male writers, whereas women more often use positive modifiers with male reference than men do. On the whole, in this material the female writers are somewhat more inclined to use modifiers with positive connotations than the male writers are.

4.7   The Mental State category: a close-up

In the previous sections, modifiers referring to females and males have been discussed chiefly from a quantitative perspective, and the analysis has focused on the broad categories of adjectives established in section 3. However, a closer look at one category, where quantitative and qualitative approaches are combined, may uncover patterns that eluded discovery in the macro-level discussion above. There are two reasons why the category that comprises modifiers denoting mental qualities and states is of great interest in this regard:

1. Mental State is the largest category in the study: it comprises 23 per cent of the total number of modifiers in the sub-corpus and includes 331 instances, evenly distributed over the three periods (cf. tables 1.6a and 1.6b). Moreover, as there are 132 instances with female reference and 199 with male reference, fairly reliable results can be obtained for both genders.
2. Modifiers belonging to the category of Mental State, such as *foolish* and *noble* (see table 1.17), frequently encode positive or negative values. This category is thus of special relevance to a study of how men and women were described positively and negatively, in relation to societal values.

The discussion starts by showing, for each period, what modifiers are used with both female and male reference (table 1.17). Then those used with only female and only male reference will be presented (tables 1.18a–1.18c). In the tables figures in brackets denote number of instances for each modifier. It is important

Table 1.17. *Mental State modifiers used with both female and male reference.*

Period	1 (1800–1830)	2 (1850–1870)	3 (1870–1900)
	affectionate (3)	good (22)	courageous (2)
	excellent (4)	kind (6)	good (12)
	fine (3)	noble (2)	happy (3)
	foolish (2)	sensible (3)	honest (2)
	good (13)	true (2)	humorous (2)
	happy (7)		kind (5)
	kind (4)		merry (2)
	noble (3)		sad (2)
	virtuous (4)		sensible (3)
	wonderful (2)		strong (2)
			weak (2)
			wise (2)
Total types/tokens	10/45	5/35	12/39

to keep in mind that for each instance the classification into a given semantic category is based on the contextual meaning of each modifier (cf. section 3).

It is interesting to note from table 1.17 that comparatively few adjectives are used with both female and male reference and that different periods mainly use different terms. There are only two adjectives, *good* and *kind*, that are used in all three periods, and three adjectives, *happy, noble*, and *sensible*, that occur in two periods. Only three of the twenty-seven adjectives in table 1.17 have negative connotations, namely *foolish* in period 1 and *sad* and *weak* in period 3. The lists of modifiers with only female or only male reference are longer and will be divided into positive items and negative items (for principles of categorization, see section 3). Modifiers from different periods will be presented in separate tables (1.18a–1.18c). The fourteen neutral modifiers in the Mental State category have been omitted, since they were not considered of interest for the present discussion.[20]

What is immediately apparent from tables 1.18a–1.18c is, firstly, that the lists of positive terms are much longer than those of negative terms and, secondly, that, with the exception of positive terms in period 3, the lists with female reference are shorter than those with male reference. In both cases, the result tallies with what has been reported earlier. Tables 1.15a and 1.15b gave proportions of positive, negative and neutral modifiers with female and male reference, respectively. If those figures are combined, we find that there are 681 positive modifiers, which is 48 per cent of all instances (681/1,419); the corresponding proportion of negative modifiers is 17 per cent (237/1,419). The comparatively short lists of negative

Table 1.18a. *Mental State modifiers only used with female or male reference in period 1.*

Positive modifiers		Negative modifiers	
Female reference	Male reference	Female reference	Male reference
careful (1)	admirable (1)	bad (1)	crazy (1)
divine (1)	disinterested (1)	fickle (1)	cruel (1)
invincible (1)	exemplary (1)	licentious (1)	faulty (1)
loving (1)	extraordinary (1)	of weaker	idle (1)
mild-natured (1)	generous (2)	intellect (1)	impatient (1)
of character (1)	good-tempered (1)	over-joyous (1)	naughty (1)
sensible (1)	honest (6)	tearful (1)	poor (1)
smart (1)	just (1)	unreasonable (1)	queer (1)
tender (1)	of admirable		savage (1)
warm-hearted (1)	resolution (1)		sinful (1)
	of real genius (1)		sly (1)
	of honour (2)		
	of intellect (1)		
	of penetration (1)		
	of resolution (1)		
	of secrecy (1)		
	of strict honour (1)		
	of the right sort of		
	principles (1)		
	peaceable (1)		
	pious (1)		
	quiet (1)		
	saintlike (1)		
	steady (1)		
	sweet (1)		
	sweet tempered (1)		
	tenderhearted (1)		
	wondrous (1)		
Types/tokens 10/10	26/33	7/7	11/11

modifiers in tables 1.18a–1.18c could thus be expected. If the proportions of positive and negative items in the Mental State category were to mirror those of the material as a whole, there would be 159 positive instances (48 per cent of 331) and 56 negative instances (17 per cent of 331). The actual figures from tables 1.18a–1.18c are 140 positive tokens and 61 negative tokens, thus fairly close to expectations.

Table 1.18b. *Mental State modifiers only used with female or male reference in period 2.*

	Positive modifiers		Negative modifiers	
	Female reference	Male reference	Female reference	Male reference
	bright (1)	affectionate (1)	dreadful (1)	coarse (1)
	careful (1)	attached (1)	foolish (2)	dangerous (1)
	cheerful (1)	brave (2)	harsh (1)	desperate (1)
	dutiful (1)	clever (4)	haughty (1)	irreligious (1)
	faithful (2)	equal to success (1)	insane (1)	lazy (1)
	great (1)	excellent (2)	mischievous (1)	melancholy (1)
	happy (1)	extraordinary (1)	obstinate (1)	soft-headed (1)
	lovely (1)	fine (1)	remorseless (1)	unhappy (1)
	motherly (1)	first rate (1)	severe (1)	
	of genius (1)	fond (1)	ungrateful (1)	
	poetic (1)	good-humoured (1)		
	proud (1)	honest (2)		
	sterling (1)	industrious (1)		
	superior (1)	intelligent (1)		
	tip-top (1)	jolly (1)		
	well-balanced (1)	observant (1)		
		of conscience (1)		
		of heart (1)		
		of noble character (1)		
		of real genius (1)		
		of sturdy action (1)		
		of virtue (1)		
		of wit (1)		
		quiet (1)		
		smart (1)		
		soft-hearted (1)		
		special (1)		
		splendid (2)		
		steady (1)		
		tender-hearted (2)		
		unworldly (1)		
		wise (1)		
Types/tokens	16/17	32/40	10/11	8/8

Table 1.18c. *Mental State modifiers only used with female or male reference in period 3.*

	Positive modifiers		Negative modifiers	
	Female reference	Male reference	Female reference	Male reference
	divine (1)	brave (1)	angry (1)	bad (2)
	faithful (1)	cheerful (1)	feeble (1)	blunt (1)
	fine (2)	conscientious (1)	froward (1)	cold-blooded (1)
	hearty (1)	generous (1)	silly (1)	cynical (1)
	innocent (1)	gentle (2)	sluggish (1)	fearful (1)
	noble-hearted (1)	harmless (1)	unhappy (3)	frivolous (1)
	patient (1)	honest (1)		haughty (1)
	plucky (1)	honourable (1)		light-hearted (1)
	pure (2)	intelligent (2)		mean (1)
	rational (1)	judicious (1)		neglectful (1)
	self-reliant (1)	kind-hearted (1)		obstinate (1)
	soft (1)	noble (1)		thoughtless (1)
	strong-minded (1)	of great humour (1)		unscrupulous (1)
	superior (1)	practical (1)		worldly (1)
	tender (1)	steady (1)		
	tranquil (1)	straightforward (1)		
	well-meaning (1)	tenderhearted (1)		
Types/tokens	17/19	17/19	6/8	14/15

What might be more interesting is how the positive and negative modifiers used only about women or only about men are distributed between female and male reference. For clarity, the figures for tokens in tables 1.18a–1.18c are repeated in tables 1.19a and 1.19b.

Of the 138 positive instances 92, or 67 per cent, refer to men, compared with an expected 56 per cent, the proportion of male reference in the material as a whole (cf. table 1.2). This means that, with the given set of modifiers, men's mental qualities and states of mind are mentioned in positive terms relatively more often than is the case for women and girls. Regarding the negative terms used only about women or only about men in each period, 50 per cent of the tokens in tables 1.18a–1.18c are used about men, again compared with the expected 56 per cent. This means that men are described as having negative mental qualities somewhat less often than women are.

Another interesting comparison of the lists above concerns time periods. In period 1, positive terms are used more than three times as often with male

Table 1.19a. *Distribution of reference for positive Mental State modifiers used only about women and only about men.*

Period	Female reference	Male reference	Total
1	10	33	43
2	17	40	57
3	19	19	38
Total	46	92	138

Table 1.19b. *Distribution of reference for negative Mental State modifiers used only about women and only about men.*

Period	Female reference	Male reference	Total
1	11	7	18
2	11	8	19
3	8	15	23
Total	30	30	60

reference as with female reference (10 vs 33). In period 2, male reference is more than twice as frequent (17 vs 40), and, finally, in period 3, the number of positive modifiers used about women only and men only is the same (19 vs 19). Although hypotheses about connections between extralinguistic events and linguistic developments must remain tentative at this stage, this apparent change might reflect the growing importance of women in society. After 1850, liberals such as John Stuart – and Harriet – Mill began to argue for an extension of the franchise (Harvie 2001: 515; *Encyclopædia Britannica*, s.v. 'Woman suffrage'). During period 2 in CONCE, woman suffrage societies were founded in many British cities, and from period 3 onwards these societies were petitioning Parliament to introduce woman suffrage (*Encyclopædia Britannica*). Although woman suffrage in Parliamentary elections was not introduced until the twentieth century, several reforms that increased the importance of women to British political life did take place before then: women taxpayers were granted the vote in municipal elections, and county and city councils became open to women (*Encyclopædia Britannica*). Married women's rights were also extended by the Married Women's Property Act of 1870.

Moreover, the life of middle-class women in late nineteenth-century Britain was beginning to change. As the average size of middle-class families decreased,

middle-class women were now both able and willing to engage in activities outside the household, and women came to play 'an important role in charities,
churches, local politics, and the arts, especially music' (Matthew 2001: 546).
Although women were largely barred from taking university degrees and entering the professions, the foundation of women's colleges at Oxford, Cambridge
and London in period 3 (Matthew 2001: 546) also testifies to the new opportunities open to women in the latter half of the nineteenth century. Impor-
tantly, all of these changes must have contributed to challenging the notion
of separate spheres for women and men. As women were increasingly active
in many areas of society of which they had not previously been a part, it is
reasonable to assume that their perceived importance increased, which may in
turn have affected the way in which they were described. However, it is important to bear in mind that these developments chiefly affected the middle class:
for instance, the larger size of working-class families, as well as economic factors, is likely to have made it much more difficult for married working-class
women than for their middle-class counterparts to engage in activities outside the
household.

Differences in descriptions of women and men in terms of mental qualities
and states can also be detected by comparing the semantic content of the items in
the lists above. Are women described as submissive and weak, and men as active
and strong, in line with the notion of separate spheres mentioned in section
1? For reasons of space, the qualitative discussion below can only be brief and
impressionistic.

For period 1, the comparison shows that women are described as *tender, warm-
hearted* and even *divine*. But men are also *sweet, tender-hearted* and *saint-like*. The
only modifiers that could be said to refer to a powerful male personality are *of
admirable resolution* and *of resolution*; yet there is also an *invincible* woman. Among
the negative items, there is a *licentious* woman, but there is also a *sinful* man. On
the whole, for the first period, the general impression is that women and men are
described in fairly similar terms, at least as far as positive mental qualities and
states are concerned.

For period 2, fewer items in both female and male lists above refer to tenderness
and peacefulness. Women are described, for instance, as *dutiful* and *faithful*, but
also as *bright, great* and *superior*, and men as *brave, clever* and *smart*. The negative
list with female reference gives a more forceful impression than the corresponding
list from period 1. In period 2, women are described among other things as *harsh,
remorseless* and *severe*. As for the negative lists with male reference, they seem
fairly similar in periods 1 and 2, with items such as *impatient, savage* and *sly* in
period 1 and *dangerous, desperate* and *irreligious* in period 2.

Regarding period 3, once more there are few modifiers with male reference
that point to the public, active, manly sphere. Among such instances items such
as *practical, judicious, unscrupulous* and *cold-bloodied* could perhaps be counted,
but on the whole, the lists for male reference in period 3 resemble those of periods

1 and 2 to a great extent. The women referred to in period 3, on the other hand, seem to be considered as stronger. It is true that modifiers such as *tender, faithful* and *feeble* still occur, but also several terms denoting various aspects of strength, such as *froward, plucky, rational, self-reliant* and *strong-minded*. Together with the fact that in period 3 the number of instances with female reference only (19+8) is closer to the number of instances with male reference only (19+15) than in periods 1 and 2, this qualitative change in modifiers used about women and girls gives an impression that, to some extent, women have gained ground in the sense that it is no longer considered inappropriate for a woman to show qualities of strength and independence. Both the quantitative and the qualitative analyses thus yield results that can be interpreted as tallying with developments in nineteenth-century British society.

5   Brief comparison with terms in an eighteenth-century corpus

It was mentioned in the introductory sections that the nouns included in this study were chosen so as to make possible some comparisons with Wallin-Ashcroft (2000). Her study is mainly an investigation of nominal terms with female and male reference used in novels from the middle of the eighteenth century. In her data, Wallin-Ashcroft (2000: 17) included collocations with prenominal adjectives for each noun. The adjectives have been categorized as positive, neutral, patronizing or negative, and for each nominal term there is an account of the adjectives collocating with that particular term.

To be able to compare the present results concerning positive, negative and neutral modifiers with those of Wallin-Ashcroft (2000), her figures for the nouns common to both studies have been collapsed in table 1.20a for adjectives with female reference and table 1.20b for adjectives with male reference; for epicene nouns, tokens with female and male reference have been separated. Wallin-Ashcroft's category of 'patronizing' adjectives has been included among the negative terms, which she herself points out would be natural in a three-part categorization (Wallin-Ashcroft 2000: 85). The tables comprise epicene and central terms; Wallin-Ashcroft gives no figures for collocations with other terms.[21]

Wallin-Ashcroft (2000: 19) states that '[t]he proportion of female and male referents is well-balanced as regards central, characterising and relational terms'. That statement refers to nouns both with and without modifiers, but, interestingly enough, when it comes to epicene and central nouns with modifiers, those with female reference comprise 60 per cent, as the total number of modifiers in tables 1.20a and 1.20b is 826. This figure is considerably higher than the corresponding figure for female reference in the present study, which is 44 per cent for the whole sub-corpus (see table 1.2).

With regard to positive, negative and neutral modifiers, the figures in tables 1.20a and 1.20b show a remarkably even distribution over the three categories of modifiers, as well as between female and male reference, in the eighteenth-century corpus. In the present sub-corpus of CONCE, however, it has been

Table 1.20a. *Distribution of positive, negative and neutral modifiers with female reference in Wallin-Ashcroft (2000).*

Term	Table	Positive	Negative	Neutral	Total
creature	1 (p. 55)	21	49	6	76
person	2 (p. 57)	9	4	1	14
child	3 (p. 62)	13	4	1	18
lady	6 (p. 81)	51	10	73	134
woman	8 (p. 87)	53	37	54	144
girl	10 (p. 97)	38	61	14	113
Total		185 (37%)	165 (33%)	149 (30%)	499

Table 1.20b. *Distribution of positive, negative and neutral modifiers with male reference in Wallin-Ashcroft (2000).*

Term	Table	Positive	Negative	Neutral	Total
creature	1 (p. 55)	2	9	4	15
person	2 (p. 57)	4	3	1	8
child	3 (p. 62)	1	–	–	1
gentleman	5 (p. 87)	19	9	9	37
man	7 (p. 86)	94	58	74	226
fellow	9 (p. 92)	4	26	10	40
Total		124 (38%)	105 (32%)	98 (30%)	327

shown that the proportion of positive modifiers is considerably larger than the proportion of negative ones: for female reference the ratio is 50/15 per cent, and for male reference 46/18 per cent in the material as a whole (cf. tables 1.15a and 1.15b). This would seem to indicate that writers in the eighteenth century were more disposed to use negative terms in connection with nouns denoting women and men than were writers in the following century. One explanation for this difference, however, might be that in the sub-corpus of CONCE, 63 per cent of the material consists of private letters, whereas Wallin-Ashcroft's corpus consists entirely of novels. It seems reasonable to assume that writers of letters are less inclined to use negative modifiers about the people they mention in their letters than are novelists when describing their characters, whose whole 'existence' depends on the writer's descriptions.

Wallin-Ashcroft (2000: 207) points to some contrasting pairs of concepts which emerge from her study, for instance that male is spirit whereas female is matter, that male is power and female is dependency, and that male inspires respect and fear, whereas female inspires tenderness and condescension. Corresponding contrasts are not found in the nineteenth-century material used for the present investigation, as has been shown above.

6   Conclusions

This study of modifiers with certain common nouns with female and male reference in a sub-set of genres in CONCE set out to answer three main questions. The first question concerned whether the ideology of separate spheres for women and men was mirrored in the way modifiers were used, with a public sphere belonging to responsible, active, powerful men, and a domestic sphere with tender, submissive and dependent women. The second question pertained to the changing role of women during the nineteenth century and whether that change was reflected in the descriptions of women and girls. The third question was directed towards possible differences in the use of modifiers between female and male writers in the material.

To pinpoint similarities and differences in the descriptions of women and men, the modifiers were grouped in two sets of different semantic categories. In the first set, the intrapersonal categories, are the modifiers which focus on individual qualities; in the second set, the interpersonal group, are the modifiers which focus on the person in relation to society and other people.

Regarding the question of separate spheres, the analysis shows that women are considerably more often referred to with modifiers belonging to the intrapersonal category of Appearance than are men, whereas men clearly dominate the interpersonal category of Situation with modifiers referring to social status. These findings could perhaps be seen as reflecting separate spheres of women and men. However, in the category called Sociability, comprising modifiers denoting attitudes, manners and behaviour, female and male reference are equally frequent. This together with the results from the detailed analysis of the category of Mental State points to fairly similar descriptions of women and men, especially towards the end of the century. Taken together, the results imply that the separate spheres are reflected in the material, but also that there are categories in the data that do not appear to be influenced by this factor. This naturally raises the question of whether any diachronic change is detectable in the data.

As regards whether the changing role of women during the nineteenth century is in any way reflected in the present material, the answer is yes, to a certain extent. Certain differences, albeit sometimes small, have been recorded between the first two periods (1800–30 and 1850–70), on the one hand, and the third period (1870–1900), on the other. For instance, in the third period more often than in earlier periods, women and girls are described with intrapersonal modifiers, denoting individual qualities, rather than by interpersonal modifiers describing them in relation to society or to other people. Another difference between periods concerns the gap in the relative frequency of modifiers with female and male reference in the category of Situation (terms denoting social status). This gap is considerably smaller in the third period than in earlier periods. A third difference occurs in the category of Mental State. Here, in the first two periods there are considerably more instances of positive terms used with male reference than with female reference, whereas in the third period as many positive modifiers are used about women as about men. Another interesting observation within this category is that in the third period both positive and negative modifiers with female reference are related to various aspects of strength of mind to a greater extent than in earlier periods. Consequently, in various ways the descriptions of women and girls towards the end of the century might reflect a stronger and more important role for women than earlier in the century: sociocultural changes such as the increasing presence of women in society, on councils and at universities may lie behind these tendencies in the data.

Finally, the third question above concerned possible differences between texts by female and male writers in the sub-corpus. Here a number of differences have been observed. To begin with, male writers use more modifiers than female writers, and for both groups there is an increase in the use of modifiers over time. For the male writers there is a steady rise, whereas for the female writers the increase only comes in the third period, 1870–1900, but then it is greater than for the male writers. Regarding the use of modifiers from different semantic categories, female and male writers are fairly similar, with two main exceptions. Women writers use relatively more modifiers belonging to the category of Sociability than male writers. The greatest difference, however, is in the category of Address. The investigation shows that women writers in the material are reluctant to address people with a modifier and a noun, and practically never address men in this way, whereas men freely use this type of address, to both women and men. This way of addressing people could perhaps be taken as a means to signal dominance and superiority, which would explain why it is seldom used by the women writers.

As regards the use of positive and negative modifiers, there was also a difference between female and male writers. Both use negative modifiers with male reference to the same extent, but with female reference the picture is different. In texts by women, the instances of negative modifiers with female reference are few, whereas in texts by men, negative modifiers referring to women and girls are three times as frequent as those used in texts by women. In texts by men, negative modifiers referring to women and girls are also more frequent than such modifiers referring to men. In other words, the male writers in the material seem to be much more inclined to mention women in negative terms than are female writers, and they also use negative modifiers about women more often than about men. Another interesting difference between female and male writers concerns reference in general. It has been shown that female reference dominates in texts by female writers, and conversely, men refer more often to men than to women in their texts.

Taken together, the results of the present study give grounds for further research. The area of modifiers in connection with terms for women and men has proved a rich field of study.

Notes

1. See Persson (1990: 46–50), for a discussion of the different age spans of the terms *girl* and *boy*. This difference explains why *girl* is more frequent than *boy*.
2. I am indebted to Christer Geisler for generous help with extracting the examples from CONCE.
3. Warm thanks are due to Erik Smitterberg for expert help with significance testing, and for helping me with a number of historical references.
4. The chi-square value is 14.945; df = 2; p < 0.001.
5. The chi-square value for table 1.5a is 13.28; df = 2; p < 0.01. For table 1.5b the value is 6.05; df = 2; p < 0.05.
6. The chi-square value is 43.718; df = 5; p < 0.001.
7. For the difference in character among the interpersonal categories, see the Method section.
8. The results obtained for female reference (table 1.7a) are not statistically significant (p > 0.05), whereas those for male reference (table 1.7b) are. The chi-square value is here 21.827; df = 6; p < 0.01. A comparison of the totals for each category in tables 1.7a and 1.7b shows statistically significant differences between female and male reference. This chi-square value is 10.869; df = 3; p < 0.05.
9. Tables 1.10a and 1.10b only comprise categories where there are instances of *of*-phrases, and no division between intrapersonal and interpersonal categories is made. Tables 1.10a and 1.10b cannot be tested for significance owing to low expected frequencies.
10. The chi-square value is 11.922; df = 2; p < 0.01.
11. The results obtained for the distribution of reference in texts by male writers are statistically significant. The chi-square value is 6.072; df = 2; p < 0.05.
12. The chi-square value is 38.132; df = 1; p < 0.001.
13. The results obtained for female and male writers' use of modifiers from different semantic categories are statistically significant. The chi-square value is 65.165; df = 9; p < 0.001.
14. The question whether this difference is due to male writers in the sub-corpus using more terms of address in general than female writers, or to more extensive use of modifiers by male writers in addressing people cannot be answered in the present study, however.
15. It should perhaps be pointed out that some of the modifiers used when addressing people occur in noun phrases with two modifiers. However, this does not alter the general picture. The number of noun phrases of address which include one or more modifiers used by female writers is thirteen and by male writers 103.
16. The chi-square value for the totals in table 1.16a is 11.041; df = 2; p < 0.01.
17. The chi-square values for female and male reference are 17.876 and 45.613, respectively; df = 4; p < 0.001.
18. The results obtained for the use of positive, negative and neutral modifiers with female reference by female and male writers are statistically significant. The chi-square value is 22.757; df = 2; p < 0.001.

19. This is also what Persson (1990: 57) suggests, although his material is not divided into texts by female and male writers.

20. The following modifiers in the Mental State category were classified as neutral in the given context: *agitated, big, impassionable, impulsive, lively, not ungrateful, of few words, of quick impulse, proud, simple* (two instances), *special* (two instances), *strange*.

21. Tables 1.20a and 1.20b cannot be tested for significance owing to low expected frequencies.

2 Words in English Record Office documents of the early 1800s

TONY FAIRMAN

1 Introduction

English County Record Offices are 'responsible for official and local authority records (both past and present) and also contain church and chapel records, the private records of businesses [and of individuals], local societies and political parties' (Dewe 2002: 38).[1] In this study I look at some of these records, which after about 1750 become plentiful for English written on all levels of 'letteracy' – minimally, partly, extensively and fully schooled.

I have restricted my research to England to avoid possible second-language interference, which could have occurred in partly schooled Welsh or Scottish English. The documents I look at are stored under three categories: (1) Church of England parish registers of baptism, marriage and burial; (2) bills written by and for artisans; (3) letters of application for relief, which members of the lower orders wrote (or got others to write) to parish overseers. Most documents were written between 1800 and 1835, but I also quote from others written earlier and later if I can connect them relevantly with those in the central period.[2]

In these documents I look at certain classes of orthographic unit – that is, a group of graphs which a writer separated from other groups by two deliberate spaces. About 90 per cent of these groups are conventionally spaced words. I argue that how a writer wrote these units depended on their[3] assumptions about the speaker and on how much and what type of schooling the writer had received. Most English words are either of Anglo-Saxon (Germanic) origin or Latinate (including Greek). I also argue that familiarity with Latinates depended on upbringing and schooling and that researchers into Late Modern English should examine the uses and users of Latinate and Anglo-Saxon words.

2 Literacy

A person who can write is commonly called 'literate'. But the terms 'literate' and 'literacy' have acquired many meanings. For one thing, if someone can write, they can also read. But my primary interest in this study is writing – the learning, the process, the product and the writers. Reading comes into focus only because writers must be readers.

Another problem with the term 'literacy' is diachronic. In the year 2005 readers who cannot write are not considered literate. But I agree with Barry Reay, the historian, that '[t]hose who made their mark [in marriage registers] included large numbers of readers and to exclude them from the category "literate" would be to fundamentally misunderstand the cultural context of nineteenth-century England, where, for the labouring population, reading was literacy' (1996: 253).

Therefore, in order to describe writing and imply nothing about reading, I use the terms 'letterate' and 'letteracy', and I place scripts (handwritten discourse), texts (printed discourse) and linguistic levels on a scale of schooledness, divided roughly into degrees of difference from whatever the textbooks and other supporting sources prescribed as the standard for writing for that time. Whole scripts can be graded for schooledness, from minimally schooled (a bill or letter, comprehensible but largely unconventional), through partly and extensively schooled (the lower and upper halves of the scale, respectively) to fully schooled (lexically very Latinate, sometimes including Latin and other languages, and often syntactically complex). Greater precision can be obtained by grading each level separately – handwriting, orthography, lexis, grammar, syntax and punctuation. 'Schooled' does not imply that the writer attended school. Many writers of extensively schooled English (women especially) were tutored at home; others were autodidacts. Writing cannot be unschooled because the skill is not acquired like speech, but always learnt in at least one of the three scholarly situations mentioned.

'Schooledness' is an achronic scale. But since schooled English changes, I add a date range if I want to limit it diachronically: for example, 'fully schooled (1750–1800)', which is the period during which most writers in my corpus became letterate. Schooled English has a wide range of supporting means, such as dictionaries, grammar books, textbooks, style books, syllabuses, teachers, schools, the complaint tradition, editors and in the last 160 years teacher training colleges and ministries of education. All these means change with time, though not all at the same time.

Letteracy can be graded as a national characteristic. But this is also too general to be useful for studies of individual or local letteracy. Letteracy rates varied widely from parish to parish and county to county. William Stephens, for example, draws up two tables for rates of signature illetteracy: his table 1.1 lists forty-four towns (excluding the 'unusual' York[4]), and table 1.2 lists thirty-two counties in which the rates have been measured in a number of rural parishes. For the period 1799–1804 the rates of signature illetteracy range between 28–72 per cent and 24–62 per cent respectively (1987: 6–9). Similarly, in my study of letteracy rates in Horsmonden and its five adjacent Kent and Sussex (south east) parishes (Brenchley, Goudhurst, Lamberhurst, Marden and Wadhurst) from 1770 to 1849, the male and female signature letteracy rates varied from 61.0 per cent to

48.3 per cent, and from 49.3 per cent to 29.3 per cent respectively. It is, therefore, more accurate to think as Reay does 'of a range of cultures, of *literacies* rather than literate, and non-literate and illiterate' (1996: 253 [Reay's italics]).

3   Handwriting

Limiting literacy to writing does not simplify the field by much when considering writing diachronically. Reay, for example, says (1996: 213), 'A vast apparatus of scholarship has been erected on a simple measurement of "literacy": a person's ability to sign his or her name', and names eleven reseachers, some of whom think ability to sign proves the signer was letterate.

But I agree with Reay that signature letteracy does not imply that a writer can write anything else. Writing is commonly divided into five subskills: orthography, lexis, grammar, syntax and punctuation. But before all these a sixth skill must be established, handwriting. Researchers have paid little attention to handwriting because it is, of course, not present in print – their main area of interest – and because most scripts they have studied are by writers who are in print. If the handwriting of such writers deteriorates to a barely legible scrawl, researchers can safely give them the benefit of any doubt about which graph they intended, if the script is schooled on the other levels. But if a script with scrawled handwriting is less than extensively schooled lexically or grammatically or syntactically, researchers must not assume it is extensively schooled orthographically. The study of handwriting is as essential for judging a writer's level of letteracy as a study of their grammar is.

For example, (1) from English Record Offices (R.Os), I have built a corpus of over 1,500 letters by several hundred writers, containing over 250,000 orthographic units. Most letters were chosen because they were written in unconventional English. About 10 per cent are in conventional English and are noted as such. Some writers of unconventional English signed in a good copperplate hand. But their teachers must have made them practise handwriting more often than anything else, because no other linguistic level is as extensively schooled (see section 5). If you examine their handwriting, you can see that some writers did not take the pen off the page only at the end of an orthographic unit, nor only after a syllable or two, as skilled writers do, but also after almost every graph. They did not so much write their words as draw them like pointillist painters, perhaps sounding each graph, as the teacher had taught them to.

(2) Other writers lacked practice as well as skill. For seven years and five months (1797–1804) the parish of Horsmonden, Kent, paid for Mary Cramp (baptized 1793) to learn to read, but not to write because she was female. However, at her marriage on 23 February 1819 she signed *Mary Crmp* (see plate I). She clearly lacked practice; note her unconventionally formed <M>, and <a>, which she wrote first as <u> and then converted to <a> by closing the top. She did not space her <y> far enough from the preceding <r>, with the result that the leading ligature of the <y> partly overlaps the <r> and looks like another

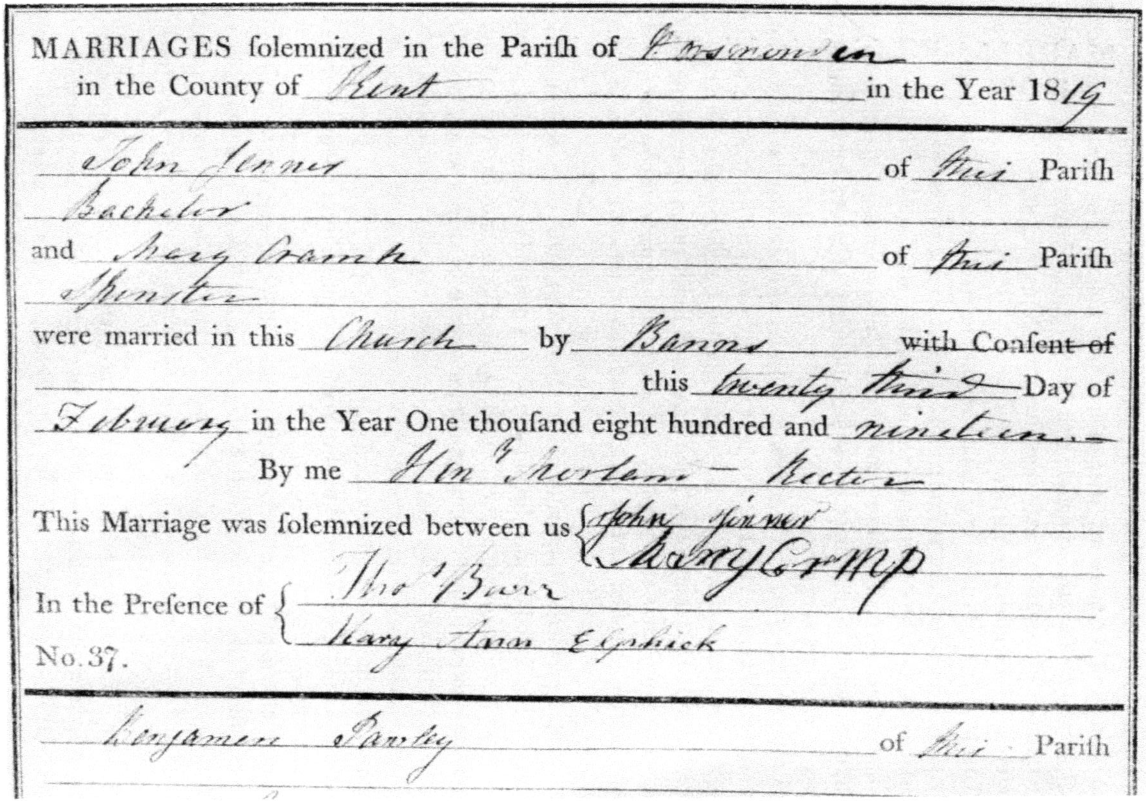

MARRIAGES folemnized in the Parifh of _Horsmonden_ in the Year 1819
in the County of _Kent_

John Turner
Bachelor of _this_ Parifh

and _Mary Cramp_
Spinster of _this_ Parifh

were married in this _Church_ by _Banns_ with Confent of
this _twenty ninth_ Day of
February in the Year One thoufand eight hundred and _nineteen_
By me _Wm Horton — Rector_

This Marriage was folemnized between us { _John Turner_
{ _Mary Cramp_

In the Prefence of { _Tho' Beer_
{ _Mary Ann Elphick_

No. 37.

Benjamin Clarke of _this_ Parifh

Plate I. Mary Cramp's signature (CKS(M): Horsmonden, P192/1/7)

<r> (compare Mary Elphick's <r> and long-ligatured <y>). After that bad start, Cramp improved in that, apart from omitting <a> and writing off-line, she formed the four graphs in her surname well. But her graph formation is pointillism of the most elementary type; she formed <p> with two strokes of the pen and her <m> also with two, probably three, perhaps dipping the pen into an inkwell for more ink after each stroke. Letteracy skills such as these are too minimal for us to conclude that Mary Cramp, despite being obviously determined not to sign her marriage lines with 'X' as many other Horsmonden brides did, could compose a letter.[5]

Unconventional handwriting can sometimes be so idiosyncratic and difficult to read that a reader must approach it as if attempting a new form of writing – must, that is, learn how **this** writer writes English graphs, before rewriting them in conventional form. To indicate that changing unconventional to conventional lettering is similar to changing Chinese signs or hieroglyphs into Roman lettering, I use the term 'transliterate'.

A transliterator's primary consistency must be with each handwriter's script, not with whatever the standard letteracy practice was at the time the document was written. Although, as Frances Austin, who has transliterated a collection of letters of mixed letteracy, says, '[t]he transfer of handwritten materials to print raises many problems and absolute consistency is virtually impossible' (1991: xiii), accurate transliteration is the precondition of accurate analysis of other levels.

Insoluble problems in transliterating handwriting arise from perilinguistic factors – blots, faded ink and discoloured or torn paper. Two potentially soluble ones arise from linguistic factors, which can be divided into two types. First, minimally schooled handwriting sometimes consists of shapes which look like no conventional graph (like Mary Cramp's upper case <M>), or, confusingly, the writer formed the wrong graph. An inexperienced writer typically did this when writing the less frequently used graphs – <j, J, q, Q, z, Z>. A few did not distinguish <u, v, w> either, but they could also fail to form common graphs conventionally.[6]

A collection of scripts, whether by the same or different writers, transliterated into less than fully schooled English may, therefore, look so inconsistent that, to reassure readers of the transliterator's and printer's reliability, transliterators should add a textual apparatus, in which they justify transliterations, explain problems, or admit inability to transliterate.

Second, inexperienced handwriters produce 'writos' – that is, unconventionalities which result from using a pen, as typos result from using a keyboard. Both hand- and keyboard-writers are likely to exchange words, or graphs, so metathesis is not a distinctive characteristic of either means of writing. But, whereas inexperienced handwriters can confuse ascenders with descenders and write, for example, <d> for <p>, they do not write <o> for <p>, as inexperienced typists do because the two keys are adjacent on the keyboard.

Sometimes the writer did not spot the error, sometimes they did, as, for example, John Wellden (or whoever wrote for him) did in Dover, Kent on *Feb 1: 1822*. The writer, whose letteracy is not extensively schooled on any level, began:

(1) *My children are very much [in want of Slo*

But after the <o>, they realised they had not completed an <h>. So, they immediately crossed out *Slo* and what you actually read is:

(2) *My children are very much [in want of ~~Slo~~ Shoes, if the Gentlemen [will Grant me the favour [. . .]*[7]

<l> for <h> is a writo, but <o> for <p> is a typo.

Writers of minimally and partly schooled Englishes usually altered their letters only for practical reasons, such as correcting nonsensical writos and rewriting something because it was not what they wanted to say. They rarely altered to produce fully schooled English, but seem to have envisaged one of their main tasks as 'putting sound on paper', i.e. representing the speech sounds they would have produced, rather than conforming to norms of conventional writing, of which they may or may not have been aware. Of 202 emendations in my corpus where the original writing can be read, only thirty-seven are towards schooled English but fifteen of these are in letters by persons who did not belong to the lowest orders and whose English was extensively schooled.

I have found it helpful to expand a concept usually expressed only in a single term – *logographic*. This term is used to describe how writing systems like Chinese or hieroglyphics function – a symbol does not signify a phoneme, but a complete word, as '&', '=' and '%' do. I have expanded this concept to a set of terms describing ways in which spellers seem to think their graphs function.

A *phonographic* speller is one who tries to spell phonemically. Minimally letterate writers are generally phonographic spellers. Phonographic spelling is common in bills which artisans made out for work they did for parishes. For example, 'Wm Halladay' billed the churchwarden of Chilham, Kent, for work he did in the church on 9 Nov 1801:

(3) *day menden Tilen & Clenen out th Guttrs self & Labar*
    (= day mending tiling & cleaning out the gutters self & labour).[8]

A *morphographic* speller is one who perceives and tries to spell a morpheme. This concept is particularly useful when some phonemes in a morpheme are not audible in a speech event – as with *-hurst* in a case to be studied (see section 6). Because of how literacy was taught in the time under study, some writers seem to have been unaware of or confused by morphographs:

(4)	Schooled	Monday, etc.	Newnham	Lancaster
	Script	Mondy	Nunam	Lankstar
	Place	*passim*	Kent	Cumbria (north west)

I have found no unconventional logographs in minimally letterate spelling.

Handwritten scripts differ from printed texts in two ways relevant to this study: one concerns the product and the other its producers. To take the producers first: print is always a joint product. Readers comment on and alter the writer's rough and fair copies; editors and typesetters make their alterations too. In addition to this external input into the writer's script, writers who can write fit for print often have available a range of means of support, such as dictionaries and grammar books. The text that gets printed is, therefore, not the product of an individual, but of a consensus, even diktat.

Handwriters may be helped by others but often write alone. Moreover, they – especially those who produced the partly schooled handwriting I examine later – were supported only indirectly and not at the time of writing by grammar books and the like.

Texts differ from scripts in that the history of the production of a printed text never exists in the text, but elsewhere – if it exists at all. But scripts, especially those by a writer too poor to buy paper for a rough copy, often include the writer's alterations. If researchers can make out a handwriter's first attempt, they can see the history of the script and try to understand what the writer tried to avoid or achieve.

4   Society and schooling

Chris Cook and John Stevenson (1996: 151) estimate that between 1700 and 1800 the population of England and Wales grew from 6.5 to 8.9 million (+37 per cent) and to 12 million by 1820 (+92.3 per cent). Patrick Colquhoun (1806: 23) calculated that the population of England and Wales in about 1803 was 9,343,561. Colquhoun listed the population by occupational groups. According to his figures, those to which (to my knowledge) writers in print most commonly belonged – peers, gentry, clergy, civil servants, people in professions – amounted to 725,665, 7.8 per cent of the population.

But many more people than that small group could write. Few of their scripts got into print, because they were not extensively schooled on all linguistic levels. These writers came from the 'lower orders', as they were called then – artisans, shopkeepers, hawkers, lesser merchants, household servants and others – who made up about 28 per cent of the population according to Colquhoun.

Some of these scripts were written in the name of a person who, being totally illiterate, or able to read but not write, told the writer what to put on the paper. Scripts in minimally and partly schooled English, therefore, provide us not only with direct evidence of the Englishes of the 28 per cent defined above, but also with better – albeit indirect – evidence than we have ever had of the Englishes of the remaining 64 per cent of the lowest orders – seamen, soldiers, labourers in husbandry, mining, manufacturing, etc., among whom were the illetterate. In sum, these scripts, written in the Englishes used by over three quarters of the population of England, enable researchers of Late Modern English to broaden the field of research beyond the small group (10 per cent, to be generous) who could write English fit to print, and whose English they have sometimes mistakenly identified with the English language as a whole.

At the same time as the population was growing, the demand for schools and schooling was growing even faster. John Caffyn, in his comprehensive documentation of schooling in Sussex, records that in the 1700s the number of charity schools increased from 32 to 85 (+165.6 per cent), and the number of a new type of school, the Sunday school, grew from almost zero in 1784 to 18 by 1797 (Caffyn 1998: 7–11). Ian Michael, who 'sought evidence mainly from textbooks and from a certain amount of general writing on education which bears directly on the teaching of English' from 'the sixteenth century to 1870', records that in the first half of the 1700s an average of 6.8 spelling- and reading-books was published every five years, in the last half 12.4 (+82.3 per cent) and from 1800 to 1820 27.7 (+307.3 per cent) (Michael 1987: 2–10). From 1750 to 1820, therefore, the demand by parents for schooling and its supply by entrepreneurs and benefactors outstripped the rise in population (at least in Sussex), and so nationwide did the demand for textbooks.

5 Schooling for letteracy

Schooling is a process with two types of direct input: (1) teachers; (2) textbooks and other teaching materials. Schools are not part of the teaching process. They are the environment within which the schooling takes place and may facilitate or hinder it.

In the 1700s either a child was taught alone at home by a full-time tutor, if the family could afford the expense, or by a parent, friend or relative, who usually had other work to do. Alternatively, it was taught with a number of others in five types of school, which are not always clearly distinguishable: (1) grammar; (2) private (including so-called dame schools, that is, a room in a private house where the inhabitant, usually a woman, taught a few pupils); (3) charity; (4) parish (often in the workhouse) and (5) from about 1784, Sunday schools (in Caffyn 1998: *passim*). In the 1700s private and charity schools outnumbered the other types of school. Grammar and some private schools accepted only letterate pupils and, therefore, are of no interest in this examination of how writing was taught.

Of home tuition – how it was done and in how many homes – we know almost nothing. But, as Caffyn says, 'without it . . . it is not possible to account for the relatively high levels of literacy that were achieved in the 18th century' (Caffyn 1998: 13).

Since the first teacher training college was not founded till 1840 in Battersea, London (Kay-Shuttleworth 1973 [1841]: 294–386), all teachers before that date were untrained, and, except for a few professional tutors, had, or had had other occupations. In Kent in 1837, for example, teachers included a 60-year-old failed farmer, and an ex-inmate of a lunatic asylum.[9] Michael, after recording 2,708 literacy textbooks and consulting 1,880 of them, concludes 'little is known of the work of these early teachers' (1987: 3). Since, therefore, direct evidence is scanty, we must try other ways to find out what teachers did.

Among these ways, a researcher's imagination is the least desirable, especially when considering drilling – that is, groups of pupils performing the same action at the same time, or the same type of action in turn. Richard Altick, writing at the time when teacher-centred methods were discouraged in favour of child-centred ones, 'imagine[d monitorial drills as] the nightmare (. . .) of automatons turning out new regiments of automatons on a mass-production line' (Altick 1957: 146).

Of all pedagogical methods, drilling was the one that teachers used most often in the early stages of teaching reading and writing, as is clear from the content of the spelling-books and what some writers recommended. Because drilling could be heard from afar, it was also the method that attracted most attention then, and it attracts attention now, though for different reasons.

There are four main objections to Altick's imagination. First, his 'pre-adolescent monitors' were themselves too young to keep drilling their pupils till they turned into automatons. Second, there is, as Rab Houston says, 'no mechanical connection between literacy and schooling' (1985: 111). Houston argues here for greater recognition of the contribution home tutors made to national 'literacy' rates. But the same can be said of the relationship between any kind of teaching and learning. Third, drilling was not out of place when, as Altick put it (1957: 143), '[i]n the age's educational theory [. . .] a man or woman of the masses was regarded solely as an atom of society, not as a person'. As pedagogical methods, drilling and – '[f]rom one dreadful extreme to the other!' (Altick 1957: 151) – catechizing (that is, learning fixed answers to a fixed series of questions) were not intended to teach children to think for themselves. Finally, if we accept the figures given above that over 70 per cent of the population in some parts of the country were at least signature-letterate at the end of the period under study, drilling may have been inefficient but it was not ineffective, even if we allow for the variety of methods which can occur in home tuition. To reject drilling simply because it suppresses individuality is to ignore what teachers who used the method achieved, and still achieve.

In order to try to connect what teachers did with examples of what their pupils wrote, I now look at the lesson material which three spelling-book writers provided for the early stages of teaching children to read.

Charles Vyse's *The New London Spelling-Book* was in print from 1776 to 1850 and was used in the Horsmonden charity schools in the early 1800s.[10] Lindley Murray, the grammarian, also wrote a spelling-book, which was in print in the first half of the 1800s and Favell Bevan's spelling-books were in print from 1836 to 1924.

All spelling-books started with the smallest units, arranged in tables (some with over 200 words). Pictures were likely to appear only at the beginning with the alphabet (A for Apple, etc.) and much later as illustrations to fables.

After the alphabet, Vyse began:

> *Table One*
> ba be bi bo bu by
> ca ce ci co cu cy
> (and so on for all consonant graphs except 'q' and 'x')
>
> *Table Two*
> ab eb ib ob ub
> ac ec ic oc uc
> (and so on for all consonant graphs except 'q' and 'v') (Vyse 1791: 2–3)

Note that a pupil learnt rare graph combinations among the common ones. For example, from Vyse's rows we can create a surname with unconventional spelling – *Akus* – which we shall meet later.

We cannot know now, of course, exactly what any particular teacher did each lesson and we rarely know which spelling-book they used. But we know from spelling-book prefaces that teachers made their pupils individually or together do any or all of three activities (I take 'ba' as a representative syllable):

1. Spell the graphs: 'bee. ay.' Spelling was regarded as so important that many textbooks had 'Spelling-book' in their title.
2. Sound graphs phonemically: /b/, and /æ/ or /a/ – or /eɪ/, which is more likely because some spelling-book writers tried to prevent children reading 'bab' as 'babe'.
3. Sound graph groups phonemically: /bæ/ or /ba/ or /beɪ/. Pupils chanted the combinations (if they rhymed, this was called 'jingling') until, as the poet John Clare put it: '[each one] gets his horn book alphebet by heart & then can say his lesson with his eyes as well shut as open' (Storey 1985: 70, Letter to John Taylor, 20 May 1820).

All writers sorted words into tables by number of syllables and place of stress. Murray graded his words very precisely and explained the rationale of most educationists in those days:

> The work is comprehended under three general divisions. One of the chief objects of the first part, is, to teach an accurate pronunciation of the elementary sounds. If this is effectually performed, in an early stage of learning, the child's future progress will be easy and pleasant; if it is then neglected, the omission will be rarely, if ever, completely supplied. To attain this important object, the author is persuaded that a considerable number of lessons, in monosyllables, is indispensable, (. . .) to inculcate the various and exact sounds of the letters – each section being confined to a short exercise on a particular elementary sound. Many persons will probably think, as the author does, that if he had intended to teach only orthography, the monosyllabic lessons would not have been too numerous. Such words are easy and familiar to children; and they constitute the radical parts of the

language. By hurrying the young pupil through this fundamental part of the language, he is often imperfectly taught, and eventually retarded in his progress. (Murray 1804: iv)

After each set of tables spelling-book writers put reading lessons. Here is part of Murray's scheme:

p. 16–17: one syllable words of three letters (tables totalling 72 words);
p. 18–19: one syllable words of four letters (90 words);
p. 20: one syllable words of five and six letters (36 words);
p. 21: one syllable words of short diphthongs (26 words: e.g. *death, said*);
(. . .)
p. 30: one syllable words of proper diphthongs (28 words: e.g. *oil, cow*);
(. . .)
p. 38: one syllable words of double consonants (77 words: e.g. *thank, that, them*);
(. . .)
p. 49: two syllable words with accent on the first syllable (138 words: e.g. *Ab sent, pack thread*. These are the first two-syllable words. All textbook writers separated the two syllables, Murray with a space, others with a hyphen);
(. . .)
p. 68: Promiscuous Reading Lessons (*Hay making. Hark! what noise is that. It is the mower whetting his sithe* (. . .));
(. . .)
p. 90: Words of three syllables with accent on the last (e.g. *Con tra dict, un der stand*. Here are the first long Latinate words and about here are the first subordinate clauses).

Murray was not a teacher, and his careful grading resulted in slow progress for the pupils.

Michael reports small differences between the schemes of work, but 'this intensely analytical approach (. . .) is almost universal' (1987: 16). But there was one significant change in the reading lessons. Until the end of the 1700s most spelling-books contained lessons with religious and moral content. This is Vyse's first lesson (1776: 4):

A bad Boy and a bad Man go in a bad Way, and put off the Law of God. All who go in a bad Way, do you no ill, nor use the ill way; for the End of it is bad.

But from about 1800 spelling-books with secular content were increasingly available, though the earlier books remained in demand for many years. Murray's reading lessons were secular, for example (1804: 42):

(. . .) There is a poor fly in the milk. Take it out. Put it on the dry cloth. Poor thing! It is not quite dead. It moves; it shakes its wings; it wants to dry them: see how it wipes them with its feet.
Put the fly on the floor, where the sun shines.
Then it will be dry and warm.
Poor fly! I am glad it was not dead.
I hope it will soon be well. (. . .)

But the limitations of a monosyllabic vocabulary meant that writers often had to use tables of unconnected sentences. This is Bevan (1836: 38; note the absence of punctuation):

I had a cat	I had a mat	I had a hat
I had a rat	I had a bat	
The cat had a rat	The cat had a mat	
A cat is in my hat	A rat is in my hat	A bat is in my hat
My cat is on the mat	My hat is on the mat	(. . .)

Some extralinguistic factors are now indeterminable, such as a pupil's intelligence and memory. Many educationists in those days thought these were the same capacity. One of the clearest and most succinct expressions of this assumption is in the report of Reverend J. A. Boodle, Diocesan Inspector, in the Log Book of Hunton National School, Kent, for 7 July 1876: 'The Catechism was written out intelligently, & the Repetition accurately (though rather too noisily) said.'[11] Educationists valued memory above other mental abilities: 'The reflecting child who argues from analogy will certainly fall into error, while the child, possessed of a mechanical memory, will be more successful' (Bevan 1836: xii). Most children want to do well; most children, therefore, must have tried their best to remember.

Information on precisely where learning to write fitted into these syllabuses is hard to find, but Caffyn records that in one Sussex school (Mayfield) pupils could remain up to three years in the readers' class before they were moved to the writers' class, and I found the same with the boys in Horsmonden. By my calculations the average lengths of time which the first 300 pupils spent reading and writing for whom Caffyn gives dates are: 234 boys (starting age: 8.5 years) 2.0 years reading and 2.5 years writing consecutively; 66 girls (starting age: 9.3 years), 1.7 years reading and 1.5 years writing, consecutively. In Horsmonden girls were not taught to write and several did nothing but read for six years.

Learning to write must, of course, have started with graph formation. But the next, and possibly only stage in the letteracy teaching was copying set texts. According to Caffyn, most, if not all, headteachers tried to attract parents by advertising 'Writing all the hands now in use' (Caffyn 1998: 214, Goldring's boys' boarding school, Petworth, 1783). Few advertised that their schools taught composition. The dozen or so epistolatory manuals I have examined contain letters which are all far above the lexical, grammatical and syntactic skills of a child from a labouring family, who attended school for three to four years.

Of course syllabuses begin with simple material. But the literacy syllabuses of the seventeen and eighteen hundreds, when combined with the teaching methods, made it difficult for children of the lower orders to become fully functionally literate. First, 'simple' was so defined that a child who began to learn to write often spent years jingling monosyllables. Second, when it began two-syllable jingles, it saw them printed as monosyllables before it saw them as whole words. Third, because such syllabuses taught 'words familiar to children' (Murray), almost all a child's early experience of literacy was of Anglo-Saxon, or of old Norman French words. Fourth, a pupil learnt few of the newer 'Inkhorn' Latinate words, ability to use which was a mark of full letteracy and of membership of the upper orders. Fifth, few spelling-books had glossaries, which defined the Latinates, and few exemplified their use in the reading lessons. Sixth, the content of the religious reading lessons was rarely such as would appeal to a child. Finally, the often child-centred content of the secular lessons was of little use in adulthood to pupils who left school by their early teens at the latest.

No matter, therefore, what educational theorists in the seventeen and eighteen hundreds said about the aims of literacy syllabuses, and no matter, either, that some wanted to improve the schooling of the lower orders, literacy syllabuses were so structured that a child of such parents could finish three years in school and still have a productive vocabulary scarcely larger than it started with. Without definitions and contextualization, reading the tables was little more than (to put it crudely) 'barking at print'. The child had had almost no training in producing scripts for a practical purpose, such as letters and bills, and none in free composition (Fairman 2005).

6   Spelling surnames

Words whose conventional spelling a writer did not know are the best sites for deducing lexical knowledge and assumptions. In practice, this means most words that minimal-letterates wrote, and many words that slightly better ones did too. But not even a writer of fully schooled English knew the conventional spelling for some surnames because there was none. Some spelling-books listed biblical family and place names and the names of British counties and large towns, but I have seen no lists of British surnames.

There were four occasions when clergymen had to record a parishioner's name in the parish registers – baptism, banns and marriage (most of them) and burial. Baptisms and marriages are usually more worth studying for linguistic purposes because we are less sure who spoke the surname at banns and burials.

If the surname speech event reminded the clergyman of a common English word – Best, Brown, Carpenter, Farmer, Fisher, Kitchen and so on – he had no problem. But some surname speech events suggested no single written version. If the speaker was letterate, they could spell their surname for the clergyman. But often (as, for example, /ˈeɪkəs/, which we shall study later) clergymen had to record the surnames of illetterate – or rather (to characterize them positively) orate – parishioners: language for them was only sound, so they could not do what we do these days: spell, or pronounce the spelling. If asked to speak more clearly, the orate speaker had no idea what the writer's problems were, so they might shout or drawl their surname, thus uttering variants, which would confuse the clergyman still further. These events caused many spellings, depending on (1) the speaker and the event; (2) the writer's ability to recall English words and orthographic systems; (3) their assumptions about unschooled speech (dialect). In the west today we rarely face this problem. But something similar happens if we hear a foreign place-name and want to look it up in an atlas index: /xabə'r.onɛ/, for example.[12] Phonologically aware researchers can scan a register and spot a surname entry which suggests events worth further study.[13] Surname events spoken by illetterate speakers are what I focus on in this section.

To distinguish orate speakers from letterate ones when someone else has to write their surnames, I call the former *name-holders* and the latter *name-owners*. Writers can rename name-holders, but name-owners control their surnames. There are, for example, now only Jenners in Kent (see Mary Cramp) and some families accepted unconventional spellings – 'Carpinter, Kitchin' and 'Mayger' are all in my local phone directory.

Contrary to what we might expect of men trained to use the same spelling for the same word, when a clergyman registered the surnames of his orate parishioners, he did not always copy the spelling the previous clergyman used, nor did he always use the same spelling in his own entries for the same family, nor even for the same person.

So, clergymen sometimes entered spellings for a name-holding family which readers might think have no connection with each other. To account for the possibility that different spellings can refer to the same person or family, genealogical reference sources – The International Genealogical Index, for example – group them in what I call a *surname cluster*. Some spellings are in a cluster for a genealogical reason – because someone has established that they have been entered for the same person or family. Others are there for phonological or orthographic reasons. For example, I include *Youens* in my Ewens cluster. Clergymen did not enter this spelling for the families I have studied in the west Kent parishes of Brenchley and Pembury, but I have noticed they did elsewhere together with the same spellings as for the families in my study. I label each cluster with the spelling that occurs first when they are ordered alphabetically.

We cannot know now, of course, what a name-holder said when uttering their surname, especially as they may have produced variants. However, after making two assumptions and taking three factors into consideration, I suggest one, or sometimes two 'very likely speech events' for each cluster, of whose consonantal values and vowel quantities I can be fairly sure, though I am less sure of vowel qualities.

My first assumption is that a writer of scripts fully or extensively schooled for that period was used to writing graphs representing phonemes they did not hear, because English spelling conventions force everyone to do this. My second assumption is that a clergyman was not likely not to spell a phoneme he did hear, especially when he was registering surnames in fulfilment of the law and in the house of God. A complicating factor is that many clergymen took charge of parishes far from their home areas, where they were not at first familiar with their parishioners' accents.

The three factors I take into consideration are: (1) the orate name-holder's probable accent; (2) the writer's assumptions about the speaker and their community; (3) the writer's use of English orthographic systems. I look first at clergymen's spelling. The clergymen studied here were all members of the Church of England and had studied Latin and Greek in Oxford or Cambridge Universities. They could, therefore, produce fully schooled English scripts.

My Ewens cluster – *Ewens, Ewings, Ewins, Hewens, Hewings, Huings, Uings, Uins, Youens* – suggests /ˈjuːənz / or ˈjuːɪnz / as very likely speech events, because clergymen would not have written *Ewens* if name-holders had always aspirated before the initial vowel and velarised the nasal consonant. A further fundamental schooled assumption was expressed by Samuel Johnson in the grammar which he attached to his *Dictionary* in 1755: 'For pronunciation the best general rule is, to consider those as the most elegant speakers who deviate least from the written words'. In his preface he judged unschooled speech by the same assumption, 'we now observe those who cannot read to catch sounds imperfectly, and utter them negligently'. If we apply Johnson's assumption to the Ewens cluster, then a clergyman – in Brenchley between 1807 and 1843 it was Andrews Kersteman and then Robert Leman – had three choices: he could (1) waive the principle of the dominance of orthography, assume that the illetterate name-holder really did know his own surname and register him as *Ewens* (both clergymen); (2) make the entry look more unconventional by waiving conventional orthographic systems too and entering *Uings* (Leman) – there are no precedents in English spelling for initial <ui->; (3) assume that the name-holder spoke negligently – as in "ewers of wood' (*Deut.* 29.11) – and register them as *Hewens* (both) or *Hewings* (Leman).[14]

The assumption that orthography determined elegant (schooled) pronunciation persisted well into the 1800s. John Walker, for example, in the preface to his influential *A Critical Pronouncing Dictionary* (1791, in print till 1873) disagreed with Johnson's fundamental assumption only in two details: (1) 'unaccented vowels, for want of the stress, are apt to slide into an obscurity of sound'; (2) 'Dr. Johnson's general rule (. . .) can only take place where the custom has not plainly decided' – i.e. where the custom of 'respectable speakers' has not plainly decided, as in the case, for example, of Walker's own surname, in which the <l> is not pronounced. Walker did not reject the assumption itself. Since, therefore, members of the lower orders – especially those who were illetterate – were not respectable, members of the upper orders did not take their pronunciations as determinants of schooled spelling. In the following case study of the Accock cluster in south west Kent I demonstrate that clergymen applied this assumption to surnames even though this implied that orate name-holders did not know their own name.

Some time before 1785 an illetterate family moved from the parish of Pembury to an adjacent parish, Brenchley, where nobody with that surname had lived till then. All keepers of the Brenchley parish books, religious and secular, recorded the surname of this family with entries that ended in <t>: *Acot, Accott, Aycut* – *Accott* being the curate Andrews Kersteman's preferred entry. On 20 October 1815 he married *Daniel Accott* and *Ann Eaton*, who made their marks in the register. But for the birth of their first child on 5 September 1816 he entered *Accock alias Alcock. Daniel & Ann. Labourer*, and then added round three margins of the parish baptism register:

> This name has been spelt by me heretofore thus (Accott) owing to the ignorance of the Parents who cd not read or write. I have reason to think that the name ought to be written <u>Alcock</u>, as the Family were so called when they lived in Pembury Parish, & I believe registered so by the late Vicar of Pembury, Mr Whitaker. A. Kersteman.[15]

Whitaker had indeed so registered the family in Pembury. But since the Brenchley writers had no elegant speakers' custom to prescribe their spelling and there is no obvious reason why they should prefer the morpheme <cot> to <cock>,[16] they followed a secondary principle and spelt what they thought they heard. Every clergyman and layman spelt the surname with no <l> in the first syllable and with a final <t>. The explanation for these early Brenchley entries must be that the name-holders said nothing in the first syllable which reminded the Brenchley writers of the word <all>. Indeed, one of them makes it plain what he did hear by starting *Ay-*. In the second syllable the name-holders used a final glottal stop, which had not then been identified as an articulatory feature and was probably part of what Johnson meant by 'utter negligently'.

However, in Kersteman's mind recording exactly what orate name-holders said was not the dominant principle. As soon as he learnt how another clergyman had recorded the speech events in their place of origin, he copied their spelling. By 'ignorance' Kersteman seems to have thought that name-holders pronounced their own surnames negligently because they were ignorant (negligent) of the elegant (determined by orthography) pronunciation.

But in Pembury *Alcock* was itself the result of the principle of schooled orthography dominating unschooled speech, but here the principle was realised in a different way. From as far back as the earliest (1638) legible entry in Pembury registers clergymen had not spelt the speech events with an <l> in the first syllable. Two entries begin <Au-> (1638 and 1663) and all the others begin either <Ak-> (1 occurrence) or <Ac-> (19 occurrences). The first entry with <l> is in 1736, one year after a clergyman took charge of the parish who spelt his own surname with an <l>: Thomas Elcock. Elcock's preferred entry was 'Alcock', which was copied by the next clergyman – John Whitaker.[17]

So far I have looked at surnames written by writers who seem to have known all or most English orthographic systems. I now include less letterate writers in a study of how another surname, which cannot be modelled on a common word, was written. From this I can point to another factor which helped determine how writers spelt surnames – the amount of knowledge of orthographic systems. To show how this factor worked, I look at how writers between 1629 and 1832 in the parishes of Bredgar, Milton Regis, Ospringe, Selling and Sheldwich in central north Kent dealt with the Accost cluster: *Accost, Accust, Acers, Ackhurst, Ackost, Acorst, Acres, Acust, Aikkers, Akars, Akehurst, Akers, Akhurst, Akres, Akurst, Akus, Aukhurst.*

One likely speech event – / 'eɪkəs / – was a problem for any writer who tried to spell what they heard: grammar does not permit an adjectival affix ('Acous') for a proper noun, nor do English orthographic systems permit *Akus*, although, as we saw, the earliest stages of some spelling-books appeared to sanction it and, perhaps as a result, it was, in fact, written in what looks like skilled handwriting.[18]

I have not found another possibility – 'A(y)cuss' or 'A(y)cass' – probably because even those who wrote minimally schooled English realised that by ortho-graphic convention a final <-ss> puts unwanted stress on the second syllable, and because the shifted stress and spelling suggest an (even in those tolerant days) unsuitable name: 'a curse'. There is plenty of evidence in spellings in 'dialect' literature that some vowel phonemes were short in the local accent (south east of London) – *hoss, puss, cuss* for 'horse, purse, curse'.

One solution, which involves perceiving the final /s/ as the voiced plural morpheme, occurred to some writers – *Acers, Ackers, Acres, Akers.* But most seem to have perceived the final sibilant as voiceless, so they still had a problem, which they solved by spelling unphonographically.

The simplest solution occurred mostly to less letterate writers – add <t> at the end, as Milton Regis shoemakers for the most part did: *Accost, Accust, Ackost.* But a third, morphographic solution (*-hurst*) demands more of a speller. The graphs in this morpheme represent four phonemes /h/, /ɜː/, /s/ and /t/, only one of which – /s/ – the writer heard. Furthermore, the syllabication is different, not / 'eɪkəs/ but / 'eɪk'hɜːst/. This was the entry of Milton Regis clergy, with shoemakers occasionally joining in.

The Accost cluster is found during roughly the same period in Selling a few miles east. Here the surely no less letterate clergy wavered between *Akars, Acust, Acers, Acres* and *Akers.* In 1813 Matthias Rutton married *Thomas* and *Mary Acust* and baptised their first son *Thomas Acust*, although in previous years in Sheldwich, an adjacent parish, where he also officiated, he had baptised and buried children of the letterate name-owners, James and Mary Akhurst. But in the next entry for the same Selling family the next clergyman, James Halke, first baptised two more children, *Benjamin* (1816) and *Isaac* (1818) as *Acres*, and then in one disastrous year (1821) baptised *Charlotte*, then buried all the children and their mother and finally remarried the father, all as *Akhurst.* In eight years, therefore, two clergymen had renamed the father from *Acust* to *Acres* to *Akhurst.*[19] The orate name-holder,

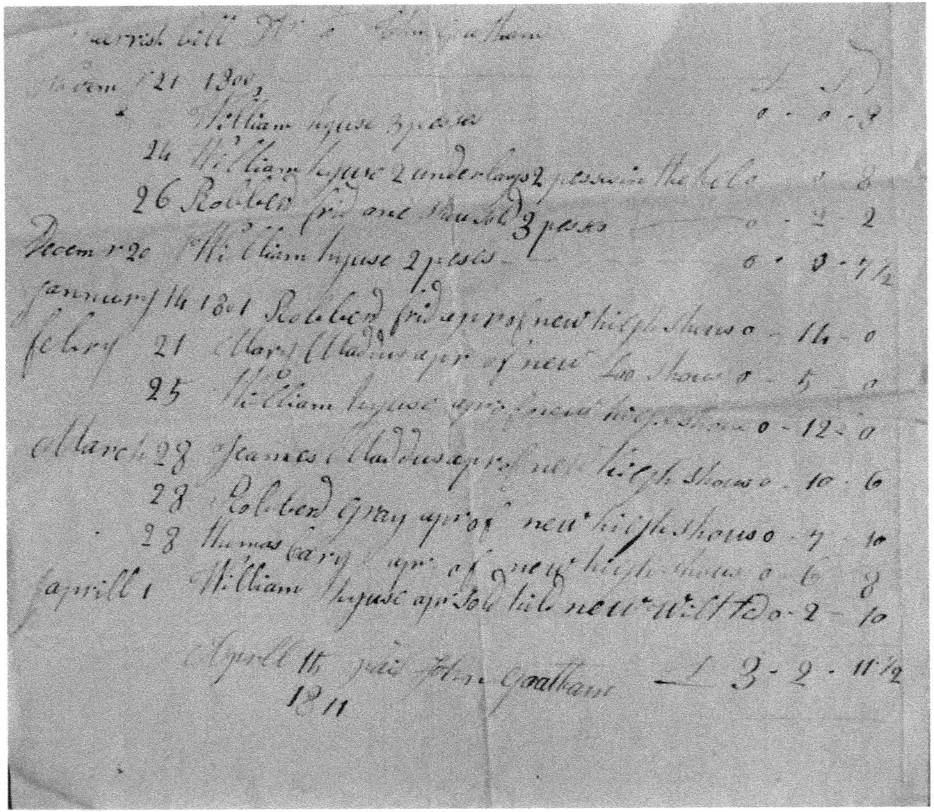

Plate II. A bill by John Goatham (CKS(M): Bredgar, P43/12/7/Bundle 5; microfilm 699)

Thomas Acust-Acres-Akhurst, probably did vary his surname allophonically, but he is not likely to have made the phonemic changes which made Halke change his spelling so that readers might assume that the three entries were the surnames of different persons and not variants of the same person's surname. The stimulus for change must have come mostly from Halke's own assumptions and his fully letterate knowledge of the possibilities in conventional English orthography.

Ability to perceive a morpheme in speech and to spell it, whether conventionally or unconventionally, grows with schooling. It is impossible to be absolutely sure about this because four linguistic levels are involved – handwriting, spelling, grammar, lexis – and writers may be good on one level but weak on another. Nevertheless, writers who are bad at morphographic writing tend to be bad on other levels of letteracy too. An example of this is shown in plate II.

Plate II shows one of seven surviving bills which John Goatham made out for shoemaking in Bredgar, Kent (1799–1803). Although he perceived the morphemes in his trade terms and in his own surname (others spelt it *Gothem*), he did not perceive any in his customers' surnames. Below I transliterate all Goatham's words and *translate* a few, where necessary:

(5) parrish bill d^tr (*debtor*) to John Goatham

Novem^r	21 1800
	William hyuse (*Hughes*) 3 pesses (*pieces*)
	24 William hyuse 2 underlays 2 pesses in the hel (*heel*)
	26 Robberd (*Robert*) Frid (*sic*, or *Freed*) one Shou Sold (*shoe soled*) 3
Decemr	20 William hyuse 2 peses[pesses
Jannury	14 1801 Robberd Frid apr (*a pair*) of new high Shous
febry	21 Mary Maddus (*Medhurst*) apr of new Loo (*Low*) Shous
	25 William hyuse apr of new high Shous
March	28 Jeames (*James*) Maddus apr of new high Shous
	28 thomas Cary apr of new high Shous
aprill	1 William hyuse apr hild (*heeled*) new Wiltted (*welted*)
Aprll	15 paid John Goatham
	1811 (*1801*)[20]

Goatham's spelling is not Kentish, nor idiosyncratic. It is typical of a partly letterate writer and follows the first (phonographic) rule found in all spelling-books. Thomas Dilworth's spelling-book (1751, still in use after 1800) was just one of several examples in which a spelling-book writer set down the rationale underlying the drilling of two- and three-graph combinations in the early lessons: '*Monosyllables* not only make the greatest Part of our Tongue, but are the substantial Parts of all Words of more than one Syllable' (Preface: vi). Fifty years later Murray put it another way in the passage I quoted above (see section 5). They all believed drilling monosyllables was the foundation for their pupils' literacy. Goatham has two graph combinations (*Hyu* and *dus*, and *-le* in *Camselle* for 'Kemsley' in another bill) which show that his feeling for which graphs cannot by convention go together in certain contexts was incomplete. But they did go together in the first pages of the spelling-books, including in Lindley Murray's.

7   Spelling other orthographic units

In one respect writing surnames was easy. All writers of whatever degree of letteracy knew that however many syllables a surname had, it was a single ortho-graphic unit (rare double-barrelled surnames excepted) although less letterate writers did not always capitalise the first graph.

But with other classes of word it was different. Speakers do not usually mark the boundaries of common words as clearly as they do those of surnames. Fur-thermore, when textbook writers introduced polysyllabic words, they did not print them as units. We must also bear in mind that, although, depending on the area, between 28 and 76 per cent of the population in the early 1800s were signature-letterate, most of these lived in what was largely an orate culture. In 1838 Frederick Liardet, for example, inspected about 350 households in three north Kent parishes and noted books (87 per cent of them 'religious') in only 26.8 per cent (94) of them.

Despite all this, the untrained teachers produced almost the desired result at least as far as writing orthographic units is concerned. In my corpus less than 10 per cent of all the orthographic units that the less letterate wrote are not words. In this small percentage of certainly deliberate, unconventionally spaced ortho-graphic units are some idiosyncrasies, some writos, and some Latinate words which writers could not reproduce conventionally – malaprops as they are dis-missively called. But some of the rest exemplify a structure which suggests what these partly letterate handwriters seem to have assumed to be a characteristic of the English word, i.e. first-syllable stress. It is therefore of interest to investigate how they represented words where the stress falls later than the first syllable; these words are chiefly Latinate in origin.

This structure is found all over England typically in minimally letterate scripts – some examples are in more letterate ones too. It is exemplified in three unschooled ways in which the least letterate writers could spell Latinate words with a weak first syllable:

- **excision of the first syllable:** *tack of feever* ([attack of fever] Berkshire (just west of London)); *prantis* and other spellings ([apprentice] *passim*); *pologise, the torney* ([apologise, attorney] Cornwall, far south west); *nockalashun, tenden, shuar ans, sistants, Grement, Plobbel* ([inoculation, attending, assurance, assis-tance, agreement, deplorable] Kent); *shord* ([assured] Buckinghamshire, just north west of London); *straining* ([destraining] *passim*); *cess, sess* ([assess], used by spellers of all degrees of schooledness, *passim*); *wesery* ([advisory] Yorkshire, north east); *form* ([perform] Durham, north east); *sponcable* ([responsible] Somerset, south west); *an old Stablish Fun* ([an old established fund], Suffolk (East Anglia)) – sometimes the excised syllable re-appears as an article, as in *put him as a prentice to [me* ([engage him to me as an apprentice] Cheshire (north west Midlands)).

- **detachment of the first syllable (aphesis):** *in form, a prentice* ([inform, apprentice] *passim*); *a Gree, a Grid* ([agree, agreed] *passim*); *Con Clude, de stress* ([conclude, distress] Cambridgeshire, East Midlands); *a quint* ([acquaint] Cornwall); *so fistient* ([sufficient] Dorset), *a Counts, a Bay* ([accounts, obey] Kent); *a plin* ([applying] Yorkshire); *de [termint De termi-nashon* ([determination] Herefordshire, West Midlands); *in Clind* ([inclined], Staffordshire (North Midlands)). Unstressed first syllables are also detached from non-Latinate words: *a nother* ([another] Berkshire); *a Nuf* ([enough] *passim* in several spellings).
- **conflation of the first and second syllables:** *Stifffitck* ([certificate] Dorset); *prish* ([parish] Cambridgeshire); *cracter* ([character] Yorkshire); *drict, druck,* and several other spellings ([direct = send to] *passim*); *preashener* ([parishioner] Herefordshire).

Two examples in these lists are especially relevant to the point I am discussing.

First, in 1821, William Wall, *Jerneyman Taylor* in Hampshire (south-central), about 130 miles (210 km) from his home parish in Herefordshire, set out his letter as such writers occasionally did, as a formal petition, ambitiously aiming at schooled syntactic structures and Latinate lexis, an aim which he did not have the ability to carry out successfully: *To the oversears of the parish of stocke to Wich [your Humble petitoener and parioshener [Wm Wall [Ø] Dose Be Long (...)* .[21] Wall wrote nineteen words beginning with a weak syllable. Among these he wrote eight conventionally, detached the first syllable from ten others, and, having – perhaps – given *parioshener* the conventional number of syllables at the beginning of his letter, did what such writers often did – spelt it differently elsewhere, conflating the first two syllables: *preashener*. He started writing 'determination' but it did not fit on the line so he continued on the next. But before he had finished, he crossed out what he had written on the second line and began the word again but divided it so that he did not begin a unit with a weak syllable:

(6) *de [termint De terminashon.*

Second, J. Headlam, (*Jen^y th 3-1834*) seems to have been copying from an official document – *I have [A abstract of the Pensioners Act by me.* But still he wrote

(7) *form* for 'perform'.[22]

The lexeme with a weak first syllable which they most often spelt unconventionally is 'direct', which occurs in various conflated spellings in nearly 12 per cent (17) of all its instances (142) in my corpus and which is unlikely to have been part of their productive spoken wordstock. 'Inform' is another such lexeme, whose syllables they separated in about 6.9 per cent (14) of all instances (204).

Aphesis is just one aspect of the larger process which I have described and which needs explaining. One contributing factor may be that the writers had seen syllables separated in their schoolbooks, and psycho-dynamic causes are also possible. But if we look at the productive wordstock of those who had not received much schooling and must, therefore, have used the same vocabulary in writing as they did in speech, we can see a similarity between this structure and the type of vocabulary they used most often, in most of which the stress is on the first syllable.

From my corpus I have chosen six letters, handwritten in minimally and partly schooled English in different parts of England by

i.   Augustin(e) Morgan, Dorset
ii.   Benjamin Brooker, Essex
iii.   Richard Jones, Herefordshire
iv.   Stephen Wiles, Kent
v.   one of the many writers for Luke Bratt, Kent
vi.   Susannah Wyld, Westmorland (north west).[23]

To match these partly schooled letters I have chosen six written in extensively and fully schooled English by

vii.   Lady Mary Armytage, a friendly handwritten letter to her future daughter-in-law
viii.   John Best, schoolboy, a handwritten model letter from some epistolatory manual
ix.   Samuel Taylor Coleridge, the opening of a letter on autobiographical and linguistic matters to H. J. Rose (now in print)
x.   Samuel Johnson's famous letter to Lord Chesterfield (now in print), telling him he had been useless as a sponsor and was not needed now the dictionary was in print
xi.   James Kay-Shuttleworth (the pioneer of universal schooling in England), a printed letter of dedication to Rev. Thomas Chalmers, D. D.
xii.   William Lushington to his father-in-law, General Lord George Harris, asking for a loan of money for a female friend.[24]

Since most grammatical words are Anglo-Saxon and are used alike in fully and minimally schooled English, I have not counted them. Table 2.1 contains the figures for the tokens of Anglo-Saxon and Latinate content words, which the twelve writers used, with Inkhorns included in the Latinates and then totalled separately. Table 2.2 contains the figures for the types.

The tables show that scripts which are partly schooled grammatically or syntactically had fewer Latinate words than did extensively schooled scripts, and that the partly letterate writers used their content lexemes more often than fully letterate writers did theirs. There are three reasons for this; first, writers were, and still are, exhorted not to use the same content word too often. Second, partly letterate writers often gave their information a ringform structure, as for example, James Lock, cordwainer, wrote from Oxford (south Midlands) to his parish in Gloucestershire (south west Midlands):

Table 2.1. *Tokens: Anglo-Saxon vs Latinate.*

Tokens	Partly schooled	Extensively schooled
All tokens	1,360	1,413
All content tokens	446	516
Anglo-Saxon content	333	188
% of content tokens	74.7	36.4
Latinate content	113	328
% of content tokens	25.3	63.6
in which is included Inkhorn content	1	59
% of content tokens	0.2	11.4

Table 2.2. *Types: Anglo-Saxon vs Latinate.*

Types	Partly Schooled	Extensively Schooled
All content types	177	391
Anglo-Saxon content	110	120
% of all types	62.2	31.7
Latinate content	67	271
% of all types	37.8	69.3
in which is included Inkhorn content	1	57
% of content types	0.6	14.6
Type/Token ratio	1:2.5	1:1.3

(8) *and she A dead [cripple, so that she cannot be mov'd* [5 lines later] *and cannot [be mov'd, on account of her affliction.*[25]

Third, whereas fully letterate writers used different Latinate verbs to express different meanings, partly letterate writers combined the same Anglo-Saxon verb with prepositions and prepositional adverbs (phrasal verbs), as in: 'get' + 'by, into, off, over, round, to, up' and 'put' + 'at, about, forward, in mind, off, on, out, to, up with, upon'.

In fact, the gap between the Anglo-Saxon and Latinate wordstocks of the two classes of writer is even more striking if one looks more closely at their Latinate words. In my classification, the term 'Latinate' includes any word from a Romance language, regardless of when it entered the English language. Some Latinates had entered the language via French with the Normans some seven hundred years earlier, if not before. By the early 1800s many of them, especially those of one or two syllables, had long been part of the productive wordstock of all users of English. But from the time of Sir Thomas Elyot in 1531 writers of schooled English began to use hundreds of neologisms from languages such as Latin and French. These imports I refer to as 'Inkhorns', the term used by those who disapproved of them at the time. The classification, 'Latinate' and 'Inkhorn', therefore, depends on the period during which each relevant word entered English, as evidenced by, for instance, the *Oxford English Dictionary* and the *Oxford Dictionary of English Etymology*. From the two tables it is clear that Inkhorns were not part of the productive vocabulary of most users of English.[26]

We can find further evidence of how unfamiliar Latinate lexis was to some less than fully letterate writers, and of their oral/aural (not literal) perception of the English language in one particular phrase – 'take it into consideration'.

All parishes dealt with applications for relief similarly. The overseer could grant the application on his own authority, but, usually he laid the letter before the monthly meeting of the parish council (called 'the vestry' because that was where it often took place), who took it into consideration and paid relief – or not, as the case may be. A member of the lower orders, especially if they lived outside their home parish, had probably never attended a vestry to plead their case before the gentlemen, and so had no precise idea of what happened. But they heard other speakers say something in their unschooled local accents, which we write as 'take it into consideration'. But they wrote:

(9) *taket in Considarchen*
    (one of John Arger's writers)

(10) *tacket in to considdertion*
     (Rich[d] Garlick)

(11) *take it into Consideration my case*
     (E[th] Heap)

(12) *Sir be so kind as take it into consideration [As I ham very ill*
     (Ellen Marks)

(13) *Take it into Consither rasion.*
     (Jhon Ashby)[27]

Sometimes the writer listed several things for the vestry to consider and immediately summed them up in the singular pronoun *it*, or they used *it* in the opening statement of the letter, with no preceding or following complement for it to refer to, as Ellen Marks did above. In the minds of some minimally letterate writers 'take it into consideration' was a formula, whose constituent parts they could not analyse conventionally, and whose precise meaning they were unclear about. The following writers, for example, had not figured out the schooled meaning of the verb *consider*:

(14) *if you [will ave the goodness to Conceder mee [somtheng to wards Clothing my small [famely*
     (arrot (= Harriet) Rayner)

(15) *you may considar [your self 7 Childer & 6 of them very smal ones*
     (Rich[d] Garlick)

(16) *gentelmen if you will [but consider me it and send [me a triful*
    (Mary Jane Stears).[28]

Latinate words were transparent to readers who had learnt Latin. They might, for example, remember that 'postpone' came from the Latin *ponere* ('place') and *post* ('after'), or that 'distract' came from the Latin *trahere, tractum* ('pull') and *dis* ('asunder, aside'). By comparison the Anglo-Saxon *put off* is opaque. Moreover, like so many Anglo-Saxon phrasal verbs, it has two meanings: 'postpone' and 'distract'. Such Anglo-Saxon opacity and ambiguity are what textbook writers had in mind when they instructed pupils how to write with 'accuracy and perspicuity', and thereby lexically separated schooled from unschooled English.[29]

8   Matters arising

If my analyses of orthographic units in scripts with different degrees of schooledness and of their causes are tenable, three topics need to be investigated.

8.1   Anglo-Saxon vs Latinate

When I began researching partly schooled scripts, I assumed that the distinction between Anglo-Saxon and Latinate lexis was of no significance. But it has turned out to have been a key marker of social status and attainment in letteracy, although few in the 1800s used the two terms. 'Anglo-Saxon' was often opposed to 'Norman'. So, it was perhaps partly to avoid a division which had complex historical, social and racial as well as linguistic connotations that its linguistic aspect was defined as a matter of syllables, and 'monosyllabic' (that is, Anglo-Saxon) became almost a term of abuse.

James Kay-Shuttleworth was one who did use this pair of terms:

> Those who have had close intercourse with the labouring classes [Kay-Shuttleworth inspected Manchester slums before Friedrich Engels did] well know with what difficulty they comprehended words not of a Saxon origin, and how frequently addresses to them are unintelligible from a continual use of terms of a Latin or Greek derivation; yet the daily language of the middle and upper classes abounds with such words. (1973 [1841]: 339)

I give the following eight instances that the distinction was and still is significant, and merits research. As pointed out in section 1, I draw on sources from before and after the early 1800s. First, in 1679 the poet and playwright, John Dryden, using the customary term, wrote in his Epistle Dedicatory to Robert Earl of Sunderland in *Troilus and Cressida*: 'we are full of Monosyllables, and those clog'd with consonants'. But it was consonantal clusters, as in /gdw/ in the quotation from his own writing, which he disliked, not monosyllables in themselves. For example, in his well-known second edition revision (1684) of his first

edition (1668) of *Of Dramatick Poesie*, he did not dislike monosyllabic prepositions, only their sentence- and occasionally their clause-final positions, as in *As
for the poor honest Maid, whom the Story is built upon* (. . .) (1668: 18), which in
1684 became *on whom the Story is built* . . . (both editions are in Boulton 1964).
So, although he moved all sentence-final prepositions, he moved only twenty-
eight (21.4%) out of 131 clause-final ones. Furthermore, only in ten instances of
the twenty-eight did he get rid of the preposition by changing the wording – as
call'd for (1668: 3) became *desired* (1684). In all the other instances he let phrasal
prepositions and other short Anglo-Saxon words 'clog' his prose.

But by the middle of the 1700s monosyllabic Anglo-Saxon lexis was being
judged unschooled. Johnson – notorious as a Latinate writer – recorded phrasal
verbs as lexemes in his dictionary, but registered disapproval of them in his
preface: 'a class of word too frequent' (1755).

Second, in a section headed 'Of the different Excellencies and Defects of different Languages', James Burnet (Lord Monboddo), who, like James Harris,
expounded the linguistic theory of the late 1700s, wrote 'a language all of monosyllables, such as the Chinese, or with very many monosyllables, such as ours,
can never have a sweet or pleasant flow' (Burnet 1773–92, 4: 8). By 1797 Murray
had written exercises for changing Anglo-Saxon phrasals to single Latinate verbs
(see note 29). In the early 1820s the poet, John Clare, having probably witnessed
the effect a monosyllabic politician made on his audience, satirized an 'orator
(. . .) at the hustings [for] bad english':

> No hungry magpie round a rotten sheep
> A longer song of nonsence up can keep
> Were small words all their utmost powers engage   [where]
> And monnysyllables swell mad with rage
> (Robinson 1985: lines 807–10)

Third, people with, or aspiring to, social status devalued Anglo-Saxon lexis and
grammar because they were the language of the lower orders. But they could not
ban them totally because they were the language of the Bible[30] and of some of the
best English literature. In 1831 the historian, Thomas Macaulay, wrote of John
Bunyan's *Pilgrim's Progress*:

> The vocabulary is the vocabulary of the common people (. . .). There is
> no book in our literature on which we would so readily stake the fame of
> the old unpolluted English language, no book which shows so well how
> rich that language is in its own proper wealth, and how little it has been
> improved by all that it has borrowed. (Macaulay 1907, 2: 410)

Fourth, phrasal avoidance strategies continued into the late 1800s. I have come
across one book in which the author, apparently unable to think of alternatives to phrasal verbs, joined almost all prepositions (and a few more lexical
classes) to the foregoing verb with a hyphen (Carpenter 1875: *passim*). But nowa-
days prepositions and adverbs are converted to nouns or adjectives and even to

verbs – totally unknown in Latin and not in any early English grammar book I have looked in. For example, the former train-operating company, Connex, used to issue a monthly newsletter called (my italics) '*Upfront*: Your local Connex *update*'. The banner headline in the May 2001 issue was 'Thank you for being *Upfront!*'.

Fifth, Dryden (1679) described one of the mechanisms which activated strategies for English usage in Early and Late Modern English:

> But how barbarously we yet write and speak, your Lordship, knows, and I am sufficiently sensible in my own English. For I am often put to a stand, in considering whether what I write be the Idiom of the Tongue, or false *Grammar*, and nonsence couch'd beneath that specious name of *Anglicisme*. And have no other way to clear my doubts, but by translating my English into Latine, and thereby trying what sence the words will bear in a more stable language

Richard Bailey (2003: 30) thinks *Anglicisme* refers to 'inept Latin'. But it doesn't. Dryden meant that, if he could not translate his own English literally into Latin or Greek, it was *specious Anglicisme*.[31] Even the translations in the simple *Cassell's Latin Dictionary* bring to mind generations of schoolboy howlers and reveal the 'sence the [*Anglicisme*]s bear' – for example, '**put**, (. . .) to – down, (fig) *ex(s)tinguere*; see DESTROY; (. . .) to – off, *differre*; see DELAY'.

Sixth, Greek – 'the finest language that ever existed' (Burnet 1773–92, 4: 2) – and Latin – 'if I could write in Latin as well as some of the scholars in England, (. . .) I would never write in English' (Burnet 1773–92, 4: 62) – provided the models for schooled English. Those who could translate English into Latin and *vice versa* had the social status and the presence in print to set a linguistic standard for those who needed one.

Seventh, Murray recorded the fact that English nouns can be converted to adjectives with no morphemic change (1795: 166, under 'Rule 8' in the syntax of adjectives), but neither he nor, so far as I know, any other textbook writer, made pupils practise it. But by the middle of the 1800s Matthew Arnold, poet, essayist and school inspector, was quite inventive with his adjectival nouns, but signalled his discomfort with his conversions by using hyphens: 'education-rate, prize-scheme, school-machinery, state-expenditure, education-societies, newspaper-test, home-training, prison-discipline', and many more (Super 1962: *passim*).

Eighth, a sensitivity to Latin and Anglo-Saxon which was still widely felt at the end of the 1800s had not disappeared entirely from written English by the end of the 1900s. For example, (1) At least one modern researcher calls the distinction *The Lexical Bar* (Corson 1985); (2) in a draft of this study, the editors of this book wrote 'in the interest of consistency (. . .) please use corpora' (I had written 'corpuses'). *Corpus* is a Latin word and now an English linguistic term, whose use linguists can control as a third declension, neuter noun: *corpus–corporis*. But the editors did not require 'syllabi' for my 'syllabuses'. 'Syllabus' is not a linguistic term, nor is it Latin (*OED*: 'a misreading of L[atin] *sittybas*'). But in the mid-1600s it was classed as a second declension masculine Latin noun and declined in English accordingly. In linguistic terminology the division – Latinate vs. Anglo-Saxon – is still active, though, as in previous centuries, it is not labelled as such.

8.2   Diffusion

A second topic for Late Modern English research is what some historians of language and society call diffusion – synchronic and diachronic.

For example, Richard Watts used the metaphor for the spread of institutional influence (my italics in this quotation and in the next):

> the significance of certain powerful social institutions through which dom-
> inant social values were not only constructed and *diffused throughout* society
> but were also built into and made part of the hegemonic practices of govern-
> ment and administration. The most influential of these social institutions
> was that of 'public' education in the form of schools and universities (. . .)
> and the grammars of English that were written specifically for it (. . .)
> (Watts 1999: 40)

Dick Leith used a related metaphor when he wrote that one remedy for the 'barbarous' nature English was thought to have in the early 1500s 'was to *inject* thousands of Latin loan-words into the language' (Leith 1997: 46).

Injected fluids typically spread throughout the system they are injected into. But English was not used as a single system. Letters by and for the labouring poor show that some three hundred years after Inkhorns had been introduced into English only a minority of the English-using community – members of the upper social orders – used them.

Second, during the period studied here, schooling, one of Watts's 'powerful social institutions', did not function as a single system either. There were at least five types of school, ranging from one like Horsmonden Charity School, which spent about fourteen shillings a year (1797–1816) teaching a pupil only to read and one pound fourteen shillings teaching them also to write,[32] to Dane John Academy in Canterbury, which was not among the most expensive schools in England, but charged General Lord George Harris £38 for 'Board and Instruction' for his fifteen-year old protégé, John Best, in the first half of 1813.[33]

Third, I have argued that, although Vyse, Murray, Bevan and other textbook writers intended their books to lead to full literacy, the consequences of their syllabuses for most pupils were not what the writers intended nor what modern educationists and researchers assume.

In the England of the 1700s and early 1800s schooled English seems to be diffused through the English-using community at isolated points, that is, among families who spoke and wrote it to each other, but had limited influence outside their circle – diffused, therefore, not like ink in English water but like safari lodges in game parks.

What value parts of the community outside this well schooled group placed on the language of the upper orders we have yet to establish. In my data there is no obvious reason why users of unschooled English should have thought they had to write schooled English. Their bills were paid and their requests for parish relief granted irrespective of their schooledness on any linguistic level. It is likely that before universal schooling most users of unschooled English were indifferent to schooled English.

Other users of unschooled English may have thought about schooled English as the poet John Clare did. He, no doubt, had been taught that his Northamptonshire (East Midlands) English did not have grammar, and wrote: 'grammer in learning is like Tyranny in government – confound the bitch Ill never be her slave' (Storey 1985: 231; letter to John Taylor 21 February 1822).

Finally, diachronic diffusion is not a matter of the simple domination of schooled over unschooled Englishes. There has been interchange between them. The declining influence of Latin and growing acceptance of Anglo-Saxon lexis and lexical operations into schooled English need to be charted.

8.3   Mainstream English

In my discussion of possible influences on a writer's spelling I did not consider one factor – dialect, or, more precisely, the writer's accent. I have four reasons for this omission.

First, my examples were written by monodialect speakers, who must have had a local accent and were probably taught by teachers who had the same accent. So, they did not think of writing, for example, <carstle>, nor <cassle>, because <castle> signified whatever they said. Only if the local allophonic variation co-incided with a conventionally different phoneme was their local accent likely to reveal itself in their spelling; for example, once or twice in Dover a *fishaman*, Harvey Worell (or his writer), addressed his letter to *New rumley* (= New Romney). Elsewhere in Kent even writers of partly schooled English sometimes wrote the Kentish <w> initially, *wery*, for the conventional <v>.

Second, only fully letterate writers had the bidialectal ability to spell so as to convey a local accent to fully letterate readers. Therefore, third, in the medium of writing the term 'dialect' has acquired a special meaning, as the catalogues of all Record Offices illustrate. Under the heading 'Dialect' archivists list dictionaries of local lexis, and texts – usually poems – written in what purports to be local lexis and grammar.[34]

I have looked at about twenty 'dialect' texts. All were, to the best of my knowledge, written either by writers who had never spoken dialect, or by bi-dialectal speakers who had been schooled out of their dialect but, later as bi-dialectals, took advantage of the market for 'dialect' literature after about 1850.[35] These texts are easy to distinguish linguistically from the scripts of unidialect speakers.

Since there was then no International Phonetic Alphabet with an agreed sound for each symbol, 'dialect' writers wrote graphs (and occasional diacritic marks) in sequences unlike any in minimally schooled scripts. They spelt not only to convey a local accent to those who could spell conventionally, but also for humour (*ottibography* (= autobiography), Richard Lower, Sussex). They did not distinguish between a local accent and 'dead' graphs, glides, elisions, conflations and mutations caused by phonological context, so the 'dialect' they wrote is sometimes no different from what all speakers say. Moreover, they did what unidialect writers rarely did – spelt the commonest words and names unconventionally, for example: *abeawt* (= about), *aw* (= all), *cud* (= could), *de* (= the), *goä* (= go), *Lunnun* (= London), *ov* (= of), *ya* (= you).[36]

Finally, although some letters from which I quote contain features whose use is geographically restricted, in most there is no sign, apart from the postmark and addresses, where the writer lived (see Fairman, 2002b and 2003). To describe the dialect features in partly schooled scripts is not, therefore, to describe one of their defining features.

Two questions arise: (1) if the scripts are not in dialect nor Standard – fully schooled (1750–1850) – English, what variety of English were they written in? (2) what factors contributed to their writing?

It is possible to regard less than fully schooled writings as interlanguages, on their way to schooled English as Jack Richards, Larry Selinker and others treated Third World Englishes as 'inter', on their way to 'native-speaker competence' in the 1970s, before they were accepted as Englishes in their own right. My corpus contains letters at many stages of schooledness, including several sequences in which the schooledness remains the same over fifteen years, but so far I have seen no example in any archive I have visited of the same writer producing scripts at different stages of letteracy.

In this study I have tried to answer the second question by discussing certain classes of orthographic unit. I have given evidence that, just as clergymen and other writers of fully schooled English spelt words according to their schooling, so writers of less than fully schooled English spelt according to their schooling. And both were influenced by what they assumed about language in general. As for the first question about variety, I am inclined to think all scripts belong to one variety – Mainstream English (Fairman 2002a).

Acknowledgements

I would like to thank the editors for their comments on drafts of this study, the diocesan offices of Canterbury and Rochester for permission to publish the photos of Mary Cramp's marriage lines and John Goatham's bill respectively, the archivists in all the Record Offices I have visited, especially those in my 'home' Record Office in Maidstone, Kent, for their unfailing help, and finally, my sister, Jenny Fairman for countless useful discussions.

Notes

1. See also (1) www.archon.nationalarchives.gov.uk/archon. (2) Jeremy Gibson and Pamela Peskett. *Record Offices: How to Find Them* (1998. 8th edn. Federation of Family History Societies.)

2. For the benefit of readers unfamiliar with the geography of England, when I mention a county for the first time, I indicate in round brackets roughly where it is. Most counties have only one Record Office (R.O.), but if, like Cumbria, they have more than one, I indicate in round brackets which R.O. contains the document. A single right-facing square bracket within a quotation means 'line-break'. Line-breaks are sites of linguistic interest.

3. I try to focus on individuals. But since I often don't know who wrote the document, I am faced with the problem of pronoun reference. Rather than avoid the problem by using plurals, I have decided to remain focused on individuals and use 'they' and 'their' where needed for singular, genderless reference.

4. Twenty-four points below the next lowest town.

5. Centre for Kentish Studies (Maidstone), hereafter CKS(M): **Horsmonden**. P192/25/2 and P192/1/7. In this one marriage register (166 marriages (1813–36), each with at least two witnesses), at least six other women produced pointillist signatures, including *Mary Lambrt*, who had been a Charity School scholar for five years and nine months, and a bride who managed to write *Mrathr* (= Martha), but then Rev. Henry Morland added *Ellis* for her. I shall refer to the *Jenner/Jinner* variants in section 6.

6. English handwriting, including distinguishing <u> from <v>, has been stable since the 1740s (see George Bickham, *The Universal Penman*. 1733). Most writers in the early 1800s will have been taught by those who themselves had learnt these stable forms. I have seen no sign of <u> for <v>, even in the most formal petitions.

7. CKS(M): **New Romney**, P309/18/16. The writer could be his wife, Mary, because there is another letter in the same handwriting but in her name.

8. Kent, Canterbury Cathedral Archives (hereafter KCCA): **Chilham**, U3/191/5/3.

9. 'Statistical Inquiries of the Central Society of Education into the Social Condition of the Working Classes'. In *Central Society of Education Papers*, 1837, pp. 338–59.

10. Parish records show that spelling-books and religious literature were the only books that parishes ordered as reading material.

11. CKS(M): **Hunton**, C/ES/197/1/1.

12. Gaborone, the capital of Botswana.

13. For example, in Godmersham, Kent, I saw a Henry Peckman (1739), so I checked back and found a Henry Pettman (1722. KCCA: **Godmersham**, U3/117/1/1-2). I am looking for further evidence of the vocalisation of /l/, as in 'Bolsher' for a family usually registered as 'Bowsher'. Berkshire R.O.: **Avingdon**, DP/11/1/1-6).

14. CKS(M): **Brenchley**, P45/12/20, Poor Relief Book, between 1803 and 1807.

15. CKS(M): **Brenchley**, P45/1/5.

16. The genital reference of *Acock* would have been no hindrance. In Dorset (south west) I have found a family called *Bastard*.

17. CKS(M): **Pembury**, P286/1/1-7.

18. CKS(M): **Bredgar**, P43/12/9/Bundle 9. *Nov. 2 1833. Robt Akus X his Mark.*

19. KCCA: **Selling**, U3/229/1/1-9: **Sheldwich**, U3/186/1/3-7.

20. 'Frid, Freed' and 'Medhurst' are all in the 2002 Medway phone directory. So is 'Selling' (a nearby village), which Goatham spelt 'Sellen' in another bill. Even Goatham's *1811* for '1801' is not idiosyncratic; another writer wrote '18010' for 1810.

21. (6) Herefordshire R.O.: **Stoke Edith**, G53/24. [Ø] = a single unidentifiable mark.

22. (7) Durham R.O.: **Durham, St. Oswald in Elvet**, EP/Du/SO/17/118. Headlam's *a* before a vowel is not idiosyncratic. It occurred all over England.

23. (i) Dorset R.O.: **Blandford Forum**, PE/BF/OV/13/1. 10 December 1804. (ii) Essex R.O. (Colchester): **Colchester, St. Peter**, D/P/178/18/23. 2 December 1825. (iii) Herefordshire R.O.: **Eardisland**, AJ/32/91. 26 December c. 1813. (iv) CKS(M): **New Romney**, P309/18/15. 2 June 1821. (v) CKS(M): **New Romney**, P309/12/45. 10 April 1814. (vi) Cumbria R.O. (Kendal): **Hawkshead**, WPR/83/File 11. 9 April 1814.

24. (vii) CKS(M): **Streatfield**, U908/C90/5. 14 October 1817. (viii) CKS(M): **Harris**, U624/C127/1. 24 December 1812. (ix) Griggs (ed.) 1956–1959, 4: 684–685. (x) Redford 1992, 1: 95. (xi) Kay-Shuttleworth. 1970 [1832]: 3–4. (xii) CKS(M): **Harris**, U624/A70. Xmas day 1819.

25. (8) Gloucestershire R.O. (Gloucester): **Blockley**, P52/OV/7/1/1.

26. Although Johnson used slightly more Inkhorns than anyone else, contrary to complaints his style is not over-Latinate overall. Best, Kay-Shuttleworth and Lushington all used more Latinates than he did. Armytage's friendly letter is the least Latinate of the fully schooled letters, but belongs to the same group.

27. (9) CKS(M): **New Romney**, P309/12/63. 12 December 1818. (10) Cumbria R.O. (Kendal): **Kirkby Lonsdale**, WPR/19/1823/17. 27 February 1823. (11) Derbyshire R.O.: **Ticknall**, D1396A/PO/39. no date, c. 1809. (12) Durham R.O.: **Barnard Castle**, EP/BC/7/272(2). 11 March 1837. (13) Sussex R.O. (Lewes): **Frant**, PAR/344/37/3. 24 September 1810.

28. (14) Buckinghamshire R.O.: **Wooburn**, PR/240/18/4/20. 25 July 1826. (15) Cumbria R.O. (Kendal): **Kirkby Lonsdale**, WPR/19/1823/17. 27 February 1823. (16) KCCA: **Preston/Wingham**, U3/245/16/54. 4 January 1835.

29. In *English Exercises* (1797, still in print in Britain in 1864 and in the USA in the 1880s) Murray included 'He stands upon security' and 'He does not hold long in one mind' in 'Exercises to promote perspicuity and accurate writing'. In his key he 'corrected' these to: 'He insists upon security' and 'He does not continue long in one mind'.

30. A count of word types beginning with <s> in Cruden's *Bible Concordance* yields the following: Anglo-Saxon 65.3 per cent, Latinate 34.7 per cent, close to the figures in table 2.1. Milton's poetry was more schooled, though not as much as the six schooled letters in my tables: Anglo-Saxon 52.7 per cent, Latinate 47.3 per cent for word types beginning with <s> (Bradshaw 1965).

31. The *Oxford English Dictionary* first defines 'Anglicism' as 'Anglicized language, such as the introduction of English idiom into a sentence in another language'. However, I take it that Dryden is using the term in its derived sense, also given by the dictionary, i.e. 'a peculiarity of the English language, an idiom specially English'.

32. CKS(M): **Horsmonden**. P192/25/2.

33. CKS(M): **Harris**, U624/C130/4.

34. See Edwards (1990). Occasionally 'dialect' seems to have another meaning: 'whatever is not standard'. Manfred Görlach, for example, collects a wide range of non-standard texts under the heading 'On Dialect' (1999: 201–214).

35. For example, Ben Brierley (1825–96) and Edwin Waugh (1817–90), both of Lancashire (north west).
36. The examples are taken from, Charles Clark Esq. (Essex) 1839, Richard Lower (Sussex), 1831, John Masters (Kent), c. 1820, Josiah Relph (Cumberland (north west)) fl. 1712–43, Alfred, Lord Tennyson (Lincolnshire (north east Midlands) 1809–92), William Makepeace Thackeray (London), 1837, Edwin Waugh (Lancashire) 1817–90. William Barnes (Dorset) 1801–86, was a noteworthy exception as a dialect writer.

3   The subjunctive in adverbial clauses in nineteenth-century English

PETER GRUND AND TERRY WALKER

1   Introduction

In Present-day English the subjunctive in adverbial clauses is rare. It is limited by and large to the verb BE (especially *were*). This was not the case in Early Modern English: in this period the subjunctive occurred quite frequently, in a variety of adverbial clauses. The path of development between these two periods has received little attention in previous research. To remedy this, our study maps the use and development of the subjunctive in adverbial clauses in an intervening period, i.e. nineteenth-century English, exemplified in (1).

(1) If the gold *be* comparatively abundant, a part will soon settle, i.e. in twenty-four or forty-eight hours; [. . .]
(Science, Michael Faraday, 1850–70, p. 413)

In our primarily quantitative investigation, we will focus on variation across time and across genre, but we will also briefly discuss the gender variable in the Letters genre. In addition, we will consider patterns of usage in different adverbial clauses headed by a variety of conjunctions, and patterns with different verbs. We define the subjunctive in morpho-syntactic terms, that is to say, this chapter is concerned with verb forms which have a distinct subjunctive marking in a specific syntactic environment. This definition enables a variationist approach to the subjunctive, and, consequently, we will examine the use of the subjunctive in relation to that of both modal auxiliary constructions and the indicative. Our data derives from CONCE, a stratified multi-genre corpus of nineteenth-century English. In this article, we will first give a brief survey of previous research on the subjunctive (section 2), and introduce our material and method (sections 3 and 4), before we present the results of our investigation (section 5).

2   Previous research

Especially in several early twentieth-century studies, it has been claimed that the use of the subjunctive in general has diminished since Old English times (for a survey of such statements, see Jacobsson 1975; Peters 1998). However, it has been shown by a number of recent studies that there is no clear line of decline up to the present day, and that the subjunctive, at least in terms of the mandative subjunctive, has even been gaining ground over the last hundred years (see Övergaard 1995; Hundt 1998; Peters 1998).

The fate of the subjunctive in adverbial clauses in Present-day English (twentieth century) has been discussed in several studies and grammars of English (for an overview, see Peters 1998). Most of them have pointed to the decline of the subjunctive in this type of clause over the century. In contemporary English grammars, such as Quirk et al. (1985), the subjunctive is mostly attributed to formal style, and claimed to be an optional, marked alternative. In Biber et al. (1999), the subjunctive is not discussed *per se*, but it is mentioned as an alternative verb form in some dependent clauses (see e.g. Biber et al. 1999: 827–8 [10.2.8.4.C]).

In the Early Modern English period, the subjunctive was still frequently used in adverbial clauses. Rissanen (1999: 304–17) notes the use of the subjunctive in a wide range of clauses, but also points out that constructions with modal auxiliaries were an alternative. Moessner (2000) remarks that the subjunctive became less frequent during the course of the Early Modern English period in her material, and claims that this is owing to a marked decline of this form in conditional clauses, as the subjunctive increased slightly in temporal and concessive clauses. Furthermore, Moessner argues that the subjunctive was more frequent in informal texts especially towards the end of the seventeenth century. However, Rissanen (1999: 228) states that textual evidence shows that the use of subjunctive forms in general increased in the following century, which he suggests is due to an increase in usage in formal style.

There is no comprehensive study of the subjunctive in adverbial clauses in the nineteenth century, to our knowledge, although a few scholars have touched upon the topic. Harsh (1968), who does not deal specifically with the subjunctive in adverbial clauses, states that at the end of the nineteenth century there was an increase in the inflected subjunctive in the drama texts making up his material (1968: 85–6). For example, Harsh notes the use of the subjunctive in clauses of purpose and clauses of result, which, according to him, is otherwise exceptional in his drama texts after the seventeenth and mid-eighteenth centuries respectively. He also states that there is a high frequency of subjunctives in conditional statements in the texts studied (1968: 86).

Dealing with the whole of the Late Modern English period, Denison (1998) observes that the subjunctive became increasingly infrequent during this period in, for example, final and consecutive clauses, and temporal clauses (1998: 295, 304). As pointed out by Denison (1998: 294), referring to Visser (1966: §837), the disuse of the subjunctive, especially the present subjunctive, goes against the recommendations by prescriptive grammarians of the nineteenth century, who advocated the use of the subjunctive in a number of adverbial clauses. Nevertheless, as is shown by the citations provided by Visser (1966: §877–95),

Denison (1998: 295–305), and Poutsma (1926: 182–200), the subjunctive still occurred in a range of clauses in the period studied.

Our investigation aims at complementing previous remarks by presenting quantified data on the development of the subjunctive, and its rival forms, in adverbial clauses. With this approach we hope to provide more detailed information on the development within the nineteenth century as well as on genre-specific variation.

3   Material

Our data are taken from the computerized corpus CONCE, which is stratified into three periods, 1800–30, 1850–70, and 1870–1900, and contains seven genres: Debates, Drama, Fiction, History, Letters, Science and Trials. This set-up makes the corpus well suited for a study of the development of the subjunctive in nineteenth-century English with emphasis on variation across time and genre (for further details of CONCE, see the Introduction to the present volume; see also Kytö, Rudanko and Smitterberg 2000).

4   Method

The data for our study were extracted from WordCruncher files of CONCE, and processed in Microsoft Excel. As the basis for our searches, we used the subordinating conjunctions that Visser (1966: §877–95) lists as possibly occurring with the subjunctive in the nineteenth century.[1] As mentioned above, we employ a morpho-syntactic definition of the subjunctive.[2] In the nineteenth century, the subjunctive was only distinguishable from the indicative in the third person singular present tense of verbs other than BE (and also occasionally in the second person singular),[3] in all present tense forms of the verb BE, and in the first and third person singular past tense of BE.[4] Therefore, only verb forms in these contexts were collected, which was done by manual checking. Examples of forms in each of these contexts, taken from the corpus, are given in (2)–(4).

(2)   – Oh, Frederick! avert that face, lest the indignant lightning of thy eye *blast* me!
(Drama, Thomas Morton, 1800–30, p. 74)

(3)   [. . .] and suggests that the molecular grouping of a chemical substance may be simplified almost without limit if the temperature *be increased*.
(Science, Norman J. Lockyer, 1870–1900, p. 260)

(4)   I then stole out of the house-door, and made my appearance, as if I *were* a customer in the shop, just to take Miss Matty by surprise, and gain an idea of how she looked in her new situation.
(Fiction, Elizabeth Gaskell, 1850–70, p. 297)

As our study is set in a variationist framework, we not only extracted subjunctive forms but also indicative verb forms and modal auxiliary constructions in these syntactic environments.[5] For examples, see (5)–(6).[6]

(5) If the Queen *was deposed*, the Regency, in the Prince's minority, would go by the custom of Scotland to the nobleman next in blood to the Crown.
   (History, James Anthony Froude, 1850–70, p. IX, 114)

(6) – I have hitherto been silent – & may probably remain so – unless something *should occur* to render it impossible.
   (Letters, George Byron, 1800–30, p. IV, 60)

However, in a variationist study it is important to have a clearly defined variable, with clearly defined variants (see e.g. Romaine 1982: 31–7; Rissanen 1986: 97–8). In the case of the subjunctive, it has been argued, for example by Övergaard (1995: 54) and Hundt (1998: 160), who both discuss the mandative subjunctive, that the subjunctive and the modal constructions are not semantically equivalent, the modal auxiliaries being more specific in meaning. In the case of the indicative, it is of course even more difficult to claim exact semantic equivalence with the subjunctive. However since it has been claimed that the subjunctive has been replaced by modal auxiliary constructions and the indicative from at least the Middle English period onwards (Plank 1984: 346; Denison 1993: 330, 339), we consider it important to take these two verbal constructions into account when investigating the development of the subjunctive. We therefore adopt a fairly wide definition of semantic equivalence.

5   Results

In the CONCE corpus, 20 different subordinating conjunctions were found that introduce adverbial clauses containing subjunctive verb forms (for a list of these conjunctions, see section 5.5, table 3.5). In accordance with our method outlined above (section 4), we also collected the instances of indicative forms and modal auxiliaries, where these verb forms occurred, in adverbial clauses headed by these conjunctions. This yielded a total of 1,625 adverbial clauses. In what follows, we will first present the distribution of subjunctive, indicative and modal auxiliary verb forms in the 1,625 adverbial clauses across the three periods in CONCE (5.1). In 5.2, the distribution among the seven genres will be discussed, and in 5.3, period and genre subsamples will be studied in combination. The third extralinguistic parameter, gender, will be examined in 5.4. In the last two subsections, linguistic variables will be considered: the type of conjunction heading the adverbial clause (5.5), and the verb type (5.6).

Table 3.1. *The distribution of the subjunctive and modal auxiliaries according to period.*

Period	Subjunctive	Modal auxiliaries	Total
1	147 (53%)	128 (47%)	275 (100%)
2	154 (59%)	107 (41%)	261 (100%)
3	74 (61%)	48 (39%)	122 (100%)
Total	375 (57%)	283 (43%)	658 (100%)

Table 3.2. *The distribution of adverbial clauses according to verb form and period.*

Period	Subjunctive	Indicative	Modal auxiliaries	Total	Frequency (per 10,000 words)
1	147 (26%)	292 (51%)	128 (23%)	567 (100%)	16
2	154 (26%)	325 (55%)	107 (18%)	586 (100%)	17
3	74 (16%)	350 (74%)	48 (10%)	472 (100%)	16
Total	375 (23%)	967 (60%)	283 (17%)	1,625 (100%)	16

5.1   Variation across time

As pointed out in section 4, it has been suggested by previous research that modal auxiliary constructions have increasingly replaced the subjunctive. Our first step is therefore to investigate the distribution of subjunctive forms and modal auxiliary constructions across the three periods.[7]

Table 3.1 illustrates the distribution of the subjunctive compared with modal auxiliaries in the three periods. It can be observed that the ratio of subjunctive verb forms to modal auxiliary constructions increases across time from 53 per cent versus 47 per cent in Period 1 to 61 per cent versus 39 per cent in Period 3. This development is surprising in the light of previous research. However, as may be noted, the actual frequency of both the subjunctive and the modal auxiliaries decreases. It is therefore necessary also to consider the use of the indicative in the adverbial clauses under investigation, in order to discover whether this drop in frequency is connected with the development of the indicative rather than simply being a result of a general decrease in the particular adverbial clauses studied.

Table 3.2 displays the distribution of adverbial clauses according to verb form and period. It is clear from the table that the normalized frequency of adverbial clauses is remarkably consistent throughout the century, which demonstrates that the drop in the subjunctive and modal auxiliaries is not related to the number of adverbial clauses.

Table 3.3. *The distribution of adverbial clauses according to verb form and genre.*

Genre	Subjunctive	Indicative	Modal auxiliaries	**Total**
Trials	22 (16%)	105 (75%)	13 (9%)	140 (100%)
Letters	117 (17%)	465 (66%)	123 (17%)	705 (100%)
Drama	31 (19%)	109 (67%)	22 (14%)	162 (100%)
History	21 (25%)	40 (47%)	24 (28%)	85 (100%)
Debates	25 (26%)	58 (60%)	13 (14%)	96 (100%)
Fiction	45 (31%)	67 (47%)	31 (22%)	143 (100%)
Science	114 (39%)	123 (42%)	57 (19%)	294 (100%)
Total	375 (23%)	967 (60%)	283 (17%)	1,625 (100%)

As can be seen in table 3.2, of the 1,625 adverbial clauses, 23 per cent (375 examples) contain subjunctive verb forms, 60 per cent (967 examples) are in the indicative, while modal constructions account for the remaining 17 per cent (283 examples). This overall pattern is repeated in all three of the periods studied: in each period the indicative is the most common, and modal constructions are the least frequent, with the subjunctive making up the middle ground. This pattern is statistically significant at the 0.001 level.[8] Over the three periods, the indicative increases from just over half to almost three quarters of the examples. Thus, the modally marked forms, that is, the subjunctive and the modal auxiliaries together, decrease from 49 per cent in period 1 to 45 per cent in period 2, and drop considerably to 26 per cent in period 3. This variation is also statistically significant.[9] The increase in indicative forms over the century is primarily at the expense of the modals, as the subjunctive remains steady at 26 per cent until after 1870, when occurrences drop to 16 per cent.[10] In order to a get a more detailed picture of the relationship between the indicative, modal constructions and the subjunctive, it is helpful to look at the distribution of adverbial clauses by verb form and genre in the nineteenth-century material as a whole, as well as in each of the three periods.

5.2   *Variation across genre*

The distribution of the verb forms studied across the seven genres in CONCE is shown in table 3.3.[11] As may be seen in this table, the subjunctive has a relatively high frequency in Science, Fiction, Debates and History, compared with Drama, Letters and Trials. In the former genres, the proportion of the subjunctive ranges from 39 to 25 per cent, while in the latter three genres the figures are very similar, ranging from only 16 to 19 per cent. In Geisler's study (2002), in which he applies Biber's (1988) multi-dimensional approach, the texts in CONCE exhibited the tendency to group in the same two categories with regard to Dimension 1, which concerns 'involved' versus 'informational' production.

Drama, Letters and Trials were shown to be clearly 'involved', that is, more personal and interactive in nature than Science, Fiction, Debates and History, genres characterized by more informational content and minimal interactiveness. Moreover, the variation *within* these two groupings is not statistically significant in our study, which seems further to support the division. Thus it seems that the subjunctive is more a feature of genres with an informational focus.

As suggested by previous research (see section 2), formality may also play a role in the use of the subjunctive, although there appear to be no clear patterns in this regard. Table 3.3 shows that the highest frequency for the subjunctive is found in Science (39 per cent), while it is also relatively high in History and Debates (25 per cent and 26 per cent respectively), all of which are formal in style. Moreover the subjunctive is less common in the more informal genres, Letters and Drama (17 per cent and 19 per cent respectively). However, the subjunctive is rarest in Trials (16 per cent), a genre which records spontaneous speech in a formal context, and rather common (31 per cent) in Fiction (see also below), arguably a more informal genre.

Regarding the frequency of the indicative, there is a division of the genres into two distinct groups: the indicative is used in less than 50 per cent of the adverbial clauses in Fiction, History and Science (ranging from 42 per cent to 47 per cent), but the figure is 60 per cent or more (up to 75 per cent) in Debates, Letters, Drama and Trials. Thus, the modally marked forms are more frequent than the indicative in Fiction, History and Science, while the reverse is true of Debates, Letters, Drama and Trials. This division may reflect a difference in usage between speech-related and non-speech-related genres. Letters may be classified as speech-related owing to a tendency to include speech-related features (see Kytö, Rudanko and Smitterberg 2000: 90). Fiction consists partially of constructed speech, but as a whole, the genre was found to be marked for narrativity – associated with non-speech-related genres – by Geisler (2002).[12] Furthermore, the variation *within* these two groupings, of speech-related versus non-speech-related genres, is not statistically significant, which would seem to lend support to this division.

Modal auxiliary constructions are consistently less frequent than the subjunctive in all genres except for History (and in Letters, where they share the same frequency of 17 per cent). Moreover, the modal auxiliaries are least common in the speech-related genres (ranging from only 9 to 17 per cent) compared with the non-speech-related genres, where the modals range from 19 to 28 per cent. Thus modal constructions may be more a feature of non-speech-related genres. However, accounting for these patterns would require an in-depth qualitative analysis of the use of modal constructions in the different genres, which is outside the scope of this study.

5.3   *Variation across time and genre*

In sections 5.1 and 5.2, we discussed variation across time, and variation across genre, in isolation. In this section, we will examine whether any overall trends are

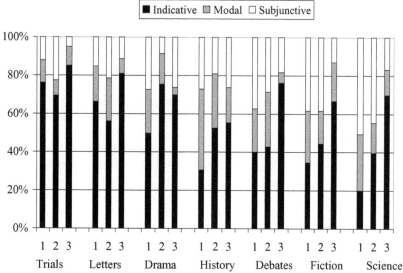

Figure 3.1. The distribution of adverbial clauses according to verb form, genre and period

discernible if the parameters of time and genre are combined. The distribution of the verb forms studied across the three periods and the seven genres in CONCE is shown in figure 3.1 (and table 3.7 in the appendix to this chapter).

Certain overall trends can be seen in figure 3.1. In all genres there is a decrease in the subjunctive between period 1 and period 3, although this decrease is only steady over the three periods in Science, Fiction and Debates. These three genres have the highest frequency of the subjunctive in period 1 (51, 38 and 37 per cent respectively), and the decrease from period 1 to period 3 is the more drastic in these genres (a fall of 34, 25 and 18 percentage points respectively). Between period 1 and period 3, the indicative rises in all genres and the modal constructions decrease. In the non–speech-related genres, Fiction, History and Science there is a continuous increase in the indicative over the three periods, while the decrease in the use of modal constructions is steady only in History and Science. There is also a consistent decrease in modals in Drama, but the frequency of the subjunctive actually increases after 1870 almost to that of period 1, which seems in line with the findings of Harsh (1968: 85–6), reported on in section 2. In all other genres there is fluctuation in the frequency of the indicative and the modals. It should be noted that only two genres, Science and Letters, have double figures for all raw frequencies. Consequently, much of the fluctuation in the data might simply be due to the low raw figures involved. In all, only Science displays consistent trends, that is, a fall in the subjunctive and the modal constructions in favour of the indicative.

The usage in individual texts does not seem to skew the results. Only six of the seventy-eight texts (from five of the genres) contained no occurrences of the subjunctive.[13] Moreover, the subjunctive rarely occurs more than ten times in any one text, the exceptions being two Science texts in both period 1 and period 2.[14] Considering the large number of texts sampled (29), the Letters genre shows a remarkable consistency in the distribution of the verb forms. However, in 5.4 we discuss possible gender differences in this genre.

5.4   Gender variation

Thus far we have considered the extralinguistic factors of time and genre, both separately and in combination. However, the design of the CONCE corpus also enables an investigation of the gender parameter. In the Letters genre, for each period there are five samples from male writers and five (four in period 3) from female writers (for details, see Kytö, Rudanko and Smitterberg 2000). Gender differences have been found in CONCE regarding, for example, the use of the progressive (Smitterberg 2005) and adjective comparison (Kytö and Romaine, this volume). It is therefore of interest to investigate whether this extra-linguistic factor influences the distribution of the verb forms used in the adverbial clauses included in this study.

As has been shown, the Letters genre, like the other speech-related genres, shows a consistent preference for the indicative over the modally marked forms. There is a rise in the frequency of the indicative between period 1 and period 3 contrasting with a decline in frequency of both the subjunctive and modal constructions in these periods, while period 2 attests the temporary reversal of this development in the Letters genre (see figure 3.1 in 5.3, and table 3.7 in the appendix). Taking the gender variable into account (see table 3.4), we can see that this pattern is repeated by both female and male writers as regards the indicative and the modal constructions.

However, there is some difference in male and female usage of the subjunctive. Male writers overall use the subjunctive slightly more than female writers do (19 compared to 15 per cent). Nevertheless, there is a steady decline in the use of the subjunctive by males (falling from 23 per cent to 21 per cent and finally to 9 per cent), but the female writers use slightly more in period 3 (13 per cent) than in period 1 (10 per cent). Thus, the usage by female writers is contrary to the pattern found for the subjunctive not only in the corpus as a whole and in the individual genres, but also by men in the Letters genre. However, it is not the increase in the frequency of the subjunctive in period 3 which requires explanation but rather the divergence from the general pattern by female writers found in period 1, with a relatively low frequency of the subjunctive (and a corresponding high frequency for the indicative), as elsewhere the frequencies for male and female writers are fairly similar. This statement is also supported in that the proportion found in the corpus for the subjunctive in period 1 is never smaller than 23 per cent, except in Trials (12 per cent), while the frequency of the subjunctive in period 2

Table 3.4. *The distribution of adverbial clauses according to verb form, gender and period in the Letters genre.*

Gender	Period	Subjunctive	Indicative	Modal auxiliaries	Total
Female	1	18 (10%)	128 (72%)	31 (18%)	177 (100%)
	2	29 (22%)	75 (58%)	26 (20%)	130 (100%)
	3	12 (13%)	69 (78%)	8 (9%)	89 (100%)
	Total	59 (15%)	272 (69%)	65 (16%)	396 (100%)
Male	1	27 (23%)	66 (56%)	24 (21%)	117 (100%)
	2	24 (21%)	63 (54%)	29 (25%)	116 (100%)
	3	7 (9%)	64 (84%)	5 (7%)	76 (100%)
	Total	58 (19%)	193 (62%)	58 (19%)	309 (100%)
Total		117 (17%)	465 (66%)	123 (17%)	705 (100%)

and period 3 for female writers is not remarkable when compared with the figures for the individual genres, or the corpus as a whole. However, to find an explanation for this gender difference, or rather the deviation by female writers in period 1 from the general pattern found in the corpus, we would need a more in-depth investigation of a range of linguistic features in the Letters genre, which does not fall within the scope of this study.

5.5   Variation according to the conjunction introducing the adverbial clause

Having discussed the extra-linguistic factors of time, genre and gender, we now consider linguistic factors that may influence the use of verb forms, namely the conjunctions found to introduce the subjunctive, and, in 5.6, the specific verbs used in the subjunctive. Table 3.5 illustrates the distribution of the conjunctions according to verb forms.

It can be observed in table 3.5 that of the twenty conjunctions only ten occur with the subjunctive more than once (though *provided* and *suppose* only occur twice with the subjunctive). These ten conjunctions introduce clauses of condition, concession and comparison. Four of these conjunctions, *as*,[15] *as if*, *even if* and *whether*, illustrated in (7)–(10), occur more often with the subjunctive than with the indicative and the modal constructions combined.

(7)   Yes, I apprehend that was at the onset or beginning, **as** it *were*, of the paroxysm.
      (Trials, William Palmer, 1850–70, p. 236)

(8)   He has spoken **as if** it *were* the absolute possession of the Nationalists; [. . .]
      (Debates, 1870–1900, p. IV, 1228)

Table 3.5. *The distribution of the verb forms according to conjunction.*

Conjunction	Subjunctive	Indicative	Modal auxiliaries	Total
as	15 (94%)	1 (6%)	0 (0%)	16 (100%)
as if	35 (56%)	25 (40%)	3 (5%)	63 (100%)
as though	1 (20%)	2 (40%)	2 (40%)	5 (100%)
even if	9 (56%)	6 (38%)	1 (6%)	16 (100%)
even though	1 (13%)	4 (50%)	3 (38%)	8 (100%)
except	1 (4%)	21 (88%)	2 (8%)	24 (100%)
if	268 (28%)	525 (56%)	149 (16%)	942 (100%)
in case	1 (50%)	0 (0%)	1 (50%)	2 (100%)
lest	1 (6%)	0 (0%)	17 (94%)	18 (100%)
provided	2 (18%)	7 (64%)	2 (18%)	11 (100%)
so long as	1 (50%)	1 (50%)	0 (0%)	2 (100%)
suppose	2 (22%)	5 (56%)	2 (22%)	9 (100%)
though	4 (2%)	164 (77%)	45 (21%)	213 (100%)
till	1 (1%)	81 (87%)	11 (12%)	93 (100%)
unless	16 (23%)	39 (57%)	14 (20%)	69 (100%)
until	1 (2%)	45 (90%)	4 (8%)	50 (100%)
whatever	3 (8%)	11 (29%)	24 (63%)	38 (100%)
whatsoever	1 (100%)	0 (0%)	0 (0%)	1 (100%)
whenever	1 (4%)	20 (83%)	3 (13%)	24 (100%)
whether	11 (52%)	10 (48%)	0 (0%)	22 (100%)
Total	375 (23%)	967 (60%)	283 (17%)	1,625 (100%)

(9) I fear I should be no great comfort to you **even if** I *were* with you, for I feel more helpless than ever [. . .]
(Letters, Geraldine Endsor Jewsbury, 1850–70, p. 391)

(10) [. . .] I can see no satisfactory solution except by equal representation for every part of the United Kingdom, **whether** it *be* in Ulster, Leinster, Munster, Yorkshire, or the Metropolis.
(Debates, 1870–1900, p. IV, 1228)

The conjunction *if* is by far the most common conjunction introducing the subjunctive, and this is especially true of Drama, History, Science and Debates where *if* makes up over 75 per cent of the subjunctive examples (see table 3.8 in the appendix to this chapter); nevertheless, the indicative occurs much more frequently than the subjunctive after this conjunction except in Science and History (see table 3.9 in the appendix to this chapter). There is some variation among the genres concerning the usage of the subjunctive with different conjunctions (see table 3.9). The conjunctions *as if* and *unless* are found with the subjunctive in all but one genre, History and Drama respectively. With regard to *as if*, however, the subjunctive is only frequent in Letters (seventeen instances) and Fiction (nine instances). The conjunction *even if* only occurs more than once in one genre,

Letters, in which the subjunctive (seven instances) is slightly more common than the indicative (five instances). Finally, despite the fact that *though* is relatively frequent in most genres, it only occurs with the subjunctive in Letters, yet even in this genre the indicative (ninety-eight instances) far outweighs the subjunctive (four instances).

There are ten conjunctions that occur with the subjunctive only once (see table 3.5). In the case of some of the conjunctions the subjunctive is a minor form, with the majority of the instances found with the indicative or the modal auxiliaries: clauses with *except*, *till*, *until* and *whenever* occur mostly with indicative forms (cf. Poutsma 1926: 183–4). *Lest* appears almost exclusively with the modal auxiliary *should*, which is in agreement with Poutsma's findings (1926: 181). There are also conjunctions which appear with as many instances of the subjunctive as with the indicative and/or the modal auxiliaries, i.e. *in case* and *so long as*. The only conjunction that occurs exclusively with the subjunctive is *whatsoever*, albeit there is only one example.

Regarding changes over time, only *as*, *as if*, *if*, *unless* and *whether* occur more than once with the subjunctive in each of the three periods (see table 3.10 in the appendix to this chapter). No patterns could be discerned for *as* and *as if*, but the other three conjunctions show a decline in use with the subjunctive over time. Occurrences of the subjunctive after both *unless* and *whether* decrease sharply after period 1 (from 69 to 19 per cent, and 64 to 18 per cent respectively), whereas occurrences after *if* decrease substantially only after 1870 (from 42 to 19 per cent). However, only the raw figures for *if* are sufficiently high for conclusions to be drawn (see table 3.11 in the appendix to this chapter): the decrease in period 3 seems to reflect a great decline in use in the Letters and Science genres (from 46 and 52 per cent in period 2 to 16 and 9 per cent in period 3 respectively).

Overall it appears that the conjunctions which occur most frequently with the subjunctive in the nineteenth century are those which may still do so in Present-day English, that is, *as* (in the formulaic phrase *as it were*), *as if* (in clauses of comparison), and *if*, *unless* and occasionally *whether* (in conditional or conditional/concessive clauses). In our data, however, the subjunctive was also found residually, for example, in temporal clauses, introduced by *till* in period 1, and *until* in period 2, where the subjunctive was commonly used in the Early Modern period.

5.6   Variation according to specific verbs

Studies of the subjunctive in Present-day English have shown that in adverbial clauses certain verbs occur in the subjunctive more frequently than other verbs (see e.g. Peters 1998: 95–6). We will therefore investigate the relationship between the subjunctive and specific verbs in this section. Table 3.6 shows the distribution of different verbs in the subjunctive. Since *be* and *were* exhibit widely different patterns, these forms have been presented separately in the table. Furthermore, owing to the small number of verbs, other than BE, in the subjunctive, the figures for these verbs have been collapsed.

Table 3.6. *The distribution of subjunctive forms according to verb type.*

Period	*Be*	*Were*	Verbs other than BE	Total
1	49 (33%)	78 (53%)	20 (14%)	147 (100%)
2	68 (44%)	78 (51%)	8 (5%)	154 (100%)
3	14 (19%)	59 (80%)	1 (1%)	74 (100%)
Total	131 (35%)	215 (57%)	29 (8%)	375 (100%)

As can be seen in table 3.6, of the 375 subjunctive forms in the corpus, BE is by far the most common verb, exemplified in (11)–(12). The forms *be* and *were* together account for 92 per cent (i.e. 35 and 57 per cent respectively) of all subjunctive forms. Apart from being the more frequent of the two forms, *were* also makes up the majority of all subjunctive examples (57 per cent).

(11) I will, at all costs, furnish it, provided I *be* there so long as I commit no canonical offence, on the strength of having his word; [. . .]
(Trials, Richard Boyle, 1850–70, p. 66)

(12) If it *were* not Richmond, I should be afraid to take such a life's gift [. . .]
(Letters, Anne Thackeray Ritchie, 1870–1900, p. 177)

In the category of verbs other than BE, seventeen different verbs were found in the subjunctive, making up 8 per cent (29 instances) of all subjunctive forms.[16] Only three of the verbs are found more than once: *come*, *have* and *please* (2, 10, and 3 occurrences respectively). For examples, see (13)–(15).

(13) Here I swear, that if the hour of trial *come*; Avondale will stand forth arrayed in all his guilt [. . .]
(Drama, Thomas Morton, 1800–30, p. 81)

(14) LET the reader, if he *have* one spark of sympathy for Edward Maxwell, just think of his feelings at this moment; [. . .]
(Fiction, Theodore Edward Hook, 1800–30, p. I.205)

(15) I shall not examine him, but leave the defendant to do so, if he *please*.
(Trials, John Singleton Copley Hill, 1850–70, p. 34)

It might be argued that the forms *be* and *were* would naturally occur more frequently as they are not restricted to the third person singular. However, in our data, this factor only partly accounts for the predominance of these two forms. Of the 131 instances of *be*, 110 (84 per cent) are in the third person singular, whereas there is only one instance in the first person singular (1 per cent), and twenty instances in the third person plural (15 per cent). Regarding *were*, of the 215 instances 179 (83 per cent) are in the third person singular, and only thirty-six occurrences (17 per cent) are in the first person singular.

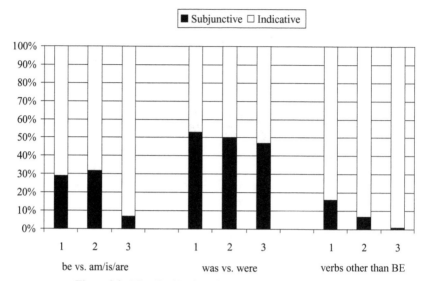

Figure 3.2. The distribution of subjunctive and indicative forms according to verb (form)

As may be seen in table 3.6, the proportion of subjunctive forms constituted by *were* increases between period 1 and period 3, whereas the proportions of both *be* and other verbs decrease. Verbs other than BE in the subjunctive disappear almost completely by period 3, whereas *be* actually exhibits an increase in period 2, but the frequency drops considerably in period 3. The variation shown in table 3.6 is statistically significant.[17] These findings are close to the results reported in Peters (1998: 95) for the twentieth century: she remarks that the *were* subjunctive is much more common than the base form subjunctives.[18]

There is some variation among the genres in the use of the subjunctive and different verbs. Of the genres with a high frequency of the subjunctive, History and Debates only have forms of BE in the subjunctive, and Fiction only contains forms of BE plus two occurrences of *have*. Science, on the other hand, which exhibits the highest frequency of the subjunctive, has eight different verbs in the subjunctive. Trials, Drama and Letters show a lower frequency of the subjunctive than the other genres, but a greater range of verbs in the subjunctive (five, seven and ten different verbs respectively) compared with History, Fiction and Debates.

In 5.1, we showed that there is an overall trend in the CONCE corpus texts for the subjunctive (and the modal auxiliaries) to decrease and the indicative to increase in the adverbial clauses studied. Consequently, since it was shown above that there is some variation in the usage of the subjunctive depending upon the type of verb or verb form used, it is of importance to investigate whether there are also some patterns in the distribution and development of the indicative with these verbs.[19] Figure 3.2 (and tables 3.12–3.14 in the appendix to this chapter) presents the results of this investigation.

Figure 3.2 reveals several notable trends. Both in the case of BE and other verbs, the proportion of subjunctive forms to indicative forms decreases between period 1 and period 3, but, as noted above, *be* shows a slight increase in period 2. However, the form *were* shows a gradual but steady decrease over time. It thus seems that the indicative increases at the expense of the subjunctive form *be* and the subjunctive of other verbs (cf. Denison 1998: 294). The form *were* appears to have been a more viable subjunctive form. The fact that this form was frequent would make it more resistant to the trend towards loss of inflection.

6   Conclusion

To sum up, we have shown that the subjunctive was used in a range of adverbial clauses during the nineteenth century. However, there was a decline in the frequency of the subjunctive over the century. The subjunctive in adverbial clauses was thus among the linguistic features undergoing change – in this case in the direction of morphological levelling – in the nineteenth century (see also Kytö and Romaine on adjective comparison in this volume). The subjunctive occurred more in Science, Fiction, History and Debates than in Trials, Drama and Letters. This seems to reflect a difference between 'informational' and 'involved' genres. However, the formality of the genre, as previous research generally agrees, may also influence the use of the subjunctive, as the subjunctive is generally more common in the formal texts. The indicative was increasingly more common than modally marked forms, and this became especially so after 1870 when the subjunctive declined most sharply. Surprisingly, the ratio of the subjunctive to the modal auxiliaries actually increased across time, since the frequency of the modals decreased even more than that of the subjunctive. Thus, it seems that the indicative rather than constructions with modal auxiliaries was the preferred alternative to the subjunctive, especially in the speech-related genres. The gender parameter was included in an investigation of the Letters genre, and was found to have some influence on variation: the overall frequency of the subjunctive was higher among male writers, although after period 1 women actually used the subjunctive slightly more than men did. Women also used the subjunctive less at the beginning than they did at the end of the century. Further research into this parameter would be worthwhile, in order to uncover possible explanations.

In our data there are some examples of the subjunctive in certain clauses, and/or with certain conjunctions, where it would not occur today but which would not be unusual in the Early Modern English period. Of the conjunctions, the subjunctive is most common after *as if*, *unless*, *as*, *whether* and *even if*, though it also appears after conjunctions such as *till*, *in case* and *so long as*. The conjunction *if* has by far the greatest number of subjunctive forms, but the indicative is nevertheless almost twice as common as the subjunctive after this conjunction. In the investigation of the specific verbs, we showed that the subjunctive form *be* and the subjunctive form of other verbs decreased considerably over the nineteenth century. Verbs other than BE in the subjunctive had almost disappeared completely by period 3. *Were*, on the other hand, was still a frequently used form at the end of the century.

This quantitative study has expanded our knowledge of a hitherto largely unexplored area of nineteenth-century English. It has also provided a link between the research carried out on the Early Modern period and the twentieth century as regards the development of the subjunctive. Studies of the mandative subjunctive and the subjunctive used in indirect questions are needed to give a complete picture of the use of subjunctive in nineteenth-century English.

Appendix

Table 3.7. *The distribution of adverbial clauses according to verb form, genre and period.*

Genre	Period	Subjunctive	Indicative	Modal auxiliaries	Total
Trials	1	3 (12%)	19 (76%)	3 (12%)	25 (100%)
	2	17 (23%)	52 (69%)	6 (8%)	75 (100%)
	3	2 (5%)	34 (85%)	4 (10%)	40 (100%)
Debates	1	13 (37%)	14 (40%)	8 (23%)	35 (100%)
	2	2 (29%)	3 (43%)	2 (29%)	7 (100%)
	3	10 (19%)	41 (76%)	3 (6%)	54 (100%)
Letters	1	45 (15%)	194 (66%)	55 (19%)	294 (100%)
	2	53 (22%)	138 (56%)	55 (22%)	246 (100%)
	3	19 (12%)	133 (81%)	13 (8%)	165 (100%)
Drama	1	11 (26%)	20 (50%)	9 (23%)	40 (100%)
	2	6 (9%)	52 (75%)	11 (16%)	69 (100%)
	3	14 (26%)	37 (70%)	2 (4%)	53 (100%)
Fiction	1	20 (38%)	18 (35%)	14 (27%)	52 (100%)
	2	20 (38%)	23 (44%)	9 (17%)	52 (100%)
	3	5 (13%)	26 (67%)	8 (21%)	39 (100%)
History	1	7 (27%)	8 (31%)	11 (42%)	26 (100%)
	2	4 (19%)	11 (52%)	6 (29%)	21 (100%)
	3	10 (26%)	21 (55%)	7 (18%)	38 (100%)
Science	1	48 (51%)	19 (20%)	28 (29%)	95 (100%)
	2	52 (45%)	46 (40%)	18 (16%)	116 (100%)
	3	14 (17%)	58 (70%)	11 (13%)	83 (100%)
Total	1–3	375 (23%)	967 (60%)	283 (17%)	1,625 (100%)

Table 3.8. *The frequency of the subjunctive after if vs other conjunctions according to genre.*

Conjunction	Debates	Drama	Fiction	History	Letters	Science	Trials	Total
if	21	24	24	17	74	94	14	268
	(84%)	(77%)	(53%)	(81%)	(63%)	(82%)	(64%)	(71%)
Other conj:s	4	7	21	4	43	20	8	107
	(16%)	(23%)	(47%)	(19%)	(37%)	(18%)	(36%)	(29%)
Total	25	31	45	21	117	114	22	375
	(100%)	(100%)	(100%)	(100%)	(100%)	(100%)	(100%)	(100%)

Table 3.9. *Instances of the ten most common conjunctions which occur with the subjunctive presented according to mood and genre.*

		Genre							
Conjunction	Mood	Debates	Drama	Fiction	History	Letters	Science	Trials	Total
as	Indicative					1			1
	Subjunctive		4			4	5	2	15
as if	Indicative	1	2	3	2	8	1	8	25
	Modals		1				1	1	3
	Subjunctive	2	4	9		17	1	2	35
even if	Indicative	1				5			6
	Modals					1			1
	Subjunctive			1		7	1		9
if	Indicative	45	74	25	16	240	63	62	525
	Modals	3	18	15	4	73	29	7	149
	Subjunctive	21	24	24	17	74	94	14	268
provided	Indicative	1				2	2	2	7
	Modals					1		1	2
	Subjunctive			1				1	2
suppose	Indicative	1	3			1			5
	Modals							2	2
	Subjunctive		1				1		2
though	Indicative		9	20	9	98	26	2	164
	Modals	1	2	5	4	14	18	1	45
	Subjunctive					4			4

Table 3.9. *(cont.)*

Conjunction	Mood	Debates	Drama	Fiction	History	Letters	Science	Trials	Total
					Genre				
unless	Indicative	2	5	2	1	19	4	6	39
	Modals	2			5	4	3		14
	Subjunctive	1		3	1	5	5	1	16
whatever	Indicative			3	1	3		4	11
	Modals	4	1	2	1	11	4	1	24
	Subjunctive				1	2			3
whether	Indicative				4	2	3	1	10
	Subjunctive	1			1	1	7	1	11

Table 3.10. *The frequency of the subjunctive after* as, as if, if, unless *and* whether *according to period.*

Conjunction	Period 1	Period 2	Period 3	Total
as	5 (33%)	2 (13%)	8 (53%)	15 (100%)
as if	7 (20%)	22 (63%)	6 (17%)	35 (100%)
if	105 (39%)	113 (42%)	50 (19%)	268 (100%)
unless	11 (69%)	3 (19%)	2 (13%)	16 (100%)
whether	7 (64%)	2 (18%)	2 (18%)	11 (100%)

Table 3.11. *The frequency of the subjunctive after the conjunction* if *according to genre.*

Genre	Period 1	Period 2	Period 3	Total
Debates	12 (57%)	2 (10%)	7 (33%)	21 (100%)
Drama	8 (33%)	4 (17%)	12 (50%)	24 (100%)
Fiction	11 (46%)	10 (42%)	3 (13%)	24 (100%)
History	7 (41%)	2 (12%)	8 (47%)	17 (100%)
Letters	28 (38%)	34 (46%)	12 (16%)	74 (100%)
Science	37 (39%)	49 (52%)	8 (9%)	94 (100%)
Trials	2 (14%)	12 (86%)	0 (0%)	14 (100%)
Total	105 (39%)	113 (42%)	50 (19%)	268 (100%)

Table 3.12. *The distribution of subjunctive and indicative forms with the verb* BE.

Period	Subjunctive (*be*)	Indicative (*am, is, are*)	Total
1	49 (29%)	118 (71%)	167 (100%)
2	68 (32%)	147 (68%)	215 (100%)
3	14 (7%)	180 (93%)	194 (100%)
Total	131 (23%)	445 (77%)	576 (100%)

Table 3.13. *The distribution of subjunctive* were *and indicative* was.

Period	Subjunctive (*were*)	Indicative (*was*)	Total
1	78 (53%)	68 (47%)	146 (100%)
2	78 (50%)	79 (50%)	157 (100%)
3	59 (46%)	68 (54%)	127 (100%)
Total	215 (50%)	215 (50%)	430 (100%)

Table 3.14. *The distribution of subjunctive and indicative forms with verbs other than* BE.

Period	Subjunctive	Indicative	Total
1	20 (16%)	106 (84%)	126 (100%)
2	8 (7%)	99 (93%)	107 (100%)
3	1 (1%)	102 (99%)	103 (100%)
Total	29 (9%)	307 (91%)	336 (100%)

Notes

1. We searched for the following words which could possibly function as conjunctions (including variant spellings) or keywords of conjunction phrases: *afore, after, albeit, although, as, before, case, condition, ere, except, however, howsoever, if, lest, notwithstanding, once, provided, providing, save, saving, soever, sooner, suppose, that, though, till, unless, until, whatever, whatsoever, when, whence, whenever, wherever, whether, whichever, whoever, whomsoever, without.* Some of these conjunctions, e.g. *whether*, can introduce clauses other than adverbial clauses. Naturally, we only include examples in which the conjunctions introduce adverbial clauses.

2. There are several reasons for adopting a morpho-syntactic definition of the subjunctive. If the subjunctive is defined as a verb form indicating that something is uncertain, unreal, improbable, impossible etc., even indicative forms could notionally be subjunctive in certain contexts. Furthermore, basing a classification on notional, semantic consideration often entails a great deal of subjectivity. For an in-depth discussion of the problems inherent in the notional approach, see Cannon (1959).

3. However, we found no examples of the subjunctive in the second person in CONCE.

4. It is not within the scope of this study to examine the possible differences between main verb uses and primary auxiliary uses of BE and HAVE.

5. Some verb forms were excluded from our data. First, in one of the Drama texts (period 3, Gilbert), dialectal speech is represented. Since it was uncertain in a number of cases whether the indicative form with zero-inflection or a subjunctive form was intended (cf. Trudgill 2001: 181–2), these instances were excluded. Secondly, instances of *don't* used in the third person singular were omitted since *don't* was frequently used in this context as an indicative form (see Harsh 1968: 97; Denison 1998: 196). Thirdly, in the case of the compound conjunction *so long as*, we only included instances where *so long as* had conditional force (cf. *OED* s.v. *long* adv. 1.b.), since the subjunctive only occurred in the conditional *so long as* clauses.

6. A third possible alternative to the subjunctive might be conjunction-headed abbreviated clauses (for this term, see Bäcklund 1984), such as *when asked, he answered*. However, it was not within the scope of this study to include such clauses in the analysis.

7. Percentages in the tables are rounded off to whole numbers. However, percentages given in the running text are based on exact calculations rather than on the rounded-off percentages presented in the tables.

8. d.f. $= 4$; χ^2 63.668; $p < 0.001$.

9. d.f. $= 2$; χ^2 61.086; $p < 0.001$.

10. We considered the possibility that a partial explanation for the rise in the indicative, and corresponding fall in the modal constructions, might be an increasing use of adverbials such as *perhaps* with the indicative, in place of certain modal auxiliaries. However, only four such examples were found, all preceded by the conjunction *though*, in period 2 and period 3. We are grateful to Professor Terttu Nevalainen for drawing our attention to this possibility.

11. The overall variation illustrated in table 3.3 is statistically significant (d.f. $= 12$; χ^2 102.531; $p < 0.001$).

12. Although not attempted here, it would of course be possible to study the representation of direct speech in Fiction separately.

13. The texts are: in period 1, Shelley (Fiction), Lyell (Science), Bowditch (Trials); in period 2, Taylor (Drama); in Period 3, Hardy (Letters), Tichborne (Trials).

14. The texts are: in period 1, Malthus and Ricardo; in period 2, Darwin and Faraday.

15. Nine of the instances of *as* occur in the formulaic phrase *as it were* (cf. Visser 1966: §890; Rissanen 1999: 317). The remaining six instances are examples of *as* with the meaning *as if* (cf. *OED* s.v. *as* 9.a.).

16. Verbs other than BE in the subjunctive are: *attach, become, blast, come, deem, do, exceed, fail, have, lie, marry, permit, please, profit, return, sell, stand*.

17. d.f. $= 4$; χ^2 29.167; $p < 0.001$.

18. Peters (1998) does not make explicit what is included in the category of the base form subjunctive. For example, it is unclear whether the discussion concerns both the base form of BE and other verbs.

19. There are several caveats that must be taken into consideration in this discussion. First of all, the modal auxiliaries have not been included at this level of analysis owing to the difficulty in many cases of deciding whether a modal auxiliary construction would be equivalent to a 'present' subjunctive *be* or a 'past' subjunctive *were*. It would have been possible to collapse the figures for the base form *be* and *were*. However, as we will show that *be* and *were* exhibit widely dissimilar trends, such an operation would skew the figures.

4   The passive in nineteenth-century scientific writing

LARISA OLDIREVA GUSTAFSSON

1   Introduction

The present study focuses on the use of the passive in nineteenth-century scientific writing as attested in CONCE, A Corpus of Nineteenth-century English (see Kytö, Rudanko and Smitterberg 2000; see also the Introduction to the present volume), and as compared to other genres included in this corpus, namely Debates, Drama, Fiction, History, Letters, and Trials. Samples from Science amount to approximately 100,000 words, which corresponds to 10 per cent of this one-million-word corpus. The corpus samples represent one genre of scientific writing, viz. scientific monographs; some of these monographs contributed to the evolution of science (see the Appendix to the present volume). A corpus comprising authors known as leaders of scientific thinking is essential for the analysis of grammar that characterizes the development of scientific style. The impetus for this study comes from statements that passive forms played a decisive role in the formation of the new impersonal style in scientific English (Bailey 1996: 239; Görlach 1999: 150). In some studies (e.g. Halliday 1988: 166), this formation is described as a recent development dating back to the nineteenth century. The evidence provided by the CONCE corpus may clarify to what extent such claims are justified.

Science deals with objective and impersonal events and entities, and the passive voice is an ideal grammatical form for discourse associated with objectivity and non-involvement. Handbooks on practical English usage point to the frequent occurrence of passives (the agentless passive, in particular) in academic and scientific writing (Swan 1995: 408). The fact that the passive voice is indispensable in academic writing, and that in Present-day English, this genre yields the largest number of BE-passive verb phrases, is acknowledged and statistically verified in many studies (e.g. Quirk et al. 1985: 166; Givón 1993, 2: 53). According to corpus findings on present-day usage reported in Biber et al. (1999: 476), 'passives are most common by far in academic prose, occurring about 18,500 times per million words. . . . Proportionally, passives account for c. 25% of all finite verbs in academic prose', and 'at the other extreme, passives account for only c. 2% of all finite verbs in conversation'. The present survey of the passive in nineteenth-century scientific writing will at various points refer to the findings of this corpus-based grammar: parallels between observations provided by different corpora help to distinguish between period-specific and non-period-specific features of scientific writing.

2   Previous research

It seems appropriate to start the discussion of the CONCE findings by referring to the results of an earlier corpus-based diachronic study of scientific writing, namely the study of samples from *The Philosophical Transactions of the Royal Society of London* included in A Representative Corpus of Historical English Registers, ARCHER (Atkinson 1996). This study covers three centuries of publications (1650–1990), and reveals a dramatic change from an author-centred rhetoric to an object-centred and more abstract strategy of scientific writing in articles published in *Philosophical Transactions* (Atkinson 1996: 359, 361). Besides other stylistic developments, this rhetorical evolution manifests itself in the increasing use of passives (Atkinson 1996: 357–8).

According to studies of the history of science, the movement towards object-centred discourse may be related to a special emphasis on scientific methods (Yeo 1981: 68–72; Atkinson 1996: 365). For instance, scientific articles published in *Philosophical Transactions* after 1825 abound in methodological descriptions. Owing to the abstract character of such descriptions, the grammar of scientific articles tends to be highly passivized (Atkinson 1996: 365). The emphasis on scientific methodology and the frequent occurrence of passives seem to go hand in hand. Yeo ascribes the emphasis of the period on methodology to the impact of John Herschel's requirement of methodological elaboration, formulated in his *Preliminary Discourse on the Study of Natural Philosophy* (1831) (Yeo 1981: 70; Atkinson 1996: 367). In this book, published as a volume in Lardner's *Cabinet Cyclopedia*, Herschel 'attempted to give a clear account of scientific method – the hallmark, in his view, of the scientific endeavour' (Yeo 1981: 65).

The distribution of passives over time attested in ARCHER reflects the movement towards passivized scientific writing as 'total counts of the three types of passives taken together [i.e. agentless passives, *by*-passives, and past participle reduced relative clauses] show steady increases across the three centuries studied' (Atkinson 1996: 357–8). However, the results provided by the ARCHER corpus do not show any statistical changes in the occurrence of passives after 1825. The nineteenth-century collection of articles from *Philosophical Transactions* seems to illustrate that a highly passivized style of scientific writing was a stable feature of this genre throughout the nineteenth century. To judge from the data provided by ARCHER, the shift towards passivized writing took place between 1775 and 1825 (Atkinson 1996: 358), as samples from other periods of the nineteenth century do not evidence an increasing use of passives. Atkinson concludes his study by stating that this '"wide-angle" approach presents a perspective which can usefully complement studies of more specific time periods and more closely delineated areas of scientific activity' (Atkinson 1996: 367). CONCE presents such a possibility of complementing Atkinson (1996) by focusing on passives in nineteenth-century scientific monographs.

The figures in table 4.1, cited from Geisler's article (2002: 252) on register variation in CONCE, seem to echo the above-mentioned findings by Atkinson. In this table, the statistical distribution of passives per period is reported in relation to all seven genres included in CONCE (a number of passives per 1,000 words is presented as 'average of passives').[1]

The figures in table 4.1 characterize scientific writing as the genre that is marked by the greatest frequency of passives. At the same time, the use of the passive in the specimens of this genre does not show any increase across the century. Moreover, the multi-feature/multi-dimensional analysis of the corpus findings (see Biber 1995: 177–9) performed by Geisler has singled out Science as the only genre in CONCE that does not change to a statistically significant degree across the century (Geisler 2002: 269). All this indicates that in nineteenth-century English, the predominance of the passive voice in scientific monographs was a stable feature of this genre of writing. If there had been any decisive turn towards the formation of the impersonal and objective style, this turn must have taken place earlier.

Table 4.1 also shows that in relation to the occurrence of passives, two groups of genres emerge: one group including Science, History and Debates – genres in which passivized discourse is statistically prominent (the expository group), and one group including Letters, Trials, Drama and Fiction – genres which contain a much smaller number of passives (the non-expository group). This grouping holds throughout the nineteenth century. Statistical fluctuations in some genres across time do not unbalance the statistical contrast within the grouping (as, for instance, in the case of Debates, which are most passivized at the beginning of the century, less in the middle, and revert to a more passivized discourse by the end of the century; see table 4.1).[2] Interestingly, three of the genres which are not associated with the passivized type of writing, Drama, Fiction and Letters, tend to become even less passivized in the course of the nineteenth century (see table 4.1). This tendency makes the frequent occurrence of passives in Science appear even more prominent, and the passive voice may thus be easily interpreted as a feature of scientific writing. At the same time, the increasing difference in the use of passives between the two groups of genres agrees with an overall tendency towards an increase in genre diversification across time that is described in Biber and Finegan (1997: 273). The distribution of passives across genres and time is part of this general tendency, and the dense occurrence of passives in scientific writing is an established grammatical feature of this genre throughout the nineteenth century.

Table 4.1. *The distribution of passives across time and genre in CONCE (based on Geisler 2002: 252).*

Period		Debates	Drama	Fiction	History	Letters	Science	Trials	Total
1	No. of text samples	11	9	7	6	10	7	15	65
	Word count	19,509	31,567	41,806	30,795	121,019	37,791	62,042	344,529
	Average of passives	13.994	6.998	7.093	12.376	6.715	16.277	5.044	
2	No. of text samples	11	5	7	7	13	5	11	59
	Word count	19,256	30,611	38,896	30,326	130,777	31,339	60,382	341,587
	Average of passives	9.815	4.461	5.989	12.034	5.105	14.383	6.958	
3	No. of text samples	11	6	7	6	9	7	17	63
	Word count	19,491	29,983	30,096	30,389	90,241	30,305	67,146	297,651
	Average of passives	10.774	4.623	5.190	11.934	4.987	15.060	4.997	
Authors per period		–	3	3	3	10	3	–	3

Table 4.2. *The distribution of* BE-*passives in Science.*

Period	Author	Domain	Word count	Raw frequencies of BE-passives	BE-passives per 1,000 words
1	Lyell	geology	11,898	280	23.5
	Malthus	demography	10,472	196	18.7
	Ricardo	economy	15,667	362	23.1
	Total		38,037	838	22.0
2	Darwin	biology	10,694	168	15.7
	Faraday	chemistry	10,084	273	27.1
	Goschen	economy	10,901	232	21.3
	Total		31,679	673	21.2
3	Bateson	biology	10,141	250	24.6
	Galton	biology	10,315	239	23.2
	Lockyer	astronomy	10,147	174	17.1
	Total		30,603	663	21.7
Total			100,319	2,174	21.7

3   Parameters of diachronic stability and textual variation

As the statistical survey of CONCE texts presents Science as a genre that maintained a highly passivized discourse without noticeable changes across the century, an analysis of the grammatical parameters of this stability may be enlightening. To obtain data about these parameters, instances of BE-passives were coded in a database, and statistical tendencies in the occurrence of these instances were detected (by using pivot tables in Microsoft Excel). The present analysis comprises finite and non-finite verb phrases with BE-passives; other types of passives (e.g. reduced relative clauses with past participles) were not included in the database. Raw frequencies and the incidence of the coded instances as well as their extralinguistic variables (i.e. author and period) are given in table 4.2.[3]

The incidences of BE-passives in table 4.2 echo the observations reported in table 4.1 cited from Geisler (2002).[4] No diachronic trends can be discerned in the occurrence of BE-passives; the incidences for the three time periods are 22.0, 21.2, and 21.6. However, in table 4.2, the scope of authorial variation is discernible. Thus, the lowest incidence of BE-passives (15.7) is provided by the samples from Darwin's *Origin of Species*, whereas the highest figure (27.1) is recorded in the samples from *Experimental Researches* by Faraday (see table 4.2). How this combination of diachronic stability and authorial variation is related to the parameters of tense, aspect and mood is commented on in what follows.

Table 4.3. *The distribution of passives in relation to grammatical parameters.*

Grammatical parameters		Period 1	Period 2	Period 3	Total
Tense	Present	634 (76%)	546 (81%)	499 (75%)	1,679 (77%)
	Past	159 (19%)	88 (13%)	111 (17%)	358 (16%)
	Future	45 (5%)	39 (6%)	53 (8%)	137 (6%)
Aspect	Indefinite	775 (92%)	600 (89%)	580 (88%)	1,955 (90%)
	Perfect	63 (8%)	71 (11%)	76 (11%)	210 (10%)
	Progressive	0 (0%)	2 (0%)	7 (1%)	9 (0%)
Mood	Indicative	699 (83%)	549 (82%)	590 (89%)	1,838 (85%)
	Conditional	138 (17%)	114 (17%)	72 (11%)	324 (15%)
	Imperative	1 (0%)	10 (1%)	1 (0%)	12 (1%)
Total		838 (100%)	673 (100%)	663 (100%)	2,174 (100%)

3.1   Parameters of tense, aspect and mood

Since the present analysis is based on the statistics provided by a database, the coding scheme needs to be commented on here. When coded in relation to the parameters of tense, aspect and mood, every instance of BE-passives was classified in accordance with the typical grammatical function of the respective verb phrase. Thus, when coded in relation to the parameter of tense, BE-passives with *will* and *shall* were coded as future passives. This coding strategy was followed even when the verb phrase had meanings other than the meaning of futurity; for example, when the use of *will* could be interpreted as having the habitual predictive meaning (as in example (2)). The reduction of the variety of uses to the set of three groups, i.e. present, past and future BE-passives, made coding feasible but led to the generalized presentation of the semantics of the verb phrase. In terms of aspect, instances were coded as indefinite, perfect or progressive. Occurrences that are associated with neither perfect (as in example (4)) nor progressive (as in example (5)) aspects were coded as indefinite BE-passives. In relation to the parameter of mood, BE-passives were coded as indicative, conditional or imperative. The hypothetical use of verb phrases with the mood markers *would* and *should* and with the past tense modals *could* and *might*, as well as the use of *be/were*-subjunctives with hypothetical or unreal meaning was coded as conditional (on *would/should* and *could/might* as 'mood markers', and on the hypothetical meaning of the subjunctive forms, see Quirk et al. 1985: 157–8, 232–3, 234–5). Statistical observations enabled by this coding scheme are shown in table 4.3. In this table, associations of BE-passives with the parameters of tense, aspect and mood are reported per period.[5]

The figures in table 4.3 demonstrate that passives are evenly distributed across time in relation to these variables. It is difficult to discern any clear diachronic trends in the material (a decrease in the occurrence of conditional passives between periods 2 and 3 will be commented on further). Some slight tendencies towards a more frequent use of future and perfect passives are noticeable, but these tendencies do not change the general distribution of forms over time. Thus, in the course of the nineteenth century, BE-passives are most common as forms of the present tense, indefinite aspect and indicative mood (see table 4.3). Whether this statistical distribution of BE-passives is passive-specific or reflects the overall proportion of associations between variables and instances of verb forms cannot be detected from my data. Example (1) illustrates the type of BE-passives most frequently occurring in the samples from scientific monographs:

(1) I believe that the ruby character of the deposit in the line of discharge, *is caused* by the same action of heat produced at the moment by the electricity passing there. In the distant parts, the deposit, rubified by after-heat, *is not imbedded* or *fused* into the glass, rock-crystal, topaz, &c., but *is* easily *removed* by a touch of the finger, though in parts of the glass plate which *are made* very hot, it will adhere.
(Science, Michael Faraday, 1850–70, p. 403)

As regards the proportion of occurrences in future and past tenses, BE-passives are more than twice as common in the past tense as in the future tense; this statistical proportion holds for the whole century (see table 4.3). In nineteenth-century scientific monographs, prognostic statements subsuming futurity, as in example (2), are infrequently a theme of BE-passives; passivized statements more often focus on descriptions of events, phenomena or experiments in reference to the past, as in example (3):

(2) If the markets be favourable for the exportation of wine from Portugal to England, the exporter of the wine will be a seller of a bill, which *will be purchased* either by the importer of the cloth, or by the person who sold him his bill; and thus without the necessity of money passing from either country, the exporters in each country *will be paid* for their goods. Without having any direct transaction with each other, the money paid in Portugal by the importer of cloth *will be paid* to the Portuguese exporter of wine; and in England by the negociation of the same bill, the exporter of the cloth *will be authorized* to receive its value for the importer of wine.
(Science, David Ricardo, 1800–30, pp. 165–6)

(3) The experiments *were conducted* as follows: [. . .] The end of the tube *was* then *drawn out* and *connected* with a Sprengel pump and *exhausted* as rapidly as possible. Hydrogen *was* then *admitted*, and the tube *re-exhausted*, and when the pressure *was* again *reduced* to a few millimetres, carefully *sealed up*. The tube thus prepared *was placed* between the slit plate of a spectroscope and a source of light giving a continuous spectrum.
(Science, Norman J. Lockyer, 1870–1900, p. 128)

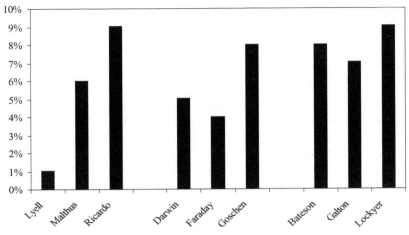

Figure 4.1. Proportion of future BE-passives.

Example (2), from Ricardo, illustrates the most frequent occurrence of future BE-passives in the present selection of samples. The samples from Goschen (period 1850–70), Bateson (period 1870–1900), and Lockyer (period 1870–1900) provide data which are close to those provided by the monograph by Ricardo; these four texts occupy the same place in the continuum of variation. The opposite extreme is the very low frequency of future passives in *Principles of Geology* by Lyell (period 1800–30).

Figure 4.1 shows the continuum of authorial variation, and to judge from this graph, there seems to be a slight overall increase in the occurrence of future passives towards the end of the century (see also table 4.2). However, contrasts of text-related frequencies are more distinct, and they may skew diachronic trends.

Findings related to the parameter of aspect evidence that perfect passives account for c. 10 per cent of all instances. A slight but steady increase in the incidence of this type of verb phrase is observable (the percentages per period are 8, 10 and 11, respectively; see table 4.2). These instances are rather evenly distributed between the present and the past perfect (13 per cent of present passives and 10 per cent of past passives are associated with the perfect aspect).[6] A closer reading of the corpus samples testifies that the distribution of perfect passives can vary markedly within a text, as some passages are permeated with successive instances of such forms. Example (4), from a section of *Materials for the Study of Variation* by Bateson, illustrates this type of passivized writing.

(4) However this may be, the fact remains, that since the first brief treatment of the matter in Animals and Plants under Domestication no serious effort to perceive or formulate principles of Variation *has been made*, and there is before us nothing but the most meagre and superficial account of a few of its phenomena. Darwin's first collection of the facts of Variation *has* scarcely

been increased. These same facts *have been arranged* and *rearranged* by each successive interpreter; the most various and contradictory propositions *have been established* upon them, and they *have been strained* to shew all that it can possibly *be hoped* that they will shew.
(Science, William Bateson, 1870–1900, p. 13)

The example from Bateson also calls for observations on the use of the present perfect in Present-day English discussed in Biber et al. (1999). According to their corpus-based findings, in present-day academic writing, the present perfect is typically used 'to imply validity of earlier findings or practices' (Biber et al. 1999: 465). In (4), this function of reference is manifest in the sequence of perfect BE-passives relating discussion to earlier scientific findings. In this example, the relation to findings is to the opposite effect, as Bateson denies the validity of earlier theories. Be it denial or confirmation of earlier findings, perfect passives typically provide references to previous research. The above-mentioned small increase of perfect BE-passives across time may be partly explained by the gradual increase of references to earlier studies. The fact that successive instances of perfect passives relating to previous research are provided by Bateson's monograph dated as late as 1894 is in agreement with the diachronic trend.

In contrast to perfect passives, passive progressives are extremely rare in scientific monographs during all three periods under study. Instances of such forms, as in examples (5) and (6), barely reach 1 per cent in the third period (see table 4.3).

(5) They think thus to increase the means of paying the debts which *are being incurred*, but the only effect is, still further to increase the evil, as importation, instead of being checked, is fostered by such a plan.
(Science, George Joachim Goschen, 1850–70, p. 73)

(6) It is most difficult always to remember that the increase of every living being *is* constantly *being checked* by unperceived injurious agencies; and that these same unperceived agencies are amply sufficient to cause rarity, and finally extinction.
(Science, Charles Darwin, 1850–70, p. 319)

As shown in Smitterberg (2005: 131), the raw frequencies of the passive progressive are low in all genres included in the CONCE corpus. Since the passive progressive was a new construction at this time (first attested in 1772; see Denison 1998: 151–8; Smitterberg 2005: 123), its frequency can be expected to be low. Nevertheless, it is surprising that the seven instances of this form recorded in the samples from Science of the last third of the century (see figures in table 4.3) provide the highest percentage of passive progressives of the genres in CONCE (Smitterberg 2005: 131–2). Smitterberg ascribes this statistical surprise to two factors: the overall frequency of passives in Science and the need, which is felt in Science more than in other genres, for lexical and syntactic precision (2005: 132). Examples (5) and (6) seem to confirm the factor of lexico-syntactic precision. At the same time, the findings provided by CONCE agree with general tendencies

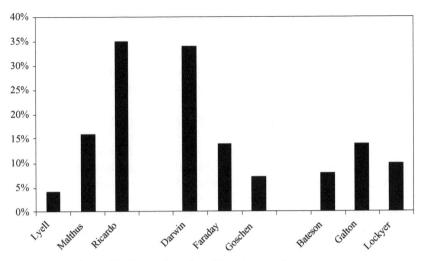

Figure 4.2. Proportion of conditional BE-passives.

in the genre-specific distribution of the auxiliary *be*. Thus, as shown in Biber et al., in academic prose the auxiliary *be* tends to mark passive voice, whereas in conversation this verb tends to mark progressive aspect (1999: 470). This overall tendency is prominent in nineteenth-century scientific writing.

In relation to the category of mood, as mentioned above, BE-passives are most often associated with the indicative mood (percentages of these forms for the three periods under study are 83, 82, and 89; see table 4.3). By contrast, imperative passives do not amount to 1 per cent; the few instances of these forms recorded in the samples from Darwin and Faraday are phrases with the verb *let*. These instances are interesting as they contain rare occurrences of *let*, which is usually associated with special imperative clauses used in the first person plural, in combination with the impersonal passive. In the present selection, BE-passives with *let* usually accompany shifts from expository to instructive discourse. Examples (7) and (8) illustrate these rare combinations of passives.

(7) *Let* it *be borne* in mind how infinitely complex and close-fitting are the mutual relations of all organic beings to each other and to their physical conditions of life. [. . .] *Let* it *be remembered* how powerful the influence of a single introduced tree or mammal has been shown to be.
(Science, Charles Darwin, 1850–70, pp. 80–1)

(8) *Let* a little oxide of copper *be dissolved* in olive-oil to form a bath, and having immersed some plates of glass, for which purpose microscope plates 3 × 1 inches are very convenient, *let* the whole *be heated* up to the decomposing temperature of the oil; [. . .]
(Science, Michael Faraday, 1850–70, p. 410)

Compared with the few instances of imperative passives, the proportion of passives associated with the conditional mood is rather substantial. This mood is essential in hypothetical statements of scientific writings, and this explains why 15 per cent of passives occur in the conditional mood (see totals in table 4.3). As scientific texts differ in their hypothetical force, the way BE-passives occur in the conditional mood appears to be a feature of authorial and textual variation. To illustrate this, percentages of passives associated with the conditional mood are reported in figure 4.2.

As shown in figure 4.2, the percentages by author vary from 4 to 35 (the present statistical extremes are provided by the samples from *Principles of Geology* by Lyell and samples from *On the Principles of Political Economy and Taxation* by Ricardo). In terms of authorial variation, the samples from the writings by Ricardo and Darwin stand out as texts saturated with combinations of the passive voice and the conditional mood. The frequent occurrence of these forms is connected with hypothetical reasoning prominent in the general character of the two monographs. Examples (9) and (10) illustrate the impersonal style of such hypothetical statements.

(9)   This, however, is only a seeming advantage to Portugal, for the quantity of cloth and wine together produced in that country *would be diminished*, while the quantity produced in England *would be increased*. Money would in some degree have changed its value in the two countries – it *would be lowered* in England, and *raised* in Portugal. Estimated in money, the whole revenue of Portugal *would be diminished*; estimated in the same medium, the whole revenue of England *would be increased*.
(Science, David Ricardo, 1800–30, p. 169)

(10)   On the other hand, we may feel sure that any variation in the least degree injurious *would be* rigidly *destroyed*. This preservation of favourable variations and the rejection of injurious variations, I call Natural Selection. Variation neither useful nor injurious *would not be affected* by natural selection, and *would be left* a fluctuating element, as perhaps we see in the species called polymorphic.
(Science, Charles Darwin, 1850–70, p. 81)

Figure 4.2 also sheds light on the decrease in the use of conditional passives between periods 2 and 3 reported in table 4.3 (from 17 to 11 per cent; see table 4.3). Compared to the frequent occurrence of this type of passives in the monographs by Ricardo (period 1) and Darwin (period 2), the samples of period 3 seem to demonstrate an overall decrease in the use of conditional passives (see figure 4.2). This decrease may be connected with a move towards objectivity in scientific writing, which, among other things, manifests itself in the increase of indicative passives. However, the present selection of samples is too small for generalizations concerning period-specific usage; the conspicuously frequent use of conditional passives in the writings of Ricardo and Darwin seems to be an idiosyncratic feature of these two monographs, and this may skew period-specific tendencies.

Table 4.4. *The distribution of* BE-*passives in relation to syntactic parameters.*

Period	1	2	3	Total
Simple sentence	41 (5%)	42 (6%)	83 (13%)	166 (8%)
Complex sentence	643 (77%)	488 (72%)	441 (67%)	1,572 (72%)
Compound sentence	154 (18%)	143 (21%)	139 (21%)	436 (21%)
Total	838 (100%)	673 (100%)	663 (100%)	2,174 (100%)

At the same time, the findings on the use of subjunctives and modal auxiliaries in adverbial clauses in CONCE as a whole have revealed a similar tendency, i.e. the overall slight decrease in the occurrence of these forms between period 1 and period 3 (see ch. 3 section 5.3, Grund and Walker in the present volume). Moreover, according to these findings, Science in CONCE is one of the genres in which this decrease is steady over the three periods (see figure 3.1 in Grund and Walker, this volume). Thus, the present study of passives and the above-mentioned findings on the use of the subjunctive and modal auxiliaries characterize Science as a genre that displays a consistent trend in favour of the indicative. However, further research is needed to find out whether we are dealing with a genre-related tendency or whether this trend pertains to a more general diachronic change in the use of the subjunctive.

To conclude this section, associations of passives with the present tense, indefinite aspect and indicative mood prevail in scientific writing during all three periods studied. Combinations with other alternatives within these variables show only slight statistical changes such as the steady but inconsiderable increase of passives in future, perfect and progressive verb phrases. Further research is needed to see whether this increase reflects general diachronic trends in the use of various, not only passive, verb forms. At the same time, the reported statistical tendencies, slight as they are, seem to reflect such movements of scientific discourse as the increase in prognostic statements, references to previous findings, and the need for linguistic precision. In other words, grammatical associations of BE-passives tend to become more varied with the development of impersonal scientific discourse.

3.2   Syntactic parameters across the nineteenth century

Figures that characterize BE-passives in terms of syntactic relations are reported in tables 4.4 and 4.5. In table 4.4, instances of passives are related to their occurrence in simple, complex and compound sentences, while in table 4.5 these instances are reported in relation to the type of clause, main and subordinate, and to the type of syntactic link, syndetic or asyndetic.[7] In this study, the syntactic parameters are distinguished in the way they are defined in Quirk et al. (1985: 719, 918–19).

Table 4.5. *The distribution of* BE-*passives in relation to syntactic parameters of simple and complex sentences.*

Period	1	2	3	Total
Simple sentence	41 (5%)	42 (6%)	83 (13%)	166 (8%)
Complex sentence				
Main clause	233 (28%)	143 (21%)	140 (21%)	516 (23%)
Subordinate clause	410 (49%)	345 (51%)	301 (45%)	1,056 (49%)
Total	643 (77%)	488 (72%)	441 (67%)	1,572 (72%)
Compound sentence				
Syndetic coordination	147 (18%)	107 (16%)	109 (16%)	363 (17%)
Asyndetic coordination	7 (1%)	36 (5%)	30 (4%)	73 (3%)
Total	154 (18%)	143 (21%)	139 (20%)	436 (20%)
Total	838 (100%)	673 (100%)	663 (100%)	2,174 (100%)

The data are analysed in terms of these parameters with the aim of highlighting period-specific tendencies.

Table 4.4 shows that complex sentences are the most frequent loci for passives across all three periods, partly because simple sentences are, in general, rare in nineteenth-century scientific writing. The percentages for BE-passives occurring in complex sentences decrease slightly but steadily from 77 to 72 to 67 per cent in the three periods respectively (see table 4.4). At the same time, a tendency for passives to occur more frequently in simple sentences towards the end of the century is also observable; the increase is from 5 per cent in period 1 to 13 per cent in period 3 (see table 4.4). However, this tendency may be ascribed to authorial variation and/or shifts in the overall proportion of simple sentences. Texts from period 1 (where BE-passives in simple sentences account for 5 per cent), e.g. *Principles of Geology* by Lyell, are sparingly interspersed with simple sentences, as in examples (11) and (12).

(11) Along the alluvial plains, and in marshy places, an immense number of cones of sand *were thrown up.*
(Science, Charles Lyell, 1800–30, p. 428)

(12) The aged Prince, with one thousand four hundred and thirty of his people, *was destroyed.*
(Science, Charles Lyell, 1800–30, p. 430)

Otherwise this clearly expository academic textbook, which classifies, as Lyell (1830: 167) states himself, 'the former changes that have taken place in the organic, as well as in the inorganic kingdoms of nature' (1830: 167), favours complex sentences. In contrast, *The Chemistry of the Sun* by Lockyer, dated as late as 1887, is more experiment oriented. In agreement with this orientation, it employs simple sentences with passives to introduce detailed descriptions of experiments, as in examples (13) and (14). The frequency of such passages in Lockyer's monograph seems to contribute to the increase of BE-passives in simple sentences in the texts studied.

(13) This experiment *was* then *varied* in the following way. Some pieces of metallic sodium were introduced into a test-tube, and a long glass tube conveying coal-gas passed to the bottom, an exit for the gas being also provided at the top.
(Science, J. Norman Lockyer, 1870–1900, p. 129)

(14) The experiment *is managed* as follows. The condenser of a Duboscq lantern being removed, a combination of a slit and lens is put in its place, the slit being placed inside the lantern close to the carbons at the principal focus of the lens.
(Science, J. Norman Lockyer, 1870–1900, p. 130)

Within this classification, the most frequent host of BE-passives is a subordinate clause. Almost half of BE-passives are recorded in this syntactic position (the percentages for the three periods are 49, 51, and 45, respectively; see table 4.5). Main clauses account for a considerably smaller number of passives; in complex sentences, passives occur twice as often in subordinate as in main clauses. In contrast to sentences containing subordination, in compound sentences, BE-passives occur less frequently; 20 per cent of instances are recorded in such sentences, whereas in sentences with subordinate clauses, these instances amount to 72 per cent (see totals in table 4.5). This statistical proportion reflects how logical relations are dealt with in scientific discourse. The coupling of syndetic subordination and passive voice potentiates the overt presentation of logical relations within a text, and this accounts for the prevailing association of passives with subordinate clauses. Example (15) from *Natural Inheritance* by Galton shows how this syntactic feature structures the logical arrangement of the passage that introduces the discussion of processes in heredity. Example (15) is also representative of the Science genre in statistical terms: associations of passives with sentence and clause structures reflect the overall proportion of such associations for Science. Thus, in (15), passives in subordinate clauses are twice as frequent as in main clauses, and compound sentences are notably less frequent hosts of passive constructions. Coordination is known to be 'the kind of link most used for optimum ease of comprehension' (Quirk et al. 1985: 1040). This kind of link is infrequent in nineteenth-century scientific writing.

(15) Natural and Acquired Peculiarities. – The peculiarities of men may be roughly sorted into those that are natural and those that are acquired. [. . .] It may be that some natural peculiarity does not appear till late in life, and yet may justly deserve *to be considered* natural, for if it is decidedly exceptional in its character its origin *could* hardly *be ascribed* to the effects of nurture. If it *was* also *possessed* by some ancestor, it *must be considered* to be hereditary as well. But 'Natural' is an unfortunate word for our purposes; it implies that the moment of birth is the earliest date from which the effects of surrounding conditions *are to be reckoned*, although nurture begins much

earlier than that. I therefore must ask that the word 'Natural' *should not be construed* too literally, any more than the analogous phrases of inborn, congenital, and innate.
(Science, Sir Francis Galton, 1870–1900, p. 4)

To judge from the data in table 4.5, the distribution of passives in compound sentences differs depending on the type of syntactic link. Thus, about 17 per cent of passive phrases are recorded in sentences with syndetic coordination (the percentages for the three periods are 18, 16, and 16, respectively). By contrast, combinations of passives with asyndetic coordination are very rare, in particular in the texts of the earliest period (1 per cent). Such combinations appear slightly more frequently in scientific writing in the second half of the century (5 per cent in period 2 and 4 per cent in period 3). They are especially visible in the samples from Faraday's writings, as in example (16).

(16)   Nor has the gold disappeared; a piece of leaf, altered in one part and not in another, *was divided* into four equal parts, and the gold on each *converted* by chlorine gas into crystallized chloride of gold; the same amount *was found* in each division.
(Science, Michael Faraday, 1850–70, p. 396)

Since asyndetic coordination is a common substitute for subordination (Quirk et al. 1985: 1042), instances as in the above-quoted example from Faraday indirectly reinforce the fact that, in scientific writing, BE-passives tend to associate with subordination.

In sum, BE-passives most often associate with subordination, and half of these forms are recorded in subordinate clauses of complex sentences. However, a tendency in the opposite direction is detectable. The number of BE-passives recorded in sentences with subordinate clauses gradually decreases in the course of the century (the percentages for the three periods are 77, 72, and 67, respectively), whereas the occurrence of passives in simple sentences increases towards the end of the century. These diachronic trends, however, do not skew the above-mentioned tendencies in the distribution of BE-passives: proportionally, the association of passives with subordinate clauses of complex sentences prevails across time, and is a stable feature of the use of passives in nineteenth-century scientific writing. Further research is necessary to reveal how this feature correlates with the overall distribution of syntactic parameters, but it is possible that we are dealing with a feature which exhibits stability across time (on stable variation see Raumolin-Brunberg 2002).

4   Lexical associations of BE-passives

In scientific writing, 'many of the verbs that most commonly occur in the passive refer to aspects of scientific methodology and analysis' or 'are used to report findings or to express logical relations' (Biber et al. 1999: 480). Although the

Table 4.6. *Past participles of verbs commonly occurring in the passive in scientific (CONCE) and academic (LSWE) writing (verb forms occurring in both corpora underlined).*

CONCE findings (raw frequencies)	LSWE findings (occurrences per million words)
Over 50 occurrences *found, made, seen*	
Over 30 occurrences *considered, increased, given, known, produced*	Over 300 occurrences *found, given, made, seen, used*
Over 20 occurrences *employed, observed, reduced, said, supposed*	Over 200 occurrences *considered, shown, taken*
Over 10 occurrences *affected, applied, brought, called, described, diminished, drawn, effected, examined, formed, introduced, left, obtained, paid, raised, shown, stated, supposed, taken, thrown*	Over 100 occurrences *achieved, associated, based, called, carried, concerned, defined, described, determined, done, expected, expressed, involved, known, measured, needed, obtained, performed, related, required, said, set*
Over 5 occurrences *bound, caused, composed, connected, determined, distributed, done, enabled, expected, expended, expressed, felt, imposed, justified, kept, limited, recognised, regarded, regulated, removed, supplied, understood, used*	Over 40 occurrences *asked, applied, brought, calculated, chosen, compared, derived, designed, developed, discussed, drawn, examined, explained, formed, held, identified, illustrated, introduced, kept, left, limited, lost, noted, observed, prepared, presented, put, recognized, regarded, replaced, reported, represented, studied, suggested, thought, treated, understood*
	Over 20 occurrences *forced, paid, sent, told*

selection of samples from CONCE does not allow generalizations similar to those found in Biber et al. (1999), which is based on the 40-million-word Longman Spoken and Written English Corpus (LSWE), the present findings provide some comparable corpus-based evidence.[8] Table 4.6 lists verbs that frequently occur in the passive in scientific writings in CONCE and verbs that are most common in the passive in present-day academic prose in LSWE (findings on present-day usage are cited from Biber et al. 1999: 478–9). To facilitate comparisons, findings from the two corpora, which are so different in size, are arranged in table 4.6 in such a way that words with a similar rate of frequency are listed, when possible, in the same row.

The findings reported in table 4.6 show that the two corpora provide a quintet of verbs that are common in passives in scientific writing, i.e. *find, give, make, see* and *consider*. This points to continuity of lexical associations in scientific writings across the two successive centuries. Monosyllabic verbs of Germanic origin are words most often used in English, and a number of these verbs, i.e. *find, give, make* and *see*, play a prominent role in the vocabulary of scientific passives.[9] Used in the passive, these verbs tend to be associated with notions related to scientific methodology, classifications and the interpretation of findings. Example (17) illustrates how the passives of these four monosyllabic verbs make up a core of phrases presenting and interpreting the scientist's findings.

(17) When the evidence is looked at as a whole it appears that no generalization of this kind *can be made*. It suggests rather that the variability of a form is, so far as *can be seen*, as much a part of its specific characters as any other feature of its organization. Of such frequent Variation in single genera or species some curious instances *are to be found* among the facts given. (Science, William Bateson, 1870–1900, p. 266)

Besides this quotation, all the instances of passives containing *found, given, made,* and *seen* which occur in Bateson's text samples in CONCE are listed in table 4.7 (these instances are given in the order in which they occur). The list demonstrates how the passives of the four activity verbs lend an impersonal tone to scientific writing.

Table 4.7 shows that the BE-passives containing *found, given, made* and *seen* are most often combined with features typical of scientific presentation of empirical facts. Such presentation requires examples and quantified data. Hence, words pertaining to this semantic domain, i.e. *examples, cases* (each recorded six times in the samples from Bateson), and *instances* (recorded twice), are the words which most often occur in phrases with *found, given, made* and *seen*. Other notions, such as *symmetry, semblance, reference,* etc., belong to the area of abstract thinking, or to the classifications of concrete phenomena, such as *duplicate teeth* or *legs of double structure* (see table 4.7). Lexical associations of this type constitute the basic vocabulary of impersonal discourse in scientific writing.

To return to the types of verbs reported in table 4.6, approximately half the verbs occur in both corpora, which testifies to the continuity of lexical associations across time (see the verb forms underlined in table 4.6). These verbs typically denote mental acts (*consider, know, observe*), the activity of communication (*call, describe, say*), acts of simple occurrence (*increase, obtain, distribute*), and concrete actions (*bring, leave, take*). Neither movement verbs nor verbs denoting bodily posture commonly associate with passives in scientific writing of the nineteenth and twentieth centuries.

Differences observable in table 4.6 should be interpreted with caution as they relate to corpora of different sizes. For instance, in contrast to the distribution of the above-mentioned monosyllabic verbs common in scientific writings of the two

Table 4.7. *Phrasal associations of* found, given, made *and* seen *in the samples from* Materials for the Study of Variation *by Bateson (1894).*

found	a semblance <u>may be found</u> (p. 18), limitations . . . <u>will be found</u> (p. 18), one feature which <u>is found</u> (p. 18), heterogeneity <u>is found</u> (p. 19), the symmetry which <u>is found</u> (p. 20), examples <u>can be</u> easily <u>found</u> (p. 267), series of repetitions <u>will be found</u> (p. 268), every condition <u>may</u> . . . <u>be found</u> (p. 270), it <u>will often</u> . . . <u>be found</u> (p. 272), this fact <u>will be found</u> (p. 272), they [instances] <u>are found</u> (p. 331), legs of double structure <u>are</u> sometimes <u>found</u> (p. 476), it <u>will be</u> generally <u>found</u> (p. 477)
given	patterns <u>are being given</u> (p. 20), the following examples <u>may be given</u> (p. 267), three cases of variation <u>were given</u> (p. 267), several examples <u>have been given</u> (p. 268), examples <u>have been given</u> (p. 272), several such cases <u>were given</u> (p. 273), <u>will be given</u> a brief notice (p. 331)
made	no . . . attempt . . . <u>has been made</u> (p. 13), effort <u>has been made</u> (p. 13), observations <u>cannot be made</u> (p. 14), supposition <u>has been made</u> (p. 16), generalization . . . <u>cannot be made</u> (p. 226), reference <u>was made</u> (p. 267), can . . . premolars <u>be made</u> (p. 273), the attempt . . . <u>should not be made</u> (p. 273), they [cases] <u>will be made</u> the subject (p. 475)
seen	symmetry <u>is seen</u> (p. 20), repetitions . . . <u>may be seen</u> (p. 20), the variability of a form . . . <u>can be seen</u> (p. 266), four cases . . . <u>were seen</u> (p. 266), further examples <u>may be seen</u> (p. 267), division . . . <u>is seen</u> (p. 267), cases of division . . . <u>are seen</u> (p. 267), duplicate teeth <u>were seen</u> (p. 268), these cases . . . <u>may be seen</u> (p. 268), cases . . . <u>may be seen</u> (p. 269), a good illustration . . . <u>may be</u> often <u>seen</u> (p. 270), phenomena <u>may be seen</u> (p. 270), spines . . . <u>are</u> generally <u>to be seen</u> (p. 270), it <u>is seen</u> that (p. 270), variation . . . <u>may be seen</u> (p. 272), conditions <u>were seen</u> (p. 272), the same <u>was</u> also <u>seen</u> (p. 272), examples <u>were seen</u> (p. 273), what <u>may be seen</u> (p. 273), it <u>will be seen</u> (p. 273)

centuries, the difference in the distribution of *increased* and *produced* is notable. Verb phrases with these participles, so frequent in CONCE, are absent from the list of verbs common in academic writing from LSWE (see the group of verbs with over thirty occurrences in table 4.6). This might be interpreted as a change in the focus of lexical associations across time. However, a closer look at the frequencies of *increased* and *produced* in CONCE reveals a text-specific distribution of phrases with these verb forms in Science. This text-related distribution is shown in table 4.8.

The text-specific frequency of *increased* and *produced* stands out in table 4.8: BE-passives of these verbs dominate in the samples from Ricardo. The dominance of *increased* is even more pronounced than that of *produced*, which is connected with the prognostic and hypothetical modality of Ricardo's classic work on political economy. Speculations on 'increase phenomena' are a frequent topic in the

Table 4.8. *Raw frequencies of* BE-*passives with past participles of* increase *and* produce *in Science.*

Period	Author	*increased*	*produced*
1	Lyell	1	1
	Malthus	3	0
	Ricardo	20	8
2	Darwin	0	2
	Faraday	2	4
	Goschen	1	0
3	Bateson	1	0
	Galton	0	0
	Lockyer	2	2

samples from this work; moreover, owing to the hypothetical treatment of this topic by Ricardo, half of the BE-passives with *increased* are associated with the modal verbs *would* and *may* (see example (9) quoted in section 3.1). Conversely, in the other works sampled in CONCE, not a single verb phrase with *increased* has such an association, and this emphasizes the text-specific distribution of verb phrases with *increased* in Science.

According to the findings reported in table 4.8, the incidence of *increased* and *produced* in samples from other texts included in Science does not characterize these verbs as especially frequent passives in the genre of scientific writing. Nevertheless, *increased* and *produced* have this statistical status in CONCE owing to their frequency in the samples from Ricardo. But for the samples from Ricardo, these verbs would not be classified as common in the passive in scientific writing. All this makes the interpretation of lexical associations reported in table 4.6 dependent on the analysis of subject-matter differences, and such analyses are beyond the scope of the present study. At the same time, the comparable corpus-based evidence reveals a good deal of continuity in the distribution of main verbs in phrases with the passive in nineteenth-century and present-day academic writing.

5   Science versus Letters: differences in usage by an individual author

One way of testing the specific nature of passivized scientific writing is to compare texts from different genres by the same author. Since CONCE contains samples from both Letters and Science by Darwin, such a case study can be based on the writings of this scientist. With the variable of author under control, genre-related differences in the occurrence of passives may reveal themselves through contrasts

Table 4.9. *The distribution of passives in samples of Charles Darwin's writing included in CONCE (period 2, 1850–70).*

Genre	Word count	BE-passives: raw frequencies	BE-passives per 1,000 words
Letters	19,349	137	7.1
Science	10,694	168	15.7

Table 4.10. *The distribution of BE-passives in relation to grammatical parameters in the writings of Darwin.*

Grammatical parameters		Letters	Science
Tense	Present	100 (73%)	147 (88%)
	Past	29 (21%)	12 (7%)
	Future	8 (6%)	9 (5%)
Aspect	Indefinite	114 (83%)	138 (82%)
	Perfect	23 (17%)	29 (17%)
	Progressive	0 (0%)	1 (1%)
Mood	Indicative	115 (84%)	108 (64%)
	Conditional	18 (13%)	57 (34%)
	Imperative	4 (3%)	3 (2%)
Total		137 (100%)	168 (100%)

in usage. The present case study involves the same variables as are discussed in the previous sections.

The frequencies of BE-passives in the letters of Darwin and in his famous work *The Origin of Species* are shown in table 4.9. As expected, the figures in table 4.9 vary greatly across genre: in the samples from Science, BE-passives are more than twice as frequent as in Letters. This contrast in individual practice agrees with the figures per genre and per period discussed earlier: in CONCE, the genre-related averages provided by Letters and Science dated 1850–70 are 5.105 for Letters and 14.383 for Science (see table 4.1). BE-passives in the writings of Darwin have the same genre-specific pattern of distribution (the incidence for Letters is 7.1 and 15.7 for Science; see table 4.9).

Observations on the grammatical parameters of this contrast are reported in table 4.10. To judge from these observations, the use of passives in Letters and Science texts written by Darwin differs markedly as regards association with the categories of mood and tense.

Table 4.10 shows that, in Science, the percentage of BE-passives in the conditional mood is almost three times higher than in the selection of Darwin's letters

Table 4.11. *The distribution of* BE-*passives in relation to syntactic parameters in the writings of Darwin.*

Syntactic parameters	Letters	Science
Simple sentence	25 (18%)	8 (5%)
Complex sentence	68 (50%)	122 (73%)
Compound sentence	44 (32%)	38 (23%)
Total	137 (100%)	168 (100%)

(see table 4.10). It is possible that the general hypothetical presentation of ideas in *The Origin of Species* accounts for this contrast, as the combination of the passive and the conditional mood is common in this monograph (see figure 4.2 discussed in section 3.1). As for the proportion of associations with the variable of tense, the following trends are notable: future BE-passives do not display a manifest contrast between the two genres (the percentages of such instances are 6 for Letters and 5 for Science; see table 4.10). Conversely, the association of passives with the past tense differs considerably with genre: Letters focus on the past more often than Science (the respective percentages are 21 and 7; see table 4.10).

In terms of syntactic associations (see table 4.11), BE-passives in Letters occur more often in simple and compound sentences compared with the samples from *The Origin of Species*. This agrees with the overall tendency of BE-passives recorded in Science; as shown earlier, complex sentences are the most frequent hosts of passives in the genre of scientific writing. The samples from Darwin's monograph provide data that accord with this distribution. The genre-specific difference is especially prominent in the association of the passive with subordination: 49 per cent of verb phrases with passives are recorded in complex sentences in Letters, whereas 73 per cent of such phrases occur in this syntactic structure in Science (see table 4.11).

Table 4.12 gives the frequencies of BE-passives recorded in main and subordinate clauses of complex sentences. Within the classification adopted, subordinate clauses are the most frequent host of BE-passives in Letters. Although subordination is not as dominant in the epistolary syntax as it is in Science, the tendency of passives to associate with subordinate clauses holds in Letters (the percentage of such instances is 39; see table 4.12). Table 4.12 also shows the proportion of passives in relation to syndetic and asyndetic types of coordination. The genre-specific difference in the frequencies of BE-passives associated with syndetic coordination is not remarkable (15 per cent of passives in Letters and 18 per cent of passives in Science are recorded in this syntactic structure; see table 4.12). In contrast, asyndetic coordination is more notable in the samples from Letters than from Science: 17 per cent of passives in Letters and only 5 per cent of passives in

Table 4.12. *The distribution of* BE*-passives in relation to syntactic parameters of compound and complex sentences in the writings of Darwin.*

Syntactic parameters	Letters	Science
Simple sentence	25 (18%)	8 (5%)
Complex sentence		
Main clause	14 (10%)	45 (27%)
Subordinate clause	54 (39%)	77 (46%)
Total	68 (50%)	122 (73%)
Compound sentence		
Syndetic coordination	21 (15%)	30 (18%)
Asyndetic coordination	23 (17%)	8 (5%)
Total	44 (32%)	38 (23%)
Total	137 (100%)	168 (100%)

Science are recorded in this syntactic structure (see table 4.12). It is possible that this difference is genre-specific. The percentage of passives in asyndetic structures also adds to the overall proportion of compound sentences with passives in Letters (32 per cent in contrast to 22 per cent in Science; see table 4.12). It is evident that the epistolary syntax favours coordination more often than does the syntax of scientific writing. Examples (18) and (19) illustrate the way BE-passives occur in asyndetically coordinated sentences in Darwin's letters.

(18) With respect to Clapham School: I think favourably of it: the Boys *are* not so exclusively *kept* to Classics: arithmetic *is made* much of: all *are taught* drawing, & some modern languages.
(Letters, Charles Darwin, 1850–70, p. 6, 346)

(19) The work is too great for me, but if I live I will finish it: indeed three-fourth *is done*.
(Letters, Charles Darwin, 1850–70, p. 7, 161)

As for the lexical repertoire of BE-passives, in the samples from Letters, instances with the verbs most common in the passives of scientific writing, i.e. *find*, *give*, *make*, *see* and *consider*, are not frequent; they do not stand out as a dominant pattern of phrases (see the list in table 4.7). In the samples from Science, not a single combination of BE-passives with an animate noun or personal pronoun is recorded. By contrast, in Letters, the percentage of such combinations amounts to forty-one. In Letters, subjects expressed by personal pronouns, as in examples

(20) and (21), frequently associate with passives; in the samples from *The Origin of Species*, such associations are not recorded.

(20) We *are* both rather *knocked up* & I have not spirits to see anyone, even you, at present.
(Letters, Charles Darwin, 1850–70, p. 7, 115)

(21) I am glad that you *were tipped* but that makes no difference in my repaying your outlay.
(Letters, Charles Darwin, 1850–70, p. 6, 434)

Of the associations of BE-passives with personal pronouns 24 per cent have as subject the pronoun *I*, which seems to be a typical distribution for letters, texts written in the first person. All these instances of BE-passives usually focus on emotion, involvement, stance and personal affect. For instance, in the selection of letters by Darwin, the passives with first person singular subjects occur in combination with *bothered, disappointed, frightened, opposed, perplexed, tempted, prostrated, quizzed*, and other verbs expressing stance, as in example (22).

(22) I *was* rather *frightened* by having heard that it was rather a rough school: but young Herschel did not agree to this; [. . .]
(Letters, Charles Darwin, 1850–70, p. 6, 346)

This type of passivized description of involvement has no parallels in the samples from the scientific writing of Darwin. In the samples from *The Origin of Species*, the personal viewpoint may be expressed by the combination of *I* with a performative verb as in example (10) quoted in section 3.1, in which Darwin states his credo of the scientist: 'This preservation of favourable variations and the rejection of injurious variations, I call Natural Selection'. Such expressions radically differ from the repertoire of passivized discourse, and they are exceptionally rare in Science.

In sum, the contrasts in usage provided by the writings of the same language user seem to reveal some cross-genre variation in the use of passives. Although the samples from the scientific writing of Darwin provide the smallest number of BE-passives in CONCE (see table 4.2 on p. 114), the way this scientist uses the passive in Science and Letters accords with the overall contrast characteristic of the two genres. As shown earlier (see table 4.1 in section 2), Science and Letters represent two extremes in the continuum of variation: Science is the most passivized genre, whereas Letters is one of the least passivized genres in CONCE. This contrast is a stable genre-specific feature of nineteenth-century scientific writing, and it is also manifest in the samples from Darwin's writings. Yet the possibility of idiosyncratic influence has to be kept in mind, since this genre-specific feature has been confirmed by the writings of only one author, however influential and representative.

The present comparison of Darwin's writings suggests that the parameters of mood and tense tend to be more indicative of genre-specific use of passives than the parameter of aspect. No genre-related difference in the frequency of perfect passives and passive progressives is observed; in contrast, the frequency of past passives seems to be genre-related, as samples from Science and Letters differ in the distribution of past passives. Associations of BE-passives with the conditional mood are also indicative of the genre-related authorial variation, as these associations are far more frequent in the samples from Science. In terms of syntactic variables, the association of BE-passives with subordinate clauses comes forth as a distinct feature of both genres, epistolary and scientific, but the statistical profile of this feature is more prominent in the scientific writings of Darwin. The most conspicuous differences are to be found in the lexical associations of BE-passives. Thus, in contrast to the impersonal character of passages with BE-passives in Darwin's *The Origin of Species*, in his letters verb phrases with passives express emotionality, involvement and personal affect.

Specimens of the writings of one nineteenth-century scientist have provided the present observations about genre-related contrasts in the use of passives. Further research is needed to find out to what extent these contrasts are period-specific and to what extent they reflect the continuum of individual styles characteristic of the writings of nineteenth-century scientists.

6   Conclusions

Scientific writings have generally been taken to constitute a semiotic space that is associated with a depersonalized tone of discourse. This tone is required by Western academic tradition (Biber et al. 1999: 477), and it is manifest in the use of, among other things, the 'suppressed person', the passive voice and avoidance of emotive features. The depersonalized tone has been stated to be a recent development dating from the nineteenth century (Halliday 1988: 166). At the same time, the findings provided by the CONCE corpus show that neither lexical nor grammatical associations of passives in nineteenth-century scientific monographs can be characterized as period-specific.

Studies of early texts have shown that even at the initial stage of scientific writing the academic tradition favours a depersonalized tone. Thus, fourteenth-century medical texts contain a striking number of passive and impersonal forms (Taavitsainen 1994: 333, 339). The present corpus-based investigation of the use of BE-passives confirms the centuries-old development of this academic tradition. The corpus findings do not testify to any considerable increase in the use of passives in the course of the nineteenth century. The frequency of verb phrases with BE-passives is rather stable for all three subperiods. Moreover, this stability is also evident in relation to the parameters of tense, mood and aspect; BE-passives seem to be fully integrated in nineteenth-century scientific writing. A slight increase in the occurrence of future and perfect passives, as well as a new grammatical form such as the passive progressive, shows the expansion of an established feature rather than a development in process. This expansion reflects

134   Larisa Oldireva Gustafsson

movements towards prognostic and aspectually exact statements in scientific writing.

The integration of BE-passives into the syntax of scientific writing is characterized by the frequent association of the passive with subordinate clauses. Considerably less frequent occurrences in simple and asyndetic compound sentences make up the opposite pole of this continuum. Presenting the data by sub-period has not revealed diachronically distinct tendencies in terms of syntactic parameters; instead, nineteenth-century scientific writing displays quantitatively stable associations between passives and sentence structure. Since these proportions are observed in the texts dated as early as 1800–30, this stability cannot be interpreted as a nineteenth-century development. All this points to the earlier periods as a formative time for the development of passivized scientific discourse. Moreover, since the present corpus findings on grammatical and lexical associations of nineteenth-century BE-passives display so many parallels with the findings on present-day academic writing there seem to be more genre-specific than period-specific tendencies at work.

Notes

1. The figures in table 4.1, from Geisler (2002: 252), are based on the observations of forms tagged as passives using the EngCG-2 tagger designed by Conexor; the tagged output files were not edited manually (Geisler 2002: 252).
2. The statistical fluctuation in the occurrence of passives in Debates may be connected with style changes in the samples from different periods: samples for period 1 and most samples for period 2 represent indirect speech, whereas debates for period 3 are in direct speech. However, the supposition that the difference in style may influence the occurrence of passives is purely tentative and requires special study.
3. In my database, coordinated passives like *is not imbedded or fused* (see example (1)) were counted and coded as separate instances.
4. Different counting techniques are the reason for differences in incidences of passives in table 4.1 and table 4.2. Thus, figures in table 4.1, which are provided by the automatic extraction of BE-passives, exclude ambiguously tagged instances (see Geisler 2002: 252). In table 4.2, which is based on a manually edited database, passive constructions with two or more words (usually modifiers) separating the auxiliary verb BE and the past participle (e.g. *was so greatly amended*) are included, whereas in table 4.1, instances of such extended constructions are not reported. In spite of the differences in counting and resultant figures, table 4.1 and table 4.2 show the same diachronic trend in the use of BE-passives in scientific writing.
5. In table 4.3, the few non-finite passives in the material were counted as present with respect to tense, indefinite with respect to aspect, and indicative with respect to mood.
6. It is reported in Biber et al. that the present perfect aspect is relatively common in present-day academic writing and that the following verbs occur with the present perfect more than 25 per cent of the time: *criticize, document, implicate, master* and *report* (1999: 463). Interestingly, the verbs most frequently recorded in the passive of scientific writings included in the two corpora, the Longman Spoken and Written

English Corpus (LSWE) and CONCE (see the forms *found*, *given*, *made* and *seen* in table 4.6) differ from this group thematically and etymologically.

7. In tables 4.4 and 4.5, instances of BE-passives are counted in relation to their immediate syntactic host. Thus, passives occurring in sentences that contain both subordination and coordination are counted and classified in the following way: instances occurring in subordinate clauses are reported under complex sentences, while instances associated with coordination are reported under compound sentences.

8. The academic prose subcorpus in LSWE (the total number of words is 5,331,800) includes both book extracts and research articles (Biber et al. 1999: 32), while Science in CONCE only comprises samples from scientific monographs. Despite this difference LSWE provides the closest comparable material available for the present study.

9. According to Biber et al., the same set of verbs is common in various, not only passive, verb phrases recorded in present-day academic writing; *make* and *give* are such verbs representing the group of activity verbs, and *see* and *find* are such verbs representing the group of mental verbs (1999: 367–8). Academic writing is so saturated with passives that analyses of its grammar are commonly accompanied by text examples with passive constructions, even if quotations do not aim at exemplifying the use of passives (Biber et al. 1999: 372).

5   Relativizers in nineteenth-century English

CHRISTINE JOHANSSON

1   Introduction

This study analyses the use of relativizers in nineteenth-century English,[1] and the distribution of *wh*-forms (*who*, *whose*, *whom* and *which*) and *that* in particular. The data are drawn from CONCE (A Corpus of Nineteenth-century English; see Kytö, Rudanko and Smitterberg 2000, and the Introduction to this volume). Three genres, very different in character, were analysed: Science, Trials and Letters. Time periods 1 and 3 were studied in order to detect a change in the use of relativizers, mainly in the distribution of the *wh*-forms and *that*.

In Middle English and Early Modern English, frequent use is made of the relativizer *that* regardless of the type of antecedent and the type of relative clause (Barber 1997: 209–16). In the fifteenth century, *which* (or the form *the which*), as an alternative to *that* occurs for example in prepositional relative constructions (see Fischer 1992: 296–8, 388–90 and Johansson 2002), but *who* is not widely used, outside certain idiolects, until the beginning of the eighteenth century (Rydén 1966: 3–4, 279–80; 1983). In Present-day English (primarily American English), the relativizer *that* is used chiefly in restrictive relative clauses, whereas *which* in particular is very rare in this type of clause (see Geisler and Johansson 2002). The results of the present study show that in nineteenth-century English, at least in the genres studied here, it is the *wh*-forms that are used much more frequently, in restrictive and nonrestrictive relative clauses, than the relativizer *that*. The predominant use of the *wh*-forms is what makes the nineteenth century stand out compared with both earlier periods of English and Present-day English. Nineteenth-century English provides us with new patterns in the use of relativizers where one strategy for forming relative clauses (*that*) is seldom used.

The study first discusses the overall distribution of *wh*-forms and *that* in nineteenth-century English (section 2). The zero relativizer is not included for the simple reason that it is problematic to retrieve in a corpus-based study such as the present one. *What* as relativizer, as in *Here's a man what's eighty*, is not discussed either since it is nonstandard (Görlach 1999: 86). The study aims at describing standard variation in the use of relativizers and, as pointed out

Table 5.1. Wh-*forms and* that *in Science.*

Relativizer	Period 1	Period 3	Periods 1+3
Wh-	461 (95%)	273 (80%)	734 (89%)
That	25 (5%)	70 (20%)	95 (11%)
Total	486 (100%)	343 (100%)	829 (100%)

earlier, particularly the distribution of *who, whom, whose* and *which* versus *that*. In sections 3–4, factors which influence this distribution will be discussed, such as the type of relative clause and the type of antecedent. In section 5, typical syntactic environments of *wh*-forms and *that* will be studied (for example, sentential relative clauses, cleft sentences and pronominal antecedents). The use of relativizers across speaker roles in Trials will be analysed in section 6. Section 7 examines gender-based differences in the use of relativizers and relative clauses in Letters.

2   The distribution of *wh*-forms and *that* in nineteenth-century English texts

The three genres included in this study differ greatly as regards the frequency of *wh*-forms (*who, whose, whom* and *which*) and *that*. Whereas the Science texts have 1,188 relative clauses with *wh*-forms or *that* per 100,000 words, there are 398/100,000 words in Trials and 804/100,000 words in Letters.

2.1   Science

In Science, the *wh*-forms are particularly frequent, occurring in 89 per cent of the cases (see table 5.1). Naturally *wh*-forms are used in formal scientific texts according to the norms for good writing. The animacy and case contrasts signalled by the *wh*-forms (see Quirk et al. 1985: 366) contribute to the kind of clarity of expression and conciseness required of a scientific text. Also in Early Modern English scientific writing, the *wh*-forms are more frequent than *that*. Towards the end of the period, they are twice as frequent as *that* in Science (in Bacon, see Barber 1997: 213). In nineteenth-century Science texts the *wh*-forms are even more frequent; the relativizer *that* occurs in only 11 per cent of the relative clauses. In the first period (1800–30), there is only 5 per cent of *that*, while in the third period (1870–1900), 20 per cent of the relative clauses are with *that*.[2] Most nineteenth-century scientists prefer, or feel obliged, to use the *wh*-forms, abiding by the norm, but there exist exceptions, as for example Sir Francis Galton's text *Natural Inheritance* (1889). It is this single text that contributes to the frequency of *that* in the third period. The use of one particular relativizer can thus be typical of an individual writer, not only of the genre.

Table 5.2. Wh-*forms and* that *in Trials.*

Relativizer	Period 1	Period 3	Periods 1+3
Wh-	183 (66%)	203 (68%)	386 (67%)
That	95 (34%)	97 (32%)	192 (33%)
Total	278 (100%)	300 (100%)	578 (100%)

The Science texts tend to be formal, informative, nonpersonal and abstract. Lockyer's text, *The Chemistry of the Sun*, from 1887, is markedly specialized as is shown by the use of chemical formulae, illustrated in examples (1) and (2).

(1) There is no break in the general line of increase, and after we have gone through the gaseous stage, *which* stops at C_3H_8, and through the liquid stage, *which* stops at $C_{15}H_{32}$, we get the solid state, and there again the same series is represented.
(Science, J. Norman Lockyer, 1870–1900, p. 265)

(2) [. . .] for instance, with cyanogen compounds of oxygen we have a simple thing like cyanic acid (CNO) say, *which* will form a series of compounds, and we have its so-called polymers, $C_2N_2O_2$, or $C_3N_3O_3$, *which* will each form a series of compounds, [. . .]
(Science, J. Norman Lockyer, 1870–1900, p. 270)

Nineteenth-century scientific texts can be specialized and technical but they may also include more informal personal comments. The relative clause in example (3) is *sentential* (cf. Quirk et al. 1985: 1258). This type of relative clause is a typical feature of an *involved* text type, as is the use of the pronoun *I* in example (3) below (see Biber 1988: 106).

(3) This illustration partly covers the analogous fact of diseases and other inheritances skipping a generation, *which* by the way I find to be by no means so usual an occurrence as seems popularly to be imagined.
(Science, Sir Francis Galton, 1870–1900, p. 12)

2.2   Trials

In Trials, *wh*-forms are used in 67 per cent of the cases but *that* is decidedly more frequent (33 per cent) here than in Science. The diachronic difference in Trials shown in table 5.2 is not statistically significant.[3] Trials are speech-related but the scribe may have influenced the text to some extent. Explicit references, that is, the use of *wh*-forms, might have been considered important in correctly reporting the case.

The Trials texts comprise dialogues with frequent references to time, place or the situation in question. The relative clauses occurring in the dialogues also often refer to people or individuals for instance in order to identify them; see examples (4) and (5).

(4) [$Mr. Serjeant BALLANTINE.$] That the present claimant is the same man *that* I saw called Roger Tichborne in the Carabineers.
(Trials, Sir Roger Tichborne, 1870–1900, p. 2408)

(5) [$JOHN OXENHAM sworn; examined by MR. SELWYN.$] Now, Sir, do you know the young lady *who* has been called here as a witness to-day? [. . .] Can you mention any other persons *who* were with you that morning?
(Trials, James Bowditch, 1800–30, p. 76)

Naturally, Trials contain formal legal language (cf. Görlach 1999: 145), such as special formulae for questions and answers. Certain identification formulae are typical of the Trials texts: *Do you think him a person that* . . . (example 6); *you were the person that* . . .; *it is not a witness of this sort that* . . .; *that is the young woman that*. . . . Moreover, a formal construction typical of legal language may be reproduced to some extent in other parts of the dialogue. When, for example, a judge asks a question using a particular relative construction such as *pied piping* (preposition + *wh*-word, as in *of which he complained*), the witness answers using the same construction and then goes on to use preposition *stranding* (*which I should attach more importance to*), as in example (7).

(6) [$Mr. Sergeant Jones.$] Do you think him a person *that* it would be safe to trust to go abroad?
(Trials, Jonathan Martin, 1800–30, p. 66)

(7) [$Sir Charles Russell.$] Yes. What were the symptoms *of which* he complained? [. . .] These were the symptoms *of which* he complained. I think you saw him, did you not, on the 19th, the 22nd, and the 26th November; the 5th December and the 10th December; and on the 7th March in the present year? [$ MR TIDY'S EVIDENCE.$] But the prominent symptoms *which* I should attach more importance *to* than anything else are those I have mentioned [. . .]
(Trials, Edwin Maybrick, 1870–1900, p. 231)

2.3   Letters

The letter writers in the corpus also use *wh*-forms much more frequently (86 per cent) than *that* (14 per cent), see table 5.3.[4] These letter writers are all famous novelists, poets or important cultural personalities. They are presented in figure 5.1.

According to Görlach (1999: 36), the language used in letters and diaries in nineteenth-century English depends to a great extent on literacy, although less educated people try to produce their best English. In the case of the relativizers, this would mean using *wh*-forms, which were looked upon as the literary norm at that time (see Murray 1795: 148–56; see also the opinions of other

Table 5.3. Wh-*forms and* that *in Letters.*

Relativizer	Period 1	Period 3	Periods 1+3
Wh-	866 (86%)	643 (87%)	1509 (86%)
That	139 (14%)	100 (13%)	239 (14%)
Total	1005 (100%)	743 (100%)	1748 (100%)

Letter writer	Period 1	Period 3
Female	Jane Austen Sara Hutchinson Mary Shelley Mary Wordsworth	May Butler Mary Sibylla Holland Christina Rossetti Anne Thackeray Ritchie
Male	William Blake Lord Byron Samuel Taylor Coleridge John Keats Robert Southey	Matthew Arnold Samuel Butler Thomas Hardy Thomas Huxley

Figure 5.1. Female and male nineteenth-century letter writers (periods 1 and 3).

eighteenth-century grammarians, such as Brittain 1788, Buchanan 1762, Eglesham 1780 and Fell 1784 [see Sundby et al. 1991: 173]). The letters contain frequent references to individual people, as in example (8).

(8) for now I long more than ever that our house should be quickly ready for the reception of those dear children *whom* I love so tenderly then there will be a sweet brother and sister for my William *who* will lose his pre-eminence as eldest and be helped third at table [. . .] How is Charles Arthur & all the little folks & womanly Victoria *whom* I do not & must not include in the list –
(Letters, Mary Shelley, 1800–30, p. 309)

As is the case with the Science texts, individuals, mainly women letter writers, contribute to a great extent to the frequency of *that* (mainly with nonpersonal antecedents, see sections 4 and 7). Mary Sibylla Holland's letters from period 3 show a frequent use of *that*, see example (9), as do the letters of Mary Shelley and Mary Wordsworth (period 1).

(9) I wish, indeed, that Lucy were with you, to gather primroses and taste the sweet air *that* blows so lightly over the wide wolds. [. . .] The ash tree *that* hangs over the stream was also pure pale gold, [. . .]
(Letters, Mary Sibylla Holland, 1870–1900, p. 129)

Table 5.4a. *Relativizers in Science, Trials and Letters (periods 1 and 3).*

Relativizer	Science	Trials	Letters
Who	77 (9%)	97 (17%)	393 (23%)
Whom	6 (1%)	15 (3%)	110 (6%)
Whose	13 (2%)	3 (1%)	42 (2%)
Which	638 (77%)	271 (47%)	964 (55%)
That	95 (11%)	192 (33%)	239 (14%)
Total	829 (100%)	578 (100%)	1748 (100%)

2.4 Forms and functions of the relativizers

In Science, Trials and Letters, the use of the relativizers differs not only in the use of *that* versus the individual *wh*-forms but also in the use of *who* (*whom, whose*) versus *which* (see table 5.4a). In the three genres studied, the most common relativizer is *which* (47–77 per cent). There are no examples of *the which*, possibly modelled on French *liquels* (see Poutsma 1926–9: 198). The construction was regarded as 'obsolete' by eighteenth-century grammarians (see Sundby et al. 1991: 367). *Which* is particularly frequent in Science (77 per cent), whereas *who* is most common in Letters (23 per cent). The forms *whom* and *whose* are infrequent in all the three genres (1–6 per cent). The relativizer *that* is more frequent in Trials (33 per cent) than in the other two genres.[5]

Only the relativizers *which* and *that* occur in different clause functions. These functions are listed in tables 5.4b–5.4c. The form *who* does not function as direct or prepositional object in the genres studied. In table 5.4b, the clause functions of the relativizer *which* are listed. Prepositional constructions with *which* function either as prepositional objects (example (10)) or adverbials (example (11)) in the relative clause. The category 'prepositional object' comprises, first, the large group of multi-word verbs (Quirk et al. 1985: 1150–68), for example, *refer to, speak of, labour under, direct one's attention to* and *owe one's origin to*. Second, adjective phrases such as *fond of, delighted with, assailed for*, complemented by a preposition, are included in this category. 'Adverbial' is a category where preposition + relativizer function as an adverbial in the relative clause.

(10) [$Mr. Clarke.$] You have mentioned something about the fire *to which* I wish to direct your attention.
(Trials, Adelaide Bartlett, 1870–1900, p. 47)

(11) [$Sir Charles Russell.$] The first article you have mentioned *in which* arsenic was found was the writing-table?
(Trials, Edwin Maybrick, 1870–1900, p. 61)

Table 5.4b. *Clause functions of the relativizer* which.

Function	Science	Trials	Letters
Subject	332 (52%)	110 (41%)	488 (51%)
Direct object	83 (13%)	64 (24%)	252 (26%)
Possessive (*the effects of which*)	14 (2%)	2 (1%)	17 (2%)
Partitive (*some of which*)	11 (2%)	1 (0%)	14 (1%)
Prepositional object	83 (13%)	32 (12%)	97 (10%)
Adverbial	115 (18%)	62 (23%)	96 (10%)
Total	638 (100%)	271 (100%)	964 (100%)

Table 5.4b shows that the relativizer *which* is most common as subject in Science, Trials and Letters (41–52 per cent). The subject position is the most accessible position for the formation of finite relative clauses (see Keenan and Comrie 1977); hence, subjects can be expected to be more frequent generally than other functions irrespective of genre.[6]

The direct object function of *which* is more common in Letters (26 per cent) and in Trials (24 per cent) than in Science (13 per cent). 'Things' are often the objects of human activity both in Letters and in Trials, for instance, as pieces of evidence (see examples (12)–(13)).

(12) [$WM. SWAINTHORPE, sworn – Examined by Mr. Archbold.$] [$Q.$]
Did he state how he kept the light? – [$A.$] With a penny candle *which* he had cut in two.
(Trials, Jonathan Martin, 1800–30, p. 28)

(13) [$Sir Charles Russell.$] Mr Addison said he would like to ask the witness to identify a bottle *which* he produced. It was the bottle sent by Dr Fuller together with the prescription.
(Trials, Edwin Maybrick, 1870–1900, p. 108)

Table 5.4b also shows that prepositional constructions with *which* functioning as adverbials or prepositional objects are slightly more frequent in Science and in Trials than in Letters. Prepositional objects and adverbials are often part of scientific descriptions. In example (14) the first two prepositional constructions function as adverbials, whereas the third functions as prepositional object.

(14) Among the causes of deviation from a straight course *by which* torrents and rivers tend to widen the valleys *through which* they flow, [...] in confirmation of the gradual nature of the process *to which* the inequalities of hill and valley owe their origin.
(Science, Charles Lyell, 1800–30, p. 172)

Table 5.4c. *Clause functions of the relativizer* that.

Function	Science	Trials	Letters
Subject	76 (80%)	135 (70%)	157 (66%)
Direct object	12 (13%)	28 (15%)	63 (26%)
Prepositional object	1 (1%)	12 (6%)	9 (4%)
Adverbial	6 (6%)	17 (9%)	10 (4%)
Total	95 (100%)	192 (100%)	239 (100%)

Adverbials are frequent in Trials, since establishing the whereabouts of people is often a crucial part of many cases (cf. the discussion of *that* below):

(15) [$Q.$] That happened only once? [$A.$] It might have been two or three nights *in which* he was obliged to do it. (p. 43) [. . .] [$Q.$] Do you forget the actual day *on which* you returned to your uncle's? (p. 44) [. . .] [$MR. JUSTICE PARK.$] You know the house *in which* William Bowditch did live, was that in a court? (p. 78)
(Trials, James Bowditch, 1800–30, pp. 43, 44, 78)

Possessive *of which* occurs in Science (2 per cent), Letters (2 per cent) and Trials (1 per cent) but is clearly infrequent. Partitive *of which* is similarly rare, occurring slightly more frequently in Science (2 per cent). Possessive and partitive *of which* can be expected to be part of a fairly complex style. The word order *NP of which* is predominant in the genitive and partitive *of which* constructions, but *of which NP* occurs when a numeral functions as head of the partitive construction. Example (16) below illustrates two partitive constructions.

(16) From his work, it appears that, in the year 1783, the number was nine hundred and forty-nine, *of which* five hundred and one were shocks of the first degree of force; and in the following year there were one hundred and fifty-one, *of which* ninety-eight were of the first magnitude.
(Science, Charles Lyell, 1800–30, p. 413)

Table 5.4c lists the clause functions of the relativizer *that*. As is clear from the table, the subject function is the most common also for *that*. It is in Science, the genre with the fewest occurrences of *that* as relativizer, that the subject function is most frequent (80 per cent). The functions of prepositional object and adverbial, which are otherwise frequent in Science, are expressed with *which* and not *that*; in other words, preposition + *wh*-form (that is, *pied piping*; see the discussion below) is the preferred pattern in the Science texts. Thus, when *that* occurs in Science, it is mainly in the functions of subject and object; prepositional objects and adverbials are expressed with *which*. This is to some extent true also of the Trials texts but here the function of

Table 5.4d. *Pied piping and stranding in Science, Trials and Letters (periods 1 and 3).*

Prepositional construction	Science	Trials	Letters
Pied piping	76 (95%)	42 (68%)	122 (77%)
Stranding	4 (5%)	20 (32%)	37 (23%)
Total	80 (100%)	62 (100%)	159 (100%)

adverbial is slightly more common (9 per cent) because *that* occurs in examples such as (17), where the adverbial is not expressed by a preposition and relativizer:

(17) [$The ATTORNEY GENERAL:$] That was the 13th or 14th February *that* you saw him at the station, was it not?
(Trials, Sir Roger Tichborne, 1870–1900, p. 2165)

In Letters, there is a somewhat more even distribution of the clause functions of *that*. The subject function is not as predominant (66 per cent) and the direct object function is decidedly more frequent (26 per cent) than in Science (13 per cent) and Trials (15 per cent); see table 5.4c. In Letters, 'things' and, to some extent, people are often referred to as exposed to human activity, that is, as direct objects in syntactic form (cf. the discussion of *which* above). Example (18) is from the letters of Mary Shelley, one of the female letter writers who uses *that* rather frequently:

(18) If you trouble yourself to answer t[/his/] impertinent billet will you let me know how your health is and if you take the exercise *that* you ought. [. . .] Your mother was infinitely nervous – she spoke with great delight of a letter *that* she had received from you.
(Letters, Mary Shelley, 1800–30, p. 17)

In prepositional constructions with *wh*-forms and with *that* as prepositional objects or adverbials, the preposition is either *pied piped* (preposition + relativizer) or *stranded* (the only alternative with *that*). As table 5.4d shows, pied piping occurs more frequently (68–95 per cent) than stranding (5–32 per cent) in the genres studied.[7]

Pied piping is particularly frequent in the Science texts (95 per cent). There are mainly two reasons for this: first, the prepositional constructions function more frequently as adverbials, and here pied piping is generally more common than with prepositional objects (see Johansson and Geisler 1998). Another reason is that stranding of the preposition is not a typical feature of scientific writing in the nineteenth-century texts studied. Pied piping seems to create a tighter sentence structure than a stranded preposition. In example (19), pied piping enables the writer to continue with the reasoning in the text between the preposition + relativizer and the nominal part *the specific and immediate remedy*. The noun phrase modified by the prepositional construction is fairly complex with coordinated premodifiers, and a stranded preposition would seem particularly unattached here: *which* [. . .] *the immediate and specific remedy for.*

(19) [. . .] the evil obviously arises, not so much from the want of capital and the means of production, as the want of a market for the commodity when produced – a want, *for which* the removal of taxes, however proper, and indeed absolutely necessary as a permanent measure, is certainly not *the immediate and specific remedy.*
(Science, T. R. Malthus, 1800–30, p. II, 365)

Stranding is most common in the speech-related genre, Trials (32 per cent). Both *wh*-forms and *that* occur, but stranding with *that*, as in examples (20)–(21), is more frequent. *Nothing that I know of* is a common answer in Trials.

(20) [$MICHAEL MAYBRICK'S EVIDENCE.$] [$Sir Charles Russell cross-examined the witness.$] – Was there anything else in that parcel ? – Nothing *that* I know *of.*
(Trials, Edwin Maybrick, 1870–1900, p. 48)

(21) [$JOSEPH BROOM, sworn.$] She came back again towards me, and held out a ring *which* she said she was going to be married *with.*
(Trials, James Bowditch, 1800–30, p. 105)

As is evident from table 5.4c, however, prepositional objects with *that* are infrequent in all three genres (1–6 per cent).[8]

In nineteenth-century English, *which* is the most common relativizer in Science, Trials and Letters. It occurs most frequently as subject but also as prepositional object and adverbial in prepositional constructions. The most noticeable difference in the use of *wh*-forms is that *who, whose* and *whom* occur in Trials and Letters but are rare in Science where people are not frequently referred to. The relativizer *that* (as subject and object) is most frequent in Trials. The factors influencing the distribution of *wh*-forms and *that* in Science, Trials and Letters will be dealt with in the following sections. First, the type of relative clause, restrictive or nonrestrictive, will be discussed in section 3.

3   *Wh*-forms and *that* in restrictive and nonrestrictive relative clauses

In nineteenth-century English as in Present-day English, the type of relative clause is an important factor influencing the distribution of *wh*-forms and *that*. Whereas *wh*-forms are used in both *restrictive* and *nonrestrictive* relative clauses, the relativizer *that* occurs mainly in restrictive relative clauses. However, compared with Present-day English, the relativizer *that* is much less frequent in the nineteenth-century data. Thus *wh*-forms are predominant not only in nonrestrictive relative clauses but also in restrictive ones.

A restrictive relative clause restricts the reference of the antecedent: it identifies and classifies the antecedent. A nonrestrictive relative clause adds information about an already identified antecedent (cf. Quirk et al. 1985: 1239–42, Poutsma 1926–9: 421–30, 966 and Rydén 1974).[9] A nonrestrictive relative clause can stand in a close relationship to the antecedent or the antecedent clause in that it may be *context-bound* and express, for example, a causal relation with the antecedent clause or fulfill the characterization of the antecedent (see Rydén 1974 and 1984).[10] With an indefinite but specific antecedent the distinction between a restrictive and a nonrestrictive relative clause may only be a question of how the writer (or speaker) wants to present the information given in the antecedent clause and relative clause (that is, *the relative clause complex*; see Rydén 1974 and Johansson 1995: 16–17). The information value of the antecedent decides whether there is one assertion, in which case the relative clause is restrictive, or two assertions, in which case the relative clause is nonrestrictive (cf. Baker 1995: 334; Jacobsson 1994: 185; Johansson 1995: 111–12). Referentially specific modifiers are likely to favour a nonrestrictive interpretation, as in example (22).

(22) It was beautiful, but as our lakes are beautiful, gray and cold, and with an unpleasant ruffling wind *which* strengthened as the evening advanced. (p. 116) [. . .] Mrs. Churchill is a pretty little woman, with two boys, one of fourteen, the other of five, an old dog and a tabby cat, *which* did me the honour to visit my bedroom at night. (p. 282)
(Letters, Matthew Arnold, 1870–1900, p. 116, 282).

In Science, Trials and Letters, the proportions of restrictive and nonrestrictive relative clauses differ as does the distribution of *wh*-forms and *that* in the two types of relative clause. The Science texts often contain logical reasoning, explanations and formulae: what is said in the preceding clause is expanded on in the next, and one step follows another. This is expressed in restrictive relative clauses, which occur in 80 per cent of the examples in this genre. Even if the relative clause is restrictive, *wh*-forms are used in more than 85 per cent of the cases. *Wh*-forms are typical of the formal scientific writing style as such, but they are also used because they convey the explicitness needed in a scientific text: see examples (23) and (24). In (25), a restrictive relative clause with *that* is exemplified.

(23) It is, indeed, a circumstance *which* enhances the geological interest of the commotions *which* so often modify the surface of Calabria, [. . .]
(Science, Charles Lyell, 1800–30, p. 414)

(24) We see in a moment that much the same condition of affairs will be brought about if, instead of using a candle, we use an electric arc or spark *in which* the pure vapour of the substance *which* is being rendered incandescent fills the whole interval between the poles, the number of particles being smaller and the degree of incandescence being less intense at the sides of the arc.
(Science, Norman J. Lockyer, 1870–1900, p. 142)

(25) There is no known limit to the number of Repetitions *that* may occur.
(Science, William Bateson, 1870–1900, p. 20)

In Trials, identification or classification of persons or objects is crucial; hence the frequent occurrence of restrictive relative clauses, as in examples (26)–(27).

(26) [$MR. JUSTICE PARK.$] Was she the lady *who* sat down on Mr. James Bowditch's knee in your presence?
(Trials, James Bowditch, 1800–30, p. 87)

(27) [$DR HOPPER'S EVIDENCE.$] [$Cross-examination.$] [$Sir Charles Russell.$] [$A.$] – I use arsenic very frequently. [$Q.$] Principally in Fowler's solution, I believe? [$A.$] – Yes. [$Q.$] Has any case come across you in this country of men *who* have used arsenic habitually?
(Trials, Edwin Maybrick, 1870–1900, p. 56)

As in Science, restrictive relative clauses occur in Trials in 80 per cent of the examples, but here 40 per cent of these clauses are introduced by *that*. This may be because Trials are speech related, but the most important factor appears to be the syntactic environments in which *that* occurs in Trials (see section 5), for example, pronominal antecedents and cleft sentences with *it is/was* [. . .] *that*, as in (28). These environments express a close link between antecedent and relative clause, and hence both the use of *that* and restrictive relative clauses are favoured.

(28) [$Mr. Poland.$] You say there was nothing else *that* you noticed? [. . .] [$Mr. JUSTICE WILLS.$] – It is not a witness of this sort *that* would understand the plan.
(Trials, Adelaide Bartlett, 1870–1900, p. 55)

In Letters, nonrestrictive relative clauses are more frequent (35 per cent) than in Science and Trials. Personal names, which take nonrestrictive relative clauses, are often used as antecedents, as in example (29).

(29) Blanche came this evening, and although it was my Thursday at home, I spent a long delightful afternoon with Mrs. Kemble, *who* sends you many messages. I should not have survived the snow wedding and the confusion and the crowds yesterday, if it had not been for Pen Browning and Henry James, *who* nobly devoted themselves to extricating me from under the horse's feet, and to finding my deaf and dumb flyman.
(Letters, Anne Thackeray Ritchie, 1870–1900, p. 193)

Furthermore, what has been written about in a letter can be commented on in a nonrestrictive relative clause, particularly in sentential relative clauses, as in example (30). Sentential relative clauses are frequent in Letters: 53/100,000 words, compared with 23/100,000 words in Science and 7/100,000 words in Trials (see also the discussion of syntactic environments of *wh*-forms and *that* in section 5).

(30) We met not a creature at Mrs. Lillingstone's, & yet were not so very stupid as I expected, *which* I attribute to my wearing my new bonnet & being in good looks. (p. 52) [. . .] Mrs. J. Austen has asked me to return with her to Steventon; I need no [sic] give my answer; and she has invited my mother to spend there the time of Mrs. F. A.'s confinement, *which* she seems half inclined to do. (p. 70)
(Letters, Jane Austen, 1800–30, pp. 52, 70)

In Trials, the function of nonrestrictive relative clauses is often to provide the background when the identity of the personal or nonpersonal antecedent has been established (see Rydén 1974). The nonrestrictive relative clauses contain information on personal relations, or other circumstances crucial to the outcome of a case, as in examples (31)–(32).

(31) [$ANNE NOBLE, sworn.$] Yes; I have said I believed it was no other than Mr. Tichborne, *who* was formerly at Tichborne Park (p. 2162) [. . .] [$ THERESA HUSSEY, sworn. $] [. . .] On the 15th day of October 1867 the above-named plaintiff called at my cottage where I saw and had some conversation with him, and I am perfectly sure that he is the same person as the said Mr. Roger Charles Tichborne *whom* I formerly knew. (p. 2407)
(Trials, Sir Roger Tichborne, 1870–1900, pp. 2162, 2407)

(32) [$Sir Charles Russell.$.] Yes. In the second hatbox, *which* you say was standing near the first, you found a glass, and there was something like milk in it with a rag?
(Trials, Edwin Maybrick, 1870–1900, p. 62)

As is the case in Present-day English, *that* occurs mainly in restrictive relative clauses in the nineteenth-century genres studied.[11] The use of *that* in restrictive relative clauses had been prescribed in the eighteenth-century grammars (see Görlach 1999: 86) and this norm was still closely followed in writing in particular. In Letters, *that* occurs exclusively in this type of clause. However, in example (33), a nonrestrictive relative clause with *that*, from Science, is illustrated.

(33) Some apparent evidence of a positive kind, *that* was formerly relied upon, has been since found capable of being interpreted in another way, and is no longer adduced.
(Science, Sir Francis Galton, 1870–1900, p. 14)

Example (33) is from Galton's text, the scientific text with the highest frequency of *that*. Galton uses *that* in cases where *which* would be expected, for example, in nonrestrictive relative clauses. This probably reflects idiosyncratic usage; *that* is used frequently regardless of the type of relative clause. Galton also uses *that* in syntactic environments where *wh*-forms could be expected to occur instead, for instance with a non-adjacent antecedent (see the discussion in section 5).

Table 5.5. Wh-*forms and* that: *type of antecedent in Trials (periods 1 and 3).*

Relativizer	Personal antecedent	Nonpersonal antecedent	Total
Wh-	117 (76%)	269 (63%)	386 (67%)
That	37 (24%)	155 (37%)	192 (33%)
Total	154 (100%)	424 (100%)	578 (100%)

Table 5.6. Wh-*forms and* that: *type of antecedent in Letters (periods 1 and 3).*

Relativizer	Personal antecedent	Nonpersonal antecedent	Total
Wh-	542 (97%)	967 (81%)	1,509 (86%)
That	14 (3%)	225 (19%)	239 (14%)
Total	556 (100%)	1,192 (100%)	1,748 (100%)

4   The antecedent of *wh*-forms and *that*

The antecedent of *wh*-forms and *that* is *personal* or *nonpersonal*. Personal antecedents are less frequent than nonpersonal ones in the genres studied. However, in Trials and Letters, about 30 per cent of the antecedents are personal, since both of these genres deal with 'persons'. In Science, on the other hand, only 10 per cent of the antecedents are personal, which is due to the subject matter treated in this genre. The personal–nonpersonal contrast is naturally shown only by *wh*-forms (see Quirk et al. 1985: 366), but the contrast itself influences the distribution of *wh*-forms and *that* in the nineteenth-century genres studied; *that* is used with a nonpersonal antecedent in more than 90 per cent of the examples. In the Science texts, all examples of *that* except two are used with a nonpersonal antecedent. Thus, this genre is not represented in the tables in this section.

Only in Trials is there a fairly large number of personal antecedents with *that*: thirty-seven instances, or 24 per cent (see table 5.5). With a nonpersonal antecedent, *that* is used in 37 per cent of the cases.[12] Trials is the genre in which *that* is generally most frequent, but *wh*-forms predominate with both personal (76 per cent) and nonpersonal antecedents (63 per cent).

Table 5.6 shows the distribution of *wh*-forms and *that* with personal and nonpersonal antecedents in Letters. Even if personal antecedents are more frequent in Letters than in Trials, they are not referred to by *that*. There are only fourteen examples of *that* with a personal antecedent. Many of the personal antecedents in Letters are proper names, which entail a nonrestrictive relative clause and a *wh*-form. With a nonpersonal antecedent, *that* occurs in 19 per cent of the cases.[13]

The possessive relativizer *whose* can refer both to a personal and nonpersonal antecedent. In the nineteenth-century genres studied, there are fifty-three examples of *whose*; most of these, forty-two instances (79 per cent), occur with a personal antecedent. The different subject matter of the genres mirrors the use of *whose* with the two types of antecedent: whereas all examples except one are with a nonpersonal antecedent in Science (see also Johansson 1995: 66–8), all examples in Trials, and 90 per cent of the examples in Letters are with a personal antecedent. In example (34), from Science, *whose* with nonpersonal antecedents is illustrated. In examples (35)–(36), from Trials and Letters, *whose* occurs with personal antecedents.

(34) [. . .] and teeth *whose* forms approach so nearly to those of other teeth in the series as to suggest that they are duplicates of them and that they may have arisen by multiplication of the same germ, cannot be accurately distinguished from extra teeth *whose* forms agree with none in the normal series.
(Science, William Bateson, 1870–1900, p. 269)

(35) [$MR. SERJEANT PELL.$] I fancy, my Lord, that means the mother *whose* name is Joan.
(Trials, James Bowditch, 1800–30, p. 17)

(36) The Brownings are like noble simple people of the past *whose* life was in their genius, <& their genius was to love too, > I scratch this out for it is too like a phrase.
(Letters, Anne Thackeray Ritchie, 1870–1900, p. 249)

Among personal antecedents, subcategories such as personal nouns, proper names and pronouns can be distinguished. For nonpersonal antecedents, there are nonpersonal abstract and concrete nouns, names of countries and pronouns (see Quirk et al. 1985: 314). These subcategories of personal and nonpersonal antecedents all occur in the nineteenth-century genres studied. Collective nouns as antecedents, which can be treated both as personal and nonpersonal (see Quirk et al. 1985: 316–17), are not found in Trials, and are rare in Science, occurring only in Galton's text *Natural Inheritance* (1889). The only collective noun that is found in this text is *fraternity* (*fraternities*) and it is treated as a nonpersonal antecedent in all instances except one (see example (37)). In Letters, on the other hand, where collective nouns are more frequent, they are treated as personal antecedents. The only exception is example (38) below from Matthew Arnold's letters (1848–88), where *family* occurs with *which* (but also with *who*):

(37) It was a necessary condition of success to have the completed life-histories of many Fraternities *who* were born some seventy or more years ago, [. . .] I took every fraternity *in which* at least one member was consumptive, [. . .]
(Science, Sir Francis Galton, 1870–1900, p. 166)

(38) The female part of the family, *who* write volumes to one another, have treated us very shabbily in the way of letters, [. . .] (p. 119) [. . .] I am very glad you like your importation, and your importation, I hear, greatly likes the family *to which* it has been consigned. (p. 230)
(Letters, Matthew Arnold, 1870–1900, pp. 119, 230)

Pets and deities may also have an intermediate status between personal and nonpersonal antecedents. They are treated as personal antecedents in Letters, which is the only genre where they occur. Pets are often written about in the letters; see example (39):

(39) We are all well here – our dog *who* is a malicious beast *whom* we intend to send away has again bitten poor little Will-man without any provocation for I was with him and he went up to him to stroke his face when the dog snapped at his fingers.
(Letters, Mary Shelley, 1800–30, p. 28)

Personal antecedents in Science are different from those in Trials and Letters. The nouns referring to people in Science mainly have generic reference (*geologists who, workmen who, labourers and manufacturers who*), as 'examples' of human types. In Trials and Letters, antecedents have specific reference: a certain person is discussed and often the antecedent is a proper name, as in example (40).

(40) [$ANNIE WALKER sworn. – Examined by Mr. Poland.$] [$Q.$] The husband of the lady *who* had originally written to you? – [$A.$] Yes. [$Q.$] Did you know that he was the gentleman *who* had written this book [$handing it to the witness.$]? – [$A.$] Yes. (p. 120) [. . .] [$Mr. THOMAS LOW NICHOLS sworn. – Examined by Mr. Wright.$] At any rate, you are the Mr. Nichols *who* published the book that has been mentioned in court? (p. 123)
(Trials, Adelaide Bartlett, 1870–1900, pp. 120, 123)

In nineteenth-century English, as in Present-day standard English, personal antecedents are referred to by the relativizer *who* and nonpersonal antecedents by *which* (see Görlach 1999: 86, Poutsma 1926–9: 969, and Kjellmer 2002). Examples (41) and (42) below are the only instances of *which* referring to a personal antecedent in Trials.

(41) [$Mr. Holroyd.$] Mrs. Jones, I believe, was the most intimate friend *which* the deceased, Miss Burns, had?
(Trials, Charles Angus, 1800–30, p. 50)

(42) [Mr. HENRY MILLS POWELL, sworn.$] There was a lady passing behind him, *which* I believe was his wife.
(Trials, Sir Roger Tichborne 1870–1900, p. 2155)

Table 5.7. Wh-*forms and* that: *type of antecedent and clause function in Trials (periods 1 and 3).*

Function		Subject		Direct + prepositional object		
Relativizer	*Who, which*	*That*	Total	*Whom, which*	*That*	Total
Personal antecedent	97	31	128	15	10	25
	(76%)	(24%)	(100%)	(60%)	(40%)	(100%)
Nonpersonal antecedent	110	104	214	96	29	125
	(51%)	(49%)	(100%)	(77%)	(23%)	(100%)

In Science, there are a few cases of *which* used with what appears to be a personal antecedent. In example (43), *writers* occurs but here *writers* stands for 'writers' works, books':

(43) [...] that the writers *which* are now most extensively read among the common people should have selected for the subject of reprobation exactly that line of conduct which can alone generally improve their condition, [...]
(Science, T. R. Malthus, 1800–30, p. II, 371–72)

In Bateson's text on *The Discontinuity in the Origin of Species* (1894), we find *individuals which* and *each individual and each type which*. These examples are illustrations of a scientific use of the noun *individual* (see Kjellmer 2002). In Malthus's *Essay on the Principle of Population* (1817), *numbers* and *crowds of children* are used in the same 'scientific' sense, treated as statistical entities rather than as personal antecedents, as in example (44).

(44) The observation of the eminent Judge is, with regard to the numbers *which* are prevented from being born, perfectly just; but the inference, that the unmarried ought to be punished, does not appear to be equally so. [...] and add to this the crowds of children, *which* are cut off prematurely in our great towns, our manufactories and our workhouses [...] (p. 49) [...] the funds for the maintenance of labour must increase with much greater rapidity than they have ever done hitherto in this country, in order to find work and food for the additional numbers *that* would then grow up to manhood. (p. 50)
(Science, T. R. Malthus, 1800–30, pp. 49, 50)

The choice between *wh*-forms and *that* according to type of antecedent and clause function in Trials and Letters is illustrated in tables 5.7 and 5.8. The clause functions included in these tables are those of subject and direct and prepositional object, since in these functions, there may be variation between *wh*-forms and *that* depending on the type of antecedent. This variation is not possible in the other functions; personal antecedents cannot function as adverbials, and *that* is not used as possessive or partitive. The tables show that personal and nonpersonal antecedents and the use of *wh*-forms or *that* pattern somewhat differently when the clause functions are considered. In Trials, with a personal antecedent, it is mainly as direct and prepositional object that the relativizer *that* occurs with some frequency as an alternative to a *wh*-form (that is *whom*): ten and fifteen instances, respectively. In the subject function, however, a *wh*-form (*who*) occurs much more frequently than *that*: ninety-seven examples or 76 per cent.

With a nonpersonal antecedent, on the other hand, *that* does not compete with a *wh*-form as direct or prepositional object but as subject: 104 examples of *that* occur (49 per cent) to be compared with 110 examples of a *wh*-form (51 per cent).[14] A *wh*-form (*which*) could be expected to have a more specialized function as relativizer, that is, to be used with a more specific antecedent such as the name of a drug referred to in a case of poisoning in Trials. However, *that* occurs just as frequently in these instances; cf. examples (45) and (46).

(45) [$Mr. Holroyd.$] And that was the tartar emetic *that* was given the week preceding her death to the maid servant?
(Trials, Charles Angus, 1800–30, p. 102)

(46) [$Sir Charles Russell$] – Did it come to your knowledge, or was it put to you, that traces of arsenic were found in one bottle of Valentine's meat juice *which* had not been administered to the deceased man. Do you recollect that?
(Trials, Edwin Maybrick, 1870–1900, p. 63)

Thus, it is as subject that the relativizer *that* functions as an alternative to *which* with a nonpersonal antecedent. The situation is different, however, when the relativizer functions as direct or prepositional object; here there are ninety-six examples of a *wh*-form (77 per cent) compared with only 29 examples (23 per cent) of *that*.

According to Fox and Thompson (1990: 303), who discuss a discourse explanation of relative clauses in spoken English, personal antecedents are often referred to by a relative clause with the relativizer as subject. This type of clause has a characterizing or identifying function, a function which is crucial in court proceedings. In table 5.7, the subject function is expressed by a *wh*-form (*who*) or *that* in 128 examples, whereas a *wh*-form (*whom*) or *that* as direct object or prepositional object is found in twenty-five examples.[15]

In Letters, the relativizer *that* is generally less frequent than in Trials. As pointed out earlier, *that* is particularly rare with personal antecedents. As subject, *that* occurs in eight examples (2 per cent) and as direct object and prepositional object in six examples (5 per cent). With a nonpersonal antecedent, *that* is used as subject in 23 per cent of the instances and as direct object or prepositional object in 15 per cent.[16] This can be compared with the Trials texts where *that* as subject

Table 5.8. Wh-*forms and* that: *type of antecedent and clause function in Letters (periods 1 and 3).*

Function	Subject			Direct + prepositional object		
Relativizer	*Who, which*	*That*	Total	*Whom, which*	*That*	Total
Personal antecedent	392	8	400	111	6	117
	(98%)	(2%)	(100%)	(95%)	(5%)	(100%)
Nonpersonal antecedent	488	149	637	349	63	412
	(77%)	(23%)	(100%)	(85%)	(15%)	(100%)

with nonpersonal antecedents (49 per cent) may be regarded as an alternative to a *wh*-form (*which*) with 51 per cent.

Thus, as is evident from tables 5.5–5.8, the relativizers in the nineteenth-century genres are mainly used with the same types of antecedents as in Present-day English (see for example Biber et al. 1999: 613–16; Huddleston and Pullum 2002: 1048–9). Only two cases of *which* with personal antecedents occur. *That* is not frequent in the nineteenth-century English data but when it occurs, it is with a nonpersonal antecedent rather than with a personal one. In Trials, *that* functioning as subject with a nonpersonal antecedent can be regarded as an alternative to *which*: in roughly 50 per cent of the examples *that* occurs as relativizer. It is worth noting that in Trials, with a personal antecedent and as subject, *that* is actually slightly more frequent than in Present-day English (see Geisler and Johansson 2002: 102–3). The reason is probably that the relativizer *that* is commonly used with nouns such as *person(s)* and with pronouns such as *anyone, nobody* and *somebody* in Trials.

In nineteenth-century English, as in Present-day English (see Biber et al. 1999: 613–14), the relativizer *that* is frequently restricted to certain types of personal and nonpersonal antecedents. With nouns such as *person(s), people, thing(s)* and pronouns, *that* is used as frequently as *who* or *which*. These types of antecedent are discussed in terms of syntactic environments in the next section.

5   The syntactic environments of *wh*-forms and *that*

Analysing the syntactic environments means studying mainly the antecedent, the antecedent clause and the relative clause in more detail to detect syntactic relations and combinations in which either *wh*-forms or *that* can be expected to be more frequent. Since it has been shown in the previous sections that the *wh*-forms predominate in the nineteenth-century genres studied, the purpose of this section is primarily to reveal typical syntactic environments of *that* and to

Table 5.9a. *The syntactic environments of* wh-*forms and* that *(Science, Trials and Letters, periods 1 and 3).*

Syntactic environment	Which (+ whose with nonpersonal antecedent)	Who (whom, whose)	That	Total
Sentential relative clause	138 (22%)	0	0	138 (11%)
Non-adjacent antecedent	335 (54%)	114 (34%)	39 (12%)	488 (38%)
Cleft sentence	1	0	39 (12%)	40 (3%)
Person(s), people, thing(s)	8 (1%)	42 (13%)	21 (7%)	71 (6%)
Pronominal antecedent	84 (14%)	142 (42%)	120 (39%)	346 (27%)
Other (*any, no, same, only,* superlative+N)	56 (9%)	37 (11%)	94 (30%)	187 (15%)
Total	622 (100%)	335 (100%)	313 (100%)	1,270 (100%)

what extent *wh*-forms encroach upon this territory. The aim is also to investigate the typical syntactic environments of *which* and *who* (*whom, whose*).

A number of syntactic environments of *wh*-forms and *that* in the three genres studied are listed in table 5.9a. The overall results will be broken down by genre in tables 5.9b–5.9d and discussed further.[17]

The first two categories to be discussed, 'Sentential relative clause' and 'Non-adjacent antecedent', are environments expected to favour *wh*-forms. A sentential relative clause, as in example (47), refers back to the content of the entire antecedent clause, the predication or parts of it or a verb phrase (see Quirk et al. 1985: 1118–20). Table 5.9a shows that a sentential relative clause is the second most common syntactic environment of the relativizer *which* (22 per cent).

(47) Hal therefore must either go on as he is – *which* is intolerable – till my father dies; or get my father to lend him capital – or take some other situation; [. . .]
(Letters, Samuel Butler [1], 1870–1900, p. 211)

In the second category, 'Non-adjacent antecedent', the antecedent noun has different postmodifying elements such as prepositional phrases, relative clauses, finite and nonfinite verb phrases. With non-adjacent antecedents and sentential relative clauses the link or connection within the relative clause complex is fairly loose, which favours the use of *wh*-forms (see Rissanen 1984: 420–1). In table 5.9a, a non-adjacent antecedent is the most common syntactic environment of *which* (54 per cent) and the second most common environment of *who* (*whom, whose*) with 34 per cent. In example (48), there are two relative clauses: the postmodifying element of the first antecedent is an *of*-phrase and of the second a finite verb phrase.

(48) On the same subject Robinson writes, 'At that boundary of the spectrum *which* corresponds to the negative electrode (and in a much less degree at the positive) extremely intense lines are seen, ... *which*, however, are short.'
(Science, J. Norman Lockyer, 1870–1900, pp. 147–8)

In example (49), an *of*-phrase and a relative clause serve as postmodifiers and the second relative clause which follows is co-ordinated by *and*.

(49) [...] for we were told the next day that the house is now a capital one; that it is gone into the hands of a gentleman of fortune, who has a taste for that sort of life, and *who* saw the capabilities of that house, and wished to make it what it ought to be.
(Letters, Mary Wordsworth [2], 1800–30, p. 56)

The next three categories, cleft sentences of the type *it is/was* [...], antecedents such as *person(s)*, *people* and *thing(s)*, without any modifiers, and pronominal antecedents, usually have a close link with the relative clause. These syntactic environments, which are illustrated in (50)–(59), normally favour *that*. Cleft sentences with *it is/was* [...], as in example (50), favour *that* and are a fairly common syntactic environment of this relativizer (12 per cent). With the antecedent *person(s)*, both *that* and *who* (*whom, whose*) are used; example (51) illustrates *the person that*. *People* occurs mainly with *who* (*whom, whose*), whereas the antecedent *thing(s)* appears with *that* in most cases, as in example (52).

(50) [$CHARLES PUDDEY sworn.$] They came to see a print we had got; it was not Mr. Bowditch *that* was with her then; it was one of her sisters.
(Trials, James Bowditch, 1800–30, p. 85)

(51) [$Court.$] Were you the person *that* brought the quilt down stairs?
(Trials, Charles Angus, 1800–30, p. 56)

(52) He replied, 'There are three postulates: firstly, things *that* are equal to the same are equal to one another; secondly, things *that* are greater than the same are greater than one another; and thirdly, things *that* are less than the same are less than one another.' (p. 217) [...] It is only now that I realise what mischief Tom could do in this way by simply destroying proof of his identity and going to some place known only to people *who* would not tell us without making us pay heavily. (p. 252)
(Letters, Samuel Butler [1], 1870–1900, pp. 217, 252)

Pronominal antecedents are frequent syntactic environments not only of *that* (39 per cent) but also of *who* (*whom, whose*) with 42 per cent. Whereas *who* (*whom, whose*) is naturally used only with pronominal antecedents referring to people (mainly indefinite pronouns, the demonstrative *those* and *same*), *that* is mostly used with pronominal antecedents with nonpersonal reference (for example *anything, something, all* and *much*). The demonstrative *those* is the most common pronominal antecedent with personal reference both with *who* (*whom, whose*) and *that*. *Those who* occurs in sixty-five out of 142 examples. Only eleven out of

120 examples of *that* with a pronominal antecedent refer to a person, and *those that* is the most frequently occurring combination, with five examples. Examples (53)–(55), from Trials, illustrate pronominal antecedents and the use of *who* and *that*.

(53) [$Mr. Clarke.$] Did you keep a record of <u>those</u> *who* visited you in England?
(Trials, Adelaide Bartlett, 1870–1900, p. 125)

(54) [$CHARLES PUDDEY; sworn.$] Yes; I was in the house when she asked me, and I went out to her, in company with <u>those</u> *that* were in the kitchen.
(Trials, James Bowditch, 1800–30, p. 83)

(55) [$Mr. Hawkins:$] <u>Anybody</u> *who* had been in your parlour might see that?
(Trials, Sir Roger Tichborne, 1870–1900, p. 2191)

That is frequent with pronominal antecedents with nonpersonal reference; but this is also a fairly common syntactic environment of the relativizer *which* (14 per cent), for example, s*omething **which**, everything **which**, any thing **which**, much **which** and those **which***. It is only with *all* that the relativizer *that* is used exclusively. Examples (56)–(59) illustrate pronominal antecedents of *which* and *that*.

(56) [. . .] Mrs. Abrey called Dr. Harris's attention to <u>something</u> *which* now leads him to this sad conclusion.
(Letters, Christina Rossetti, 1870–1900, p. 116)

(57) [$MATTHEW WILSON, SWORN.$] Yes; I then referred to <u>something</u> *that* was said in the newspapers [. . .]
(Trials, Jonathan Martin, 1800–30, p. 32)

(58) You know I am a valiant eater, and having retained my appetite as well as my spirits during this confinement, I eat <u>everything</u> *which* is put before me.
(Letters, Robert Southey, 1800–30, p. 396)

(59) [. . .] but as the general stock out of which each man's riches are drawn, is diminished in quantity, by <u>all</u> *that* any individual takes from it, other men's shares must necessarily be reduced in proportion as this favoured individual is able to appropriate a greater quantity to himself.
(Science, David Ricardo, 1800–30, p. 382)

The last category, 'Other', consists of different subcategories of antecedents. It includes antecedents with indefinite determiners (such as *any, no, some*); antecedents with *all*, both as indefinite determiner and as predeterminer with the definite article; and antecedents with *same, very, only, first* and superlatives.[18] These categories of antecedents tend to express a close link with their relative clauses and are often regarded as favouring the use of *that* in both early grammars (see for example Murray 1795: 149) and present-day grammars (see for example Huddleston and Pullum 2002: 1052–4 and Biber et al. 1999: 615–17). Table 5.9a shows that 'Other' is a common syntactic environment of *that* (30 per cent). In

Table 5.9b. *The syntactic environments of* wh-*forms and* that *(Science, periods 1 and 3).*

Syntactic environment	Which (+*whose* with nonpersonal antecedent)	*Who* (*whom, whose*)	*That*	**Total**
Sentential relative clause	16 (7%)	0	0	16 (5%)
Non-adjacent antecedent	148 (65%)	13 (23%)	15 (34%)	176 (54%)
Cleft sentence	1	0	2 (5%)	3 (1%)
Person(s), people, thing(s)	4 (2%)	6 (10%)	1 (2%)	11 (3%)
Pronominal antecedent	25 (11%)	34 (60%)	8 (18%)	67 (20%)
Other (*any, no, same, only,* superlative+N)	33 (15%)	4 (7%)	18 (41%)	55 (17%)
Total	227 (100%)	57 (100%)	44 (100%)	328 (100%)

examples (60)–(62), antecedents with indefinite determiners and *only* occur; in example (63) a superlative expression is illustrated.[19]

(60) In order to explain the second limitation which is to be introduced it is necessary to refer to some phenomena *which* are characteristic of the forms of organisms, and to separate them from the group with which we shall deal first.
(Science, William Bateson, 1870–1900, p. 18)

(61) The Master is a puppet in their hands and as a Scholar is nobody – and there is no candidate *that* can possibly oppose H.
(Letters, Mary Wordsworth [2], 1800–30, p. 14)

(62) The best of all reasons for the breach of a promise, is, the absolute impossibility of executing it; indeed it is the only plea *that* can ever be considered as valid.
(Science, T. R. Malthus, 1800–30, p. II, 353)

(63) [$MR. TUCKETT.$] The most affectionate girl *that* ever lived; devoted to her mother and my children.
(Trials, James Bowditch, 1800–30, p. 49)

The following subsections discuss those syntactic environments of the *wh*-forms and *that* which are typical of Science, Trials and Letters.

5.1   Science

The syntactic environments in which the *wh*-forms and *that* occur in Science are listed in table 5.9b. In the Science texts, there seems to be no typical syntactic

environment of the relativizer *that*, perhaps because there are few examples
of *that* in this genre (see table 5.1 in section 2 above). *That* occurs in 'Other'
(eighteen instances, or 41 per cent) but this category includes many subcategories
of syntactic environments (see the list above), and the relativizer *that* is not
frequent in any of them; moreover, in most of them, *which* is also found. 'Other'
is a fairly common syntactic environment of the relativizer *which* (15 per cent).
In the three examples of antecedents with superlative + noun that occur, *that* is
used, and *same* occurs with *that* in the combination *at the same time that*.

An environment favouring *wh*-forms (*which*: 65 per cent; *who, whom, whose*:
23 per cent) is the category 'Non-adjacent antecedent'. Table 5.9b shows, however, that 34 per cent of the instances of *that* also occur in this syntactic environment. Eleven out of the fifteen instances are from Galton's *Natural Inheritance*
(1889), which, as mentioned earlier, is the scientific text where *that* is generally
frequent. *That* is thus used here even in a syntactic environment typical of *wh*-
forms. Galton has nine examples of *which* with a non-adjacent antecedent and
that and *which* seem to function as alternatives: consider example (64), where a
relative clause, a prepositional phrase with a preposition other than *of*, and an
of-phrase exemplify the postmodifying elements.

(64) The unborn child together with the growth to which it is attached, and *which*
      is afterwards thrown off, have their own vascular system to themselves,
      entirely independent of that of the mother. [. . .] Again, not only is the
      unborn child a separate animal from its mother, *that* obtains its air and
      nourishment from her purely through soakage, but its constituent elements
      are of very much less recent growth than is popularly supposed. [. . .] But
      we may predict average results with great certainty, as will be seen further
      on, and we can also obtain precise information concerning the penumbra of
      uncertainty *that* attaches itself to single predictions.
      (Science, Sir Francis Galton, 1870–1900, pp. 15–17)

Non-adjacent antecedents are frequent in Science. Postmodification of the noun
is apparently one of the typical features of the scientific writing style of that time.
Of-phrases, which are structurally fairly simple postmodifiers, make up nearly
40 per cent of the postmodifying elements in Science (for example *the distribution
of property*, *an excess of births*, *the degree of continuity* and *the planes of division*). A
more complex type of postmodification is exemplified in (65)–(67). Here relative
clauses themselves serve as postmodifiers, making the antecedent non-adjacent
to a second relative clause which is co-ordinated with the preceding clauses and
introduced by *and* or *but*.

(65) Some of its members drop out of sight at every step, and a new rank is ever
      rising up to take the place vacated by the rank that preceded it, and *which*
      has already moved on.
      (Science, Sir Francis Galton, 1870–1900, p. 164)

In example (66), both *of*-phrases and relative clauses are postmodifiers of the antecedent. The first relative clause may have a *wh*-form, as in example (66), or *that*, as in (65), but the second relative clause introduced by *and* always has a *wh*-form. Possibly, *that* in *and that* (or *but that*) is avoided, as it could be interpreted as a relativizer or a demonstrative. Both relative clauses generally occur with a *wh*-form; example (65) above is the only exception. The example is again from Galton, who uses *that* more frequently.

(66) But the moment we reascend the cliff, the spell is broken; for we scarcely recede a few paces, before the ravine and river disappear, and we stand on the black and rugged surface of a vast current <u>of lava, which seems unbroken,</u> and *which* we can trace up nearly to the distant summit of that majestic cone [. . .]
(Science, Charles Lyell, 1800–30, p. 179)

In example (67), two relative clauses serve as postmodifiers of the antecedent. The third relative clause is co-ordinated with *but*.

(67) We appear, then, to be severally built up out of a host of minute particles <u>of whose nature we know nothing, any one of which may be derived from any one progenitor,</u> but *which* are usually transmitted in aggregates, considerable groups being derived from the same progenitor.
(Science, Sir Francis Galton, 1870–1900, p. 9)

The fairly complex type of postmodification described in examples (65)–(67) is typical of the Science texts. However, it also occurs to some extent in Letters; compare example (49) above.

The relativizer *who* (*whom, whose*) is not common in the Science texts. When it occurs, it is chiefly with a pronominal antecedent (59 per cent). Pronouns are particularly common as antecedents of *who* (*whom, whose*) in Science: thirty-four out of a total of ninety-six instances of *who* (*whom, whose*) are pronouns (see table 5.4a in section 2 above). *Those who* is here the most frequent combination. It seems that the reference to a person is less specific in Science (see the discussion of personal antecedents in Science in section 4 above). Pronouns such as *any one, somebody, nobody* and *those*, illustrated in example (68), are common as antecedents.

(68) <u>Any one</u> *who* cares to glance at the works of <u>those who</u> have followed Darwin in these fields may assure himself of this.
(Science, William Bateson, 1870–1900, p. 13)

A pronoun with nonpersonal reference is a fairly frequent syntactic environment of *that* (18 per cent) and of *which* (11 per cent) in Science. *That* can also be used with a pronoun which refers to a person, but there is only one example (*those that*). Examples of *something which/that, anything which/that* and *everything which/that* are found, but *all* always occurs with *that*.

Table 5.9c. *The syntactic environments of* wh-*forms and* that *(Trials, periods 1 and 3).*

Syntactic environment	Which (+whose with nonpersonal antecedent)	Who (whom, whose)	That	Total
Sentential relative clause	9 (15%)	0	0	9 (4%)
Non-adjacent antecedent	35 (57%)	16 (30%)	9 (8%)	60 (27%)
Cleft sentence	0	0	28 (26%)	28 (13%)
Person(s), people, thing(s)	0	18 (33%)	12 (11%)	3 (13%)
Pronominal antecedent	14 (23%)	14 (26%)	36 (34%)	64 (29%)
Other (*any, no, same, only,* superlative+N)	3 (5%)	6 (11%)	22 (21%)	31 (14%)
Total	61 (100%)	54 (100%)	107 (100%)	222 (100%)

5.2   Trials

That is more common in Trials than in Science and in Letters (see for example tables 5.2 and 5.4a in section 2 above). This can be partly explained by the fact that many of the syntactic environments in which *that* occurs are typical environments of *that* in general, as well as of the dialogue in the courtroom. Examples are cleft sentences with *it is/was* [. . .], pronominal antecedents, antecedents such as *person(s)*, and *same*, both as determiner and pronoun.

Cleft sentences could generally have been expected to be a more frequent syntactic environment of *that*. In table 5.9a, which shows the overall frequencies of the syntactic environments in the three genres, cleft sentences occur only in 12 per cent of the cases. This is because cleft sentences of the type exemplified in (69) occur mainly in Trials: twenty-eight out of thirty-nine examples of *that* and this syntactic environment in table 5.9a are from Trials. Thus, cleft sentences are a common syntactic environment of *that* only in this genre (26 per cent, see table 5.9c).

(69) [$JANE NICKSON, SWORN.$] Sir, <u>it was the Cook</u> *that* was trying the salt, and said there was not a pewter plate to put the salt upon, [. . .]
(Trials, Charles Angus, 1800–30, p. 82)

The most common syntactic environment of *that* in Trials is with a pronoun as antecedent (thirty-six instances or 34 per cent). The pronoun has nonpersonal reference in twenty-nine of the thirty-six examples, and *any thing that, something that* and *all that* are frequent combinations; see example (70).

(70) [$WM. SWAINTHORPE, SWORN.$] I told him, that he was not to say <u>any thing</u> *that* was to criminate himself.
(Trials, Jonathan Martin, 1800–30, p. 27)

In the dialogue of the courtroom, many questions begin with the sequence *are you a person that*. *Person(s)* as antecedent is most frequent in the category *person(s)*, *people*, and *thing(s)* with eight examples out of twelve. The antecedent *person(s)* is also a common syntactic environment of *who* (*whom*, *whose*) with eighteen instances or 33 per cent. In example (71), *that* and *who* are used with *persons* in questions asked by the same judge.

(71) [$MARGARET ORTON, SWORN. – Cross-examined by Mr. Alderson.$]
     [$Q.$] Is it not common with persons *that* are insane, to be greatly displeased at being proved to be insane? – [$A.$] Yes, I believe it is. [$Q.$] They are generally angry with persons *who* endeavour to shew it?
     (Trials, Jonathan Martin, 1800–30, p. 54)

In the category 'Other', the determiner/pronoun *same* is frequent. It occurs in questions and answers in the dialogues, to establish or clarify a person's identity, as in example (72).

(72) [$The ATTORNEY-GENERAL:$] Except that he was much stouter, was he the same man *that* you remembered?
     (Trials, Sir Roger Tichborne, 1870–1900, p. 2165)

Which occurs most frequently (57 per cent) with a non-adjacent antecedent, which is also a fairly frequent syntactic environment of *who* (*whom*, *whose*), with 30 per cent. Antecedents with postmodifying elements inserted before the relative clause indicate a formal style, similar to that used in Science. Most examples of *which* with a non-adjacent antecedent are found in fairly technical or scientific statements from doctors as witnesses describing the symptoms of a disease or of arsenic poisoning. Example (73) shows that the relativizer *that* is also used to some extent (8 per cent; see table 5.9c). The postmodifiers in example (73) are an *of*-phrase, a nonfinite verb phrase, and finally a finite verb phrase.

(73) [$MR. TIDY'S EVIDENCE.$] This was a case of acute poisoning by arsenic *that* occurred in 1863, and it illustrates the condition of the stomach in arsenical poisoning. [. . .] (p. 234). Yes, but a great many substances introduced into the body kill *which* are not poison. (p. 240)
     (Trials, Edwin Maybrick, 1870–1900, pp. 234, 240)

In example (74), a relative clause and an *of*-phrase serve as postmodifiers.

(74) [$Rev. JOHN VAUSE, sworn.$] He said, he supposed she must have died in a fit – that her complaint was the fluor albus, under which she had long laboured, and *which* had weakened her excessively. (p. 94) [. . .] – He said, that what he had given her was in the preceding week; and that he meant by the black puke, the contents of the stomach *which* had been thrown up – (p. 97)
     (Trials, Charles Angus, 1800–30, pp. 94, 97)

Table 5.9d. *The syntactic environments of* wh-*forms and* that *(Letters, periods 1 and 3).*

Syntactic environment	Which (+*whose* with nonpersonal antecedent)	*Who* (*whom*, *whose*)	*That*	Total
Sentential relative clause	113 (34%)	0	0	113 (16%)
Non-adjacent antecedent	152 (45%)	85 (39%)	15 (9%)	252 (35%)
Cleft sentence	0	0	9 (6%)	9 (1%)
Person(s), people, thing(s)	4 (1%)	18 (8%)	8 (5%)	30 (4%)
Pronominal antecedent	45 (14%)	90 (41%)	76 (47%)	211 (29%)
Other (*any, no, same, only,* superlative+N)	20 (6%)	25 (12%)	54 (33%)	99 (14%)
Total	334 (100%)	218 (100%)	162 (100%)	714 (100%)

When *who* (*whom, whose*) occurs with a non-adjacent antecedent in the Trials, it is often to establish relations, origin or status, something that is of great importance in the court proceedings; see examples (75)–(76). The postmodifiers are prepositional phrases.

(75) [$Rev. JOHN VAUSE SWORN.$] A surgeon <u>of great eminence in Liverpool</u>; and *who*, I understand, has always attended the family.
(Trials, Charles Angus, 1800–30, p. 91)

(76) [$JOHN OXENHAM SWORN.$] I remember preparing a marriage settlement for a daughter <u>of Mrs. Bowditch,</u> *who* married a person of the name of Scarlett.
(Trials, James Bowditch, 1800–30, p. 79)

Sentential relative clauses are a fairly frequent syntactic environment of *which* in the Trials (nine examples or 15 per cent). Sentential relative clauses often finish off a statement, as in example (77).

(77) [$MARIA GLENN SWORN.$] I saw the two Bowditches in the kitchen, and Mrs Bowditch took from the table a cup which had something black in it. She then desired me to drink it, *which* I did.
(Trials, James Bowditch, 1800–30, p. 35)

5.3   Letters

In Letters, the relativizer *that* is not a frequent relativizer (see for example table 5.3 in section 2 above) and largely restricted to two syntactic environments, 'Pronominal antecedents' (47 per cent) and 'Other' (33 per cent). With pronominal antecedents, seventy-three of the seventy-six examples with *that* have nonpersonal reference. The most frequent combination is *all that*. The relativizer *which* also occurs in this syntactic environment (forty-five instances or 14 per cent), in for example *something which*, *everything which* and *much which*. However, *which* mainly occurs in the combination *that which*, where the use of *that* would be awkward. The distribution of relativizers with pronouns is thus rather clear in Letters, and in the other two genres studied: *that* and, to some extent, *which* occur with pronominal antecedents with nonpersonal reference, whereas *who* (*whom*, *whose*) is used with pronouns referring to a person. A pronominal antecedent with personal reference is the most common syntactic environment of *who* (*whom*, *whose*) in Letters with ninety instances or 41 per cent. *Those* as antecedent occurs frequently, as in example (78).

(78)   I do not understand the feeling which could create such a desire on any personal grounds, save those of affection, and the natural yearning to be near even in death to *those whom* we have loved. And on public grounds the wish is still less intelligible to me. One cannot eat one's cake and have it too. *Those who* elect to be free in thought and deed must not hanker after the rewards, if they are to be so called, which the world offers to *those who* put up with its fetters.
(Letters, Thomas Huxley, 1870–1900, pp. 19–20)

In Letters, personal pronouns (mainly *I*, *you*, *her* and *they*) quite often serve as antecedents, since letters are frequently about specific individuals; see example (79). This is also evident from the fact that the antecedent *person(s)*, which without modification conveys a general meaning, is a rare syntactic environment of *that* and *who* (*whom*, *whose*) in Letters.

(79)   You will and must miss your sister unspeakably; still you will have some comfort, as time goes on, in the warm affection which so many of us bear both to her *who* is gone and to you *who* survive. Believe me always, my dear Mima, sincerely and affectionately yours, MATTHEW ARNOLD.
(Letters, Matthew Arnold, 1870–1900, p. 145)

In 'Other', the second most frequent syntactic environment of *that*, superlative + noun is most common. Both personal and nonpersonal antecedents occur. The antecedent *thing(s)* is found together with a superlative in *the best thing*, *the wisest thing* and *the best and happiest thing*, as in example (81). Superlative expressions are more frequent in Letters than in Science and Trials, and they are often found in personal comments on different topics in Letters; see examples (80)–(81).

(80)   I am grown a great Jesuitophilist, and begin to think that they were the most enlightened personages *that* ever condescended to look after this 'little snug farm of the earth'.
(Letters, Robert Southey, 1800–30, p. 56)

(81) Some people have delightful qualities, but let them float and waste, but your brother's kindness grew into love, and his good taste and love of art into zeal for the House of God, and so on – and this seems <u>the best and happiest thing</u> *that* can come to a human soul, [. . .]
(Letters, Mary Sibylla Holland, 1870–1900, p. 149)

A non-adjacent antecedent is a frequent syntactic environment not only of *which* (45 per cent) but also of *who* (*whom, whose*), with 39 per cent. The postmodifiers in example (82) are first, a finite verb phrase (*would tell*) and second, a relative clause (*which I have long outgrown*). The relative clause which then follows is introduced by *and*. Lastly, a prepositional phrase (*for his supper*) functions as postmodifier.

(82) What a different story Sir Robert Wilson <u>would tell,</u> *who* has kept the field with his legion of Portuguese, through all the perilous season. (p. 56) [. . .] It contains the statement of opinions <u>which I have long outgrown,</u> and *which* are stated more broadly because of this dramatic form. (p. 279) [. . .] Whether it were so, or by some instinct in a Roman Catholic bug it knew me for a heretic of the first class, so it was, that the said bug fixed on that very joint <u>for his supper,</u> *which* ill-fortune had, I suppose, rendered tender and so to her liking. (p. 405)
(Letters, Robert Southey, 1800–30, pp. 56, 279, 405)

In example (83), a prepositional phrase, which denotes professional location, serves as postmodifier.

(83) This morning we all came up by the train, the Greek professor <u>at Harvard,</u> *whom* I think Walter knows, and a pleasant Professor Child, a great authority on ballad poetry, being of the party.
(Letters, Matthew Arnold, 1870–1900, p. 274)

Example (84) is one of the few instances of *that* and a non-adjacent antecedent. These examples are mainly found in those letters with a frequent use of *that* generally, as in Mary Wordsworth's letter collections, illustrated in (84). The postmodifying element is a relative clause and the pattern is similar to that expressed by the last two relative clauses in example (82) above. It is worth noting that the first relative clause in example (84) is introduced by *which* and the second by *that*. The opposite relationship would have been expected since *that* expresses a tighter link with the antecedent and should thus normally occur close to it (see Rissanen 1984: 424). In the other examples of this type of postmodification, the relative clause with *that* comes first, or both relative clauses occur with a *wh*-form, as in example (82). In addition, the indefinite determiner *every* + noun, which is a syntactic environment favouring *that*, occurs in example (84).

(84) That thy best thoughts will go with me I am well assured – & that every object <u>which I see</u> *that* gives me pleasure will be ten thousand times more dear to me [. . .]
(Letters, Mary Wordsworth [1], 1800–30, p. 197)

As mentioned in the discussion of restrictive and nonrestrictive relative clauses in section 3, sentential relative clauses, as in example (85), are particularly frequent in Letters. This is the other syntactic environment where *which* often occurs in Letters (113 instances, or 34 per cent).

(85) He always speaks warmly & kindly of you, & when I asked him to come in to meet you at tea – *which* he did – he spoke very heartily –
(Letters, May Butler, 1870–1900, p. 223)

5.4   Summary of the syntactic environments of wh-*forms and* that *in the three genres*

In most of the syntactic environments listed in tables 5.9a–5.9d, the *wh*-forms are used more frequently than *that*. There are, however, a number of typical syntactic environments of *that* in Science, Trials and Letters. First, *that* occurs in cleft sentences of the type *it is/was . . . that*, mainly in the Trials texts. Second, pronominal antecedents with nonpersonal reference occur with *that*, but *which* is also used here and the only combination where *that* occurs exclusively is *all that*. Third, the antecedent *person(s)* is a frequent syntactic environment of *that*, though only in the Trials. *Person(s)* is also very commonly used with *who* (*whom, whose*) in this genre. Fourth, in the category of 'Other', *that* occurs with superlative expressions in all cases but one in the three genres. With the remaining subcategories in 'Other' (indefinite determiners, *very, only, first* + noun), the *wh*-forms are used as frequently as *that*. The examples of a non-adjacent antecedent and *that* are mainly found in texts where *that* is generally frequent, for example Galton's scientific text and Mary Wordsworth's letters.

The syntactic environments of *that* are mainly the same in the nineteenth-century English genres studied as in Present-day English, but in the nineteenth-century data, *that* is possibly more restricted to its typical environments. The use of *that* in cleft sentences, with *person(s)*, *people*, *thing(s)*, with pronouns and 'Other' (274 examples, see table 5.9a) makes up more than 50 per cent of the total number of instances of *that* (526). *Which* occurs in cases where *that* would be preferred today (for example with *anything, everything* and *much*). In the following two sections the syntactic environments of the *wh*-forms and *that* will be included in the discussion of the use of relativizers across speaker roles and gender.

6   The use of *wh*-forms and *that* across speaker roles

In Trials, speakers of different social ranks or roles are represented, mainly judges, or other members of the legal profession, and doctors and servants as witnesses. It is possible to study the use of the relativizers and relative clauses with reference to these different social roles and professional backgrounds (termed *speaker roles* in table 5.10a). As can be seen in table 5.10a, 'Members of the legal

Table 5.10a. *The use of* wh-*forms and* that *across speaker roles in Trials (periods 1 and 3).*

Relativizer	Members of the legal profession	Others	Total
Wh-	208 (66%)	178 (68%)	386 (67%)
That	109 (34%)	83 (32%)	192 (33%)
Total	317 (100%)	261 (100%)	578 (100%)

profession' use more relative clauses in their speech (317 instances versus 261 for other professions). The reason could be that they speak more, or that their speech simply contains more relative clauses, which would indicate that it is syntactically more elaborate. Table 5.10a shows that *wh*-forms predominate in the speech of both 'Members of the legal profession' (66 per cent) and people with other speaker roles (68 per cent).[20]

Doctors as expert witness, who are included in 'Others', use a fairly scientific or technical style in their speech when crimes like poisoning, or diseases, are discussed, as in example (86). This fact may partly explain why *wh*-forms predominate in the group 'Others' as well as among 'Members of the legal profession'.

(86) [$DR. BALDWIN WAKE, SWORN.$] I have known many instances of monomania, I know that at certain times they have lucid intervals, and will be conscious of the error they have committed, and the delusion *under which* they labour; of this I know a striking case, if it were necessary on this occasion to state it.
(Trials, Jonathan Martin, 1800–30, p. 70)

Judges, prosecutors or lawyers use *that* in 34 per cent of the cases, and members with other occupational or social backgrounds use *that* slightly less frequently (32 per cent). The rather high frequency of *that* in the speech of, for example, judges can be explained by the fact that the syntactic environments in which *that* occurs are not only typical of *that* but also of the dialogue in the courtroom. *That* is used with *person(s)* in the formulae for questions and answers (see example (87)), and with pronouns, which are common antecedents in the legal dialogue, as in example (88). In (88), the use of *that* in *him that* might reflect the language used by members of the lower classes (one Charlotte Holder).

(87) [$The ATTORNEY-GENERAL.$] Yes. In the Alresford circle you are a person *that* everybody knows ?
(Trials, Sir Roger Tichborne, 1870–1900, p. 2153)

Table 5.10b. *The use of relativizers across speaker roles in Trials (periods 1 and 3).*

Relativizer	Members of the legal profession	Others	Total
That (nontypical use)	31 (41%)	36 (52%)	67 (46%)
Whom	7 (9%)	7 (10%)	14 (10%)
Which (personal antecedent)	1 (1%)	1 (1%)	2 (1%)
Pied piping	29 (38%)	13 (19%)	42 (29%)
Stranding	8 (11%)	12 (18%)	20 (14%)
Total	76 (100%)	69 (100%)	145 (100%)

(88) [$CHARLOTTE HOLDER, sworn.$] [$Cross-examined by the ATTORNEY-GENERAL.$] Do you say you are quite sure he is the same man? – As him *that* went away; as I saw before he went away. Just the same? – I am convinced it is the same *that* went abroad.
(Trials, Sir Roger Tichborne, 1870–1900, p. 2449)

That also occurs frequently in cleft sentences including both references to people and adverbial expressions, when a particular time or place of a crime has to be identified, as in example (89). Jacobsson (1994: 190) points out that a relative clause with *that* and a proper noun in a cleft sentence, illustrated here by example (89), could be the equivalent of, in this case, *It was Jonathan Martin, the one that has done it.*

(89) [$Mr. Brougham.$] Was not the first thing you said to your wife when you heard the Minster was burnt, 'surely it is not Jonathan Martin *that* has done it?' (p. 15) [. . .] [$Mr. Alderson.$] Was it in your presence *that* he read it? (p. 24)
(Trials, Jonathan Martin, 1800–30, pp. 15, 24)

However, it is of special interest to consider cases where *that* occurs outside typical syntactic environments. These cases, which are termed 'nontypical' in table 5.10b, show a different use of *that* with the speaker roles, a use where *that* occurs more freely. Besides the nontypical use of *that*, the use of *whom* is also analysed, as are the use of *which* with personal antecedents and the frequency of pied piping versus stranding in relative prepositional constructions. In table 5.10b, only cases where there is a choice between pied piping and stranding are included.

The nontypical use of *that* is less frequent in the speech of members of the legal profession (41 per cent) than with people with other speaker roles (52 per cent). This indicates that when judges or lawyers use *that*, it is mainly in its typical syntactic environments. Members of professions other than the legal one seem

to use *that* more freely, with personal and nonpersonal antecedents, as in examples
(90)–(91).

(90) [$MARIA GLENN SWORN.$] The man *that* had the paper, and said the
marriage would not be lawful, again looked over the large paper, and said
'Never mind, you can be married just the same,' and looked at the parties
and smiled.
(Trials, James Bowditch, 1800–30, p. 38)

(91) [$MARY CADWALLADER'S EVIDENCE.$] There was a new bottle of
vanilla *that* I thought had not been opened; but, when I came to look at it,
I found that it was.
(Trials, Edwin Maybrick, 1870–1900, p. 97)

The antecedent *person(s)* is a typical syntactic environment of both the relativizer *that* and *whom* in Trials. Four out of the seven instances of *whom* spoken
by a judge are of this type, all from the first period (1800–30). Judges seem to use
whom (seven instances or 9 per cent) as frequently as people with other occupations (seven instances or 10 per cent). However, as is the case with *that*, judges
or other members of the legal profession use *whom* more frequently in a typical
syntactic environment (*a/the person **whom***), possibly for the sake of precision, as
in example (92).

(92) [$MR. JUSTICE PARK.$] You are certain that was a person *whom* you had
not seen before?
(Trials, James Bowditch, 1800–30, p. 29)

As is the case in Present-day English, the relativizer *whom* was regarded as
formal in nineteenth-century English (see Schneider 1996a: 492–3). Görlach
(1999: 67) notes that *whom* was disappearing during the nineteenth century and
was being replaced by *who*. In Trials, there are no examples of *who* for *whom*;
on the other hand, there are instances of the opposite: *whom* used for *who*. This
suggests that people were not certain how to use *whom* but that they regarded it
as formal and particularly suitable in certain contexts because it seemed 'more
correct' than *who*. In Present-day English (as in nineteenth-century English),
this so-called hypercorrect use of *whom* is found in *push-down relative clauses*; this
term denotes that the modifying relative clause is itself embedded in a clause (see
Quirk et al. 1985: 368, 1050). The relativizer has the double function of subject
and object: **That is the man **whom** we thought was not coming* (hypercorrect) and
*This is the man **whom** we thought to be difficult* (see Quirk et al. 1985: 1050, 1298–9).
Two of the fourteen examples of *whom* are hypercorrect. Both instances are found
in the speech of members of the legal profession:

(93) [$The ATTORNEY-GENERAL.$] Then you saw a man *whom* you were
told was Sir Roger coming out of door?
(Trials, Sir Roger Tichborne, 1870–1900, p. 2447)

Table 5.10c. *Pied piping and stranding across speaker roles in Trials (periods 1 and 3).*

Speaker role	Pied piping	Stranding	Total
Members of the legal profession	29 (78%)	8 (22%)	37 (100%)
Others	13 (52%)	12 (48%)	25 (100%)
Total	42 (68%)	20 (32%)	62 (100%)

(94) [$Mr. Addison$] No. For instance, this gentleman, *whom* you say looked like Mr Maybrick, he used to take it on the way down to the office, so that it could not do him any harm?
(Trials, Edwin Maybrick, 1870–1900, p. 226)

The use of *which* with reference to an individual was probably looked upon as nonstandard usage in nineteenth-century English, as it is in Present-day English (but cf. Kjellmer 2002). There are, however, only two examples in Trials. One example is found in a question asked by a judge, the other in the evidence given by a friend or a neighbour of the defendant (see examples (41) and (42) in section 4).

The use of pied piping versus stranding in relative prepositional constructions might depend on different speaker roles. Pied piping is regarded as a more formal feature than stranding in cases where variation between the two constructions is possible (see Johansson and Geisler 1998). Overall, pied piping is twice as common (29 per cent) as stranding (14 per cent) in table 5.10b. This seems to imply that both 'Members of the legal profession' and 'Others' use fairly formal speech (see example (86) above, spoken by a doctor). However, as can be expected, the speech of judges or lawyers may be even more formal since table 5.10b shows that pied piping is used by 'Members of the legal profession' in twenty-nine examples and in thirteen examples by 'Others'. Stranding is used almost as frequently (twelve instances, or 18 per cent) as pied piping (thirteen instances, or 19 per cent) by witnesses. Members of the legal profession, on the other hand, use stranding in only eight instances (or 11 per cent) and pied piping in twenty-nine examples (or 38 per cent); see table 5.10b.

Table 5.10c compares only pied piping and stranding across the speaker roles. As table 5.10c shows, in prepositional constructions, pied piping is generally more frequent than stranding (68 per cent vs 32 per cent). As stated earlier, judges or lawyers use pied piping more frequently (78 per cent) than doctors, or neighbours, friends or servants of the defendant (52 per cent).[21] Stranding accounts for only 22 per cent in the speech of 'Members of the legal profession', while 'Others' use pied piping and stranding nearly to the same extent. Examples (95)–(96) illustrate stranding with *that* in the speech of 'Others'.

(95) [$JOHN BURROUGHS; SWORN.$] This young man *that* I have been talking *about*.
(Trials, James Bowditch, 1800–30, p. 100)

(96) [$THOMAS LOW NICHOLS SWORN.$] Not at all. I always gave persons to understand what my position was. If they insisted upon my seeing a child or a patient *that* I thought I could be useful *to*, I ordinarily would go, but that was very rare.
(Trials, Adelaide Bartlett, 1870–1900, p. 125)

However, when judges ask questions using pied piping, the witness may answer using the same construction (see also example (7) in section 2.2). In the dialogue in example (97) from the trial of Charles Angus, a witness uses a relative prepositional construction with stranding. The question asked later on by a member of the legal profession exemplifies pied piping. In example (98), *allude to* is used with both stranding and pied piping by the same professional group (the legal profession).

(97) [$ANN HOPKINS, SWORN.$] [$Examined by Mr. Raine.$] [$Q.$] Had she no wrapper on – you tell me, on the Sofa there was a flannel wrapper, what do you mean by that? [$A.$] One *that* she was laid *on*, Sir. [$Q.$] Did you collect the clothes that were taken from her? [$A.$] I took them altogether, Sir. [$Court.$] Was that which you call a flannel wrapper, *on which* she lay, was that Mr Angus's morning gown?
(Trials, Charles Angus, 1800–30, p. 63)

(98) [$Mr. Alderson.$] These two documents, the tickets and the notes *that* have been alluded *to* in the evidence of the witness are in these words. (p. 39) [...]
[$Mr. Brougham.$] Have you had any practice, in respect to insanity, except upon those accidental occasions *to which* you allude? (p. 42)
(Trials, Jonathan Martin, 1800–30, pp. 39, 42)

The *wh*-forms are predominant regardless of speaker role. It may seem somewhat surprising at first that the relativizer *that*, usually looked upon as an indicator of informality, occurs frequently in the speech of members of the legal profession. This is because *that* occurs chiefly in its typical syntactic environments in Trials; with *person(s)* or a pronoun as antecedent and in cleft sentences with adverbial expressions of time and place, which are important in a legal case (*are you sure it was shortly before six o'clock that . . . ?*). The use of *that* in Trials is thus typical of the genre rather than of a particular speaker role.

It was not possible to perceive any gender-based differences in the use of relativizers in Trials since the only speaker role in which women are represented is that of witnesses (servants, neighbours and friends of the defendant). In the nineteenth century, women were, by and large, excluded from the legal profession and from the professions that expert witnesses in court were taken from (see Smitterberg 2005: 85 and references therein). In nineteenth-century letter

Table 5.11. Wh-*forms and* that *in women's and men's letters (periods 1 and 3).*

Relativizer	Female letter writer	Male letter writer	Total
Wh-	729 (84%)	780 (89%)	1,509 (86%)
That	139 (16%)	100 (11%)	239 (14%)
Total	868 (100%)	880 (100%)	1,748 (100%)

writing, on the other hand, it is possible to study men's and women's use of the relativizers.

7   Gender-based differences in the use of relativizers in nineteenth-century letter writing

Women are often claimed to use more conservative and tentative language than men (see Coates and Cameron 1988: 15, and Biber and Burgess 2000). For nineteenth-century English, however, Geisler (2003) shows that female letter writers can be looked upon as linguistic innovators, in introducing features of a new writing style, such as a more frequent use of stranding of a preposition with relativizers or a more frequent use of the progressive (cf. Rydén and Brorström 1987: 201–2; Labov 2001: 292–3; Romaine 1999: 175–7; Smitterberg 2005). This section will investigate differences in the use of relativizers and relative clauses in letters written by women and in letters written by men, and consider whether there is a change over time. As regards the frequency of relative clauses with *wh*-forms and *that*, women use fewer such clauses than men do in their letters, an indication that female letter writing is slightly less elaborate. Female letter writers use seventy-four relative clauses with *wh*-forms or *that* per 10,000 words in the first period, and sixty-seven per 10,000 words in the third period. Men, on the other hand, use ninety relative clauses with the *wh*-forms and *that* per 10,000 words in 1800–30 and continue to use relative clauses more frequently than women in the third period with ninety-nine per 10,000 words.

Table 5.11 presents the use of *wh*-forms versus *that* by nineteenth-century female and male letter writers. As stated earlier, the *wh*-forms are predominant (86 per cent), whereas *that* is used in only 14 per cent of the cases. Görlach (1999: 150) points out that private letters may contain informal language, an example of which could be a frequent use of *that*. In table 5.11, we find that women use *that* more often (16 per cent) than men do (11 per cent), and hence their letter writing might be looked upon as more informal.[22]

However, if both women's and men's letters are considered together, the use of *that* is infrequent: the figure is 14 per cent, which is closer to the proportion of *that*

Table 5.12a. Wh-*clauses and* that-*clauses in women's letters (periods 1 and 3).*

Period	Period 1		Period 3	
Function	Subject	Direct + prepositional object	Subject	Direct + prepositional object
Wh-clauses	232 (80%)	149 (84%)	203 (85%)	66 (84%)
That-clauses	57 (20%)	28 (16%)	35 (15%)	13 (16%)
Total	289 (100%)	177 (100%)	238 (100%)	79 (100%)

Table 5.12b. Wh-*clauses and* that-*clauses in men's letters (periods 1 and 3).*

Period	Period 1		Period 3	
Function	Subject	Direct + prepositional object	Subject	Direct + prepositional object
Wh-clauses	240 (87%)	138 (91%)	192 (87%)	100 (84%)
That-clauses	35 (13%)	13 (9%)	29 (13%)	19 (16%)
Total	275 (100%)	151 (100%)	221 (100%)	119 (100%)

in Science (11 per cent) than the one in Trials (33 per cent). The low frequency of *that* in letter writing can probably be explained by the high frequency of nonrestrictive and sentential relative clauses in this genre (see section 3).

Tables 5.12a–5.12b show the use of *wh*-forms and *that* in relative clauses in women's and men's letters from period 1 to period 3. Only the clause functions of subject and direct + prepositional object have been included. It is mainly in these functions that variation between the *wh*-forms and *that* occurs, and it is also of importance to show how these two clause functions influence the variation between *who, whom* and *which*, on the one hand, and *that*, on the other, from period 1 to period 3.

The *wh*-forms naturally predominate in periods 1 and 3 as subjects, direct and prepositional objects in both letters written by women (80–85 per cent) and letters written by men (84–91 per cent).[23] It is possible, however, to see some change as regards the frequency of *that*. In women's letters, there is a slight decrease in the use of *that* over time. In period 1, women use 16–20 per cent *that* in their letters; in period 3 *that* occurs in 15–16 per cent of the cases.[24] The highest frequency of *that* is as subject (20 per cent) in period 1. In letters written by men, there is, instead, a slight increase of *that* over the two periods. In period 1, they use 9–13 per cent *that*, and in period 3 they use 13–16 per cent *that*.[25] Most occurrences

Table 5.13a. Wh-*clauses and* that-*clauses in women's letters (period 1).*

Relative clause	Austen	Hutchinson	Shelley	Wordsworth
Wh-clauses	65 (86%)	125 (89%)	60 (78%)	174 (79%)
That-clauses	11 (14%)	16 (11%)	17 (22%)	45 (21%)
Total	76 (100%)	141 (100%)	77 (100%)	219 (100%)

Table 5.13b. Wh-*clauses and* that-*clauses in men's letters (period 1).*

Relative clause	Blake	Byron	Coleridge	Keats	Southey
Wh-clauses	76 (83%)	100 (94%)	64 (85%)	54 (87%)	147 (94%)
That-clauses	16 (17%)	6 (6%)	11 (15%)	8 (13%)	9 (6%)
Total	92 (100%)	106 (100%)	75 (100%)	62 (100%)	156 (100%)

of *that* in men's letters are as direct and prepositional objects (16 per cent) in period 3, whereas the same clause functions have the lowest frequency of *that* (9 per cent) in period 1.

During the nineteenth century, women change their writing styles to a greater degree than men do with regard to the use of relativizers. As a result of the changes, a gender difference is no longer clear in period 3, according to tables 5.12a–5.12b. In period 1, women use restrictive relative clauses with *that* more frequently than men do (*that* occurs exclusively in restrictive relative clauses in Letters; see section 3). Female letter writers use *that* not only in typical syntactic environments, such as nonpersonal antecedents, pronouns with nonpersonal reference, and with a superlative + noun (see sections 4 and 5.3 above), but they also seem to choose a *that*-clause, that is, a clause with a closer link with its antecedent than a *wh*-clause, in 'nontypical' environments. The nontypical syntactic environments of *that* are, for example, personal antecedents and pronouns with personal reference, as in (99). Compare also examples (100)–(102) below.

(99) If you are going to lead a London life, you had better go everywhere and see everyone *that* is worth seeing.
(Letters, Mary Sibylla Holland, 1870–1900, p. 160)

In period 3, women seem to conform more to the norm, that is, the use of relative clauses with *wh*-forms.[26] In other words, their writing style becomes more similar to that used by the male letter writers. It is important, however, to consider *individual* writing styles as well as female versus male use of *wh*-forms and *that*. In tables 5.13a–5.13b, female and male letter writers from period 1,

Table 5.14a. Wh-*clauses and* that-*clauses in women's letters (period 3)*.

Relative clause	Butler	Holland	Rossetti	Thackeray Ritchie
Wh-clauses	43 (90%)	62 (70%)	65 (96%)	135 (90%)
That-clauses	5 (10%)	27 (30%)	3 (4%)	15 (10%)
Total	48 (100%)	89 (100%)	68 (100%)	150 (100%)

Table 5.14b. Wh-*clauses and* that-*clauses in men's letters (period 3)*.

Relative clause	Arnold	Butler	Hardy	Huxley
Wh-clauses	83 (90%)	155 (84%)	39 (91%)	62 (89%)
That-clauses	9 (10%)	29 (16%)	4 (9%)	8 (11%)
Total	92 (100%)	184 (100%)	43 (100%)	70 (100%)

1800–30, are listed to illustrate the individual patterns in the use of *wh*-forms and *that* in relative clauses.

As shown in tables 5.13a–5.13b, two female letter writers stand out with a more frequent use of *that*-clauses in their letters: Mary Shelley and Mary Wordsworth. They use *that* fairly often, 22 per cent and 21 per cent respectively. William Blake is the male letter writer with the highest frequency of *that* (17 per cent) in period 1, whereas Lord Byron and Robert Southey use only 6 per cent *that*. A letter writer may also vary his or her use of *wh*-forms and *that*, possibly according to the topic of the letter. The two letter collections by Mary Wordsworth show a different frequency of *wh*-forms and *that*. In her love letters to William, *that* is twice as frequent (28 per cent) as in her other letters (14 per cent). The two letter collections are conflated in table 5.13a, giving 21 per cent as regards the use of *that*-clauses. In period 1, the use of *that*-clauses ranges from 11 to 22 per cent among the female letter writers and from 6 to 17 per cent among the male letter writers.

Tables 5.14a–5.14b present the use of relative clauses with *wh*-forms and *that* by female and male letter writers in period 3. In period 3, two female letter writers are very different in their use of *wh*-forms and *that*. Mary Sibylla Holland's letters might be considered as representing a new writing style with 30 per cent *that*, especially when compared to those of Christina Rossetti, where the proportion of *that*-clauses is only 4 per cent. This is the lowest frequency of *that* in either of the two periods. In period 3, the two letter collections by Samuel Butler show a different frequency of *that*. Butler uses *that* slightly more often in *The Family Letters* (19 per cent) than in the letters to his sister May (13 per cent). The two letter collections have been

Table 5.15a. *The use of relativizers in women's and men's letters (periods 1 and 3).*

Relativizer	Female letter writer	Male letter writer	Total
That (nontypical use)	59 (40%)	30 (20%)	89 (30%)
Whom	24 (17%)	23 (16%)	47 (16%)
Pied piping	40 (27%)	82 (55%)	122 (41%)
Stranding	23 (16%)	14 (9%)	37 (13%)
Total	146 (100%)	149 (100%)	295 (100%)

conflated in table 5.14b, giving 16 per cent. The male letter writers in period 3 show a more even distribution in the use of *that* (9–16 per cent); for the female letter writers, the use of *that* ranges from 4 to 30 per cent, as mentioned above.

Table 5.15a shows the extent to which four constructions (nontypical *that*, *whom*, pied piping and stranding) are used by female and male letter writers respectively (cf. table 5.10b in section 6). As the table shows, the nontypical use of *that* is more frequent in women's letters (59 instances, or 40 per cent) than in letters written by men (30 examples, or 20 per cent). Two of the three female letter writers who use the relativizer *that* most frequently display a nontypical use of *that*. In Mary Wordsworth's letters, twenty-five of forty-five examples of *that* are not in their typical syntactic environments. Her letters also contain instances of *that* used with a personal antecedent, which is very rare in Letters (see section 4). In example (100), *that* is used with a pronoun with personal reference (*those*). A pronoun is a typical syntactic environment of *that* only when it refers to a nonpersonal antecedent (see section 5). In Mary Shelley's letters also, *that* is used more freely. Examples (100) and (101) illustrate a use of *that* which is not restricted to typical syntactic environments.

(100) All I beg with much earnestness is that you wilt take care of thyself – but compare thyself with those *that* are well in things wherever you can agree & not with those *that* are ill –
(Letters, Mary Wordsworth, [1], 1800–30, p. 166)

(101) How very happy shall I be to possess those darling treasures *that* are yours –
(Letters, Mary Shelley, 1800–30, p. 16)

In Mary Sibylla Holland's letters, which contain most instances of *that* in Letters, the relativizer *that* is used in its typical syntactic environments, such as cleft sentences, indefinite determiners or *same* + noun and superlative + noun.[27] In example (102), one of the few instances of the nontypical use of *that* is illustrated. Compare also example (99) above.

(102) You were a great pleasure to me as a babe – and at twenty months old you showed a sort of serious vivacity *that* gave me great pleasure.
(Letters, Mary Sibylla Holland, 1870–1900, p. 116)

The use of *whom* and pied piping in relative prepositional constructions is an indicator of a formal writing style. The relativizer *whom* is fairly frequent in comparison with the other constructions in table 5.15a, in both women's (twenty-four examples, or 17 per cent) and men's letters (twenty-three examples, or 16 per cent). On the one hand, Mary Shelley's letters have most occurrences of the formal *whom* in period 1; on the other hand, her letters also show a frequent use of *that*, which may be regarded as an informal relativizer compared to *wh*-forms. There are no examples of hypercorrect *whom*. Using hypercorrect *whom* could be a sign of the linguistic insecurity thought to be particularly typical of female writing and speech (cf. Coates and Cameron 1988: 17, and Romaine 1999: 155). *Who* as direct object is found once in Mary Shelley's letters (the second relative clause with *who* in example (103) below), which is probably not an example of objective *who* but a form influenced by the other instances of *who* in the sentence.

(103) He says the children are to go to this old clergyman in Warwickshire *who* is to stand instead of a parent – and [\sic\] old fellow *who* no one knows and [\ who\] never saw the children this is somewhat beyond credibility did we not see it in black & white – (p. 28) [. . .] You will see I doubt not some old friends there, for somehow or other people pop up in that city *whom* you imagined hundreds of miles off – [. . .] (p. 263)
(Letters, Mary Shelley, 1800–30, pp. 28, 263)

As mentioned above, Holland's letters may be looked upon as innovative in the frequent use of *that* but they are conservative and rather formal in other respects: the relativizer *whom* is found, and stranding does not occur in Holland's letters.

The use of pied piping versus stranding in prepositional constructions may not only depend on different speaker roles, as in Trials, but may also reflect gender-based differences in the use of relativizers. Of the features listed in table 5.15a, pied piping constructions make up 55 per cent in letters written by men and 27 per cent in letters written by women. This may be interpreted as male letter writers using a more formal writing style than female letter writers. Table 5.15b focuses on the proportions of pied piping and stranding by female and male letter writers (cf. Table 5.10c in section 6).

Table 5.15b shows, first, that pied piping is generally more frequent than stranding in prepositional constructions, and second, that pied piping and stranding are used differently by female and male letter writers (cf. Geisler 2003).[28] Pied piping constructions are more frequent in letters written by men (85 per cent) compared with letters written by women (63 per cent). A good representative of a male letter writer who uses pied piping constructions is Lord Byron. In all eighteen examples of prepositional constructions, pied piping occurs. In thirteen of these, there is a choice between pied piping and stranding.

Table 5.15b. *Pied piping and stranding across gender in letters (periods 1 and 3).*

Letter writer	Pied piping	Stranding	Total
Female	40 (63%)	23 (37%)	63 (100%)
Male	82 (85%)	14 (15%)	96 (100%)
Total	122 (77%)	37 (23%)	159 (100%)

(104) I have gotten a very pretty Cambrian girl there *of whom* I grew foolishly fond, & Lucy & Bess became very greeneyed on the occasion. [. . .] There is the whole history of circumstances *to which* you may have possibly heard some allusion from those who knew me in the earlier part of my life – (Letters, George Byron, 1800–30, p. II, 155)

Stranding, on the other hand, is more frequent among female letter writers (37 per cent) than among male letter writers (15 per cent). However, Mary Sibylla Holland's and Christina Rossetti's letters contain no examples of stranding. Pied piping is used even if there is a choice between pied piping and stranding in the prepositional constructions. In example (105), from Jane Austen's letters, it is possible to see variation between pied piping and stranding.

(105) He was seized on saturday with a return of the feverish complaint, *which* he had been subject *to* for the three last years; [. . .] A Physician was called in yesterday morning, but he was at that time past all possibility of cure – & Dr. Gibbs and Mr. Bowen had scarcely left his room before he sunk into a Sleep *from which* he never woke. (p. 62) [. . .] Oh! dear Fanny, your mistake has been one *that* thousands of women fall *into*. (p. 173) (Letters, Jane Austen, 1800–30, pp. 62, 173)

The most varied use of stranding in relative prepositional constructions is found in a letter written by a man. In Samuel Butler's letters to his family, we find three different types: *which*, *whom*, and *that* with stranded preposition (*that I see and that I am hurt by* is here regarded as an expansion of *that I see and am hurt by*).

(106) I believe May would like this very well, and for this reason if no other think it better not to notice things *that* of course I see and am hurt *by*. [. . .] I was compelled to Miss Sayans after all, and have only half done a copy of a drawing after Holbein in the Museum at Basle *which* I have long had my eye *on* [. . .] I have lost my friend Miss Savage *whom* you have often heard me speak *of*, and no words of mine can express how great a loss this is. (Letters, Samuel Butler [1], 1870–1900, p. 258)

Some women's writing styles, in which *that* is used more frequently, differ from the writing styles in letters by men. In period 1, more than 60 per cent of the instances of *that* are found in letters written by women. In period 3, only Mary Sibylla Holland has a more frequent use of *that* than all the women writing in period 1. In period 3, 50 per cent of the instances of *that* are found in letters written by men. It is not probable, however, that women were looked upon as models in their letter writing.[29] Rather, the use of the relativizer *that* is a feature of the individual letter writer, male or female. In Mary Wordsworth's and Mary Shelley's letters (period 1), *that* is used fairly frequently and freely. In contrast, in Mary Sibylla Holland's letters (period 3), which display the highest frequency of *that* in Letters, *that* is used in typical syntactic environments, and her letters may be regarded as rather formal since she uses *whom* and pied piping constructions. Letters from different periods and by different writers, male or female, may also be very similar. For instance, in both Lord Byron's letters (period 1) and Christina Rossetti's letters (period 3), *that* is very rare, formal *whom* occurs rather frequently and only pied piping is used in prepositional constructions. In period 3, women letter writers do not continue to use *that* more frequently than men. If they had done so, they could possibly have been looked upon as introducers of a new, less formal style in nineteenth-century letter writing.

8   Conclusion

Two strategies or patterns are available for relative clause formation in nineteenth-century English and in Present-day English: *wh*-forms (*who*, *whose*, *whom* and *which*) and *that* or zero (see Quirk et al. 1985: 366; the zero construction is not discussed in this paper). In nineteenth-century English, the *wh*-forms, i.e. the more explicit strategy with animacy and case contrast, predominate. One reason, or at least a tentative explanation, could be found in the development of relative clause strategies towards the latter part of the Early Modern English period. This is when the *wh*-forms started being used more frequently than *that*, particularly in formal (Latinate) writing (in, for example, the works of Bacon and Locke; see Barber 1997: 213–14). It is unexpected that the *wh*-forms predominate to such a great extent in the nineteenth-century English texts examined in this study; a *wh*-form occurs in more than 80 per cent of the relative clauses overall, and in nearly 90 per cent of the relative clauses in nineteenth-century scientific writing. *Which* is mainly used with a nonpersonal antecedent; it is the most frequent relativizer (occurring in about 60 per cent of the relative clauses), and is particularly predominant in the Science texts. Here *that* is rare, even if it is with a nonpersonal antecedent that it could be said to compete with the *wh*-forms (*which*), at least to some extent.

The *wh*-forms for personal reference, *who* (*whose*) and *whom*, occur in about 20 per cent of the relative clauses. Most examples of *who* (*whose*) and *whom* are found in the Letters since here mainly persons are the topics.

Besides the fact that the relativizer *that* is infrequent in nineteenth-century texts, what else can be said about it? *That* does occur in 20 per cent of the relative clauses, and an explanation for this might be that it is fairly frequent in the nineteenth-century Trials (33 per cent). Trials are speech-related but the occurrence of *that* cannot be attributed to the speech-like character of the Trials, with speakers who can be expected to speak more informally (mainly different categories of witnesses). Instead, *that* is frequent in the Trials because it is used in its particular syntactic environments, for example in cleft sentences, with pronominal antecedents and with the antecedent *person(s)*, both by 'Members of the legal profession' and by people with other occupations.

That the relativizer *that* is largely restricted to its typical syntactic environments is naturally even more evident in written nineteenth-century English, both in scientific texts and letter writing. It seems to be the case that nineteenth-century writers are more careful to observe the norm to use *wh*-forms or are more sensitive to it than are writers in the Early Modern English period. Individual nineteenth-century scientists (Sir Francis Galton) or letter writers (Mary Shelley, Mary Wordsworth and Mary Sibylla Holland) use *that* in their writing. It is interesting to note that female letter writers use *that* slightly more frequently than male letter writers, particularly at the beginning of the nineteenth century, but they do not continue to do so. Towards the end of the century, they conform to the norm instead, which prescribes the use of *wh*-forms.

Nineteenth-century writers (and possibly also speakers) seem to prefer a more explicit method of referring to an antecedent by using a *wh*-form. The preference for the *wh*-forms also entails a frequent use of pied piping constructions (preposition + *which/whom*), which is particularly typical of the Science texts. It seems likely that stranding in its turn entails the use of *that*; examples with *which/whom* and stranding are rare. In Present-day English, the development of the relativizers has been towards a frequent use of *that* (in some cases this is also the norm, see Biber et al. 1999: 616). At the end of the nineteenth century, however, this development had not yet begun to any great extent.

Notes

1. I am grateful to Christer Geisler for his help in providing the material from the CONCE corpus and for his comments on earlier versions of this study. I also want to express my thanks to the editors for their comments and, in particular, to Erik Smitterberg for his help with statistical tests.
2. The figures in table 5.1 are statistically significant; d.f.: 1, chi-square: 46.175 and $p < 0.001$.
3. d.f.: 1, chi-square: 0.220 and $p = 0.639$.
4. The figures in table 5.3 are not statistically significant; d.f.: 1, chi-square: 0.050 and $p = 0.823$. However, when the distribution of *wh*-forms and of *that* is tested across the three genres, the results are statistically significant: d.f.: 2, chi-square: 141.434 and $p < 0.001$.
5. The figures in table 5.4a are statistically significant; d.f.: 8, chi-square: 291.479 and $p < 0.001$.
6. Finite relative clauses where the relativizer functions as subject are the easiest to form, according to the ACCESSIBILITY HIERARCHY for relativization as presented by Keenan and Comrie (1977) and by Comrie (1989). The hierarchy is described as follows in

Comrie (1989): SU>DO>non-DO>Poss (> = 'more accessible than'; SU = subject, DO = direct object, Poss = Possessor). Poss (i.e. *whose*; *of which* is not discussed in Keenan and Comrie 1977) is the least frequent relativizer (1–2 per cent, see table 5.4a) in the nineteenth-century data (see also Johansson 1995: 249–52).

7. The cross-genre differences in table 5.4d are statistically significant; d.f.: 2, chi-square: 17.944 and p < 0.001.

8. Stranding seems obligatory with prepositional objects when the meaning expressed by the verb is figurative (see Sopher 1974, and Johansson and Geisler 1998), as in [\$Mr. Poland.\$] *There is a matter* **which** *I passed over. I ought to have asked you –* (Trials, Adelaide Bartlett, 1870–1900, p. 46). Pied piping is more or less obligatory in certain adverbial expressions, with antecedents such as *way*, *degree* and *extent*. Here *way* is the most common antecedent, as in *The only difficulty was* **the way in which** *the effects of that high temperature could be measured* (Science, J. Norman Lockyer, 1870–1900, p. 267). Pied piping also seems to be obligatory with certain prepositions such as *under, during* and *beyond* (see Johansson and Geisler 1998), as in *but there is probably always an interval,* **during which** *some effect is produced on the rate of interest.* (Science, David Ricardo, 1800–30, p. 413).

9. Görlach (1999: 88) points out that in nineteenth-century English, nonrestrictive relative clauses are mostly enclosed by commas. In my data, a comma may be missing even if the clause is clearly nonrestrictive, as in the first relative clause in example (22) and the second relative clause in example (31). However, it has not been possible to verify the transcriptions given in the printed editions against the manuscript readings.

10. Rydén (1984) and Jacobsson (1994) state there is a type of relative clause that provides important information about the antecedent, or characterizes it, but which must be regarded as nonrestrictive, since the antecedent is already identified. One of Rydén's (1984: 20) examples is *New York is a pulsating, dynamic heart-of-the-world city that changes its face almost daily.* Examples of such relative clauses from the nineteenth-century data are most frequent in Letters. As can be seen from Rydén's example and the examples from the nineteenth-century data below, the antecedent is premodified, and the relative clause expands on the premodification: *to contract a sort of snipt, convulsive style, that moves forward by short repeated PUSHES* (Letters, Samuel Taylor Coleridge, 1800–30, p. 506) and *on Monday Evening we would have mocked the unkind God who introduced such confusion into my ill-formed pot-hooks* (Letters, Mary Shelley, 1800–30, p. 320). Rydén (1966: lii) calls these clauses *augmentative.*

11. According to Jacobsson (1963) and (1994), *that* in nonrestrictive relative clauses is more frequent in twentieth-century prose than generally assumed. Nonrestrictive *that*-clauses are rarely described or commented on by scholars. Reasons for this might be unreliable criteria for the distinction of restrictive and nonrestrictive relative clauses and the fact that *that*-clauses are automatically regarded as restrictive (Jacobsson 1994: 195).

12. The figures in table 5.5 are statistically significant; d.f.: 1, chi-square: 7.996 and p = 0.005.

13. The figures in table 5.6 are statistically significant; d.f.: 1, chi-square: 85.952 and p < 0.001.

14. The difference between *wh*-forms and *that* according to clause type is statistically significant for nonpersonal antecedents; d.f.: 1, chi-square: 21.351 and p < 0.001.

15. Restrictive and nonrestrictive relative clauses are not discussed by Fox and Thompson (1990) although terms such as *characterizing* and *identifying* are used. Fox and

Thompson (1990: 303) further state that nonpersonal antecedents are 'anchored' in discourse, for example as direct objects, to some personal activity or location. In Trials, however, nonpersonal antecedents are more frequent as subjects than as direct and prepositional objects. Compare table 5.7: a *wh*-form (*which*) or *that* as subjects: 214 examples; and a *wh*-form (*which*) or *that* as direct object and prepositional object: 125 examples.

16. Statistically significant; d.f.: 1, chi-square: 10.178 and p = 0.002.
17. The syntactic environments of *wh*-forms and *that* are discussed both in early grammars (for example Murray 1795) and Present-day English grammars (for example Quirk et al. 1985, and Huddleston and Pullum 2002). There is of course a relationship between, on the one hand, close links and restrictiveness (the use of *that*) and, on the other hand, loose links and nonrestrictiveness (the use of *wh*-forms, see Rissanen 1984).
18. Rydén (1970) discusses the semantics of indefinite determiners + noun and restrictive/nonrestrictive relative clauses. As opposed to Smith (1964), Rydén shows that antecedents with indefinite determiners can occur not only in restrictive relative clauses but also nonrestrictive ones.
19. Premodified antecedents generally do not favour either a *wh*-form or *that*, except in Trials. In this genre, *that* is largely restricted to antecedents without modification, such as *a person*, *people* or pronominal antecedents. See section 5.2. In Science, thirteen out of sixteen premodified antecedents + *that* occur in Galton's text. Compare the discussion of this text in sections 2.1, 3 and 5.1.
20. The figures in table 5.10a are not statistically significant; d.f.: 1, chi-square: 0.431 and p = 0.512.
21. The figures in table 5.10c are statistically significant; d.f.: 1, chi-square: 4.751 and p = 0.030.
22. The figures in table 5.11 are statistically significant; d.f.: 1, chi-square: 8.006 and p = 0.005.
23. The variation in the syntactic distribution of *wh*-clauses is statistically significant for women's letters (d.f.: 1, chi-square: 15.126 and p < 0.001) but not for men's letters (d.f.: 1, chi-square: 0.368 and p = 0.544).
24. The diachronic difference is not statistically significant; d.f.: 1, chi-square: 0.494 and p = 0.483.
25. The diachronic difference is not statistically significant; d.f.: 1, chi-square: 1.688 and p = 0.195.
26. Compare Steele's 'The Humble Petition of *Who* and *Which*' (*Spectator* No. 78, 1711), in which the *wh*-forms are described as of noble origin compared with the jacksprat *that*. According to Görlach (1999: 15), Lindley Murray's grammar (1795) was one of the most influential in the nineteenth century. In Murray's grammar, the use of *wh*-forms is described in detail (1795: 148–56); see also Görlach (2001: 126–7).
27. '[A]fter an adjective in the superlative degree and after the pronominal adjective *same* it [that] is generally used in preference to *who* and *which*' (Murray 1795: 149).
28. The figures in table 5.15b are statistically significant; d.f.: 1, chi-square: 10.240 and p = 0.001.
29. Literary works by women were also looked upon as being of inferior quality in the nineteenth century. Romaine (1999: 313–14) gives the example of the Brontë sisters, who wrote under pseudonyms.

6   Anaphoric reference in the nineteenth century: *that/those* + *of* constructions

MARK KAUNISTO

1   Introduction

The anaphoric pronouns *that/those* in connection with a following *of*-phrase suggest a notable degree of formality to many native speakers of English. It has been observed that in relation to corresponding genitival constructions, the use of the *of* construction in general is thus also more common in those genres usually associated with a greater level of formality. This tendency has been seen in texts from earlier centuries (for instance, in seventeenth-century texts, see Altenberg 1982: 251–5). The comparatively even more formal nature of the combined *that of/those of* constructions is evident in the present day, and has been noted by several authors (e.g. Schibsbye 1970: 118; Perttunen 1986: 168; Biber et al. 1999: 307). Comparing expressions as regards their differing shades of formality, Perttunen (1986: 168) considers constructions with *that of* and *those of* 'very formal'. In a similar vein, Biber et al. (1999: 307–8) argue that these constructions are 'felt as overwhelmingly associated with careful expository writing and hence inappropriate to conversation', and thus the notion of formality in this chapter is to be determined extralinguistically, i.e. depending on the situation of communication.

A typical instance of anaphoric *that/those* followed by an *of*-phrase can be seen in the following sentence, culled from CONCE (= A Corpus of Nineteenth-century English; see the Introduction to this volume):

(1)   To the outward observer, Lawrence's <u>situation</u> was almost as difficult as *that of* his brother at Lucknow.
(History, Spencer Walpole, 1870–1900, p. VI, 310)

In (1), the preceding word that the pronoun *that* refers to is *situation*. In this case the repetition of the word is avoided. The construction is parallel to the so-called elliptic genitive (as in e.g. *I thought Peter's <u>drawing</u> was much better than* GERALD's), to which it is usually regarded as an alternative (see e.g. Aarts and Aarts 1982: 88; Zandvoort 1948: 128; Jespersen 1949: 331; Leech and Svartvik 2002: 290). Here the elliptic genitive is also possible, i.e. the sentence in (1) could read *Lawrence's* <u>*situation*</u> *was almost as difficult as* HIS BROTHER'S. However, both formulations are not possible, or at least not likely, in all cases. Instead, the choice between the elliptic genitive and the *that/those* + *of* construction depends to some extent on the same kind of factors as that between the normal *s*-genitive and *of* construction (see e.g. Quirk et al. 1972: 628–30; Lass 1987: 148–52). For example, the genitive is not usually found in connection with mass nouns, and thus only the *that* + *of*-phrase construction can be used in the following case (i.e. **the action differed considerably from phosphorous'*):

(2) Hydrogen was employed to reduce some of the metals, their solutions being placed in an atmosphere of the gas. The <u>action</u> differed considerably from *that of* phosphorus, as might be expected.
(Science, Michael Faraday, 1850–70, p. 410)

As regards the observation on the formality of *that/those* + *of*-phrase constructions, the elliptic genitive, when possible, is indeed less formal.

As well as being associated with formality, the linguistic structure in question has also been considered complex and even clumsy (which is probably a significant factor in the association; see e.g. Poutsma 1914: 98). As the structure involves an anaphoric use of the demonstrative pronouns *that/those*, it could be argued that the distance between the pronoun and its referent ('anaphoric distance') is also relevant, contributing to the overall impression of complexity of the expression. Following the example of Biber et al. (1999: 239), who examined the anaphoric distance in different types of anaphoric expressions, a similar study is performed here in relation to *that/those* followed by an *of*-phrase.

The aim of this paper is therefore to examine the use of sequences with *that/those* + *of*-phrase from a corpus-linguistic viewpoint. For this purpose, the material in the CONCE corpus was examined. Containing a variety of different genres, such as parliamentary debates, trial transcripts, fiction, scientific writings and letters, the corpus is a useful tool for examining how the observations made on the formality and complexity of the constructions in question correspond with their use in historical texts of different genres. More specifically, special attention will be paid to the relative frequencies of such constructions, the average distance between the anaphoric *that/those* + *of*-phrase constructions and their referents in different genres, and the question of whether these factors can be seen as correlating with each other.

The nineteenth-century material can be regarded as suitable for the study also because, in this period, the use of *that of/those of* structures had already become fully established, at least as regards its relative frequency. In the Early Modern English section of the Helsinki Corpus of English Texts (covering the period 1500–1710, containing approximately 551,000 words), only fifteen instances could be found of the sequences in question, while CONCE (1800–1900; approximately 1,050,000 words) contained as many as 241 such occurrences. The diachronic development of their use is a matter worthy of closer investigation, and can be further examined with the aid of corpora of other historical periods (e.g. the Century of Prose Corpus). In section 2 of the present paper, attention will be paid to structures which may be considered alternatives to the *that/those* + *of*-phrase constructions, with comments on the stylistic differences between the variants. Section 3 examines the different semantic aspects involved in the use of the constructions in question, as well as the types of NPs usually encountered in the *of*-phrase. Sections 4 and 5 will introduce the methodology used in the study, and present and discuss the findings respectively.

2   Alternative structures

There are some constructions in English (used in the nineteenth century as well as today) with anaphoric *that/those* which may be considered comparable to those studied in this paper. Biber et al. (1999: 584–5) mention cases where *that/those* with anaphoric reference may be followed by a relative clause beginning with the pronoun *which*, as in *They describe a different event from that which the author chose to describe*. Instances of this type were also found in the corpus studied. In some cases – though perhaps not in all – the sequences with *that/those* + *which/who* may be expressed with a construction with *that/those* + *of*-phrase instead. *That of/those of* is generally viewed as suggesting a considerably stronger impression of formality, as can be seen from the following set of sentences with the two parallel sequences (those with *that/those* + *which* being examples in Biber et al. (1999: 585), on which I have modelled the corresponding sentences with *that/those* + *of*):

1.   They describe a different <u>event</u> from *that which* the author chose to describe.
1′. They describe a different <u>event</u> from *that of* the author's own choice.
2.   He soon discovered that every <u>movement</u> by the man, even *those which* were obviously stupid, functioned along lines of scientific exactitude.
2′. He soon discovered that every <u>movement</u> by the man, even *those of* obvious stupidity, functioned along lines of scientific exactitude.

As shown by the examples above, forming a corresponding structure with *that/those* + *of* usually requires nominalization of some elements in the clause postmodifying the pronoun. This further suggests an increased level of formality, as nominalizations have been associated with this feature (see e.g. the findings in Geisler 2002). The pronoun can also be followed by a participial clause, as in *They describe a different event from that chosen by the author himself*, modelled after sentence 1. Such constructions are likewise usually regarded as less formal than the alternatives with *that of/those of*.

In addition to the preposition *of*, anaphoric *that/those* can occasionally be followed by comparable constructions with other prepositions, such as *at, by, for, from, in, on* etc., exemplified in the following passages from CONCE (see also Poutsma 1914: 83; Perttunen 1986: 168):

(3) The deposits consist of <u>particles</u> of various sizes, *those at* the outer parts of the result being too small to be recognized by the highest powers of the microscope.
(Science, Michael Faraday, 1850–70, p. 401)

(4) When <u>the demand</u> for silks increases, and *that for* cloth diminishes, the clothier does not remove with his capital to the silk trade [. . .]
(Science, David Ricardo, 1800–30, p. 84)

(5) <u>Fluids</u> thus prepared may differ much in appearance. *Those from* the basins, or from the stronger solutions of gold, are often evidently turbid, looking brown or violet in different lights.
(Science, Michael Faraday, 1850–70, p. 413)

(6) Under this fostering government <u>the schools</u> flourished, *those in* Sura and Pumbeditha were crowded with hearers: [. . .]
(History, Henry Milman, 1800–30, p. III, 271)

Sometimes a preposition following the preceding referent may be different from that of the anaphoric expression, as in example (7):

(7) He believed every one would allow, that <u>the battle</u> *of* Aboukir was much more glorious and decisive than *that at* Talavera; [. . .]
(Debates, 1800–30, p. XV, 459)

However, unlike anaphoric *that/those* + *of* constructions, the use of anaphoric *that/those* with other prepositions has not been described as being notably formal, and their occurrence in CONCE is not included in the analysis here.

3   Different types of anaphoric *that of/those of* constructions

I will here briefly discuss the different types of anaphoric *that of/those of* constructions that were attested in CONCE. In the same way as *of* constructions in general, combinations of anaphoric *that/those* and the *of*-phrase show different kinds of relations between the referent of *that/those* (sometimes with a notion of definiteness added by the pronouns) and the NP in the following *of*-phrase. Most typically the *of*-phrase has a specifying or identifying function, often denoting 'a relation of possession, origin or agency' (Poutsma 1914: 98).

On a more practical level, most often the use of *that of/those of* involves comparison of two things, and the preceding referent may include an expression of possession, origin, etc. For example, in (8), the referent *moral code* is modified by the possessive pronoun *my*. Explicit expressions of this type are, however, not required in the referent, as shown by example (9):

(8) I hope my <u>moral code</u> is nearly as good as *that of* my neighbours.
(Drama, Thomas Holcroft, 1800–30, p. 75)

(9) Hastings returned from India at the close of the war with the hope of <u>rewards</u> as great as *those of* Clive.
(History, John Green, 1870–1900, pp. IV, 275–6)

In some cases, the relation between the preceding referent and *that* + *of*-phrase is appositional:

(10) Now, though calomel is usually the best medicine in such cases, it is not always so; and I know one <u>instance,</u> *that of* Mrs. Clarkson, wherein by immediately procribing [^FOR: proscribing^] it and prescribing something else, Beddoes checked the disease, and saved the patient.
(Letters, Robert Southey, 1800–30, p. 115)

(11) Two <u>counties,</u> *those of* Hereford and Stafford, sent not a penny to the last.
(History, John Green, 1870–1900, p. III, 91)

In example (11), one could actually question the necessity of the sequence *that of* from a present-day point of view, as omitting it would be perfectly acceptable (or even preferable, as the *that of/those of* sequences in these cases may seem to some overly pompous). Poutsma (1914: 98–9) considers sequences of *that of/those of* markedly clumsy when followed by a proper name. However, in spite of their possible clumsiness, such instances were not at all uncommon in the nineteenth century material, see examples (9)–(11).

4   Principles employed in the analysis

Of all the sequences of *that of/those of* in the material, some are not relevant to the present study, namely those where *that* is a subordinating conjunction, as in example (12):

(12) It has been asserted, *that of* the best short-beaked tumbler-pigeons more perish in the egg than are able to get out of it; [. . .]
(Science, Charles Darwin, 1850–70, p. 87)

(13) [$Q.$] We have heard, that some time ago he endeavoured to escape from the City Jail?
[$A.$] Yes.
[$Q.$] Do you know *that of* your own knowledge?
(Trials, Jonathan Martin, 1800–30, p. 61)

In instances such as (13), *that* refers to a situation described in a clause, and no single noun or noun phrase can be regarded as the preceding referent of the pronoun. The sequence of *that of* in such cases is both syntactically and semantically different from those where the referent is a clearly distinguishable element, and therefore such examples were excluded.

As mentioned earlier, Biber et al. (1999: 239) studied the distances between anaphoric expressions and their referents. Their main aim was to analyse the differences in anaphoric distance between different forms of anaphoric expressions. Their results showed that of the expressions studied, demonstrative pronouns used anaphorically had the smallest average number of intervening words, while sequences of *the* + repeated noun allowed the greatest distance between the anaphoric expression and its preceding referent in almost all genres (for examples of the expressions, see Biber et al. 1999: 237–40).

An issue given less attention in the discussion of the results in Biber et al. (1999) is the differences between registers with regard to anaphoric distance. In relation to the present study, their results include one interesting detail: the anaphoric distance appeared to depend more on the type of expression than on the register. In other words, there was no consistency between registers with regard to anaphoric distance. For example, in the case of demonstrative + synonyms, the lowest number of intervening words was seen in academic texts, whereas with sequences of demonstrative + repeated noun, the shortest anaphoric distance was found in conversations. In addition, the number of anaphoric expressions was not always in direct correlation with the anaphoric distance; i.e. if a type of anaphoric expression occurred most frequently in, say, academic writings, the average anaphoric distance in them was not necessarily the largest among the four registers studied. Thus no direct connection could be made between, for instance, the formality of the expression and either its frequency of use or the average anaphoric distance perceived.

As regards determining the number of intervening words between the *that of*/*those of* sequences and their referents in the CONCE material, the principles employed in the analysis require some explanation. For example, somewhat problematic cases involve multiple uses of the anaphoric expressions for the same preceding referent:

(14) The whole taxes for Scotland were now about 1–11th of *those of* England, and on looking back to the Union, it would be found that they had considerably increased in favour of Scotland, they being at that period only 1–14th of *those of* England.
(Debates, 1800–30, p. XV, 439)

The sentence in example (14) includes two instances of anaphoric *those* + *of*-phrase constructions. The preceding referent in both cases is the phrase *the whole taxes*, and in the first case the number of intervening words between *taxes* and *those* is seven (*1–11th* regarded in this case as one lexical unit). In the latter case, however, one could argue that the reference to *the whole taxes for Scotland* is 're-introduced' or 'reinforced' with the anaphoric pronoun *they*. Following this view, which is also adhered to in the analysis of the whole material, the anaphoric distance value for the second instance of *those of* would be seven as well, instead of the considerably greater number if one goes as far back as the phrase *the whole taxes* (or the previous instance of *those*).

The nineteenth-century material shows some degree of variation in anaphoric distance. In some cases the number of words between the referent and *that*/*those* may be as low as zero, as in examples (10) and (11) cited above. The greatest anaphoric distance in the material studied was found in the following extract, with twenty-six words between the referent (*proportion*) and *that* + *of* (*per cent* being considered in this case one lexical item):

(15) Where neither parent was consumptive, the <u>proportion</u> in a small batch of well marked cases that I tried, was as high as 18 or 19 per cent., but this is clearly too much, as *that of* the general population is only 16 per cent. (Science, Sir Francis Galton, 1870–1900, p. 173)

For the sake of comparability with previous research chapter, the method applied in measuring the anaphoric distance in the present chapter follows that of Biber et al. (1999), although the idea of paying attention to the number of words may be questioned. It could, in fact, be argued that instead of all words, one could look into the number of intervening lexical words (i.e. excluding grammatical words or 'function words') or noun phrases so as to give more weight to the elements with more semantic content.

5   Results and discussion

The results of the study on *that of/those of* constructions in the CONCE material are presented in tables 6.1–6.4. Tables 6.1–6.3 first present the results according to the periods represented in the corpus, namely, 1800–30, 1850–70 and 1870–1900. Although there was no reason to expect that there would be any significant changes in different genres as regards the use of the particular structures studied here, it is nevertheless interesting to examine the consistency and coherence of the results in the three subsections of the corpus. As described further below, for the most part, similar differences between the genres can be seen in all periods. Table 6.4 then combines the results of all three subsections together.

The frequency of *that of/those of* sequences in the material studied was as low as 0.23 per 1,000 words in the whole corpus. However, notable differences between genres were visible. In tables 6.1–6.4, both the absolute numbers of occurrences (= N) and numbers of occurrences per 1,000 words (= N/1,000) are given. The column of figures on the right-hand side refers to anaphoric distance, 'Mean' denoting the average number of intervening words between *that/those* and the preceding referent. The N/1,000 figures are the organizing principle of the tables, i.e. the genres in each table are presented in descending order according to these figures.

As regards the relative frequencies (occurrences per 1,000 words) of anaphoric *that of/those of* in different genres, the figures in tables 6.1–6.3 show notable consistency in that in all subsections of the corpus, the sequences in question occur most frequently in Debates, Science and History. The genres with the fewest occurrences of *that of/those of* per 1,000 words were likewise the same ones (Letters, Drama and Trials) in all three subsections.

In the period 1850–70, as presented in table 6.2, the incidence of the sequences is, somewhat surprisingly, considerably lower than in the other two subsections of the corpus. However, the same overall differences between the genres manifest themselves.

Table 6.1. *Anaphoric* that of/those of *constructions in the*
CONCE *corpus, period 1 (1800–30).*

Genre	N	N/1,000	Mean
Debates	32	1.60	7.4
History	27	0.87	6.7
Science	20	0.53	7.7
Fiction	7	0.16	5.7
Letters	13	0.10	6.0
Drama	3	0.08	4.0
Trials	3	0.04	3.3
All genres	105	0.28	6.8

Table 6.2. *Anaphoric* that of/those of *constructions in the*
CONCE *corpus, period 2 (1850–70).*

Genre	N	N/1,000	Mean
Science	18	0.56	6.2
Debates	4	0.20	6.8
History	5	0.16	3.4
Fiction	4	0.10	5.3
Letters	12	0.09	6.0
Trials	5	0.08	4.8
Drama	2	0.05	1.5
All genres	50	0.14	5.5

It is also worth noting that *that of/those of* constructions are consistently more frequent in Fiction than in Letters, as far as N/1,000 is concerned. The absolute number of occurrences is greater in Letters in CONCE as a whole, which is due to the fact that this section of the corpus is also considerably larger than that representing Fiction. There is a clear difference between these two genres regarding the use of *that of/those of* constructions, despite the fact that the writers of the letters in the corpus are mostly novelists. Interestingly enough, the corpus also contains samples of letters written by a historian (Thomas Babington Macaulay) and a scientist (Charles Darwin), whose texts are included in the genres of History and Science as well, providing an additional opportunity to look into the use of the constructions on an individual level. It is also worth pointing out that the use of *that of/those of* by the two writers in different genres was not parallel. Whereas Macaulay used *that of/those of* constructions in both his

Table 6.3. *Anaphoric* that of/those of *constructions in the* CONCE *corpus, period 3 (1870–1900).*

Genre	N	N/1,000	Mean
Science	30	0.97	8.0
Debates	15	0.75	5.5
History	22	0.71	4.3
Fiction	7	0.23	5.0
Drama	3	0.08	5.0
Letters	7	0.07	3.3
Trials	2	0.02	1.5
All genres	86	0.27	5.7

letters and historical works, Darwin used the constructions only in his scientific writings (eight occurrences), although the sample of Darwin's correspondence is larger in size than the extract from his *Origin of Species*. More detailed research could be done on the different types of texts written by scientists. An interesting parameter in studies of scientists' letters would be the nature of correspondence, depending to a great extent on the addressee: the expressions a scientist uses when writing to a colleague are likely to be different from the ones directed to a family member.

Considering the use of *that of/those of* in the corpus on the whole, with the results of the three subperiods combined (see table 6.4), it would seem that the constructions are relatively more frequent in works of a scientific nature (the genres Science and History). The clear difference between genres in the corpus is notable. As regards the genre of Debates, the high frequency of *that of/those of* is perhaps not an unexpected result, the institution itself, with its prestigious and official nature, prompting a certain formality. In addition, the speeches made in the British Parliament were possibly to some extent written well in advance, thus being actually far from resembling spontaneous speech (not to mention the possible effect of editing before the transcripts were published).

From the viewpoint of the use of *that of/those of*, the language used in Trials shows a contrast to Debates in that it appears to be closer to ordinary, less formal spoken language. Although one could assume that court proceedings as formal occasions themselves would raise certain expectations on the language used, and result in a greater number of formal expressions, the sequences studied here are, in fact, not at all frequent. However, the formality of the court may be partly reflected in the actual occurrences of *that of/those of* in the texts, as the people using the constructions are, in fact, more often lawyers (who, to some extent, could also prepare their questions in advance) than witnesses examined. Drama texts are written to be spoken on the stage, thus inherently aiming to give an

Table 6.4. *Anaphoric* that of/those of *constructions in the CONCE corpus.*

Genre	N	N/1,000	Mean
Debates	51	0.85	6.8
Science	68	0.67	7.4
History	54	0.58	5.4
Fiction	18	0.16	5.3
Letters	32	0.09	5.4
Drama	8	0.07	3.8
Trials	10	0.05	3.7
All genres	241	0.23	6.1

impression of spontaneity, and therefore the low number of occurrences of *that of/those of*, associated with formality, seems perfectly logical.

The difference between the attested instances of the constructions in question is very interesting in light of the results of Geisler (2002), who examined register variation in the CONCE materials. Carrying out a factor score analysis – based on Biber's framework – on a number of linguistic features (*wh*-questions, hedges, third person pronouns, nominalizations, *by*-passives, to name but a few) associated with 'Involved versus Informational Production', 'Narrative versus Non-narrative Concerns', 'Elaborated Reference versus Situation-dependent Reference', and 'Impersonal versus Non-impersonal Style', he makes observations on the major difference between Debates and Trials remarkably similar to the ones made in the present paper. In his study, it was shown that Trials manifested more speech-based characteristics, whereas Debates were very close to the expository registers Science and History.

Another interesting observation can be made from table 6.4, as it appears that there is some correspondence between the relative frequency of the *that of/those of* sequences and the anaphoric distance allowed in such instances in different genres. In those genres where sequences of anaphoric *that/those* + *of*-phrase are comparatively common, the average number of intervening words between the pronoun and its preceding referent is also greater. The average anaphoric distance is highest in Debates and Science, and lowest in Drama and Trials, with History, Fiction and Letters representing an intermediate position. As noted earlier, on the basis of the study in Biber et al. (1999: 237–40), no direct connection could be perceived between anaphoric distance and the frequency of the expressions in any register, and consequently no direct link could be seen between anaphoric distance and formality either. However, in the case of *that of/those of* constructions studied here, it is interesting to note that the two factors measured show almost parallel tendencies between genres. This would suggest that with this particular anaphoric construction, an association between formality and greater anaphoric distance could perhaps be made.

6   Concluding remarks

The study of anaphoric *that/those* + *of*-phrase sequences in the nineteenth-century material shows that, in the CONCE data, there is no consistent trend in the frequency of their use across time. However, clear frequency differences can be seen in their use according to the genre. As a starting point, it was claimed on the basis of research on twentieth-century usage that the constructions in question are associated with formality. Therefore it is not surprising in itself that the expressions studied were indeed more common in those genres where formal language is more expected. Considering this fact and the possible avenues of further research on the topic, it would be interesting to take a closer look into the diachronic development in the use of the constructions, e.g. to examine the rate at which the increase in their use took place in different genres from the early seventeenth century onwards, contributing to the larger study of the evolving nature of genres as individual types of writing.

Alternative types of anaphoric expressions in corresponding contexts were also discussed, and comparative studies of such expressions of a less formal nature (i.e. *that/those* + *which/who* and *that/those* + participial clause) might likewise be interesting when examining the difference in the levels of formality between genres. Based on the results of the present paper, the issue of anaphoric distance is also worth paying close attention to in further studies on the matter. In comparison with the results of Biber et al. (1999), who examined the demonstrative pronouns as one group of anaphoric expressions, the results of the present study suggest that there might be notable differences between individual expressions with demonstrative pronouns. In this study the anaphoric distance occurring in different genres appears to correspond with the relative frequency of the expression itself, which in turn reflects the level of formality.

7 Adjective comparison in nineteenth-century English

MERJA KYTÖ AND SUZANNE ROMAINE

1 Introduction[1]

The patterns of variation in adjective comparison in a synchronic and diachronic perspective is a topic which has recently attracted a good deal of attention (see Kytö 1996a; Kytö and Romaine 1997, 2000; Leech and Culpeper 1997; and Mondorf 2002 and 2003, for a selective sample of studies). This variation involves competition between the inflectional comparative/superlative (e.g. *happier/happiest*), historically the older form, and the newer periphrastic construction (e.g. *more/most elegant*).[2] The double comparative (*more quicker*) and double superlative (e.g. *most delightfulest*) forms were much less frequent in the history of English. They are now considered non-standard. In this chapter we will extend our analyses by considering patterns of variation in adjective comparison in nineteenth-century English, in the light of the data drawn from the CONCE corpus and, in reference to our earlier work on the topic, the ARCHER corpus (for A Representative Corpus of Historical English Registers, see Biber et al. 1994a and 1994b).

In our studies we have identified some of the major linguistic and extralinguistic factors constraining variation, in particular, word structure and genre. As far as word structure is concerned, we looked at word length and the nature of the word ending as major grammatical determinants influencing the variation, although there are other linguistic factors in need of consideration, as we will show later on in the present study (for earlier observations, see e.g. Leech and Culpeper 1997: 357–8, 366–9, and Mondorf 2002 and 2003).

Our aims in the present study are three-fold. Firstly, we will provide what we hope is 'the very *most delightfulest* tour' (to use one of the rare examples of double forms in the corpus) through CONCE. Our examination of CONCE allows us to extend our understanding of variation in adjective comparison by looking closely at nineteenth-century English, a generally neglected period, at the same time as it allows us to test the potential of CONCE for this type of cross-genre comparative work. The inclusion of texts representative of different genres and, in particular, the inclusion of a large number of personal letters written by both women and men, provide an opportunity to look at both genre and gender-related variation (see section 5). It is not coincidental that the double superlative form cited above was produced by a woman (Anne Thackeray Ritchie). Female letter writers in CONCE use more instances of adjective comparison, both comparatives and superlatives. We will show how certain patterns of adjective comparison, particularly in epistolary formulae, function as stylistic markers of affect.

Secondly, we will examine adjective comparison against patterns of register-related variation, in the light of a multi-dimensional analysis of the genres carried out on a tagged version of CONCE (see Geisler 2002). Although our earlier work illustrates genre as a relevant factor in constraining variation, our examination of ARCHER revealed that the influence of genre is not entirely straightforward (see Kytö and Romaine 2000). Thirdly, we will take a look at the role played by two further linguistic factors determining the variation, i.e. the syntactic function of the forms, and the ensuing clause or expression introduced by *than*. Finally, we will note some remaining issues and problems requiring further research and suggest some ways of investigating them. To begin with, however, we will provide a brief overview of adjective comparison across the history of English.

2 Brief summary of developments in adjective comparison in English

Adjective comparison is treated in quite general or enumerative terms in most grammars of contemporary English (see e.g. Quirk et al. 1985: 458–69; Biber et al. 1999: 521–6), and this also holds for a number of the standard handbooks on the history of English (see e.g. Poutsma 1914; Jespersen 1949). In addition, there are a few specialist philological works, which address the origin of the newer periphrastic constructions with *more* and *most* (e.g. *more/most delightful*; see Knüpfer 1922) and the distribution of the newer forms with the older pattern making use of inflectional endings (e.g. *greater* and *greatest*; see Pound 1901).

In Old English, comparative and superlative forms of adjectives were marked by inflectional endings (apart from a few possible instances of periphrastic forms referred to by Mitchell 1985: 84–5). In the thirteenth century, the periphrastic forms emerged, possibly as a result of Latin (and to a lesser extent French) influence (for a discussion, see Mustanoja 1960: 279). After the fourteenth century until the beginning of the sixteenth century, their use increased steadily, and by the 1500s, they were in as frequent use as in Present-day English (Pound 1901: 19).

The new periphrastic constructions also added one more variant to the system, the multiple or double comparative. In these hybrid comparatives or superlatives, *more* and *most* appear together with the inflectional adjective, e.g. *more easier* and *most boldest*.[3] Three alternative forms of comparison for an adjective such as *happy* were then possible in the Middle and Early Modern English periods: inflectional (*happier/happiest*), periphrastic (*more happy/most happy*) and double (*more happier/most happiest*). The use of these double forms was marginal, both earlier and now. Kytö (1996a), for instance, found no instances of double forms for the post-1640s subperiod of the Early Modern English period represented in the Helsinki Corpus. Due particularly to the continuing influence of standardization, and the condemning of the construction as non-standard by eighteenth-century grammarians, they gradually but nevertheless virtually disappeared from standard written English. Today the double forms are found primarily in the most colloquial registers of spoken English. Thus, the primary variants have always been the inflectional and periphrastic types.

There were only three clear instances of double forms in CONCE, the first from Thomas Morton's play 'The School of Reform' from 1805, and another two from Anne Thackeray Ritchie's letters from the 1870s on:

(1a) – Now I think, if one of them was just to set about talking a little of London kindheartedness and London charity, it would be rather *more truerer*, and quite as becoming.
(Drama, Thomas Morton, 1800–30, p. 70)

(1b) I needn't tell you that Hester and Billy instantly sprang from their beds when I appeared the messenger of sweetness and delight. The bonbon tongs had an immense success, the bonbons are an immenser, and Hester says those red ones are 'the *most deliciousest* things she ever ate.'
(Letters, Anne Thackeray Ritchie, 1870–1900, p. 192)

(1c) Mrs. Ritchie presents her compliments to Monsieur Denis. She also hugs him and gives him a kiss.
His father has piles of maps of Normandy and Brittany and is making out the very *most delightfulest* tour.
(Letters, Anne Thackeray Ritchie, 1870–1900, p. 247)

Our previous studies reveal that after the newer forms were introduced, variation between the newer and older forms proceeded in different directions. After an initial upsurge in the use of the new periphrastic type of comparison in some environments, the newer forms eventually replaced the older ones completely. However, in certain other environments, the newer forms gave way again to the older inflectional type. Thus, we have an interesting case of competition between the two variants. We found that the use of the newer periphrastic forms peaked during the Late Middle English period, but the older inflectional type has been regaining lost ground since the Early Modern period. In that period both types compete rather evenly. By the Modern English period, however, the inflectional forms have reasserted themselves and outnumber the periphrastic forms by roughly 4 to 1, as illustrated in figure 7.1 (adapted from Kytö and Romaine 1997: 335–6). We have established that the crucial period during which the inflectional forms increase and the periphrastic forms decrease to achieve their present-day distribution occurs during the Late Modern English period, i.e. post 1710 (see Kytö 1996a, and Kytö and Romaine 1997, for a more detailed discussion of the main lines of historical development which have shaped the modern system).

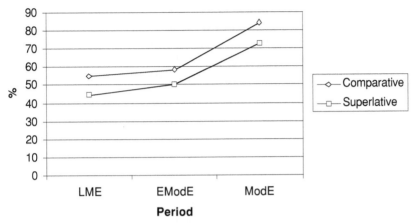

Figure 7.1. Per cent of inflectional forms of adjective comparison from Late Middle English to Modern English (based on table 3 and figure 1 in Kytö and Romaine 1997: 335–6).

Despite observations from linguists writing in the 1950s and 1960s, such as Barber (1964: 131), Fries (1940: 96) and Potter (1969: 146–7), who seemed to think that periphrasis was in the process of replacing inflection entirely, Strang (1970: 58) noted that '[they] may be right, but we lack precise numerical information on the subject'. Our quantitative analyses of ARCHER and the British National Corpus (BNC), in particular, cast considerable doubt on the claims made by Barber, Fries and Potter about the tendency towards increasing use of periphrasis in the latter half of the twentieth century. Although from a typological point of view, the elimination of the inflectional comparative would certainly be a reasonable prediction in line with a more general loss of inflectional morphology over the centuries as English drifted gradually towards a more analytical syntax, the majority of both comparative and superlative adjectives are now of the inflectional type. Nevertheless, variation still exists, with some adjectives (especially those containing more than two syllables) overwhelmingly showing a preference for the newer periphrastic mode of comparison, some (especially monosyllabic adjectives) for the older inflectional form, while some fluctuate between the two. Bauer (1994: 60) concludes that what we have here is a case of 'regularization of a confused situation', resulting in comparison becoming more predictable.

As we have extended our studies to an increasing number of corpora, some of the extralinguistic dimensions of the change have become clearer. For one, our examination of five genres representing both British and American English from the subperiods 1750–1800, 1850–1900, and 1950–90 in ARCHER has revealed that British English is slightly ahead of American English at each subperiod in terms of implementing the change towards the inflectional type (Kytö and Romaine 2000).

As far as genre is concerned, our earlier work has led us to suspect that the periphrastic form has its origin in written registers and that it spread from there to the spoken language, because its use prevailed in more rhetorical texts such as philosophical and religious treatises, as well as correspondence. At this point, however, we turn to CONCE to see what additional light it can shed on these findings from our previous work.

3   Overview of data

This study is based on the CONCE corpus, described in the Introduction to the present volume (see also Kytö, Rudanko and Smitterberg 2000). Contrasting the beginning of the nineteenth century with the rest of the century makes it possible to address some style-related research questions (see Görlach 1999: 158-9) and the transition from eighteenth-century usage to that of Victorian England. Our analysis relies on the classification of adjectives adopted in our previous work in order to facilitate direct comparison. Thus, tables 7.1a and 7.1b show the number of comparative and superlative forms for non-defective adjectives only, together with the percentage of inflectional and periphrastic forms and incidence of occurrence per 100,000 words. The non-defective adjectives include cases where forms of comparison are based on the same root as the positive form. Instances of comparative forms containing 'umlaut' (e.g. *elder/older, eldest/oldest*) are included in the group of non-defective adjectives. The excluded defective group contains cases where the comparative and superlative are not from the same root as the positive (e.g. *good/better/best*).[4]

CONCE contains a total of 1,779 tokens of comparative adjectives and 1,901 superlative adjectives. Overall, the inflectional forms predominate over the periphrastic forms for both comparative and superlative adjectives; 63 per cent of comparatives and 60.2 per cent of superlatives are inflectional (compared with 37 per cent and 39.8 per cent periphrastic respectively). This distribution matches fairly closely the distribution we found for ARCHER in the period 1850–1900 (see Kytö and Romaine 1997: 337). By the end of the twentieth century the proportion of inflectional in relation to periphrastic comparatives increases somewhat more. In contemporary written English, as seen, for example, in the BNC (British National Corpus), inflectional forms account for 74.7 per cent of the instances of comparative forms (and periphrastic forms for 25.3 per cent; Leech and Culpeper 1997: 373).

There is, however, some variation across the subperiods in CONCE. We can observe a steady increase in the inflectional comparatives from period 1 to period 3 (from 57.1 to 67.8 per cent). The superlatives show an increase in inflectional forms from period 1 to period 2 (from 51 to 65.8 per cent), but decline slightly in period 3 (to 63.7 per cent). Nevertheless, for both comparatives and superlatives the trend is towards increasing use of the inflectional forms. The results in both tables 7.1a and 7.1b are statistically significant.[5]

Table 7.1a. *Inflectional versus periphrastic comparative forms in the CONCE corpus; the incidence of the forms per 100,000 words.*

Period	Inflect.	Periphr.	Total	Inflect. %	Periphr. %	Words	Incid. inflect.	Incid. periphr.	Total
1	351	264	615	57.1	42.9	346,176	101.4	76.3	177.7
2	388	214	602	64.5	35.5	341,842	113.5	62.6	176.1
3	381	181	562	67.8	32.2	298,796	127.5	60.6	188.1
1–3	1,120	659	1,779	63.0	37.0	986,814	113.5	66.8	180.3

Table 7.1b. *Inflectional versus periphrastic superlative forms in the CONCE corpus; the incidence of the forms per 100,000 words.*

Period	Inflect.	Periphr.	Total	Inflect. %	Periphr. %	Words	Incid. inflect.	Incid. periphr.	Total
1	333	320	653	51.0	49.0	346,176	96.2	92.4	188.6
2	499	259	758	65.8	34.2	341,842	146.0	75.8	221.7
3	312	178	490	63.7	36.3	298,796	104.4	59.6	164.0
1–3	1,144	757	1,901	60.2	39.8	986,814	115.9	76.7	192.6

To conclude this empirical overview, a methodological note on knockout and other factors is in order. This concerns the superlative uses, in particular, as the category displays a great range of semantic shades that alone or combined with other linguistic factors may promote the use of one variant form or the other. A case in point is the 'absolute' or 'intensifying' meaning of the superlative, as in 'You are very helpful and *most kind*'. The grammar of these expressions is not entirely straightforward in Present-day English; for instance, in the case of evaluative adjectives, when used without a definite determiner, a sentence such as *Della is most efficient* remains ambiguous, meaning either that 'Della is the most efficient of all' or that 'Della is extremely efficient', see example (2) (Quirk et al. 1985: 466). The 'intensifying' interpretation seems only to hold for the periphrastic category in Present-day English and not for inflectional uses (according to native speakers of standard English).

(2) Della is *most efficient*. [='the most efficient of all' or 'extremely efficient'] (Quirk et al. 1985: 466)

However, nineteenth-century English displays more variation in the grammar of superlatives. In addition to instances of periphrastic superlatives used with the indefinite article, as in (3a), to indicate intensified meaning, an instance of inflectional use was recorded, given in (3b).

(3a) – altogether make me think Dr. Lane innocent & that it is *a most cruel* case.
(Letters, Charles Darwin, 1850–70, p. VII, 116)

(3b) I leave it to T[om] M. to make my apologies for troubling you with a commission – which is to procure me 5 shades of drab rug worsted from the darkest drab nearly black to white included – 2 pounds of each shade; and 6 pounds of *a lightest* bright yellow.
(Letters, Sara Hutchinson, 1800–30, p. 54)

Moreover, inflectional forms in attributive uses (without the indefinite article) can also convey the intensified meaning, as in example (4).

(4) The walls are painted a delicate French gray, relieved by a four-foot dado of ebonised panelling, and the ceiling of *palest* primrose.
(Fiction, Mary Braddon, 1870–1900, p. II, 98)

As in Present-day English, nineteenth-century English periphrastic forms with the definite article can convey either the intensifying meaning, as in example (5a) or the superlative meaning proper, as in example (5b).

(5a) Here he adopted a strange and desperate measure; he sent four papers to his father, filled with the *most extravagant* and *improbable* treasons, in all of which he avowed his participation, [. . .]
(History, Henry Milman, 1800–30, p. II, 119)

(5b) I think he was the *most generous* man I have ever known; the *most forward* to praise what he thought good, the *most willing* to admire, the *most free* from all thought of himself in praising and in admiring, and the *most incapable* of being made ill-natured, or even indifferent, by having to support ill-natured attacks himself.
(Letters, Matthew Arnold, 1870–1900, p. 140)

There are also ambiguous instances allowing both readings, as in (6).

(6) Even then it is often impossible to determine whether an elevation or depression even of several feet has occurred, because there is nothing novel in a band of sand and shingle of unequal breadth above the level of the sea, marking the point reached by the waves during springtides or the *most violent* tempests.
(Science, Charles Lyell, 1800–30, p. 416)

Owing to this variation, our approach has been to consider the superlative category a morpho-syntactic variable that in terms of semantics operates along a continuum of similarity of meaning. A rather broad view of semantic equivalence has been set here on the sameness of meaning of syntactic variables (as proposed by Jacobson 1980: 27; cf. Romaine 1984: 410–11, for a discussion), and all instances of superlative forms have been included in the present analysis. Further screening rounds are needed in order to pin down the influence of semantic constraints.

4   Genre variation

Naturally, there is a great deal of variation across the seven genres and three subperiods, as shown in tables 7.2a and 7.2b. Overall, the use of the inflectional type is on the increase, but there are exceptions to this general trend. In period 1, for instance, Debates have more periphrastic comparatives (60.6 per cent) than inflectional comparatives, as do Drama, Fiction and History with 62.5, 52.4, and 57.4 per cent periphrastic comparatives respectively. Similarly, in period 2, Trials also have more periphrastic (73 per cent) than inflectional (27 per cent) comparatives. Overall, the rate of occurrence of inflectional comparatives ranges from as low as 27 per cent in Trials in period 2 to as high as 87.4 per cent, also in Trials, but in period 3. Some of the genres also show a higher incidence of inflectional comparatives in period 2 than period 3 (e.g. Drama, Fiction, and Letters), and Science has the highest occurrence of inflectional forms in period 1. The results for Trials, Drama and History are statistically significant.[6]

As far as the superlative adjectives are concerned, we can see in table 7.2b that Debates in period 1 again show more periphrastic (80.3 per cent) than inflectional forms, and so do History and Science with 65.9 per cent and 55 per cent periphrastic forms. Likewise, in period 2 History displays more periphrastic (53.8 per cent) than inflectional superlatives, and so does Science, with 51.5 per cent periphrastic superlatives. Again, as noted in connection with the comparative adjectives, the superlatives also show great variation in the range of inflectional forms from a low of 19.7 per cent in Debates in period 1 to a high of 79.6 per cent in Fiction in period 3. In addition, some genres also show a higher incidence of superlative comparatives in period 2 than in period 3, namely Debates, Trials and Letters. The results for History are again significant for the superlative forms, as they are for Debates, Letters and Fiction.[7]

The above-mentioned exceptions to the general trend towards increasing use of the inflectional type suggest that some genres such as Trials, Debates and Science may not be internally homogeneous. Some of the anomalies may also be due to a range of factors, among them the nature of the texts included in each genre, and/or insufficient data as well as the word choices made by individual writers. The Science texts, for example, represent different fields of science such as Chemistry, Geology, population studies, etc., Debates and Drama have much lower word counts than other genres, and the Letters genre accounts for nearly a third of the material in CONCE. Furthermore, the Debates texts in period 1 have only indirect speech, while those in period 3 have direct speech, and period 2 contains both direct and indirect speech. Overall, the distribution of the superlative forms in Debates runs counter to the prevailing pattern due to the very high incidence of periphrastic forms (80.3 per cent) in period 1. In Letters the high frequency of inflectional superlatives (74.3 per cent) in period 2 is due to the occurrence of *dearest* in 200 (60.6 per cent) out of the 330 forms (see section 5). Both History and Science show a slight preference for the use of periphrastic superlatives over inflectional ones, thus constituting exceptions to the general trend in favor of inflectional forms.

Table 7.2a. *Inflectional versus periphrastic comparative forms in the seven genres and three subperiods; the incidence of the forms per 100,000 words.*

Genre	Period	Infl.	Peri.	Total	Infl. %	Peri. %	Words	Incid. infl.	Incid. peri.	Total
Debates	1	13	20	33	39.4	60.6	19,908	65.3	100.5	165.8
	2	28	19	47	59.6	40.4	19,385	144.4	98.0	242.5
	3	27	17	44	61.4	38.6	19,947	135.4	85.2	220.6
	Total	68	56	124	54.8	45.2	59,240	114.8	94.5	209.3
Trials	1	21	8	29	72.4	27.6	62,360	33.7	12.8	46.5
	2	10	27	37	27.0	73.0	60,570	16.5	44.6	61.1
	3	76	11	87	87.4	12.6	67,588	112.4	16.3	128.7
	Total	107	46	153	69.9	30.1	190,518	56.2	24.1	80.3
Drama	1	3	5	8	37.5	62.5	31,311	9.6	16.0	25.6
	2	21	4	25	84.0	16.0	29,543	71.1	13.5	84.6
	3	17	8	25	68.0	32.0	29,090	58.4	27.5	85.9
	Total	41	17	58	70.7	29.3	89,944	45.6	18.9	64.5
Fiction	1	39	43	82	47.6	52.4	42,032	92.8	102.3	195.1
	2	47	23	70	67.1	32.9	39,045	120.4	58.9	179.3
	3	20	15	35	57.1	42.9	30,113	66.4	49.8	116.2
	Total	106	81	187	56.7	43.3	111,190	95.3	72.8	168.2
Letters	1	95	87	182	52.2	47.8	121,624	78.1	71.5	149.6
	2	131	74	205	63.9	36.1	131,116	99.9	56.4	156.4
	3	93	73	166	56.0	44.0	90,891	102.3	80.3	182.6
	Total	319	234	553	57.7	42.3	343,631	92.8	68.1	160.9
History	1	43	58	101	42.6	57.4	30,904	139.1	187.7	326.8
	2	35	22	57	61.4	38.6	30,504	114.7	72.1	186.9
	3	54	27	81	66.7	33.3	30,564	176.7	88.3	265.0
	Total	132	107	239	55.2	44.8	91,972	143.5	116.3	259.9
Science	1	137	43	180	76.1	23.9	38,037	360.2	113.0	473.2
	2	116	45	161	72.0	28.0	31,679	366.2	142.0	508.2
	3	94	30	124	75.8	24.2	30,603	307.2	98.0	405.2
	Total	347	118	465	74.6	25.4	100,319	345.9	117.6	463.5

Table 7.2b. *Inflectional versus periphrastic superlative forms in the seven genres and three subperiods; the incidence of the forms per 100,000 words.*

Genre	Period	Infl.	Peri.	Total	Infl. %	Peri. %	Words	Incid. infl.	Incid. peri.	Total
Debates	1	12	49	61	19.7	80.3	19,908	60.3	246.1	306.4
	2	23	17	40	57.5	42.5	19,385	118.6	87.7	206.3
	3	14	11	25	56.0	44.0	19,947	70.2	55.1	125.3
	Total	49	77	126	38.9	61.1	59,240	82.7	130.0	212.7
Trials	1	17	8	25	68.0	32.0	62,360	27.3	12.8	40.1
	2	33	14	47	70.2	29.8	60,570	54.5	23.1	77.6
	3	9	7	16	56.3	43.8	67,588	13.3	10.4	23.7
	Total	59	29	88	67.0	33.0	190,518	31.0	15.2	46.2
Drama	1	20	12	32	62.5	37.5	31,311	63.9	38.3	102.2
	2	20	17	37	54.1	45.9	29,543	67.7	57.5	125.2
	3	41	14	55	74.5	25.5	29,090	140.9	48.1	189.1
	Total	81	43	124	65.3	34.7	89,944	90.1	47.8	137.9
Fiction	1	43	36	79	54.4	45.6	42,032	102.3	85.6	188.0
	2	24	20	44	54.5	45.5	39,045	61.5	51.2	112.7
	3	39	10	49	79.6	20.4	30,113	129.5	33.2	162.7
	Total	106	66	172	61.6	38.4	111,190	95.3	59.4	154.7
Letters	1	177	117	294	60.2	39.8	121,624	145.5	96.2	241.7
	2	330	114	444	74.3	25.7	131,116	251.7	86.9	338.6
	3	131	88	219	59.8	40.2	90,891	144.1	96.8	240.9
	Total	638	319	957	66.7	33.3	343,631	185.7	92.8	278.5
History	1	28	54	82	34.1	65.9	30,904	90.6	174.7	265.3
	2	36	42	78	46.2	53.8	30,504	118.0	137.7	255.7
	3	40	18	58	69.0	31.0	30,564	130.9	58.9	189.8
	Total	104	114	218	47.7	52.3	91,972	113.1	124.0	237.0
Science	1	36	44	80	45.0	55.0	38,037	94.6	115.7	210.3
	2	33	35	68	48.5	51.5	31,679	104.2	110.5	214.7
	3	38	30	68	55.9	44.1	30,603	124.2	98.0	222.2
	Total	107	109	216	49.5	50.5	100,319	106.7	108.7	215.3

In cases such as these a more sophisticated analysis of the genres can be helpful. Further evidence in support of the anomalous behavior of Trials in period 2, in particular, comes from Geisler's (2002) multidimensional analysis of the CONCE genres. Using the multi-dimensional register analysis of the type pioneered by Biber (1988), Geisler identified three very different dimensions, the 'involved', 'narrative' and 'non-abstract' dimensions, on which these trials show high values.[8] He also found a number of linguistic features with extremely high values for Trials in period 2, e.g. modals, suasive verbs (e.g. *command, demand, instruct*, etc.), demonstratives, present tense verb forms, first person pronouns, nominalizations, passives, *wh*-relatives, pied piping and attributive adjectives. The co-occurrence of high values for both first person pronouns and passivization is odd. Also odd is the low score for *wh*-questions for Trials in period 2 because otherwise they score high in this genre, as one would expect, given the primary function of Trials in establishing who has done what to whom, where, when, and why. Thus, Geisler's multi-dimensional analysis shows that Trials behave oddly in several respects, independently of variation in adjective comparison. However, further study of this genre (as yet not investigated synchronically or diachronically using multi-dimensional analysis) will be needed to determine whether possible differences in cross-examination techniques and other variable factors might come into play in the patterning of various linguistic features including adjective comparison in trial proceedings.

Meanwhile, a closer look at the four texts included in Trials in period 2 reveals that three of the cases are civil cases (e.g. libel, perjury, etc.) and the fourth is a criminal case of poisoning, one of the most famous criminal cases in English legal history. The occurrence of a large number of instances of periphrastic comparatives (73 per cent) is due to the testimony of a surgeon's assistant. He uses a large number of adjectives, whose structure favours periphrastic forms on grounds of length measured in terms of number of syllables (e.g. *aggravated, comfortable, difficult, complicated, convenient*, etc.). Words of three or more syllables are almost always compared periphrastically. Moreover, this surgeon's assistant also uses periphrastic comparison for some disyllabic and monosyllabic adjectives (e.g. *more long, more easy*), which one would normally expect to be compared inflectionally (see (7)). In contemporary English, monosyllabic adjectives are nearly always compared inflectionally.

This shows that it would be short-sighted to neglect the importance of stylistic factors such as speakers' needs for emphasis and clarity. Although some scholars have touched on this, it has not been systematically investigated. Some time ago Curme (1931: 504), for instance, argued that the periphrastic form had a stylistic advantage because the use of a separate word (*more/most*) instead of an inflectional ending allowed speakers to place additional stress on the comparative element rather than on the adjective and its meaning (see also Jespersen 1949: 347–9 for some observations on speaker choice). This could certainly be a factor in Trials, where establishing degree is a critical factor in certain kinds of evidence. In (7), for instance, *more long* is used to specify more particularly the size and shape of a book that is the subject of questioning. We will turn to the role of the syntactic factors that may lead to the use of periphrastic forms of monosyllabic adjectives (cf. Leech and Culpeper 1997: 357) in section 6.

(7) – Will you describe what sort of a book it was? A dark book, with a gold band round the edge. – About what sized book was it? Not a very large one, with a clasp at one end: it was not exactly a square one; rather *more long*. – Had you seen him in possession of it when he had stopped at the Talbot Arms before? Yes. – On his way to the Liverpool races? Yes. – The same book? The same book. – I think you said it was rather *more long*, with a gold border or band? Yes.
(Trials, William Palmer, 1850–70, p. 41)

Looking at the examples in Debates for period 1 we can also see at least one reason why periphrastic superlatives are more common than inflectional superlatives. Here again, word structure plays a role, as most of the adjectives are polysyllabic; only eleven out of forty-nine (22 per cent) of the adjectives are disyllabic, and one monosyllabic adjective, *dead*, appears in the periphrastic form *most dead*. Word endings are also important in favouring the periphrastic forms. Adjectives ending in *-ous* (e.g. *gracious*) and *-ful* (e.g. *painful*) almost always form both the comparative and superlative periphrastically by the Early Modern English period. A further three of the eleven adjectives have these endings. Generally speaking, periphrastic superlatives greatly outnumber the inflectional ones from the Late Middle English period onwards (see Kytö and Romaine 1997).[9]

5   Male and female usage

As we mentioned at the outset, the Letters in CONCE present a good opportunity for the study of individual linguistic features, and in particular, for a comparison of male and female usage. They may also offer us a potential window into more informal and colloquial language, as has been noted by a number of historians of English such as Wyld (1936). Görlach (1999: 149–50), for example, writes that letters are interesting because 'they reflect the social and functional relations between sender and addressee to a very high degree – only spoken texts can equal this range'. Multi-dimensional analysis of the type used by Biber (1988) also confirms that although personal letters are written and thus share some features with other written genres, on the whole they are closer to spoken genres than other forms of writing. They usually have an involved (rather than informational) focus, for instance, and share many of the interactive and affective characteristics of conversation (e.g. high frequency of personal pronouns *I* and *you*, contractions, emphatics (including *more* and *most*), and private verbs such as *feel*, *love*, etc.).[10]

In Biber's study (1988) personal letters scored higher in terms of the use of these features characteristic of conversation than did all other non-conversational spoken genres such as broadcasts. Like Trials, Letters are high in *wh*-questions, as one would expect, because these are used primarily in interactive discourse.

Geisler's (2002) multi-dimensional analysis of the CONCE genres confirms that Letters (along with Drama and Trials) score high on Dimension 1 (involved vs informational production), expectedly, but rather low on Dimension 5 (abstract vs non-abstract information). Similarly, in their study of 500 texts and twenty-four genre categories, Biber and Finegan (1989) found that personal letters turned out to be considerably more affective than conversation, a finding also supported by Besnier's (1989) research on personal letters written on the Nukulaelae atoll in Tuvalu. Of Biber and Finegan's texts only fifteen (3 per cent) made extensive use of affect markers; seven of the fifteen texts were personal letters, comprising 70 per cent of the cluster they designated as 'emphatic marking of affect'.

Indeed, some of these more general characteristics of personal letters as opposed to other written genres have also been identified as features of women's conversational style, e.g. involvement, display of emotions and personal affect (see e.g. Coates 1996). The greater use of these features reflects the functions conversation serves for women, with an emphasis on concern for others and for maintaining solidarity and co-operative relationships. In fact, in one of the first works to discuss the notion of 'women's language', Lakoff (1975) mentioned quite some time ago the use of what she called 'empty' adjectives expressing speaker's feelings, and emphasis. Although Lakoff did not collect data to support her claims, and Biber and Finegan did not explore the dimension of gender, the latter (1989) included adjectives as a linguistic feature contributing to affect in English texts. It is interesting that the female letter writers in CONCE use more instances of adjective comparison, both comparatives and superlatives (4.6 instances per 1,000 words, N = 834) than men (4.2 instances per 1,000 words, N = 676).[11]

Tables 7.3a[12] and 7.3b[13] display the incidence of inflectional and periphrastic comparatives and superlatives in men's and women's letters for the three time periods (for the word counts used for calculations, see the Introduction to the present volume). Although there are differences between men and women in the use of inflectional and periphrastic comparatives, it is of interest to note that the use of superlative forms peaks noticeably in period 2 for both men and women and that women lead in the use of the inflectional superlatives over men in all three periods (table 7.3b).

We have already pointed out that the high frequency of inflectional superlatives in period 2 is due to the occurrence of *dearest* in 200 (60.6 per cent) out of 330 instances, most of which occur in opening and closing formulae. The superlative can be considered a highly marked affective form contrasting with the unmarked formula *dear*, as can be seen in example (8) from a letter written by William Makepeace Thackeray to Harriet Thackeray.

(8) My *dearest* Minnykins. I am in beautiful rooms that are so awfully noisy that they drive me out of the town and yesterday I ran away to a place called Balloch at the end of Loch Lomond and had a row on the lake for 3 hours with Mr. James in attendance and could not see Ben Lomond for the mist: [. . .]
(Letters, William Thackeray, 1850–70, p. 33)

Table 7.3a. *Inflectional and periphrastic comparatives in men's and women's letters; incidence per 1,000 words.*

	Men						Women				
Period	Infl.	Incid.	Perip.	Incid.	Total	Incid.	Infl.	Incid.	Perip.	Incid.	Total	Incid.
1	50	1.0	45	0.9	95	1.8	45	0.6	42	0.6	87	1.3
2	60	0.9	26	0.4	86	1.3	71	1.1	48	0.8	119	1.9
3	37	0.9	27	0.7	64	1.6	56	1.1	46	0.9	102	2.0
1–3	147	0.9	98	0.6	245	1.5	172	0.9	136	0.7	308	1.7

Table 7.3b. *Inflectional and periphrastic superlatives in men's and women's letters; incidence per 1,000 words.*

	Men						Women				
Period	Infl.	Incid.	Perip.	Incid.	Total	Incid.	Infl.	Incid.	Perip.	Incid.	Total	Incid.
1	75	1.4	56	1.1	131	2.5	102	1.5	61	0.9	163	2.4
2	144	2.1	74	1.1	218	3.2	186	3.0	40	0.6	226	3.6
3	46	1.1	36	0.9	82	2.0	85	1.7	52	1.0	137	2.7
1–3	265	1.6	166	1.0	431	2.7	373	2.1	153	0.8	526	2.9

Most of the men use *dearest* in addressing women, usually wives, sisters or mothers, and only rarely for male addressees. Women, however, address each other as well as men (usually husbands) with *dearest*. Women also end their letters with formulae containing inflectional and periphrastic superlatives such as *Yours with the truest and most heartfelt affection, Yours with the deepest and truest love, With the fondest affection, the deepest love, Your own most deeply attached* (Eliza Wilson). Sometimes the women even use forms such as *dearest, dearest*, or *dearest dear*, or the superlative followed by title rather than first name, e.g. *My dearest Mrs. Martin*. In fact, in terms of frequency it is the simple form *dear* which is marked, as both men and women use *dearest* more frequently. This is an indication of the intimate nature of the letters included in CONCE.

Although both men and women use *dearest*, women use the form to a much greater extent, as can be seen in table 7.4, which shows the figures for inflectional superlatives for men and women after all the tokens of *dearest* have been removed. Removing tokens of *dearest* reduces the amount of data from 638 examples to 319, eliminating 319 adjectives, or half of the data. In the case of the women's data, only 144 superlative adjectives are left once 229 examples (61 per cent of the data) are removed from the original total of 373. For the men, the reduction

Table 7.4. *Inflectional superlatives in men's and women's letters (instances of* dearest *removed from the figures); incidence per 1,000 words.*

Inflectional superlatives	Men	Incidence	Women	Incidence
1	61	1.2	59	0.9
2	79	1.1	51	0.8
3	35	0.9	34	0.7
Total	175	1.1	144	0.8

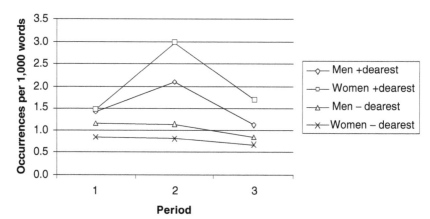

Figure 7.2. Inflectional superlatives in men's and women's letters (with and without *dearest*).

is less dramatic; after removing ninety tokens of *dearest* (34 per cent of the data) from a total of 265, 175 superlatives are left. As figure 7.2 shows, it is men's rather than women's greater usage of the inflectional superlatives in periods 1 and 2 which needs explanation.

Again, we need to look at actual examples to illuminate the quantitative findings; for space limitations, in what follows we will focus on period 2. The adjectives contained in the men's inflectional superlatives are overwhelmingly monosyllabic (e.g. *dull, great, kind, large, long*), and hence favour inflectional forms. Over a quarter of the data consists of the form *kindest*, which quite often occurs as a closing formula, as in *kindest love, kindest regards*, etc. Only four adjectives are not monosyllabic (*gentle, pleasant, simple, curious*). Those ending in syllabic /l/ such as *gentle* and *simple* favour inflectional comparison; *curious* would be expected to show preference for periphrastic comparison on account of its ending, but appears here as *curiousest* (see (9a); for an instance of *pleasantest*, see (9b)).

(9a) – Didn't I tell you what a great girl Susy has grown and Johnny is greater
than ever for his age: and I have been staying these last 2 days here with
Mr. Reid who was an officer on board the Prince Regent and brought me
to my Aunt Ritchie from the ship – a kind old affectionate gentleman with
the *curiousest* love of children, and faithful memory of old times.
(Letters, William Thackeray, 1850–70, p. 97)

(9b) – Think over this well & deliberately, & do not be guided by fleeting
motives. You shall settle for yourself, whatever you think will be really best,
not *pleasantest*, shall be done –
(Letters, Charles Darwin, 1850–70, p. VI, 434)

By contrast, most of the superlative adjectives which are compared periphrastically are polysyllabic, with the exception of three which are monosyllabic (i.e. *kind*,
glad and *cruel*) and twenty which are disyllabic (e.g. *attached, blessed, likely, gloomy,
happy, sincere, humble, pious, charming, clever, useful, splendid, friendly, stupid,
irksome, striking, monstrous*); some of the disyllabic ones would favor periphrastic
comparison owing to word endings such as *-ous, -ful*. The few instances of *most
kind* occur in syntactic contexts which promote the use of the periphrastic form,
as in (10a) and (10b). In addition to the syntactic position favouring the use of
the periphrastic form in these examples, attention will also need to be paid to
semantic considerations (for absolute superlatives, see section 3, above).

(10a) I have received your letters. I cannot think now on subject, but soon will.
But I can see that you have acted with more kindness & so has Lyell even
than I could have expected from you both *most kind* as you are.
(Letters, Charles Darwin, 1850–70, p. VII, 121)

(10b) But you are too generous to sacrifice so much time & kindness. – It is most
generous, *most kind*.
(Letters, Charles Darwin, 1850–70, p. VII, 122)

The women's inflectional superlative adjectives are also predominantly monosyllabic and include some of the same adjectives as the men use (e.g. *true, kind,
long*). However, there are not so many instances of *kindest*; women prefer instead
deepest (which the men do not use at all) and *truest* (which is used only twice by
the men); for examples, see (11a)–(11b).

(11a) Don't give me up, dear Mr. Ruskin! My husband's *truest* regards, and
farewell from both of us! I would fain be
Your affectionate friend,
ELIZABETH BARRETT BROWNING.
(Letters, Elizabeth Barrett Browning, 1850–70, p. 215)

(11b) Mama sends her kind regards and I dare say Sophy would have thought
of doing the same had she not been cross at my writing to you instead of
Claverton, which however I am going to do now.
Yours with the *deepest* and *truest* love,
ELIZA WILSON
(Letters, Eliza Wilson, 1850–70, p. 460)

Table 7.5. *Inflectional and periphrastic comparative forms in disyllabic adjectives.*

Period	Inflectional	%	Periphrastic	%	Total
1	25	21.9	89	78.1	114
3	50	40.0	75	60.0	125
Total	75	31.4	164	68.6	239

There are only six adjectives that are not monosyllabic (*clever, happy, hasty, noisy, pleasant, simple*); of these, the ones ending in -*y* generally favour inflectional comparison. When we look at the superlative adjectives that are periphrastic in form, we find that they are also predominantly polysyllabic. Only thirteen are disyllabic (e.g. *anxious, cordial, gentle, happy, heartfelt, intense, rambling, striking, thankful, sovereign*). There are two instances of *most kind*, both in contexts promoting the use of the periphrastic form, e.g. *She is most kind*.

6   Comparative forms: syntactic position and the ensuing *than*

So far we have touched upon the syntactic position of the adjective as a factor influencing the choice of the superlative form. With comparative forms, a more systematic survey was carried out in order to compare the results with those presented for Present-day English by Leech and Culpeper in their 1997 study.

In their study, Leech and Culpeper set out to examine contexts '[w]here there is a fairly even and realistic choice between the inflectional and periphrastic forms', with the intention of discovering 'what factors determine preference for one or the other form' (1997: 364). They decided to focus on disyllabic words, in particular, examining a subset of the ten most frequent adjectives found in the 90-million-word written component of the British National Corpus, totalling 261 instances of inflectional comparative forms and 490 instances of periphrastic forms (the adjectives were: *deadly, friendly, handsome, lively, polite, ready, remote, stupid, tender, unhappy*).

As the discussion of men's and women's use of adjectives in CONCE already gave reason to believe, disyllabic words remain the locus for most variation. In our data, in monosyllabic adjectives inflectional forms prevail in 96 per cent of the instances (N = 671), and in adjectives with more than two syllables, periphrastic comparison is the rule in 99 per cent of the instances (N = 239).

In table 7.5, the results are presented for period 1 and period 3, to focus on the situation at the beginning and at the end of the century (the figures are statistically significant).[14] We can see that the number of inflectional instances doubles across the century; the figure obtained for period 3 is close to the corresponding figure obtained by Leech and Culpeper for their data, 35 per cent (N = 751).

Table 7.6a. *Disyllabic comparative forms: attributive uses.*

Period	Inflectional	%	Periphrastic	%	Total
1	15	31.3	33	68.7	48
3	29	56.9	22	43.1	51
Total	44	44.4	55	55.6	99

Table 7.6b. *Disyllabic comparative forms: predicative uses.*

Period	Inflectional	%	Periphrastic	%	Total
1	10	15.2	56	84.8	66
3	21	23.4	53	71.6	74
Total	31	22.1	109	77.9	140

In their study, Leech and Culpeper found that predicative rather than attributive function favoured the periphrastic comparative form. They included in their final figure instances of predicative complements as in 'The gas lamps looked *brighter*, the spiked railings *more friendly*' and instances such as in 'make me *more unhappy* and ashamed', 'Much *more friendly*, don't you think my dear?', and 'Someone younger and *more handsome*' (p. 366). The majority of the comparatives in attributive position were inflectional, 57.7 per cent, whereas the majority of those in predicative position (according to their broad definition), 67.2 per cent, were periphrastic. The corresponding figures obtained for disyllabic adjectives in the CONCE corpus are given in tables 7.6a and 7.6b (the results in table 7.6a are statistically significant).[15]

We can see that the figure of 56.9 per cent obtained for inflectional forms in attributive uses for period 3 closely resembles that obtained for Present-day English (57.7 per cent); there is a rise in the figures across the century. Correspondingly, in predicative uses periphrastic forms dominate, with 71.6 per cent, a figure slightly higher than the 67.2 per cent obtained for Present-day English. The syntactic position of the adjectives was thus already of importance in nineteenth-century English (when tested against each other, the totals in tables 7.6a and 7.6b proved statistically significant).[16]

The final linguistic factor included in this quantitative survey is the influence of ensuing *than*. According to Leech and Culpeper, and as claimed in standard grammar books, 'there would be a tendency to prefer periphrastic forms when the comparative was followed, whether immediately or more remotely, by a *than*' (as in 'some *more deadly* reason *than* that'; 'looking both younger and *handsomer than* you remember'; p. 367). Perhaps somewhat disappointingly, their results were roughly the same for both forms of comparative, 22.7 per cent for periphrastic and 21.8 per cent for inflectional forms. The following *than* is obviously less frequent, overall, than one might intuitively presume, the authors concluded. In the CONCE corpus, the corresponding figures were somewhat higher, 34.8 per cent for periphrastic forms (N = 164) and 28 per cent for inflectional forms (N = 75) (however, the results were not statistically significant). Either the influence of the factor has weakened over the twentieth century or else differences in the genre and other corpus compilation parameters may be at work here.

7   Concluding remarks

Our analysis of patterns of variation in adjective comparison in CONCE establishes a steady increase in the use of inflectional forms throughout the nineteenth century, with a significant difference in the proportion of inflectional to periphrastic forms at the beginning and end of the century. Even by the end of the nineteenth century, however, the system does not match the present-day distribution exactly.

We have tried to show that a micro-linguistic quantitative examination of only one feature, albeit a complicated one such as adjective comparison, can easily lose sight of the larger picture unless it makes reference to the influence of genre as well as individual choice. With respect to genre, it has been illuminating to have a multi-dimensional analysis to refer to as a baseline for addressing questions of internal homogeneity of genres. As far as individual choice is concerned, we have shown that without careful examination of the data it would have been all too easy to conclude that there were significant gender differences in patterns of adjective comparison. The analysis of syntactic functions and the use of comparative forms showed that usage in the last decades of the nineteenth century already came close to present-day usage whilst that of the early decades of the century still belonged to the past in this respect. This ties in well with what Görlach has said about the pre-1830 period, i.e. that '[e]arly 19th-century writers largely built on 18th-century foundations, in literary and expository texts, and this continuity makes many pre-1830 texts look quite "classical"' (1999: 158–9).

Notes

1. Sections of this paper have been presented at the *Determinants of Grammatical Variation in English Symposium* in Paderborn (Germany), on 23–4 June 2000, and at the *Late Modern English Conference* in Edinburgh, on 29 August–1 September 2001. We are grateful for the feedback and ideas that the organizers and participants of these conferences generously gave us.
2. In fact, no inflection is involved in the forms we are calling 'inflectional' (Pound 1901: 2), but we follow conventional terminology (see Quirk et al. 1985; Biber et al.

1999). Our study is limited to gradable adjectives, excluding adverb comparison. Our study also excludes negative adjective comparisons with *less/least* because there is no corresponding inflectional form. They are in any case rare.

3. Technically speaking, most of these forms are periphrastic, apart from those involving defective adjectives such as *worser*, *bestest*, etc., which are inflectional.

4. For observations on the use of the non-defective and defective forms of adjective comparison in the history of English, see Kytö and Romaine (1997: 331–3). Owing to lack of space, we will need to discuss the use of the defective forms in CONCE in another context.

5. The chi-square values for table 7.1a and table 7.1b are 15.343 and 35.584, respectively; $p < 0.05$; df $= 2$.

6. The chi-square values are as follows: 45.041 (Trials), 6.478 (Drama; as some of the expected values are less than 5, the chi-square result may not be valid for this genre) and 11.706 (History); df $= 2$; $p < 0.05$.

7. The chi-square values are as follows: 16.627 (History), 18.388 (Debates), 21.865 (Letters) and 9.351 (Fiction); df $= 2$; $p < 0.05$.

8. A linguistic dimension consists of a grouping of linguistic features identified as having a partly shared functional load. A small number of dimensions define a continuum of variation, and can be used to specify textual relations among different kinds of texts. Thus, face-to-face conversation and telephone conversations have relatively high scores on the dimension of involved vs informational production but academic prose and official documents have low scores. Fiction scores high on the dimension of narrative concerns, while academic prose and official documents score low, etc.

9. One way of overcoming some of the discrepancies in sample size would be to pool the data for speech-related genres such as Trials and Drama, and for academic written genres such as History and Science, and compare these with Letters, a genre occupying in certain respects an intermediate position between speech and writing. However, as this did not lead to greater clarity, there is little point in discussing those results further.

10. Professional letters are, however, quite different in terms of their degree of involved vs informational focus. Biber (1988: 132–3), for instance, found that they contained fewer features that refer directly to personal emotions or to the interaction between readers and writers. Moreover, professional letters can be highly informational and are often written and revised with considerable care. Thus, they often show a greater degree of lexical variety and informational density compared with personal letters.

11. However, these overall incidence figures are not statistically significant ($p < 0.05$). As no statistical significance tests can be carried out on normalized figures directly, the numbers of the occurrences in the categories have here been tested against the word counts in the respective samples. It was deemed possible to use the word counts as such even though the figures included the actual occurrences of the comparative and superlative forms. This was because the numbers of occurrences were relatively small compared with the word counts and because exploratory calculations carried out with reduced word counts did not show major differences in the chi-square values obtained.

12. The differences over time in table 7.3a are not statistically significant.

13. The results obtained for the women's use of superlatives are statistically significant (the chi-square value is 24.925; d.f. = 2; p < 0.001).
14. The chi-square value is 9.041; d.f. = 1; p < 0.01.
15. For table 7.6a, the chi-square value is 6.57; d.f. = 1; p < 0.05.
16. The chi-square value is 13.395; d.f. = 1; p < 0.001.

8 Nonfinite complement clauses in the nineteenth century: the case of *remember*

CHRISTIAN MAIR

1 Introduction

The vast and complex system of nonfinite clausal complements in Present-day English has attracted scholarly attention from syntacticians of virtually every theoretical persuasion. While not understood in every detail, the major outlines of present-day usage, including regional and stylistic variation, have been documented and analysed satisfactorily. What is covered far less well, however, is the history of this complicated system, in particular in its more recent stages since c. 1800. This is all the more surprising since in contrast to word order or the forms of questions and negation, where after rapid developments during the Early Modern English period a degree of stabilization set in in the early nineteenth century, there is every indication that usage of infinitives, participles and gerunds has continued changing with unabated vigour also in the past two centuries.

In two related studies (Mair 2002a, 2002b), I have shown this to be the case for (a) the use of gerunds and infinitives with the verbs *begin* and *start*, (b) the variable use of *from* with gerunds dependent on *prevent*, and (c) the use of bare vs *to*-infinitives with *help*. In the present paper I propose to look at the complementation of *remember*; as in the companion studies, the *OED* quotation base on CD-ROM will be used as a 'corpus', making possible the study of change and variability which – for lack of sufficient data – cannot be investigated on the basis of smaller standard historical corpora such as ARCHER.

2 The functional division of gerunds and infinitives after *remember*

As any pedagogical or scholarly grammar of modern standard English will unfailingly point out, the gerund complement with *remember* is 'retrospective', implying that what is expressed is chronologically prior to the act of remembering, while the infinitival complement is 'prospective', giving the verb *remember* the sense '(take care) not to forget'. Thus, Quirk et al. state:

For three verbs *forget*, *remember*, and *regret*, the 'potentiality'/'performance' distinction becomes extended into the past so that there is a temporal (as well as in part modal) difference between the two constructions. The infinitive construction indicates that the action or event takes place after (and as a result of) the mental process denoted by the verb has begun, while the reverse is true for the participle construction, which refers to a preceding event or occasion coming to mind at the time indicated by the main verb. (1985: 1193)

A sentence such as – to choose their example –

(1) I *remembered to fill* out the form.

means 'I remembered that I was to fill out the form and then did so', while:

(2) I *remembered filling* out the form.

can be paraphrased as 'I remembered that I had filled out the form'. In (2), perfectivity can be expressed tautologically, as it were, by inserting the appropriate form of the auxiliary *have*:

(2a) I *remembered having filled* out the form.

There is, as Quirk et al. point out in another context (1985: 239), no contrast in meaning between (2) and (2a). The analogous operation in (1), on the other hand, yields a result which is unacceptable in Present-day English:[1]

(1a) * I *remembered to have filled* out the form.

A minor complication is introduced by the fact that – at least in formal styles – *remember* also allows a 'fused' (or 'raising') construction in which the infinitive may be retrospective:

(3a) We *remember them to be* honest.
(3b) We *remember them to have been* honest.

Extraction of the linking element in the fused construction in (3b) through questioning and relativization will give rise to structures in which *remember* and a clearly 'retrospective' infinitive are directly adjacent:

(3c) Who(m) do we *remember to have been* honest?
(3d) [. . .] someone (who(m)/ that) we *remember to have been* honest [. . .]

Needless to say, such forms can in no way be construed as counter-examples to the otherwise rock-solid division of labour between gerunds and infinitives in Present-day English.

    In view of its very solidity, it is all the more surprising to realize that, historically, the functionally and semantically determined distribution of the two complement types is in fact extremely recent. As will be shown, sentences of the type represented by (1a) above were common in the nineteenth century, and it is in fact not difficult at all to find actually attested instances from the first half of the twentieth century, when most speakers and writers were beginning to converge on present-day norms. Following Mair (2002a) and (2002b), I shall argue that, once again, the nineteenth century turns out to be a crucial phase in the emergence of present-day norms in the use of nonfinite clausal complements.

3   The syntax of *remember* in the nineteenth century: previous scholarship

The complementation of *remember* does not figure prominently in the handbooks on recent grammatical change in English. It is not a topic of discussion in two recent introductory treatments of nineteenth-century English, namely Bailey (1996) and Görlach (1999), nor is it mentioned in Strang (1970), which otherwise does draw attention to the spread of gerunds as an important trend in nineteenth-century English. Writing on grammatical changes from '1970–1770'[2], Strang notes that:

> [i]n the use of gerundial *–ing* or the *to*-infinitive after other verbs there is at present some divided usage; generally, the gerund has been gaining ground, and two centuries ago would not have been found in a number of structures where it is now required – *fell to eat(ing)*, *with a view to prevent(ing)*; the trend goes back into earlier centuries. (1970: 100)

The issue does not receive coherent treatment in Jespersen, either, who attests some retrospective infinitives with *remember* 'in the same sense' as the gerund alternative (1961: 199), but leaves any further interpretation or analysis implicit. 'Retrospective' *remember* does rate a brief mention, though, in Denison's magisterial chapter on syntax in the fourth volume of the *Cambridge History of the English Language*, where, following on from Strang's observation quoted above, he supplies two examples of 'retrospective' infinitives from 1819 and 1904 (1998: 265).

Regarding handbooks and general works of reference, the best current analysis of the recent history of gerunds and infinitives after *remember* still seems to be the one presented in Visser (1963–73: 1323, 1876, 2315, 2357). He notes the long history of *remember to* and records two late occurrences of retrospective infinitives from Lawrence's 1913 *Sons and Lovers* (p. 1323). As for *remember* + *–ing*, he points out that 'in the first half of the 19th century the form in *–ing* was frowned upon as an improper innovation by the grammarians', giving Goold Brown's compendium *The Grammar of English Grammars* (1851) as a source, and then provides attestations beginning with one early outlier of 1535 and proceeding with continuous documentation from 1823 to the present (p. 1876).

In addition, there have been a number of specialist studies on the complementation of prospective and retrospective verbs in Early Modern and Modern English. Schneider (1996b) surveys prospective verbs in Early Modern English, but has little to say about *remember* in particular (p. 216). Vosberg (2003: 308–12) provides rich corpus evidence for the spread of gerund complements after *remember* in the course of the eighteenth and nineteenth centuries in British and American data, with his particular aim being to demonstrate that the transition from the infinitive to the gerund is impeded by certain types of syntactic complexity. Fanego (1996), on the other hand, provides an empirically rich and theoretically informed survey of the history of *remember*. She argues that the verb *remember* occupied a pivotal role in the rise of the Modern English gerund and the functional distribution between gerundial and infinitival complements, and that 'the disappearance of the perfect infinitive after retrospective *remember*, and its complete replacement by an *–ing* form, could thus be interpreted as yet another manifestation of this widespread linguistic trend' (1996: 77).

It is her account which, together with that of Visser, will provide the point of orientation for the present study.

4   The syntax of *remember* in the *OED* quotation base 1700–2000

As a first step in the critical review of Visser's account it is naturally desirable to check the validity of his collection of examples against results from corpora designed for the study of the recent history of English. An obvious candidate for investigation is ARCHER ('A Representative Corpus of Historical English Registers'). However, neither *remember to* nor *remember + –ing* is frequent enough to allow statistical analysis in this corpus. The whole of ARCHER contains thirteen instances of *remember + V-ing*, and eleven instances of *remember + to*-infinitive, both in the prospective and retrospective senses. In addition, there are ten gerundial constructions in which the gerund is preceded by its notional subject, either in the possessive or in the common case (if a noun) or in the possessive or the objective case (if a pronoun other than *you*). It is clear that the dearth of examples in this case makes it impossible to use ARCHER for the purpose it was compiled for – namely to study the changing usage of forms or constructions in fifty-year stages in two different varieties, British and American English, or in different genres.

CONCE, which was consulted as another promising resource, proved unsuitable because of an unexpected bias introduced by the textual composition of this corpus. While, at nine instances (one retrospective and eight prospective), *remember + to*-infinitive occurred at the expected levels of frequency, there were more than fifty instances of *remember + V-ing*, almost all of them from the same text-type, legal cross examinations, in which witnesses were questioned about what they remembered.

In view of the limitations of ARCHER and CONCE as sources of data for the present study, the quotation base of the *OED* was consulted, in full awareness of the limitations of this type of dictionary-aided corpus-linguistics.[3] Firstly, it is impossible to determine the precise amount of material contained in the quotation base (although the procedure outlined in the appendix to this chapter will allow an approximation sufficient for practical purposes). Secondly, it is not practical to differentiate results obtained from the *OED* quotation base according to style or genre, or even major regional varieties such as British or American English. Any generalization derived from the data in the *OED* quotation base will therefore concern the history of the English language at a very general level of abstraction, focusing on the tendencies in the language as a whole rather than developments limited to individual regional varieties or registers. On a practical level, the *OED*'s search software, though impressive in its performance, falls short of state-of-the-art corpus linguistic retrieval programs such as WordSmith. This makes it difficult or impossible to retrieve some rare or special instances of a construction, such as, for example, those cases in which material intervenes between the verb *remember* and the gerund or infinitive. However, I hope that the results presented below will help allay misgivings about the 'corpus' used.

The quotation base from 1701 onwards was searched for all occurrences of *remember* to* and *remember* *ing* (where * stands for 'any sequence of characters not divided by a space'). This strategy could be relied on to find the majority of relevant instances; it would miss rare cases in which *remember* and its complement were separated by adverbials or other intervening material (e.g. *remember never to tell those kinds of people the truth*) and, more problematically, all those cases in which the gerund was accompanied by its notional subject (*remember him/his being there*). In accord with Visser (1963–73: 2357) I will assume that the latter type is as an elaboration of plain *remember –ing* and did not play a major role before the end of the nineteenth century. All instances thus collected were classified as 'prospective *to*' and 'retrospective *–ing*', the two extant types, and as 'retrospective *to*', the formerly attested but now obsolete type. (The fourth logically possible combination, a 'prospective' use of the gerund, is not attested.) Table 8.1[4] gives the results arranged by quarter century.

The perfective auxiliary *have* is present in all attested instances of retrospective infinitival complements, but only in seven out of a total of seventy-five gerunds. Apart from this, not too much should be read into these figures as the amount of quotation text available for each quarter century varies drastically. Nevertheless, it is clear from the table that the critical period of the transition was the years between 1775 and 1875. Before 1775, retrospective *–ing*-complements are not attested, and after 1875 retrospective *to* is rare.

However, despite its limitations as a corpus, the *OED* quotation base yields insights that go beyond those marshalled in the sources reviewed in section 3 above. Firstly, *remember –ing* can be antedated to the late eighteenth century,

Table 8.1. *Gerunds and infinitives after* remember *in the* OED *quotation base (approximate frequencies based on simplified search procedure).*

		Prospective *to*	Retrospective *-ing*	Retrospective *to*
Eighteenth	1701–1725	1	–	4
century	1726–1750	5	–	–
	1751–1775	1	–	6
	1776–1800	2	3	–
Nineteenth	1801–1825	1	1	3
century	1826–1850	4	4	5
	1851–1875	6	8	5
	1876–1900	6	12	2
Twentieth	1901–1925	2	8	1
century	1926–1950	6	13	1
	1951–1975	9	21	2
	1976–2000	7	6	–

which is almost fifty years earlier than the 1823 'first modern case' in Visser. These are the relevant quotations:

> 1776 T. Twining in Country Clergyman of the 18th C. (1882) 31, I *remember slumping* on a sudden into the slough of despond, and closing my letter in the dumps.

> 1778 Boswell in London Mag. Feb. 58/1, I *remember hearing* a late celebrated infidel tell that he was not at all pleased when the infidel wife of his friend, a poet of some eminence, addressed him in a company in London, 'we Deists'. – Speak for yourself, Madam, said he abruptly.

Secondly, the material holds a surprise at the other end of the timescale, as well, namely the two authentic instances of retrospective *to* from the second half of the twentieth century:

> 1969 Daily Tel. 7 Mar. 21/1 It is the first play in which I *remember to have encountered* an actor with a jockstrap which squeaks when pushed.

> 1974 R. Adams Shardik xi. 79 Bel-ka-Trazet walked with the help of a long thumb-stick which Kelderek *remembered to have seen* him trimming the evening before.

While the 1974 example could be argued to be the result of a desire to avoid two consecutively embedded *-ing* complements (more or less along the lines of Rohdenburg's not uncontroversial principle of *horror aequi* – cf. e.g. Rohdenburg

Table 8.2. *Gerunds and infinitives after* remember *in the* OED *quotation base – normalized frequencies (including all relevant constructions, and rounded to the first decimal).*

	Prospective *to*	Retrospective *–ing*	Retrospective *to*
Eighteenth century	5.5 (15)	1.8 (5)	4.8 (13)
Nineteenth century	2.2 (17)	4.1 (31)	2.1 (16)
Twentieth century	5.8 (28)	12.0 (58)	0.8 (4)

NB: figures in brackets show the absolute frequencies as given in table 8.1, plus the 'extra' examples found in the search for the gerundial constructions with a notional subject; see note 4.

and Schlüter 2000: 461–8), the 1969 example is structurally straightforward and stylistically 'mainstream', from a major British newspaper.

At a further stage in the present investigation, I shall turn to gerundial constructions containing their own notional subjects (in the objective or genitive case). These constructions are impossible to retrieve automatically in the *OED* quotation base, and so all instances of *remember** had to be scanned manually. A further advantage of this procedure was the identification of all those instances of *remember** followed by the plain gerund and infinitive which had escaped notice in the original search owing to the presence of intervening material separating the matrix and complement verbs. These instances are six and four cases of prospective *to* for the eighteenth and twentieth centuries respectively; three, six and ten cases of the gerund for the eighteenth, nineteenth and twentieth centuries; and three and one cases of retrospective *to* for the eighteenth and nineteenth centuries.

These additional examples in no way influence the conclusions drawn on the basis of the results of the simplified search, but in the following statistical analysis of the data they will be included in the interest of maximal numerical accuracy. Table 8.2 presents the evidence by century, giving normalized frequencies of the constructions as 'n/100,000 quotes' obtained by a procedure described in the appendix to this chapter.

What these figures show is:

- fluctuation for prospective *to*,
- a slow and steady decline for retrospective *to*, and
- a steep increase in the frequency of innovative *remember V-ing*.

To judge by these numbers, retrospective *remember + –ing* has not merely taken up the functional load of the outgoing retrospective infinitival construction but – together with its elaborated variant *remember someone('s) V-ing* – may have encroached on territory previously held by finite subordinate clauses (*remember + that/how*).

Such speculation, however, is difficult to substantiate with the available data from the *OED*. First, finite subordinate clauses have been more common than nonfinite ones after *remember* throughout the whole period under review here. Second, the increase in the frequency of gerunds in the twentieth century is parallelled not by a decrease but by an increase in the frequency of finite complements.[5] As the following twentieth-century examples from the Dictionary make clear, the gerundial construction may be in the ascendant, but it is not a direct competitor for the finite clause complement in all uses. In many cases it is still ruled out for a variety of semantic, structural and stylistic reasons. It is not used when *remember* has the meaning 'bear in mind the fact' rather than 'recall past experience'. This is self-evident if the complement clause has present or future reference, but this is so also if the complement clause refers to past experience:

> 1909 Belloc Pyrenees v. 169 *Remember that*, in Alpargatas, you will always end the day with wet feet.

> 1963 Camb. Rev. 27 Apr. 386/2 Teachers must *remember that* they are dealing with learners, which is another animal altogether.

> 1975 Church Times 25 Apr. 1/5 The Bishop tells charismatics:.. *Remember that* you have not a monopoly of the Holy Spirit.

> 1904 Kipling in Windsor Mag. Dec. 10/1 Whatever 'e's done, let us *remember that* 'e's given us a day off.

> 1975 W. M. MacMillan My S. Afr. Years 143 There was I remember one terrible case of a horrible old rascal who sold his step-daughter to a Hottentot. I *remember that* the schepsel was soundly punished.

> 1960 Farmer & Stockbreeder 9 Feb. 125/2 Mr. Thornber *remembered that* the poultryman slept for 21 days with the first mammoth they installed.

In terms of structure and style, a high degree of elaboration works against reformulating a finite complement clause as a gerundial construction even in cases where the meaning of *remember* is clearly that of 'recall'. Compare the original attestations in (4) and (5) with their attempted reformulations in (4a), (4b) and (5a), which are all either extremely clumsy stylistically or downright unacceptable:

(4) Users of the popular miniature cameras may *remember that* some years ago their choice lay between a fine-grain emulsion with a slow speed, necessitating a longer exposure, and a coarse-grained one that did not enlarge so well but had a faster speed. (\ 1937 Discovery Jan. 22/2)

Table 8.3. *Notional subjects in gerundial constructions after* remember.

Period	Objective case (NP)	Objective case (pronoun)	Possessive (NP)	Possessive (pronoun)*
1801–1825	2	–	–	2 (1)
1826–1850	4	1	–	3 (1)
1851–1875	1	–	–	3
1876–1900	4	1	–	1
1901–1925	3	–	–	–
1926–1950	6	–	–	–
1951–1975	12	4	1	–
1976–2000	6	–	1	1 (1)

* Figures in brackets give instances of ambiguous *her* included in the totals.

(4a) ? users [. . .] may *remember* their choice some years ago *lying* between a fine-grain emulsion with a slow speed, necessitating longer exposure, and a coarse-grained one that did not enlarge so well but had a faster speed

(4b) ? users [. . .] may *remember* some years ago their choice *lying* between a fine-grain emulsion with a slow speed, necessitating a longer exposure, and a coarse-grained one that did not enlarge so well but had a faster speed

(5) The readers will *remember that* in the heyday of non-co-operation, the terms 'Mr.' and 'Esquire', were dropped by Congressmen and the nationalist press, and 'Shri' was the title largely used for all, irrespective of religion. (\ 1938 M. K. Gandhi in D. G. Tendulkar Mahatma (1952) IV. 348)

(5a) ? readers will *remember* the terms 'Mr.' and 'Esquire' *being dropped* by Congressmen and the nationalist press, and 'Shri' being the title largely used for all, irrespective of religion, in the heyday of non-co-operation

However, the most interesting question about gerundial constructions with their own notional subjects is not whether they can be paraphrased as finite clauses (or vice versa), but whether the subject appears in the genitive or in the objective case, as this latter issue has aroused a lot of prescriptive concern in the past and continues to occupy language purists today.[6] Although, as has been mentioned, there is no easy way of retrieving the relevant constructions automatically from the *OED* quotation base, I decided to extract these manually by post-editing the search output for *remember**, chiefly in order to test the plausibility of prescriptive claims against the empirical record of language history. The results of the search are presented in table 8.3. The table covers the nineteenth and twentieth centuries because no relevant constructions were found for the eighteenth century.

Two points may be deduced from the figures in table 8.3: first, *remember* +
NP + *V-ing* is on the increase, but, second, it has certainly not spread at the
expense of a supposedly 'correct' constructional alternative in which the notional
subject of the gerundial construction is in the genitive/possessive. The only
two cases of an NP subject appearing in the genitive date from the second half
of the twentieth century, thus most likely representing conscious homage to
prescriptive teaching requiring the genitive. Even with pronominal subjects,
where the possessive/genitive is, admittedly, somewhat more of a genuinely
idiomatic development, it is not really possible on the basis of the small number of attestations to establish a clear historical anteriority. Consider the earliest
examples of the *remember* + NP + *V-ing*-construction (from 1801–25[7]), which
suggest its probable origin:

> 1825 in Hone Every-day Bk. I. 292, I *remember the old squire and his sporting
> chaplain casting* home on spent horses.

> 1809 M. Edgeworth Manœuvring i, I *remember her manœuvring* to gain a
> husband, and then manœuvring to manage him.

> 1817 Lady Morgan France i. (1818) I. 63, I *remember our having alighted*
> from our carriage to spare its springs in a sort of 'crack-scull-common'
> road.

In the 1825 attestation the genitive is *prima facie* unlikely because of the complexity of the noun phrase, which would require a group genitive. In addition,
however, there is a deeper reason for why the genitive construction would be
difficult to use here, and in similar examples with a simpler syntax: it does not
fit the underlying syntactic structure. *Remember* as used here does not offer an
instance of a monotransitive pattern of complementation in which a direct object
is premodified by a genitive, as would be the case in *I remember dancing and
shouting*, which might reasonably be expanded into *I remember their dancing and
shouting*. Rather, what we have in the 1825 attestation is the complex-transitive
pattern of complementation also found with verbs like *see, hear, find* or *catch*
(cf. *I saw/heard/found/caught them running away*). Re-casting the common-case
NP in the genitive with these verbs produces a result that is obviously unacceptable with these verbs (cf. **I saw/heard/found/caught their running away*) and
clumsy and unidiomatic with *remember*. The example from the *OED* thus shows
that in many cases the choice between genitive and common case/objective may
not just be a matter of choosing a formal or informal (or archaic and neutral)
alternative in the same constructional type. It is rather that two possible underlying syntactic structures have to be taken into account – a monotransitive one in
which the possessive is a natural option, and a complex-transitive one in which
the genitive is basically ruled out but may occur as the result of hypercorrection
induced by the influence of prescriptive recommendations. The second example, with *her* as an ambiguous objective/possessive, is difficult to analyse, but
a reading in which the speaker remembers 'her while she was manoeuvering

and, subsequently, managing' (i.e. the complex-transitive interpretation) is at least as likely as the monotransitive one, in which the speaker remembers 'her manoeuvres'. The only clearly monotransitive case, the 1817 example, represents a special constellation in which the common case of the pronoun would be problematic even today, because the referential overlap between the pronoun *us* and the main-clause subject *I* would probably trigger the use of a reflexive (cf. *?I remember us alighting* vs *I remember ourselves alighting*). Thus, the form *I remember our alighting* (possessive, as in the original, but with the perfective auxiliary of the original left out) would still be the most acceptable way of expressing the idea even today.

Additional 'early' examples from the second quarter of the nineteenth century tend to confirm that complex-transitive *remember* + NP + *V-ing* is not a recent development but was a firmly established construction type at the time, emerging simultaneously with the related construction with the genitive/possessive. In the first two attestations below adverbial and parenthetical material freely intervenes between NP and *V-ing*:

> 1827 L. T. Rede Road to Stage 56, I *remember Miss S–, at Drury*, from neglecting this precaution, *having to pay* one hundred and ninety-eight pounds, out of her ticket money alone, to her co-partner in the benefit.

> 1831 in Gen. P. Thompson Exerc. (1842) I. 475, I *remember a deputy, a good ultra too, once saying* . . that Charles X was losing the confidence and affection of his people.

> 1850 Robertson Serm. Ser. iii. ix. (1857) 133 *Remember Him pausing* to weep . ., unexcited, while the giddy crowd around Him were shouting 'Hosannas to the Son of David!'

This means that any prescriptive argument rejecting the common case in gerundial constructions depending on *remember* which is founded on the supposed historical anteriority of the possessive is clearly misguided in the case of full noun-phrases, and – as the 1850 example quoted above shows – problematical even for pronouns. That the genitive subsequently established itself at all in formal written English seems to be one of the many small and often temporary victories of the prescriptively minded stylistic conservatives. On a more general level, it should be pointed out that, while the verb *remember* is fairly common, at least one of the constructions investigated here, namely *remember* + NP(*'s*) + *V-ing*, is surprisingly rare in absolute terms. The fact that the huge amount of material in the *OED* quotation base yielded a mere fifty-six relevant attestations (the total in table 8.3) shows that large corpora are indispensable for historical studies of English grammar and will probably play an increasingly important role in the future.

5   Conclusion

The present study has shown that, in spite of its acknowledged limitations as a historical corpus, the *OED* quotation base has provided useful data for the study of the disappearance of a formerly thriving grammatical construction, namely retrospective infinitival complements after *remember*. Quantitative data obtained from an analysis of the quotation base show that it was during the nineteenth century that the way was prepared irreversibly for the emergence of conventions for present-day usage. Additionally, the data suggest that the development did not merely consist in a replacement of infinitival complements by gerunds but that there was additional growth of the gerund, presumably at the expense of finite-clause complements. As for longstanding prescriptive reservations about using common-case notional subjects in gerundial constructions after *remember*, the evidence from the *OED* shows that such reasoning is based on arbitrary aesthetic and stylistic judgements and can claim no basis in the facts attested for the history of language. The syntax of *remember* has proved far from stable in the period under review here. In addition to the expected shifts in statistical preferences there has been one categorical change, namely the elimination of the retrospective infinitive. Similar case studies may show that not just this verb, but the entire system of non-finite clausal complementation deserves more scholarly attention – as one of those areas in which there has been much previously unnoticed grammatical change in the recent history of English.

Appendix

The following table lists the number of quotations in the *OED* quotation base per quarter century from 1701 to 2000.[8] Assuming an average length of ten words per quotation, which is a conservative estimate, one can easily see that the material accessible through the *OED* is much more copious than that provided by standard historical corpora such as ARCHER, the *OED* offering almost three, eight and five million words respectively for the eighteenth, nineteenth and twentieth centuries (for a detailed assessment of the *OED* as a historical corpus, see Hoffmann 2004).

Period	Number of quotations
1701–1725	73, 341
1726–1750	56, 520
1751–1775	64, 884
1776–1800	78, 998
Total eighteenth century	**273, 676**

1801–1825	111, 374
1826–1850	174, 073
1851–1875	222, 261
1876–1900	256, 498
Total nineteenth century	**763, 987**
1901–1925	104, 297
1926–1950	122, 313
1951–1975	208, 900
1976–2000	46, 182
Total twentieth century	**481, 376**

In order to make the frequency of occurrence of the relevant constructions with *remember* comparable across the three centuries under review, normalized values of 'instances/100,000 quotes' were calculated from the absolute figures given in table 8.1. These are the values given in table 8.2 of the text.

Notes

1. Jørgensen (1990) seems to be alone in considering such usages as acceptable in Present-day English, backing up his contention with a few actually attested examples from the second half of the twentieth century. A recent corpus-based study of Present-day American English (Tao 2001) emphasizes that the complement-taking uses of *remember* which have such a high profile in reference grammars and the linguistic literature are in fact rather rare, especially in the spoken language, when compared to the overall frequency of *remember*, but the author does not question the existence of a rigid semantic contrast in those cases in which infinitives and gerunds are used.
2. In giving the dates, I follow the logic of my source, which proposes to narrate the history of English backwards, from the present to Old English.
3. Counts are based on the CD-ROM version, to avoid an admittedly minor risk that the database might be changed during or after the study as a result of the continuous updating of the online version of this electronic dictionary.
4. The figures in table 8.1 represent the output derived on the basis of the search procedure described in the preceding paragraph. For manually post-edited frequencies based on an analysis of **all** instances of *remember** retrieved from the quotation base for the period in question see table 8.2.
5. Since finite complement clauses are not the focus of this paper, I will restrict myself to giving a few orientational frequencies. A search for *remember** *wh** and *remember** *how*, i.e. targeted at indirect question clauses, revealed an incidence of 6.9 cases per 100,000 quotes for the eighteenth and nineteenth centuries, and of 16.8 per 100,000

for the twentieth century. The output for the search for *remember* that*, which, owing to the homonymy between the subordinator and the pronoun *that*, will admittedly contain many spurious cases, reveals a similar general trend: normalized frequencies of 8.4, 10.3 and 21 per 100,000 quotes respectively for the eighteenth, nineteenth and twentieth centuries.

6. *Remember* + NP + *V-ing*, of course, merely represents a special instance of the 'fused participle', which was rather polemically denied its status as an authentic English grammatical construction by the Fowler brothers in their *King's English* (1908) and Henry W. Fowler's influential usage guide *Modern English Usage* (first published in 1926). More recent usage guides, including the revised version of Fowler's guide, generally take a more lenient view but tend to argue in favour of the possessive for (unstressed) pronouns, proper names and other short noun phrases, especially in formal and written English. For a comprehensive and balanced account of the debate, compare the entry 'possessive with gerund' in the 1989 *Websters Dictionary of English Usage* (pp. 753–5).

7. There are four examples in all. The corresponding figure for the period in table 8.3 is five, however, because the 1825 instance is used in another entry in abbreviated form and hence was counted twice.

8. As some quotations are assigned to more than one specific year, there are minimal discrepancies between the figures obtained when searching for the number of citations in a given period directly, and those obtained when adding up the figures for individual sub-periods of the same period. These discrepancies, however, are not such as to affect the present argument in any way.

9 The *in -ing* construction in British English, 1800–2000

JUHANI RUDANKO

1 Defining *in -ing* complements

In recent years there has been a renewal of interest in issues of complementation, generated in large part by the increasing availability of new electronic corpora.[1] Some of this work has had a purely synchronic focus on Present-day English, but there has also been renewed attention paid to diachronic aspects of the system of English predicate complementation, and how it has developed over time (see also Mair, this volume). The present article offers a contribution to the latter area of research and takes up a particular aspect of verb complementation in the nineteenth and twentieth centuries on the basis of corpus evidence, in order to investigate stability and change in this part of English grammar.

Consider sentence (1), taken from the Bank of English Corpus:

(1) The Titans delight *in upsetting* the odds, [. . .]
 (*Times*/UK)

The pattern of sentence (1) essentially involves the preposition *in* and a following *-ing* clause. (The term 'clause' is used here to refer to a subordinate sentence.) Adopting the label first introduced in Rudanko (1991) and also used for instance in Francis et al. (1996: 194–5), the pattern may be called a type of the *in -ing* pattern. The particular *in -ing* pattern in question is the one where the pattern is associated with a matrix verb, as with *delight* in sentence (1).

There are a number of properties of the *in -ing* pattern as illustrated in sentence (1) that should be emphasized here. First, there are two sentences in (1), the higher sentence and the lower sentence. The higher sentence includes the whole string, and within that string there is a lower or subordinate sentence. The preposition *in* of the pattern is part of the higher sentence and outside of the lower sentence. The verb of the higher sentence is *delight*, that of the lower sentence is *upsetting*. The subject of the higher sentence is of course the NP *the Titans*. However, the subject of the lower sentence is not overtly expressed. The idea that not all subjects are overt is a somewhat controversial one, but it is made by many linguists working on complementation today. It was also made by many traditional grammarians.

For instance, Jespersen, using the term 'gerund' for the *-ing* form, as in sentence (1), wrote:

> Very often a gerund stands alone without any subject, but as in other nexuses (nexus-substantives, infinitives, etc.) the connexion of a subject with the verbal idea is always implied. (Jespersen (1961 [1940]: 140))

Once it is accepted that the *-ing* clause in a sentence such as (1) has an understood subject, there arises the question of how to represent such a covert subject. Here the representation PRO is used. This representation was not used by traditional grammarians, but is often found in the relevant literature today.

Using PRO to represent the understood subject in the pattern of sentence (1), it is possible to say that in the sentence PRO is coreferential with the subject of the matrix sentence.

It is also important to notice that in the pattern of sentence (1) the *in -ing* construction functions as a complement of the matrix verb *delight*. This means that there is a close grammatical connection between the higher verb, *delight* in sentence (1), the preposition *in*, and the *-ing* clause with its understood subject. To shed further light on the notion of a complement, it is also possible to say that the higher verb, *delight* in (1), syntactically selects the preposition *in*, with an immediately following *-ing* clause. The *-ing* clause, forming part of the complement, may be termed a complement clause.

The focus of the present study on a pattern of complementation means that adverbial clauses are excluded. This is worth noting here because the preposition *in* is quite capable of standing in front of an *-ing* clause which is not a complement but an adverbial clause. For instance, consider sentences (2a)–(2b), also from the Bank of English Corpus:

(2a) In English, we use the past tense *in talking* about past events.
      (usbooks/US)

(2b) At first it was easy to believe Republican Dick Armey when he said he had merely 'stumbled' *in referring* to the openly gay congressman Barney Franks as Barney [. . .]
      (*guard*/UK)

The sentences in (2a)–(2b) contain the sequence *in -ing*, in *in talking* and *in referring*, respectively. Further, the predicates introduced by the *-ing* forms in (2a)–(2b) undoubtedly have their own understood subjects, and in each case, the understood subject and the following predicate constitute a clause. However, in the case of (2a)–(2b) the *in -ing* constructions have an adverbial function, and the clauses in question are adverbial clauses. It is perhaps possible to feel an intuitive difference between for instance *delight in doing something* and *stumble in doing something*. In the case of *delight*, the following clause expresses the content of what someone delights in. By contrast, in the case of *stumble* the *-ing* clause expresses an adverbial notion. As regards the nature of the notion, there may be a number of semantic relations or elements of meaning involved in adverbial -*ing* clauses introduced by the preposition *in*, as has been noted (cf. Poutsma 1905: 703; 1929: 952; Rudanko 1996: 10), but in the case of (2a)–(2b) the notion of time seems prominent.

There are also other ways to support the distinction. For instance, it is often possible to find an *in* -*ing* sequence at the beginning of a sentence, and in general this position is more readily possible when an *in* -*ing* sequence has an adverbial function, where the connection between the higher verb and *in* -*ing* is less close. For instance, we might consider sentences (3a)–(3b), again from the Bank of English Corpus.

(3a) The first traceable reference to trout in caves is in an unpublished manuscript prepared by John Strachey in about 1730. *In referring* to Wookey Hole, he writes: This cave gives harbour to very fine trouts which [. . .] (brbooks/UK)

(3b) *In referring* to the 'compassion' of Queenslanders, [. . .] Justice Chesterman depends [. . .] on assertions unworthy of a person of his legal standing. (oznews/OZ)

In (3a)–(3b) the *in* -*ing* sequence is at the beginning of the sentence. It would be hard to imagine this position in the case of a complement construction. For instance, consider sentence (4), an invented sentence modified from (1):

(4) ??*In upsetting* the odds the Titans delight (enormously).

A less traditional way to motivate the distinction concerns the extraction of a constituent out of an *in* -*ing* clause. Such extractions tend to be easier out of complement clauses than out of adjunct clauses (cf. McCloskey 1988: 31–41). We might compare *I wonder what he said he wanted* (from McCloskey 1988: 31) with *?Who did you lie while praising* (from McCloskey 1988: 41). Applied to the present data, this criterion yields a contrast of the type *These are the odds/the opponents that the Titans delighted in upsetting*, which is conceivable, and *?These are the events that we use the past tense in talking about*, which seems slightly more doubtful.

It is easy enough to make the distinction between complement and adverbial constructions in the case of sentence (1), on the one hand, and of sentences (2a)–(2b) and (3a)–(3b), on the other. There are other cases where the distinction is harder to make, but the existence of marginal cases does not affect the status of the distinction as a basis for the study of syntactic selection and in this chapter the distinction is assumed.

The *in* -*ing* pattern of complementation is a sentential pattern. It may be noted that many matrix verbs selecting the pattern also select nominal complements of the *in* NP type, as in *delight in one's success*. However, the sets of matrix verbs selecting the two types of complement are not coextensive. For instance, we might consider the verb *end* when it selects the preposition *in*. The verb easily permits an *in* NP complement, as in *The scheme ended in disaster*, but does not easily permit a sentential complement, as witness the strain of *??The scheme ended in coming to nothing*. There is thus a need to make a distinction between nominal and sentential complements introduced by the preposition *in*. Leaving the subject of nominal *in* NP complements for a future study, the present investigation, in the tradition pioneered by Poutsma (1905: 651–6; 1929: 896–903; MS), focuses on the sentential *in* -*ing* pattern selected by matrix verbs. A further reason for this choice of focus is that it makes it possible to examine the properties of PRO, which is only present in the sentential pattern.

2   Evidence from electronic corpora

Having identified the *in* -*ing* pattern in section 1, it is now possible to turn to examining its recent history. In any such investigation, computer corpora of English are invaluable and indispensable sources of data, provided that they are used with care. This cautionary note is needed, because in electronic corpora, as in other natural language data, the investigator often comes across sentences that look relevant but are not on closer inspection. For instance the following sentence is found in the Bank of English corpus:

(5) [. . .] they had taken Dai to a doctor who gave him a meticulous examination, declared him in good health, and prescribed vitamins. The adoptive grand-mother went to great pains to prepare Mexican dishes with an Asian flavor and insisted *in making* Dai swallow the same cod-liver oil with which she had tortured her own six infants – but none of this had any results. (brbooks/UK)

The example is authentic. However, caution must be exercised in assessing it. Quite clearly there is a strong preference in English for the verb *insist* to select *on* -*ing* complements. We know this by consulting corpora or by asking native speakers. Native speakers simply do not in general accept *in* -*ing* with the matrix verb *insist*. Sentence (5) thus affords an illustration of how care needs to be taken when using corpus evidence. As regards the sentence, there are two possibilities: it is either a misprint or perhaps the clause should be interpreted as an adjunct, that is, the sentence should be interpreted as something like 'insisted when making Dai swallow the oil'.

I have examined aspects of *in* -*ing* in my earlier work, especially in Rudanko (1991), (1996, chapter 2) and (1999, chapter 3). The present chapter is offered as a follow-up to, and as an extension of, this earlier work. Here the focus is on the use of the pattern in British English in the nineteenth century and in the second half of the twentieth century. The former period is explored on the basis of the Corpus of Nineteenth-century English (CONCE), and the latter on the basis of the LOB (Lancaster-Oslo/Bergen) corpus and two major subcorpora of the Bank of English Corpus (version of May/June 2002). The first of the subcorpora is the London *Times* newspaper segment and the second is the spoken British English segment of the Bank of English Corpus.

A comment may be inserted here on the selection of the four corpora for the present study. At one level, all four corpora are similar in that they consist solely of British English material. From another point of view, it may be noted that the Corpus of Nineteenth-century English is one of the relatively few corpora covering nineteenth-century English not limited to one genre and choosing it here is a natural decision. The LOB Corpus similarly covers a number of genres. These are not identical with those of the Corpus of Nineteenth-century English, but some genres in the two corpora are similar, and as long as we remember the differences between them, it is possible to examine the two corpora together. As regards the subcorpora selected out of the Bank of English Corpus, they do not feature the same variety of genres, but they represent newspaper English and the spoken language respectively, and these corpora can be expected to give some clues as to the way that the *in -ing* pattern is developing in the language at this time.

Starting by examining the *in -ing* pattern in the Corpus of Nineteenth-century English, it may be observed that the type of adverbial construction identified above and illustrated with present-day examples is also found in the nineteenth century. Here are two examples:

(6a)   The servants who live in the families of the rich, have restraints yet stronger to break through *in venturing* upon marriage.
       (Science, Thomas Robert Malthus, 1800–30, p. 61)

(6b)   *In estimating* the proportional mortality the resident population alone should be considered.
       (Science, Thomas Robert Malthus, 1800–30, p. 58)

Setting such adverbial constructions aside and turning to examples where the *in -ing* pattern functions as a complement, we might consider some relevant examples:

(7a)   [. . .] I have been obliged to add more cloathing to my bed – though I have still persisted *in doing* without a fire – the Gees have one constantly.
       (Letters, Sara Hutchinson, 1800–30, p. 190)

(7b)   Though one of the most peaceable persons in the world, and careful ones, too, in such things, I cannot always succeed *in keeping* the peace there; [. . .]
       (Letters, Robert Southey, 1800–30, p. 404)

(7c)   The MARQUESS of LONDONDERRY rose to move the adjournment of the House as a mark of respect for the loss of that inestimable person the Duke of Cambridge, as had been done in another place on the death of a great statesman and patriot. He trusted that their Lordships would not fail *in expressing* their regret in a form which he suggested.
       (Debates, 1850–70, p. 112, 1139)

Table 9.1. *The occurrence of* in -ing *patterns by matrix verb in CONCE.*

Verb	Occurrences
succeed	34
assist	8
persist	8
agree	6
concur	5
fail	3
consist	1
help	1
hesitate	1
operate	1
persevere	1
unite	1
Total	70

(7d) Here are wide-awake men (some of them most anti-spiritual to this hour, as to theory) who agree *in giving* testimony to facts of one order.
(Letters, Elizabeth Barrett Browning, 1850–70, p. 247)

(7e) By all that I can learn, the decision will certainly be in Lord Talbot's favour, unless, within a few months, some other Earl of Shrewsbury is produced, – a most improbable event, and one which your opponents will certainly not assist *in bringing* about.
(Letters, Thomas Babington Macaulay, 1850–70, p. 106)

(7f) The data in A and B somewhat overlap, but for the most part they differ.
They concur *in telling* the same tale, namely, that it is totally impossible to torture the figures so as to make them yield the single-humped 'Curve of Frequency' [. . .]
(Science, Sir Francis Galton, 1870–1900, p. 175)

The sentences in (7a)–(7f) illustrate various matrix verbs that are found with *in* -*ing* complements in nineteenth-century English. However, in order to shed further light on the characteristic position of the *in* -*ing* pattern within the system of English predicate complementation in the nineteenth century, it is also important to consider the frequencies of the pattern with individual verbs. Table 9.1 presents the numerical figures in the corpus.

The picture that emerges from examining the use of the pattern in the Corpus of Nineteenth-century English emphasizes the predominance of the verb *succeed* among the matrix verbs selecting the pattern. This verb alone accounts for almost

Table 9.2. *The occurrence of* in -ing *patterns by matrix verb in LOB.*

Verb	Occurrences
succeed	20
consist	4
assist	3
agree	2
be	2
believe	2
delight	2
cooperate	1
excel	1
fail	1
rejoice	1
result	1
share	1
specialize	1
vie	1
work	1
Total	44

half of the instances of the pattern, and it is several times more frequent than any other matrix verb.

From a more qualitative point of view, it is worth considering the senses of matrix verbs selecting the pattern. The sense of 'perform the act of', 'carry out the activity of' or 'engage in' was identified in Rudanko (1999: 47) as one semantic category relevant to senses of matrix verbs selecting *in -ing*. The general gloss is then supplemented with more specific glosses for individual verbs. For instance, *succeed* was glossed 'do so successfully' in Rudanko (1999: 47). For this class of matrix verbs, the *in -ing* complement expresses the area or field of action or activity in which the referent of the higher subject does something.

Prototypical members of the 'engage in' class that are found in table 9.1 include *succeed, assist* and *persist*. The predominance of these verbs, in terms of frequency, in nineteenth-century English emphasizes the importance of the class at this stage of the history of English.

Another qualitative aspect of the *in -ing* pattern prevalent in the nineteenth century concerns the interpretation of PRO in the pattern. To judge by the examples of nineteenth-century usage in (7a)–(7f), the understood subject of the lower clause was typically interpreted as coreferential with the higher subject.

Turning now to the position of the *in -ing* pattern in British English in 1961, as revealed by the LOB Corpus, table 9.2 presents the figures indicating the frequency of occurrence of various matrix verbs with *in -ing* in the LOB Corpus.

In terms of sheer quantity, the verb *succeed* is again the most frequent matrix verb selecting the pattern by a very long way, though its predominance may be slightly less pronounced than in the nineteenth-century corpus.

As regards meanings of matrix verbs, verbs of the 'engage in' type are again predominant in terms of overall frequency of occurrence, largely because of the high incidence of the verb *succeed*. However, two other semantic classes have assumed more prominence than they had in the Corpus of Nineteenth-century English. The first of these are verbs such as *consist* and *be*. An example of each is worth adducing here:

(8a)   Our error is not *in training* scientists who are unaware of the classical outlook: it is *in training* them in all sorts of assumptions which are still unconsciously derived from it.
(LOB G64 95–8)

(8b)   It must be possible to characterize that internal impression without invoking any reference to the so-called object of the desire, no less than the action that consists either *in getting* or *in trying* to get that object.
(LOB J54 10–13)

The sense of the matrix verb is clearly not of the 'engage in' type. Rather the sense might be characterized on the basis of the relevant sense of the verb *consist*, which is given as 6.d in the *OED*:

(**d.**) To be comprised or contained in (actions, conditions, qualities, or other things non-material); to be constituted of. Now the usual sense.
(*OED*, sense 6.d)

The first part of the gloss, and especially the phrasing 'to be contained in' seems particularly appropriate to the sense of the verb in (8b). Much the same sense is observed in the case of *be* in (8a). This gloss is interesting because it contains an echo of the ordinary or prototypical sense of the preposition *in*, as for instance in a prepositional phrase such as *in a box* or *in a building*, where its sense might be glossed as 'inside' or 'enclosed by'.

Verbs of the 'be contained in' type with the *in -ing* pattern did not first come into existence in the twentieth century. One example of *consist* was encountered in the CONCE material, as listed above, and, in other work, I have shown that verbs of this type can be found in eighteenth-century English (Rudanko 1999: 29). However, the present investigation suggests that verbs of this semantic type have gained in relative prominence in relation to their role in the nineteenth century.

Identifying the semantic class of verbs of the 'be contained in' type is also important from the point of view of interpreting the reference of PRO, the understood subject in the pattern. It was noted above that in a sentence such as (1) above PRO is coreferential with the subject of the matrix sentence. Reference assignment for PRO in this case is stated in terms of a syntactic relation and is thus syntactic in nature.

However, this is not the case in the sentences of (8a)–(8b). For instance, in sentence (8a) the higher subject is the NP *our error*, but this of course is not understood as the subject of the lower sentence. After all, an error does not train scientists. More appropriately, PRO is coreferential with the possessive pronoun of the higher subject, that is, with *our*, in a manner that is regular enough (cf. Rudanko 1996: 36). For verbs of the 'be contained in' type, it is also possible for PRO to get its reference from even further away. For instance, we might imagine a little narrative of this type: *Last year we committed an error. It was in training scientists with a classical outlook.* Here PRO is again coreferential with *we*, even though the pronoun is now in an earlier sentence (cf. Rudanko 1996: 36–7).

Reference assignment for PRO in (8a)–(8b) is not syntactic in nature, since it can go beyond sentence boundaries. Instead, it may be called 'context dependent'.

The context-dependent interpretation of PRO identified here on the basis of (8a)–(8b) is clearly associated with matrix verbs of the semantic type of 'be contained in'. This study thus suggests that as the result of the increasing prominence of verbs of the semantic type of 'be contained in', there has been a corresponding tendency since the nineteenth century for context-dependent interpretations of PRO to gain ground in relation to the strictly syntactic principle of reference assignment.

Another semantic type that has gained in prominence, albeit in a limited way, is certain verbs of emotion with *in -ing*. An example is given in (9):

(9) There are plenty of people – both sexes – who delight *in showing* their knowledge.
    (LOB F03 97–8)

Delight, as in (9), illustrates a third major semantic type of matrix verb, different from both the 'engage in' and the 'be contained in' types. *Delight* is a verb expressing an emotion, with its subject having the semantic role of Experiencer, and in this case the *in -ing* construction simultaneously expresses both the source of the emotion and the goal towards which it is directed.

Turning now to the more recent corpora, the Bank of English Corpus affords an opportunity to study the construction both in written and in spoken language. As mentioned above, for this study, I examined two major subcorpora of British English within the Bank of English Corpus, the *Times* Newspaper segment, of some 50 million words (51,884,289 words, to be exact), and the Spoken British English segment, of some 20 million words (20,078,901 words, to be exact). A search was carried out on the material in these subcorpora using the search string 'in + VBG,' where the abbreviation 'VBG' stands for a verb ending in *-ing*. This search string produced 3,662 hits in the Spoken British English segment, and 20,132 hits in the *Times* subcomponent.

To keep the discussion within reasonable limits, the first thousand examples yielded by each search were examined for this study, that is, the first thousand of the 3,662 hits in the Spoken English search and the first thousand of the 20,132 hits of the *Times* search.

Table 9.3. *The occurrence of* in -ing *patterns by matrix verb in the* Times *subcorpus.*

Verb	Occurrences
succeed	21
specialize	16
lie	7
believe	5
persist	5
delight	4
consist	2
assist	1
glory	1
indulge	1
result	1
unite	1
Total	65

Unfortunately, in each case most of the one thousand examples were irrelevant to the present investigation for various reasons, including for instance the many examples of *interested in* Verb*ing*, where the *in -ing* pattern, while a complement, is selected by an adjective. However, there were also numerous relevant examples found.

Table 9.3 presents the results of the search for the *Times* subcorpus. Some examples, especially of verbs not illustrated above, may be worth adducing from the subcorpus:

(10a) American experience shows that control of the House of Representatives by the Democrats resulted *in piling* one bad policy on another until the welfare system became so bloated, and the military so starved, that [. . .] (*Times*/UK)

(10b) From China, where fires were lit along the entire length of the Great Wall, to Mexico City, where hundreds of thousands of people swarmed jubilantly down the Reforma boulevard into the Zocalo, the world's largest square, a culturally diverse world united *in marking* the passing of the 20th century with lavish celebrations that paid homage to the accomplishments of the 20th century while anticipating the challenges of the 21st. (*Times*/UK)

(10c) The answer lies *in expanding* the pool of doctors and in having the political courage to accept that we cannot ask the impossible, even of doctors. (*Times*/UK)

Table 9.4. *The occurrence of in -ing patterns by matrix verb in the Spoken British English subcorpus.*

Verb	Occurrences
succeed	9
believe	8
persist	3
lie	2
assist	1
consist	1
help	1
revel	1
specialize	1
Total	27

(10d) [. . .] whereas Wilson ultimately came out and gloried *in being* gay in his later fiction, [. . .]
(*Times*/UK)

The results of the corresponding search for the Spoken British English sub-corpus are shown in table 9.4. Two examples of *believe* may be sufficient as illustrations:

(11a) By the way in case you are wondering I am nothing to do with banks at all I am a retired schoolmaster and I don't like banks. Mm. But I believe *in beating* them at their own game. Oh yes.
(brspok/UK)

(11b) I don't believe *in banning* television completely and I don't believe *in* completely *banning* programmes but [. . .]
(brspok/UK).

This look into the Bank of English Corpus reveals that the *in -ing* pattern selected by matrix verbs is found both in written English and in spoken English today. If the two varieties are compared, the pattern appears to be considerably more frequent in the written subcomponent. This conclusion is based on the difference in overall figures in tables 9.3 and 9.4, coupled with the proportionately larger figure of hits for the written subcorpus (20,132 hits for 51,884,289 words versus 3,662 hits for 20,078,901 words).[2]

As regards more fine-grained findings, *succeed* is still the most frequent matrix verb selecting the pattern both in the written and the spoken sample. However, in the written material *specialize* is comparatively frequent. As for the spoken material, the high frequency of *believe* is of interest. The fact that the verb selects *in -ing* has of course been remarked on before (cf. Poutsma (MS, s.v. *(dis)believe)*; Rudanko 1996: 19), but not its high frequency of occurrence in the spoken language. The finding is also of interest in a more qualitative sense, because the interpretation of PRO with *believe* is often more general than for instance with *succeed*. The examples in (11a)–(11b) illustrate this point. In these the reference of PRO may perhaps include that of the higher subject, but it is hardly limited to it and is instead broader and less definite.[3]

Believe of course commonly also selects *that*-clause complements, and if we for instance consider (11b), a sentence such as *I don't believe that television should be banned completely* is also conceivable. The increasing prominence of the *in -ing* pattern with *believe* may be seen as an aspect of what Günter Rohdenburg has recently termed the Great Complement Shift, for an important aspect of the Shift concerns the spread of *-ing* forms, both 'straight' and prepositional, as Rohdenburg (2004) emphasizes, and the present case comes within the scope of the Shift as a prepositional *-ing* form.

A context-dependent interpretation of PRO obtains in the case of the verb *lie*. This is as expected, for this verb is an example of the semantic type 'be contained in'. For instance, in the example given in (10c), PRO is of course not coreferential with the higher subject, *the answer*, for an answer does not expand the pool of doctors. In this case the reference of PRO cannot be recovered from the single sentence.

Regarding the semantics of matrix verbs more generally, verbs of the three groups identified above – 'engage in', including *succeed* and *persist*, 'be contained in', with *lie* as a case in point, and verbs of emotion, with *revel* as a case in point – are all found in the subcorpora. Of the three types, verbs of the 'engage in' type are predominant in both spoken and written English. Another similarity between the two varieties is that verbs of emotion are relatively rare in both of them. As for the verb *believe*, it does not sit easily in any of the three semantic groups identified, and its prominence may indicate the need for the identification of a fourth semantic type in Present-day English.

3   Concluding observations

This article examines the status of one particular construction, the *in -ing* pattern, in the system of English predicate complementation over the last two centuries. The pattern is examined mostly from the point of view of matrix verbs selecting it, and generalizations are offered regarding the semantic types of relevant verbs and on changes that have taken place in this respect over the last two hundred years.

One generalization suggested by this study concerns the interpretation of the understood subject in the *in -ing* pattern. The evidence of the Corpus of Nineteenth-century English indicates that in the nineteenth century the understood subject tended to be interpreted as coreferential with the higher subject. However, twentieth-century data, both from LOB and the Bank of English

Corpus reveal an increasing scope for understood subjects that are not necessarily coreferential with the higher subject. It was argued that reference assignment for PRO is a function of the semantic type of matrix verb. For an increasingly prominent type of matrix verb, with the semantic property of 'be contained in', reference assignment was argued to be context dependent.

A further type of non-specific reference assignment was observed to have become increasingly prominent with the matrix verb *believe*, especially in the spoken language. This finding about change may be seen as an aspect of what Günter Rohdenburg (2004) has recently called the Great Complement Shift, for an important part of the Shift concerns the spread of prepositional *-ing* forms.

Beyond the grammatical properties of the *in -ing* pattern, this article raises some broader methodological issues. It highlights the role of the analyst even in the age of computers, since the distinction between complement and adverbial constructions cannot be made by a computer. At the same time, this article also emphasizes the need to use corpus evidence in investigating the system of English predicate complementation, both in defining the pattern under investigation and in examining it.

Notes

1. I am happy to acknowledge that funding from the Academy of Finland promoted the completion of this study. I also owe a deep debt of gratitude to the editors for their help. However, I am responsible for all remaining shortcomings.
2. The following formula, worked out by Erik Smitterberg, suggests itself here: $(65 \times 20{,}132) / (1{,}000 \times 51{,}884{,}289)$ vs $(27 \times 3{,}662) / (1{,}000 \times 20{,}078{,}901)$.
3. An anonymous referee draws attention to the parallel increasing use of unattached participles in this context. An example, from Huddleston and Pullum (2002: 611), of such an unattached participle is given in (i):

   (i) Bearing in mind the competitive environment, this is a creditable result.

   Regarding the interpretation of the understood subject of the *-ing* clause in a sentence of this type, Huddleston and Pullum (2002: 611) remark that 'there is still an understood subject roughly recoverable from the context as the speaker or the speaker and addressees together'.

   As noted, the reference of the understood subject of the *in -ing* pattern with *believe* may include that of the higher subject, but there is lack of specificity regarding the interpretation of PRO in both types of constructions. An unattached participle is an adjunct and not a complement, whereas the *in -ing* constructions considered here are complements; whether the nonspecific interpretation of PRO in an unattached participle may have fostered the spread of a nonspecific PRO in a complement clause construction merits further investigation.

10 Partitive constructions in nineteenth-century English[1]

ERIK SMITTERBERG

1 Introduction

In English, partitive constructions are frequently used to quantify or characterize noncount and plural count nouns, as in (1).

(1) [\$Gen.\$] Why, I own your case is singular; but I'll give you a *bit of advice*, I have often received advice from you –
(Drama, Thomas Morton, 1800–30, p. 32)

Such partitive constructions, or, simply, partitives, consist of a partitive noun followed by the preposition *of* and the complement of this preposition: in (1) above, *bit* is the partitive noun and *advice* the prepositional complement. Partitive constructions typically encode a part/whole relationship, where the partitive noun represents a part of the whole denoted by the complement.[2] It is of interest to describe the use of partitives in English in order to enable future cross-linguistic comparisons. For instance, there are similarities between partitives and classifiers in classifier languages, such as Vietnamese (Svensson 1998: 200–2).

The aim of the present study is to analyse the use and distribution of partitive constructions in nineteenth-century English. The 1800s constitute an important period regarding the occurrence of partitives containing *lot/s* (Smitterberg 2003). The same time span could also be expected to have been important to the English partitive construction from a more general perspective.

Partitive constructions have not received a great deal of attention in the scholarly literature (Svensson 1998: 198): in order to open up this field of research more fully, I therefore adopt a broad methodological approach in the present study. I will investigate three different aspects of partitive constructions in nineteenth-century English, using a combination of quantitative and qualitative methods.

I will first look at whether the overall frequency of partitives varies with the extralinguistic parameters of time, genre and gender. It has been shown that the frequency of nouns and prepositions, which make up partitive constructions, in texts differentiates genres throughout Modern English as well as in Present-day English: 'literate' genres exhibit higher frequencies of these linguistic features than 'oral' genres (see e.g. Biber 1988; Biber and Finegan 1997). Moreover, the extent of the differentiation increases across time. The genre parameter can thus be hypothesized to be of special relevance in this context. The results will also be compared with those of two recent factor score analyses of the CONCE corpus, which was used for the present study (Geisler 2002; 2003). This comparison will show with what other linguistic features partitive constructions tend to co-occur in texts.

However, considering overall frequencies alone will not provide us with a complete picture of the use of partitives. The partitive construction is heterogeneous with respect to its meanings: in addition to expressing a part of a whole, partitives often encode other semantic elements, such as time and space (Svensson 1998: 197–8). I will therefore categorize the partitive constructions in my material into semantic subgroups, in order to enable a more fine-grained analysis of their distribution. As we shall see, the overall figures hide a number of distributional differences in this respect.

Finally, I will look at verbal concord with partitives where the partitive noun and the complement of the preposition *of* do not agree in number. The complement is often the notional head of a partitive construction; in (1) above, for instance, *advice* carries more semantic weight than *bit*. This may lead to language change in which the complement, rather than the partitive noun, governs verbal concord (see Denison 1998: 121–3). This type of change is related to grammaticalization, as, syntactically, the partitive noun goes from being the head of the partitive construction to being part of a complex determiner of the head (which, in turn, started out as a prepositional complement). In order to see whether such change can be identified in the material, I will devote a case study to comparing nineteenth-century and late twentieth-century English regarding concord with partitives with *number* as partitive noun.

The main research questions of the present study are thus the following:

1. Does the frequency of partitive constructions in nineteenth-century English vary with time, gender and genre?
2. Do all semantic subgroups of partitive constructions exhibit the same pattern of occurrence, or is there variation with extralinguistic parameters in their distribution?
3. Is there any evidence from verbal concord for linguistic change in which the complement of the preposition *of* replaces the partitive noun as the syntactic head of the partitive construction, or do other factors influence the choice between singular and plural concord?

The organization of the results section matches the order of the three research questions above. However, as the partitive constructions were retrieved semi-automatically for the present study, and as several syntactic and semantic criteria were used to select partitives for inclusion in the counts, a few words on the corpus set-up and on the retrieval and classification of data are in order before the results are presented.

2   Material and data

2.1   Material

The texts examined in the present study make up part of the Corpus of Nineteenth-century English (CONCE), which includes seven genres: Debates, Drama, Fiction, History, Letters, Science and Trials (for a description of the corpus, see the Introduction to the present volume; see also Kytö, Rudanko and Smitterberg 2000). The texts in the CONCE corpus are divided into three periods: period 1 includes texts published, or, for some genres, produced between 1800 and 1830, period 2 between 1850 and 1870, and period 3 between 1870 and 1900. Since the retrieval of partitive constructions from the material was based partly on semantic criteria, thus necessitating close readings of all potential partitives (see section 2.2), the retrieval process proved to be highly time-consuming. Consequently, owing to limitations of time, only parts of CONCE could be drawn on for data. Periods 1 and 3 were selected in order to maximize the diachronic spread of the results. This subsample of CONCE will be referred to as 'the subcorpus' henceforth. As mentioned in section 1, gender differences in the use of partitive constructions will also be analysed. The Letters genre in CONCE has been stratified into texts produced by women and by men, which makes such an analysis possible.[3]

2.2   Retrieving and classifying the data

2.2.1 The retrieval process.   Given the high frequency of both nouns and the preposition *of* in the English language, it proved necessary to restrict the collection of data in two ways in order to obtain a manageable amount of information. As mentioned in section 2.1, data were drawn from a subcorpus consisting of periods 1 and 3 of CONCE. In addition, the retrieval of data was restricted to cases where *of* was both immediately preceded and immediately followed by a noun. Thus, partitive constructions where the prepositional complement included a determiner, as in *a page of a book*, or an attributive adjective, as in *a bunch of red flowers*, were not retrieved. There were two main reasons for restricting the retrieval in this way. First, by constraining the retrieval on linguistic grounds, I would still be able to include all genres in CONCE in the study. Second, the operation could be carried out automatically, as the CONCE corpus has been tagged using the EngCG–2 tagger (see Karlsson et al. 1995 for an introduction to the Constraint Grammar framework).[4]

Most of the retrieval process outlined above was based on the tagged version of the subcorpus, from which 'noun + *of* + noun' sequences were retrieved using the WordSmith Tools concordancer program.[5] However, there were two exceptions to this method. First, some sequences, including *a lot of*, are coded as complex determiners by the EngCG–2 tagger, which means that *lot* in such sequences is not retrieved as a noun. Second, the tagger classifies many nouns ending in -*ing* (for example, *feeling*) as -*ing* forms, with no further specification, rather than as nouns. Additional searches were run in order to find potential partitive constructions including such sequences and forms.

The next step was to go through the output of the retrieval procedures to include only relevant partitive constructions in the counts. As mentioned above, partitive constructions where the head of the prepositional complement was preceded by a determiner or an adjectival premodifier were excluded from the automatic retrieval process. In order to obtain a consistent set of data, I also excluded cases like *a flood of spring rain*, where the preposition *of* was followed by a noun other than the head of the prepositional complement. In addition, some set phrases, such as *man of war* meaning 'armed ship', were excluded from the counts.

As Svensson (1998: 198) points out, in a partitive construction the prepositional complement is typically either a noncount mass noun, as in (1), also cited in section 1, or a plural count noun, as in (2).

(1) [$Gen.$] Why, I own your case is singular; but I'll give you a *bit of advice*, I have often received advice from you –
    (Drama, Thomas Morton, 1800–30, p. 32)

(2) A *flight of steps* leads up to the low wooden door, innocent of knocker or bell.
    (Fiction, Mary Braddon, 1870–1900, p. II, 78)

In the interest of consistency, I therefore excluded partitives such as *parts of London*, where the complement is a proper noun with unique reference, from the analysis.

Svensson (1998: 198) also seems to take the line that the partitive noun should be either a singular count noun preceded by the indefinite article or a plural count noun. In contrast, Quirk et al. (1985: 1278) give an example of a partitive noun preceded by a demonstrative determiner (*this kind of research*). In the present study, the influence of the determiner, if any, was not taken into account in the classification. Partitive nouns preceded by definite articles, as in (3), were thus included, provided that they met the other criteria for selection.

(3) Upon the return of the Maxwells to the drawing-room, the first *burst of surprise* and sorrow – if there were any – having subsided, the members of the family were able to converse upon the topics, so new and so deeply interesting to them, with calmness and composure.
    (Fiction, Theodore Edward Hook, 1800–30, p. III, 308)

There were two main reasons for this decision. First, the part/whole relationship is discernible regardless of whether the partitive noun phrase is definite or indefinite. Secondly, as will be shown in section 3.3.2, the difference between definite and indefinite partitives affects verbal concord, which makes the inclusion of definite partitive noun phrases relevant to the discussion of this matter.

The most difficult part of the selection process was the classification of the remaining constructions as partitive and non-partitive. For instance, the sequence 'noun + *of* + noun' may be genitive rather than partitive, as in *the colour of boats*. Given that this part of the classification process was carried out by means of close readings of each potential partitive construction, scholars may disagree as regards the classification of individual cases; for the purposes of this study, I focused on making the classification internally consistent. The constructions were classified as partitive if their semantics matched one of the five semantic subgroups identified in the present study. Section 2.2.2 is devoted to a description of these subgroups.

In some cases, other linguistic constructions have functions similar to those of partitives. For instance, although factors such as sentence type and the stylistic level of the text affect the distribution, some quantifiers, e.g. *much, (a great/good) many* and *plenty of*, can be more or less equivalent to a partitive construction with *lot/s* or *deal* as partitive noun (see Quirk et al. 1985: 262–3; Biber et al. 1999: 275–6). In addition, a structure with premodifier + head may be a frequent alternative to some partitive constructions, e.g. *a news item* for *an item of news*. The former type of variation is addressed in a separate paper (Smitterberg 2003). Owing to the high frequency of noun + noun sequences in the English language, accounting for the latter also falls outside the scope of the present study, which centres on partitive constructions proper.

2.2.2 Subgroups of partitive constructions.   As mentioned in section 1, Svensson (1998: 197–8) argues that partitive constructions 'go beyond merely express-ing simple part-whole relations'. Svensson classifies partitive constructions into eight subcategories based on the semantics of the partitive noun.[6] For my study, however, although the partitive noun was given the most weight in the classi-fication, I also took the semantics of the prepositional complement and of the context into account. In my modified version of Svensson's (1998) typology, five types of partitive constructions were included:

- Qualitative partitive constructions, e.g. *a sort of journal*.
- Quantitative partitive constructions, e.g. *a piece of sodium*.
- Partitive constructions of shape, e.g. *a ball of wool*.
- Partitive constructions of time, e.g. *months of anxiety*.
- Partitive constructions of intensity, e.g. *the first burst of surprise*.

The first group thus comprises qualitative partitive constructions, as in (4).

(4) I had meant to have kept a *sort of journal* for you, but I have not been calm enough; . . .
   (Letters, Samuel Taylor Coleridge, 1800–30, p. 456)

Qualitative partitives refer to a type, rather than an amount, of the prepositional complement. The most common partitive nouns in qualitative partitives are *kind* and *sort*.

In the second group we find quantitative partitives, as in (5).

(5) This was accomplished by volatilising a *piece of sodium* in a glass tube in an atmosphere of hydrogen and observing its absorption spectrum.
(Science, Norman J. Lockyer, 1870–1900, p. 128)

The partitive noun in quantitative partitive constructions refers to a quantity of the prepositional complement. This is a heterogeneous subgroup, which covers both partitives with short, vague partitive nouns such as *bit*, *piece*, *lot* and *number*, and partitives with longer and/or more precise partitive nouns such as *proportion* and *pair*. As will become clear in section 3.2, partitives of quantity constitute a very frequent type of partitive construction.

Partitive nouns in partitives belonging to groups three, four and five tend to have more specific meanings. Group three, exemplified in (6), contains partitive constructions of shape.

(6) ... for I, so far from being bound down, take the world with me in my flights, & often it seems lighter than a *Ball of Wool* rolled by the wind.
(Letters, William Blake, 1800–30, p. 34)

These partitives are closely related to quantitative partitives, but retain a more specific idea of shape. Common partitive nouns in partitives of shape include *drop* and *line*.

The members of the fourth group, partitives of time, are also close to quantitative partitives. Partitives of time encode an amount of duration, as in (7).

(7) What *months of anxiety* you have had; there is something so exhausting in the concentration of one's thoughts on a sick person.
(Letters, Mary Sibylla Holland, 1870–1900, p. 115)

As with quantitative partitives, this group includes both vague partitive nouns like *period* and more specific ones such as *month* and *hour*.

To the fifth and last group belong partitives of intensity, as in (3), also quoted in section 2.2.1.

(3) Upon the return of the Maxwells to the drawing-room, the first *burst of surprise* and sorrow – if there were any – having subsided, the members of the family were able to converse upon the topics, so new and so deeply interesting to them, with calmness and composure.
(Fiction, Theodore Edward Hook, 1800–30, p. III, 308)

These not very frequent partitives are close to partitives of time. However, their partitive nouns are even more specific, and stress the limited duration and intensity of the prepositional complement. Apart from *burst*, as in (3), *fit* and *attack* are comparatively common partitive nouns in partitives of intensity.

In addition to the above groups, Svensson (1998) separates generic partitive nouns, such as *piece* in *a piece of paper*, and partitive nouns of configuration and collection, for instance *team* in *a team of players*, from quantitative partitive

Table 10.1. *Partitive constructions by period and genre in the subcorpus.*

Period	Debates	Drama	Fiction	History	Letters	Science	Trials	Total
1	28	39	104	65	169	330	80	815
3	54	39	84	63	187	178	133	738
Total	82	78	188	128	356	508	213	1,553

Table 10.2. *Partitive constructions by period and gender in the Letters genre in the subcorpus.*

Period	Women	Men	Total
1	69	100	169
3	114	73	187
Total	183	173	356

nouns; he also includes partitive nouns of sensory impressions/expressions, like *gasp* in *a gasp of astonishment*, in his analysis. Generic partitives have partitive nouns that are used with a variety of prepositional complements and that have little lexical meaning of their own (Svensson 1998: 207). Partitives with central partitive nouns such as *bit* and *piece*, as well as partitives with less clear-cut partitive nouns such as *case*, belong to this category. However, in the absence of large-scale corpora of nineteenth-century English, which could be used to measure the scope of the variety of prepositional complements used with a given partitive noun, the borderline between generic and quantitative partition was difficult to draw. As regards the extent to which the partitive noun has lexical meaning, it will be shown in section 3.3.2 that the relative semantic weight of the partitive noun and the complement may vary although the partitive noun is the same. Consequently, I classified Svensson's (1998) central generic partitive nouns together with quantitative partitive constructions. More peripheral members were often excluded from the data, as the part/whole relationship was frequently unclear in these expressions. Similarly, Svensson's (1998) partitives of configuration and collection were classified as quantitative partitives in my study, as these two groups proved difficult to separate. In contrast, Svensson's partitives of sensory impressions/expressions were not included in the counts, since the part/whole relation was difficult to discern in many of these constructions.[7]

A total of 1,553 partitive constructions were included in the analysis. Table 10.1 presents the results for period and genre subsamples; the results for women and men letter-writers in Letters are given in table 10.2.

Table 10.3. *Partitive constructions per 1,000 words by period and genre in the subcorpus.*

Period	Debates	Drama	Fiction	History	Letters	Science	Trials	All genres
1	1.41	1.25	2.47	2.10	1.39	8.68	1.28	2.35
3	2.71	1.34	2.79	2.06	2.06	5.82	1.97	2.47
1 + 3	2.06	1.29	2.61	2.08	1.68	7.40	1.64	2.41

3   Results

3.1   *The frequency of partitive constructions by period, genre and gender*

In order to compensate for differences in text length between samples of the subcorpus, the raw frequencies of partitive constructions were normalized to a text length of 1,000 words. The results of the normalization process are presented in table 10.3.

As table 10.3 shows, on average there are 2.41 partitives per 1,000 words in the subcorpus. The frequency of partitives increases only slightly between periods 1 and 3, from 2.35 to 2.47 partitives per 1,000 words. The overall frequency of partitive constructions is thus relatively stable in diachrony. This result implies that partitives constitute a well-established feature of Late Modern English syntax, something which may perhaps be expected. The result may also indicate that, during the nineteenth century, there were no major shifts in the relative distribution of partitive constructions and other means of encoding similar meanings, such as noun + noun sequences of the type *a news item*. However, this matter requires further investigation.

There is more variation in the frequency of partitives across the genre parameter. Table 10.3 shows that Drama, Letters and Trials have less than two partitives per 1,000 words, while Debates, Fiction, and History have between two and three. Science stands out from the other genres with over seven partitives per 1,000 words. This may be expected considering that scientific writing is characterized by high frequencies of nouns and prepositional phrases (see e.g. Biber and Finegan 1997); but the clear difference compared with History, the other non-speech-related expository genre in CONCE, is nevertheless noteworthy. According to Biber (1988: 171), Present-day English academic prose (an umbrella term that would encompass both Science and History) is a genre which includes 'several well-defined sub-genres', and which exhibits a great deal of internal linguistic variation that 'is due in part to variation among the sub-genres'. The difference between History and Science in the frequency of partitive constructions shows that such variation also existed in nineteenth-century English. Further research is needed to establish whether variation of this type is a panchronic feature of academic prose, or whether changes – such as that from a more to a less personal style which, Görlach (1999: 150) claims, took place in scientific writing in the nineteenth century – have increased the internal linguistic differentiation of this genre.

These cross-genre results can be compared with those obtained by Geisler (2002), who carried out a factor score analysis of the CONCE corpus based on the functional dimensions identified in Biber (1988). Dimensions 1, 3 and 5 of the analysis were given the labels 'Involved vs Informational Production', 'Explicit vs Situation-dependent Reference' and 'Abstract vs Non-abstract Information' in Biber (1988). Biber and Finegan (1997: 260) claim that Dimensions 1, 3 and 5 'can be considered "oral"/"literate", in that they distinguish between stereotypically oral (conversational) registers at one pole, and stereotypically literate (written expository) registers at the other pole'. On these three dimensions, Geisler (2002) showed that the expository genres Debates, History and Science were closer to the literate poles – informational production, explicit reference and abstract information – than the non-expository genres Drama, Fiction, Letters and Trials. Although Fiction occupied an intermediate position between the expository group and the other three members of the non-expository group on Dimension 1, there was no overlap between the expository and the non-expository groups of genres on any of the three dimensions (Geisler 2002).

Comparing Geisler's (2002) results with those presented in table 10.3, it is found that, apart from the relatively high frequency of partitives in Fiction, the expository genres have higher frequencies of partitives than the non-expository genres. It thus seems that high frequencies of partitive constructions are, on the whole, characteristic of literate, expository genres.[8] Given the comparatively high frequency of partitives in Fiction, it may be possible to link partitive constructions with Dimension 1 in particular, i.e. 'Involved vs Informational Production', where Fiction took an intermediate position with respect to the expository and non-expository groups of genres in Geisler's (2002: 258) analysis. A high frequency of partitive constructions would then be characteristic of informational production, and a low frequency of involved production. On the textual level, partitive constructions thus tend to co-occur with linguistic features such as nouns and prepositions (which are part of all partitives), and attributive adjectives, indicating a 'nouny' style with complex noun phrases. In contrast, the incidence of features such as private verbs, contractions, present-tense verbs and second-person pronouns, which imply a 'verby' style with a speech-related structure and dialogic turn-taking, can be expected to be comparatively low in texts where partitives are common.

As regards changes in individual genres, table 10.3 shows that the frequency of partitives is relatively stable in Drama, Fiction and History over the century. Letters, Trials and, in particular, Debates display increasing frequencies, whereas Science exhibits a decrease in the frequency of partitive constructions. Thus there seems to be no clear division between expository and non-expository genres when

Table 10.4. *Partitive constructions per 1,000 words by period and gender in the Letters genre in the subcorpus.*

Period	Women	Men	Women + men
1	1.00	1.91	1.39
3	2.27	1.79	2.06
1 + 3	1.53	1.86	1.68

the parameters of time and genre are combined. It is probable that differences in subject matter underlie the variation attested; however, analyses of such factors were beyond the scope of the present study.

As regards gender differences in the frequency of partitives, the results are presented in table 10.4. The table shows that partitive constructions are more common in men's than in women's letters in period 1, whereas the situation is reversed in period 3. When compared with the results Geisler (2003) reached in a factor score analysis of women's and men's letters in CONCE, this finding further strengthens the connection between the frequency of partitive constructions and dimension scores on Dimension 1, 'Involved vs Informational Production', of Biber's (1988) factor analysis. Geisler (2003: 94) found that men's letters were more informational than women's in period 1, when the frequency of partitive constructions was also higher in men's letters; the opposite holds for period 3, concerning both dimension scores and the frequency of partitives. In other words, across the parameter of genre as well as that of gender, low frequencies of partitive constructions correlate with high dimension scores on Dimension 1 and vice versa. High frequencies of partitive constructions thus characterize informational texts, whereas there tend to be few partitives in texts that are marked for personal involvement. The other two oral/literate dimensions do not match the results as closely as does Dimension 1. Women's letters display more situation-dependent reference than men's in both period 1 and period 3 (Geisler 2003: 99). On Dimension 5, the result is rather the opposite of what might be expected against the background of the frequency of partitive constructions: women's letters exhibit a more abstract information focus than men's in period 1, but a less abstract focus in period 3 (Geisler 2003: 103).[9] I will discuss the connection between the frequency of partitive constructions and Dimension 1 of the factor analysis further in section 4.

3.2 Semantic subgroups of partitive constructions

The aim of the following analysis is to uncover differences in the distribution of partitives across the five semantic subgroups distinguished in this study,

Table 10.5. *Partitive constructions by subgroup and period in the subcorpus (row percentages within brackets).*

Period	Quality	Quantity	Shape	Time	Intensity	Total
1	175 (21%)	524 (64%)	72 (9%)	25 (3%)	19 (2%)	815
3	158 (21%)	469 (64%)	73 (10%)	18 (2%)	20 (3%)	738
Total	333 (21%)	993 (64%)	145 (9%)	43 (3%)	39 (3%)	1,553

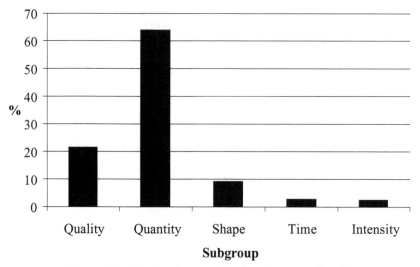

Figure 10.1. The distribution of the five subgroups of partitive constructions in the subcorpus.

differences which may not be apparent from the overall figures. As will become clear, the subgroup of quantitative partitives comprises more than half of the partitive constructions included in the counts; this dominance of quantitative partitives in the data may have obscured differences in the distribution of the less frequent but semantically more specific subgroups. At the same time, it is also of interest to look more closely at quantitative partitives precisely because they dominate the results. Given the low raw frequencies of partitives belonging to the subgroups of space, time and intensity, in what follows I will only discuss the parameters of time, genre and gender in isolation.

3.2.1 Differences in diachrony.   Table 10.5 presents the results per period for the subcorpus; the percentage of all partitives accounted for by each subgroup in periods 1 and 3 together is also given in figure 10.1.

Table 10.6. *Partitive constructions by subgroup and genre in the subcorpus (row percentages within brackets).*

Genre	Quality	Quantity	Shape	Time	Intensity	Total
Debates	16 (20%)	63 (77%)	2 (2%)	1 (1%)	–	82
Drama	14 (18%)	51 (65%)	7 (9%)	1 (1%)	5 (6%)	78
Fiction	39 (21%)	102 (54%)	30 (16%)	10 (5%)	7 (4%)	188
History	25 (20%)	79 (62%)	11 (9%)	9 (7%)	4 (3%)	128
Letters	93 (26%)	197 (55%)	40 (11%)	11 (3%)	15 (4%)	356
Science	73 (14%)	373 (73%)	48 (9%)	7 (1%)	7 (1%)	508
Trials	73 (34%)	128 (60%)	7 (3%)	4 (2%)	1 (0%)	213
Total	333 (21%)	993 (64%)	145 (9%)	43 (3%)	39 (3%)	1,553

As figure 10.1 makes clear, partitives of quantity constitute the most frequent subgroup of the five. In my discussion of cross-genre differences, I will therefore focus on the distribution of quantitative partitives, although the other subgroups will also be commented on. As for these other subgroups, roughly every fifth partitive construction is a partitive of quality, and every tenth a partitive of shape. Partitives of time and intensity are rare in the material. As shown in table 10.5, the subgroups exhibit quite remarkable consistency in diachrony. No group displays a difference of more than one percentage point between periods 1 and 3, and these differences are not statistically significant at the 0.05 significance level, which will be used throughout the present study.[10]

3.2.2 Cross-genre differences.   As was the case for the overall frequency of partitive constructions (see section 3.1), the genre parameter reveals more conspicuous differences than that of time. The distribution of the five subgroups across this parameter is given in table 10.6; figure 10.2 shows the percentage of quantitative partitives in each genre.

The results presented in table 10.6 and figure 10.2 indicate that a high proportion of quantitative partitives is characteristic of expository genres, with non-expository genres having a slightly more even distribution across the five categories. The main exception to this pattern is Drama, with the third highest percentage of quantitative partitives in the material. As will be shown, however, cross-genre differences in what types of quantitative partitives occur in texts may lie behind this seeming discrepancy. The expected frequency of partitives of time and intensity in the data is so low that the results presented in table 10.6 cannot be tested for statistical significance using the chi-square test. However, if the groups of shape, time and intensity are pooled together, with the rationale that the partition expressed by the members of these three groups is more specific

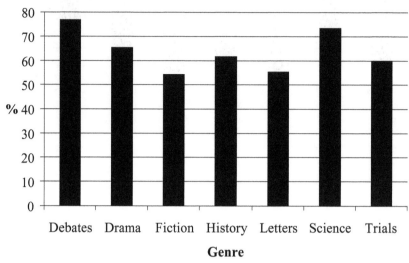

Figure 10.2. The percentage of quantitative partitives by genre in the sub-corpus.

than that expressed by qualitative and quantitative partitives, the results can be tested, and these cross-genre differences are significant.[11]

A closer look at the individual genres reveals further genre-specific patterns.

Debates

Partitives of quantity account for 77 per cent of all partitive constructions in Debates, the highest percentage for this subgroup in CONCE (see table 10.6). In Debates, the most common partitive noun in partitives of quantity is *number*, as in (8), with twenty-two instances.[12]

(8) I could multiply cases – perhaps not so extreme as that – in which persons possess and record a *number of votes*, . . .
   (Debates, 1870–1900, p. IV, 1185)

Other frequent partitive nouns belonging to this category in Debates are *system*, *body* and *share*, with six, six and five occurrences respectively, as in, for instance, *large bodies of voters*. Overall, the most common function of partitives of quantity in Debates appears to be the creation of a more or less unspecific entity, such as the number of votes in example (8).

Subgroups other than quantity and quality, the two most frequent subgroups, are less well represented in Debates. There are no partitives of intensity in Debates; the genre also has the lowest percentage of partitives of time and space in the subcorpus. This may be due to the expository nature of the Debates texts, which contain few narrative passages that would favour the occurrence of these more descriptive partitive constructions.

Drama

As mentioned above, the distribution in Drama goes against the overall trend in the material for non-expository genres to have a comparatively low percentage of quantitative partition. In Drama, partitives of quantity account for 65 per cent of all partitives, a higher figure than for the expository genre History. However, an investigation of the quantitative partitive constructions that are used in Drama evinces some differences compared with the expository genres: the most frequent quantitative partitive noun in Drama is *bit*, as in example (9), with eight instances, followed by *glass* (five instances), as in *a glass of Madeira*.

(9) [$CH.$] Then there's another little fireside game which is great fun. We each take a *bit of paper* and a pencil and try who can jot down the nicest dinner for ninepence, and the next day we have it.
    (Drama, W. S. Gilbert, 1870–1900, p. 29)

As indicated by the high frequency of these partitive nouns, partitives of quantity in Drama tend to denote a concrete quantity and/or a specific amount. In addition, eight out of the fourteen instances of partitives with *bit* as their partitive noun in the subcorpus occur in Drama, a genre that approximates informal speech in some respects. The wide semantic and stylistic range of quantitative partitives may thus explain the high proportion of this subgroup in Drama. A more fine-grained analysis of this subgroup falls outside the scope of the present study, but it seems probable that such an analysis would reveal clear signs of stylistic grading such as those hinted at above.

Drama also has the highest percentage of partitives of intensity in the material; however, the raw frequency is only five. The only partitive noun that occurs twice in partitives of intensity in Drama is *fit*, as in (10).

(10) [$Trus.$] Ah, sir, if I escape a *fit of illness*, after the fright I have suffered, it will be a miracle.
     (Drama, John Poole, 1800–30, p. 29)

Partitives of intensity typically emphasize the suddenness, intensity and/or unexpectedness of events: they can thus be expected to occur with a comparatively high frequency in a genre that consists of writing often intended to reflect colloquial speech.

Fiction

In contrast to Drama, Fiction has the lowest percentage of quantitative partitives of all genres in the subcorpus (54 per cent). Fiction exhibits the same percentage of qualitative partitives as the corpus mean: the unexpectedly high frequency of partitive constructions in this genre thus chiefly reflects the occurrence of partitives belonging to the semantically more specific subgroups of shape, time and intensity. Nonetheless, quantitative partitives account for more than half of all partitive constructions in the genre, and the partitive nouns in these quantitative partitives are quite varied. The most frequent nouns are *couple*, *thing* and *deal* (as in, for instance, *a great deal of time*) with four occurrences each, for instance (11) with *couple*.

(11)   An oval pond of stewed calves' head, dotted with dirt balls, and surrounded by dingy brain and egg pancakes, stood next the fish, and a *couple of rabbits*, smothered in onions, next the soup.
(Fiction, Theodore Edward Hook, 1800–30, p. I, 230)

Of the genres in the subcorpus, Fiction has the highest percentage of partitives of shape, 16 per cent. The only partitive nouns that occur more than once in this subgroup are *grain*, *sprig* and *line*, as in example (12) with *sprig*, with two instances.

(12)   The pale lustre yet hanging in the north-western heaven was sufficient to show that a *sprig of ivy* had grown from the wall across the door to a length of more than a foot, delicately tying the panel to the stone jamb.
(Fiction, Thomas Hardy, 1870–1900, p. I, 325)

The high percentage of partitives of shape in Fiction may be due to the many passages of narrative description in this genre. By using a partitive of shape, the writer of a Fiction text can combine the presentation of textual information and visual description. Fiction also has the second highest percentage of partitives of time, another subgroup that is often used for narrative description, in the subcorpus; only History has a higher percentage in this respect.

History
In the History genre, partitives of quantity account for 62 per cent of all partitive constructions. The most frequent partitive noun in partitives of quantity in History is *crowd*, as in example (13), with six instances, followed by *number*, *succession* and *sum* (four occurrences each), as in *a small number of names*, *a long succession of princes* and *large sums of money*.

(13)   Arches were thrown across the streets, tapestry, plate, and arms were suspended from the windows, and the road was lined with *crowds of spectators*.
(History, John Lingard, 1800–30, p. III, 80)

As may be expected of a genre where the passage of time is central to the text, History has a higher percentage of partitives of time than any other genre (as mentioned above, Fiction has the second highest percentage). In these partitives, only *month*, as in example (14), occurs twice as a partitive noun. Partitives of time seem to convey a combination of added emphasis and factual information.

(14) *Months of labour* and of battle were indeed still in store before the mutineers were finally dispersed and order was completely restored.
(History, Spencer Walpole, 1870–1900, p. VI, 317)

Letters
In Letters, partitives of quantity make up 55 per cent of all partitive constructions, the second lowest figure in the subcorpus. The most frequent partitive nouns in partitives of quantity are *deal* (e.g. *a great deal of trouble*) and *piece* (see example (15)) with thirteen instances each.

(15) As a *piece of gossip* I must tell you that Mrs Calvert says that the dear Doctor actually offered himself to Mrs Kennedy – she being an heiress – Mary had forgot the Lady's name but it must have been Miss D. from the time, her being an heiress, having a mother, and being a ward of old Mitchinson of Carlisle.
(Letters, Sara Hutchinson, 1800–30, p. 50)

It is noteworthy that, in Letters, these two most frequent partitive nouns in partitives of quantity have little semantic weight of their own, and are typically used to quantify uncountable nouns.[13] Other frequent partitive nouns belonging to this category in Letters are *quantity* and *couple* (eight occurrences each).

Letters and Drama can both be described as comparatively informal, speech-related genres: while Drama texts intend to reflect speech, Letters may contain speech-like language owing to the informal production circumstances of a private letter. Letters have the second-highest percentage of partitives of intensity in the subcorpus; as mentioned above, Drama exhibits an even higher proportion. There may be a connection between the informal, speech-related language of these genres and the occurrence of a type of partitive construction that emphasizes suddenness, unexpectedness etc. Such a connection would further indicate that not all partitives are characteristic of informational rather than involved production.

Science
Of the genres in the subcorpus, Science exhibits the second highest percentage, 73 per cent, of partitives of quantity. The most frequent partitive noun in these partitives of quantity is, in fact, *quantity*, with sixty-four instances, as exemplified in (16).

(16) If every man were to forego the use of luxuries, and be intent only on accumulation, a *quantity of necessaries* might be produced, for which there could not be any immediate consumption.
(Science, David Ricardo, 1800–30, pp. 404–5)

Other common partitive nouns in this category are *number* (as in for instance *an indefinite number of varieties*), *proportion* and *rate*, with fifty-four, forty and forty occurrences respectively. As in Debates, partitives of quantity in Science appear to occur chiefly in more or less unspecific contexts.

Trials

Partitives of quantity account for 60 per cent of all partitive constructions in Trials. The most common partitive noun in these partitives is *glass*, as in example (17), with seventeen instances. However, the high incidence of this partitive noun in Trials is partly due to genre-specific constraints. A given partitive construction is sometimes returned to in several question/answer adjacency pairs in the cross-examinations, as in (17) with *glass of water*.

(17) Then I am to understand that you recollected the voice when he asked you
      for a *glass of water*? – When I looked round I remembered the voice directly.
      Directly he asked for a *glass of water*? – Yes.
      Did he come into the cottage? You were in the parlour, were you not? –
      No; I was just coming out of my back kitchen into my front; the kitchen door
      was open, and he said, 'Will you oblige me, ma'am, with a *glass of water*?'
      (Trials, Roger Tichborne, 1870–1900, p. 2190)

Apart from *glass*, the most frequent partitive nouns include *number* (as in for example *a great number of people*), *piece*, *quantity* and *pair*, with twelve, ten, ten and nine occurrences respectively. Partitives of quantity in Trials thus express a mix of specific and unspecific partition.

Among the genres in the subcorpus, Trials have the highest percentage of partitives of quality, 34 per cent. The most common partitive noun in these partitives is *sort*, as in (18), with thirty-three instances, followed by *kind* with nineteen, as in *all kinds of music*.

(18) [\$Q.\$] It was a *sort of levee*, was it not? – [\$A.\$] Indeed it was.
      (Trials, Jonathan Martin, 1800–30, p. 63)

The high incidence of partitives of quality in Trials may be due to a need to clarify previous statements in cross-examinations. Most partitives of quality occur in questions rather than in answers from the witness, and the cross-examiner typically uses qualitative partitives either to settle a point, as in (18), or to ask the witness to specify a previous statement further, as in (19):

(19) [\$Q.\$] During that time had you opportunities of seeing him every day? –
      [\$A.\$] Yes, in the morning or at night; in the daytime he was out selling
      books.
      [\$Q.\$] What *sort of books* did he sell? – [\$A.\$] His own life.
      (Trials, Jonathan Martin, 1800–30, p. 13)

Table 10.7. *Partitive constructions by subgroup and gender in the Letters genre in the subcorpus (row percentages within brackets).*

Gender	Quality	Quantity	Shape	Time	Intensity	Total
Women	45 (25%)	98 (54%)	22 (12%)	7 (4%)	11 (6%)	183
Men	48 (28%)	99 (57%)	18 (10%)	4 (2%)	4 (2%)	173
Total	93 (26%)	197 (55%)	40 (11%)	11 (3%)	15 (4%)	356

Summary

The analysis of differences among genres with respect to the distribution of semantic subgroups, and nouns within these subgroups, has shown that not all types of partitive constructions are uniformly distributed across texts. A high percentage of quantitative partitives with unspecific partitive nouns appears to be characteristic of many expository texts in the subcorpus, whereas the non-expository genres display a lower percentage of quantitative partitive constructions and/or a tendency towards more specific or informal partitive nouns in partitives of quantity. Other genre-specific constraints can also be observed; for instance, the combination of speech-related and informal language in Drama and Letters appears to promote the occurrence of partitives of intensity. Although the genres do not pattern in the same way with respect to the overall frequency of partitive constructions and to the percentage of quantitative partitives, the tendency towards a division between expository and non-expository genres is present in both analyses.

3.2.3 Gender differentiation. The final extralinguistic parameter whose effect on the distribution of the subgroups was investigated is gender. Table 10.7 presents the results of this analysis.

The results in table 10.7 show a slight difference between women and men in that women letter writers use comparatively more partitives of shape, time and intensity, whereas men use more partitives of quality and quantity. This would mean that women might be using partitives with more specific meaning to a greater extent than men. However, the variation attested in the data is not statistically significant: there is thus no reliable evidence that women and men letter writers use different subgroups of partitive constructions to differing degrees.[14]

3.3 Verbal concord

3.3.1 Tendencies in the nineteenth-century material. When occurring in subject position, partitive constructions where the partitive noun and the complement of the preposition *of* do not agree in number can cause uncertainty among language users as regards which of the two nouns the verb should agree with in number. If the verb agrees with the partitive noun, the noun is followed by a postmodifying prepositional phrase with *of* + complement; in contrast, if the verb agrees with the complement, the partitive noun can be characterized as part of a complex determiner of the complement head (Denison 1998: 121). The partitive noun can then be said to have grammaticalized, as some of its lexical status has been lost. Denison (1998: 121) also argues that '[f]or quite a number of phrases, the historical development has been a classic process of replacement': first the partitive noun governs concord, then comes a period with vacillation between concord with the partitive noun and with the prepositional complement, and finally a stage where only the complement governs verbal concord (see section 3.3.2 for a case study of nineteenth-century and late twentieth-century English in this respect).

It can be argued that constructions where the verb agrees with the prepositional complement are not, strictly, partitive, as the partitive noun may have been reanalysed as part of a determiner. However, in the present study, all constructions that met the syntactic and semantic criteria for inclusion (see section 2.2) were classified as partitive, regardless of whether the verb agreed with the partitive noun or the complement. The distinction between partitive nouns and complex determiners can only be made on syntactic grounds for a small subset of all partitive constructions in the material, viz. those that both exhibit variation in number between the partitive noun and the complement and act as the subject of a verb phrase that shows number contrast. For this reason, this distinction was not made in previous sections. Instead, the present section is devoted to a detailed discussion of that subset.

Of the 1,553 partitive constructions in the material, 161, or 10 per cent, both act as the subject of a clause and exhibit number difference between the partitive noun and the prepositional complement (i.e. either the partitive noun is singular and the complement plural or vice versa). These 161 partitives thus present the language user with a potential choice between singular and plural verbal concord. Of these, however, 61 (38 per cent of the total of 161) do not involve any actual choice.[15] Owing to the low raw frequency of relevant verb phrases, and to the likelihood that semantic factors will influence the results, my approach in the following discussion will be both qualitative and quantitative.

Of the 100 relevant verb phrases, seventy-nine (79 per cent) agree with the partitive noun and twenty-one (21 per cent) with the prepositional complement. The tendency for the verb phrase to agree with the partitive noun is especially pronounced when the partitive noun is plural and the complement singular: none of these thirty verb phrases agrees with the complement. In contrast, of the seventy cases where the partitive noun is in the singular and the prepositional complement in the plural, the verb phrase agrees with the complement in twenty-one cases (30 per cent). Moreover, the results indicate change between periods 1 and 3 in this respect. In period 1, only six of thirty-nine verb phrases, or 15 per cent, agree with a plural complement rather than with a singular partitive noun;

in period 3, fifteen of thirty-one verb phrases (48 per cent) do so. The difference between the period samples is statistically significant.[16]

However, this significant result may be due to variation in the distribution of partitive nouns and prepositional complements rather than to language change, since partitive nouns and complements will differ with respect to their tendency to control verbal concord. In addition, semantic factors are likely to influence the results: the noun that is given more semantic weight in a given case is more likely to control verbal concord (see Denison 1998: 121 for an example with the partitive noun *majority*). Further investigation of the results is thus called for. The present investigation will focus on partitives where the prepositional complement, rather than the partitive noun, controls verbal concord, as the change between periods 1 and 3, if any, is likely to involve the complement replacing the partitive noun as the head of the partitive construction (see Denison 1998: 121).

In period 1, the only partitive nouns that could control verbal concord but do not do so are *class* and *number* (two occurrences each), as well as *couple* and *sort* (one occurrence each). For exemplification, see (20)[17] and (21).

(20) In time of peace, on the contrary, the operations of the sinking fund, the unwillingness, which a particular *class of persons* **feel** to divert their funds to any other employment than that to which they have been accustomed, . . .
(Science, David Ricardo, 1800–30, pp. 413–14)

(21) There **are** a vast *number of ways* of making the agreeable in society, and several of these pleasant knacks did Godfrey Moss himself possess; . . .
(Fiction, Theodore Edward Hook, 1800–30, p. II, 164)

Of those four partitive nouns, *class* (one occurrence) and *number* (nine instances) also occur with singular concord, as in (22).[18]

(22) When however, by the encouragement which high wages give to the increase of population, the *number of labourers* **is** increased, wages again fall to their natural price, and indeed from a re-action sometimes fall below it.
(Science, David Ricardo, 1800–30, p. 92)

In period 3, there are eight different singular partitive nouns that fail to control verbal concord, in a total of fifteen cases: *number* (eight occurrences), and *army*, *body*, *group*, *handful*, *line*, *majority* and *set* (one occurrence each). Of these nouns, *number* (seven occurrences) and *group* (one instance) also occur with singular concord; the other members of this set are *series* (two instances), and *crowd*, *family*, *flight*, *kind*, *preponderance* and *stream* (one occurrence each). Although semantic factors enter into the choice between singular and plural concord, the transition to more plural marking in period 3 may be revelatory of language change. One factor that was perhaps influential in this context is the prescriptive attitude of nineteenth-century grammarians. Dekeyser's (1975: 146–9) investigation of grammarians' views on verbal concord with plural complements shows that, when the partitive noun is a collective, plural concord was more heavily censured in the first half of the nineteenth century than after 1850.[19] Another factor that could be at work here is the principle of attraction: if the prepositional complement is closer than the partitive noun to the finite verb form, this may favour verbal concord with the complement rather than with the partitive noun. Jespersen (1914: 179–80) discusses the influence of attraction on verbal concord in general, and claims that it occurs '[v]ery frequently in speech, and not infrequently in literature'. However, Dekeyser's (1975: 151) narrower investigation of non-collective nouns modified by *of* + complement indicates that 'examples of attraction in 19th century prose are very scarce' in this category.

A structural factor that may influence the distribution is whether or not the clause containing the partitive construction is introduced by existential *there*, as in example (21) above. In Present-day English as well as nineteenth-century English, existential *there* may govern concord in informal language (Quirk et al. 1985: 1405; Dekeyser 1975: 165). Dekeyser's (1975: 166–7) list of examples implies that *there* is more likely to govern concord when the verb is *be* and the contracted form *-'s* occurs, as in *There's no tigers here*, a pattern Dekeyser (1975: 167) describes as belonging 'to the substratum of loose colloquial speech' in nineteenth-century English. Jespersen (1914: 182) argues that sentence-initial *there is* or *there's* may become 'a fixed formula to indicate the existence of something', regardless of whether the notional subject is a singular or a plural NP, although he also states that concord with *there* is colloquial. It can thus be hypothesized that, at least in informal, speech-related genres, existential *there* might encourage singular rather than plural concord in the CONCE data. However, as mentioned above, a plural partitive noun always governs concord in my material. Nor does existential *there* appear to influence the results when the partitive noun is singular and the prepositional complement plural. The seventeen relevant sentences with existential *there* have a plural verb phrase in six cases (35 per cent), whereas the fifty-three sentences without existential *there* only display plural verbal concord in fifteen cases (28 per cent). The difference in the distribution is not statistically significant; however, as with the overall figures, variation in the distribution of partitive nouns and prepositional complements that control verbal concord to differing degrees may influence the results.[20] Looking at all clauses where *there* is followed by a form of *be* and a plural notional subject, Dekeyser (1975: 165) notes a shift towards more singular verb phrases over the nineteenth century, but claims that factors such as idiolectal preferences may have influenced his results (see, however, section 3.3.2 for some individual examples where the presence of existential *there* may be influential).

As regards the parameters of genre and gender, the low raw frequencies for the relevant subsamples preclude definite conclusions. However, since three of the six instances of verbal concord with a plural complement rather than with a singular partitive noun in period 1 are from Science, a formal written genre, there seem to be no stylistic restrictions on the occurrence of this type of construction. Similarly, women and men letter writers alike exhibit both singular and plural concord in such cases; but the total number of instances (nine) is obviously too low to allow any conclusions in this respect.

3.3.2 Concord with number: *a case study of nineteenth- and late twentieth-century English.* In this section, I will compare some of the results from the nineteenth-century subcorpus with data from the FLOB corpus (the Freiburg 1990s 'clone' of the Lancaster-Oslo/Bergen corpus), comprising texts published in the early 1990s, so that language change between the nineteenth and late twentieth centuries, if any, can be detected. As *number* is the only partitive noun in the subcorpus that both governs and fails to govern verbal concord with any frequency, I will examine verbal concord with partitive constructions with *number* as partitive noun.

Reid (1991) gives a functional account of verb and noun number in Present-day English, including a discussion of variation between singular and plural verbal concord with partitives with *number* as partitive noun (Reid 1991: 280–3).[21] Reid (1991: 217, 280) claims that the choice between singular and plural concord is dependent on whether the situation applies more directly to the partitive noun or to the prepositional complement. Consider (23) and (24):

(23) Again, a large *number of diseases* are conveyed by germs capable of passing from the tissues of the mother into those of the unborn child otherwise than through the blood.
   (Science, Francis Galton, 1870–1900, p. 15)

(24) The total *number of skulls* examined for the purpose of this inquiry was about 3000.
   (Science, William Bateson, 1870–1900, p. 265)

Thus, according to Reid, the choice of *are* rather than *is* in (23) signals a closer link with *diseases* than with *number*, while the choice of *is* over *are* in (24) indicates a closer link with *number* than with *skulls*. Poutsma (1914: 283) claims that plural concord is 'regular, or all but regular' when a collective noun, a category in which Poutsma includes *number*, 'denotes mere number'.[22]

In order to obtain results comparable with the data from the subcorpus, a search was run for the sequence *number of* in FLOB; I then went through the output of the retrieval process manually using the same criteria as were described in section 2.2. Table 10.8 presents the overall results of the comparison of the subcorpus and FLOB regarding verbal concord.

As table 10.8 makes clear, there is little difference between the two corpora in this respect: the small difference is not statistically significant.[23] The overall frequency of relevant partitive constructions with *number* as partitive noun is c. four occurrences per 100,000 words in both corpora, despite differences in time and genre make-up. The tendency in the subcorpus for scientific writing to contain many partitive constructions also seems to be present in the

Table 10.8. *Partitives with* number *as partitive noun: singular vs plural concord in nineteenth- and late twentieth-century English (row percentages within brackets).*

Century	Singular	Plural	Total
Nineteenth	16 (62%)	10 (38%)	26
Twentieth	25 (57%)	19 (43%)	44
Total	41 (59%)	29 (41%)	70

twentieth-century data from FLOB: fifteen of the forty-four instances come from the category J (Learned and scientific writing). However, despite these similarities, it is possible that differences between the subcorpus and FLOB in terms of sampling universe, genre make-up etc. influence the distribution of singular vs plural concord. But since Reid (1991: 252) found no essential differences between the spoken and written parts of his material, and since there were no clear signs of genre differentiation in the subcorpus with respect to verbal concord, it does not seem likely that such differences have influenced the results in any substantial way.

Reid (1991: 280–1) claims that a verb like *increase* in (22) is 'particularly suitable for predications about numerical quantities', which favour singular verb phrases by emphasizing the numerical aspect of the partitive construction.[24] This claim proved difficult to test empirically, as Reid's list of verbs that imply 'an arithmetic figure' (Reid 1991: 282) does not seem to be exhaustive, perhaps because it focuses on the types that occurred in his material: for instance, he does not mention cases where the verb *be* is followed by a numeral. Rather than trying to decide whether each verb phrase would match Reid's criteria, which would involve a great deal of subjectivity, I decided to focus on another contextual feature that affects concord choice. Reid (1991: 281) refers to Celce-Murcia and Larsen-Freeman's (1983) claim that *a number of* selects plural concord and *the number of* selects singular concord, and shows that his data match this claim. However, Reid (1991: 282) argues that this description of the distribution is less satisfactory than his functional explanation. Nonetheless, as it matches his data and is well suited to objective classification, I classified my data on this parameter in order to see whether the results for the subcorpus and FLOB match one another in this respect. Table 10.9 presents the results of this analysis.

Owing to low expected frequencies, it is not possible to test the results for statistical significance regarding differences between the subcorpus and FLOB within the *a number of* or *the number of* groups; nor can the differences between the *a number of* and *the number of* groups in the subcorpus be tested. The difference in verbal concord between partitives containing *a number of* and *the number of* in FLOB is statistically significant, however; so is the same difference in the total

Table 10.9. *Verbal concord with partitives containing the sequence* a(n) (. . .) *number of or the* (. . .) *number of in nineteenth- and late twentieth-century English (row percentages within brackets).*[a]

| | a number of | | | the number of | | | |
Century	Singular	Plural	Total	Singular	Plural	Total	Total
Nineteenth	4 (29%)	10 (71%)	14	12 (100%)	–	12	26
Twentieth	2 (11%)	17 (89%)	19	22 (96%)	1 (4%)	23	42
Total	6 (18%)	27 (82%)	33	34 (97%)	1 (3%)	35	68

[a]In the twentieth-century data, one example occurs in a newspaper heading and has no article; another occurs with the determiner *any* instead of the indefinite or definite article. These examples were excluded from the counts in the table.

figures.[25] There is thus clear evidence that the distinction between *a number of* and *the number of* influences verbal concord. Partitives containing *the number of* exhibit a particularly strong tendency for the partitive noun to govern concord, possibly because, as Reid (1991) suggests, such partitives occur with verbs that tend to emphasize arithmetic number.

From a qualitative perspective, it may be especially worthwhile examining the seven instances in the subcorpus and FLOB that seem to go against the predictions in more detail. It is possible that Reid's (1991) hypothesis concerning the implication of an arithmetic figure can explain why these cases do not follow the overall trend in the material. If we begin by looking at the FLOB data, the only instance of *the number of* where *number* fails to govern concord is (25):

(25) Even though approximately the same *number of species* **have** become extinct as have originated during the progress of evolution, scientists have given their attention almost exclusively to origination.
(FLOB F32, 11–14)

It is likely that the word *extinct* triggers plural concord in (25): it is linked more strongly with *species* than with *number*, as species rather than numbers become extinct. Reid (1991: 281) includes subject complements of linking verbs in his Occurrences (see note 24 for an explanation of this term), which indicates that they may influence the choice between singular and plural concord.

The two instances in FLOB where the partitive noun *number* governs verbal concord despite its occurring in the structure *a number of*, (26) and (27), share three linguistic characteristics.

(26) DESPITE a resurgent interest in breastfeeding, there **is** a significant *number of women* who do not breastfeed their babies.
(FLOB E33, 139–40)

(27) Even at High Court level there **is** a remarkable *number of judges* aged
over 65.
(FLOB G72, 69–70)

First, (26) and (27) both occur in clauses introduced by existential *there*. Secondly, the partitive noun is premodified by an attributive adjective. Thirdly, the
complement of the preposition *of* is postmodified. As regards existential *there*, as
mentioned in section 3.3.1, this feature may govern concord in informal language,
especially in the pattern *there's* + plural notional subject. (However, the language
in (26) and (27) does not seem informal, and the verb phrase is not contracted.)
Furthermore, the premodifying adjectives seem to emphasize the salience of the
numerical information, perhaps making the verb relate more directly to *number*
than to *women* or *judges*, along the lines of Reid's (1991) hypothesis. Moreover,
the adjectives also increase the distance between the finite verb form and the
prepositional complement, which may make singular concord through attraction to the partitive noun more likely. The influence of the postmodifier of the
complement, if any, is more difficult to discern.

Interestingly, (26) and (27) show great similarities with the four instances
of singular concord with partitives containing the sequence *a number of* in the
subcorpus, which thus go against the predictions:

(28) In all rich countries, there **is** a *number of men* forming what is called the
monied class; . . .
(Science, David Ricardo, 1800–30, p. 84)

(29) She is lucky in disposing of it so soon, as there **is** an astonishing *number of
houses* at this time vacant in that end of the Town.
(Letters, Jane Austen, 1800–30, p. 66)

(30) [$A.$] There **was** a great *number of people* about, but I did not see them take
any notice.
(Trials, James Bowditch, 1800–30, p. 100)

(31) . . . but I fancy this is due to the fact that there **is** an infinitely greater *number
of cases* of arsenical poisoning than of any other poisoning, . . .
(Trials, Edwin Maybrick, 1870–1900, p. 231)

The partitives in (28)–(31) all occur in clauses with existential *there*. In addition,
in all except (28) the partitive noun is premodified by an adjective, and the complement of the preposition *of* is postmodified in all except (30), provided that the
nonfinite *-ing* clause in (28) is taken to postmodify *men* rather than *number*. In
(29), (30) and (31), the choice of singular concord is probably influenced by the
verb relating more closely to *number* than to the prepositional complement, as the
adjective serves to highlight the partitive noun; in addition, in (31), the prepositional complement (*cases*) does not carry much semantic weight. Moreover, (30)
and (31) come from Trials, a speech-related genre, and it is thus possible that the
use of singular concord is part of the witness's dialect.[26]

The singular concord in (28) is slightly more difficult to explain: *men* seems to be more closely related than *number* to the verb *form*. Nor does singular concord seem to be an idiolectal feature in this case. If we consider all partitive constructions in this text, there are eight cases where the partitive noun is singular and the prepositional complement plural, and there is an overt choice between singular and plural verbal concord: the writer, David Ricardo, uses plural concord on three of these eight occasions. In this context, note also that existential *there*, a premodifying adjective, and a postmodifier of the prepositional complement do not automatically result in singular verbal concord, as evidenced by (21), also cited above:

(21) There **are** a vast *number of ways* of making the agreeable in society, and several of these pleasant knacks did Godfrey Moss himself possess; . . .
(Fiction, Theodore Edward Hook, 1800–30, p. II, 164)

Further research is needed to identify other factors, linguistic as well as extralinguistic, that may affect concord in these structures.

To sum up, in partitives where *number* is the singular partitive noun and the prepositional complement is plural, there is a clear tendency in both nineteenth- and late twentieth-century English for the partitive noun to govern verbal concord if the partitive noun phrase is definite and for the complement to govern concord if the partitive noun phrase is indefinite. Most exceptions to this general trend seem to be due to information structure: the strength of the connection between, on the one hand, the verb phrase and, on the other hand, either the partitive noun or the prepositional complement is a stronger conditioning factor than the definiteness of the partitive noun phrase on the choice between singular and plural concord. Clauses with existential *there* also seem to favour concord with the partitive noun rather than with the prepositional complement.

4   Summary and discussion

When the frequency of partitive constructions across genres was analysed, a high frequency of partitives was found to be more characteristic of expository genres, Science in particular, than of non-expository genres. Fiction, however, stood out from the other non-expository genres in having a comparatively high frequency of partitive constructions. A comparison of these results with Geisler's (2002) factor score analysis of CONCE led me to hypothesize that a high frequency of partitive constructions is characteristic of genres that display informational rather than involved production on Dimension 1 of Biber's (1988) factor analysis. This hypothesis was further strengthened by an analysis of the occurrence of partitive constructions in private letters written by women and by men. Men letter writers displayed both a higher frequency of partitives and more informational production than women letter writers in period 1, whereas the opposite was found in period 3.

The distribution of the five semantic subgroups of partitive constructions was then added to the analysis. While the parameters of time and gender were found to be of lesser importance, the genre parameter exhibited statistically significant differentiation in this respect. The occurrence of partitives of quantity appeared to be especially important, as this subgroup accounted for nearly two thirds of all partitives in the material. The expository genres Debates, History and Science, as well as the non-expository genre Drama, had high percentages of quantitative partitives: Debates and Science both had percentages above seventy, and Drama and History lay between sixty and seventy. However, there were semantic and stylistic differences between the Drama genre and the expository genres regarding the types of quantitative partitives that occurred in the material. Genre-specific constraints were found to affect the distribution of the other subgroups of partitive constructions. Overall, the analysis of the subgroups helped to refine the picture afforded by the investigation of overall frequencies. For instance, the unexpectedly high frequency of partitive constructions in the non-expository Fiction genre was shown to be partly due to the high proportion of semantically specific partitives of space and time, while the percentage of quantitative partitives was low in this genre.

The above results indicate that a high frequency of partitive constructions, in combination with a high percentage of more or less unspecific, quantitative partition, is characteristic of expository genres that display informational rather than involved production on Dimension 1 of Biber's (1988) factor analysis. Features that indicate informational production, and thus great information density, on Dimension 1 include nouns and prepositions. By combining a part/whole relation and an indication of quantity in a 'noun + preposition + noun' sequence, quantitative partitives contribute to this information density. Although other types of partitives have the same syntactic make-up, many of these seem to have functions that are less information-focused (e.g. emphasis) and/or more specific (e.g. the expression of space or time). However, the semantic and stylistic scope of quantitative partition is quite large, and quantitative partitive constructions constituted the biggest subgroup of partitives in all genres considered in the present study.

The third results section concerned verbal concord with partitive constructions where the partitive noun and the complement of the preposition *of* do not agree in number. Time proved to be the most interesting extralinguistic variable in this context. When the partitive noun was plural and the prepositional complement singular, no instances that exhibited verbal concord with the prepositional complement were found in either period. In contrast, where the partitive noun was singular and the prepositional complement plural, the results indicated a tendency towards more verbal concord with the prepositional complement in period 3 than in period 1. Such a change would be in line with the general tendency for some partitive nouns to go from being the head of the partitive construction to being part of a complex determiner of the new head, i.e. the prepositional complement (see Denison 1998: 121). However, a qualitative analysis indicated that semantic factors also influence the choice between singular and plural concord.

Special attention was devoted to partitives with *number* as partitive noun, as they exhibited most variation between singular and plural verbal concord. No evidence of diachronic change between nineteenth- and late twentieth-century English was found in the data. Instead, several syntactic and semantic factors, including those of whether the partitive noun phrase was definite or indefinite and whether the verb related more directly to the partitive noun or to the prepositional complement, were found to influence the choice between singular and plural concord. Interestingly, all cases where an indefinite partitive noun phrase with *number* as partitive noun selected singular concord occurred in clauses introduced by existential *there*, which may indicate that this factor does condition the choice between singular and plural concord even though it did not have a significant impact on the nineteenth-century data.

Some potentially interesting parameters fell outside the scope of the present study, including an investigation of alternatives to partitive constructions and further semantic/stylistic subdivision of quantitative partitives (see sections 2.2.1 and 3.2). Nevertheless, the results of the present study reveal that partitive constructions in English constitute an important field of study as regards cross-genre variation and language change. It is hoped that future studies based on larger corpora of nineteenth-century and Present-day English will confirm the tendencies outlined in the present study. Studies of early twentieth-century English would also be of great value.

Notes

1. This chapter is based in part on a paper presented at the International Conference on the English Language in the Late Modern Period 1700–1900, held at the University of Edinburgh during 29 August–1 September 2001. I thankfully acknowledge a part-time research grant from Örebro University which made it possible for me to develop my ideas further.
2. The definition of partitive constructions used in the present study is based largely on the treatments in Svensson (1998) and Quirk et al. (1985). However, studies differ with respect to what types of structures are classified as partitive (see, for instance, Huddleston and Pullum 2002 for a different approach to partitive constructions).
3. See the Introduction to the present volume for word counts for period, period/genre, and period/gender subsamples.
4. The tagged output has not been post-edited manually in order to reduce the number of erroneous tags. However, a manual check of c. 3 per cent of CONCE revealed that only roughly 1.3 per cent of all words in the corpus had been classified erroneously, while c. 2.5 per cent of all words had been given more than one possible output reading (Smitterberg 2005: 50–1). Moreover, the type of partitive construction included in the counts consists of an easily identifiable syntactic pattern. It can thus be assumed that the error rate is comparatively low, and that the results are only marginally affected by tagging errors.

5. I am indebted to Dr Christer Geisler for writing Perl scripts that made the automatic retrieval of 'noun + *of* + noun' sequences possible.

6. Some groups are also subdivided further in Svensson's (1998) classification. Such subdivisions are beyond the scope of the present study; however, I will discuss different types of quantitative partitives in section 3.2.2.

7. To some extent, Svensson's (1998) classification of partitive constructions is influenced by an attempt 'to link the partitive construction to a theory of embodiment' (Svensson 1998: 207). This factor was not relevant to the classification in the present study, which may help to explain the differences between our classification frameworks.

8. However, as will become clear when I discuss the semantic subgroups in the data, this generalization does not hold for all partitives.

9. However, the overall cross-gender differences on Dimension 5 are not statistically significant (Geisler 2003: 102).

10. d.f. $= 4$; $\chi^2 = 1.272$; p $= 0.866$.

11. d.f. $= 12$; $\chi^2 = 89.312$; p < 0.001.

12. See section 3.3.2 for a discussion of verbal concord with partitives where *number* is the partitive noun.

13. As pointed out in section 2.2.1, *deal* occurs in constructions such as *a good/great deal of*, where it is an alternative to *much*. In Present-day English, the multal quantifiers *much* (with noncount nouns) and *many* (with count nouns) are often avoided in assertive contexts (Quirk et al. 1985: 262–3; Biber et al. 1999: 275–6); the alternatives include partitive constructions with *deal* and *lot/s* as partitive nouns.

14. d.f. $= 4$; $\chi^2 = 4.309$; p $= 0.367$.

15. In four of these cases, the finite verb form or the entire verb phrase is not mentioned explicitly, but must be inferred from the context; in four instances, the partitive construction is co-ordinated with another noun phrase as subject, and a plural verb phrase may thus indicate agreement with the plurality of subject noun phrases; in eight cases, the verb phrase is nonfinite; and in forty-five instances, the verb phrase is finite, but its finite verb form is a past tense verb form (the only verb in the data that shows number contrast in the past tense is *be*) and/or a modal auxiliary.

16. d.f. $= 1$; $\chi^2 = 8.958$; p $= 0.003$.

17. Note that (20) also exhibits plural pronominal concord (as evidenced by the determiner *their* and the pronoun *they*).

18. See section 3.3.2 for a case study of partitives with *number* as their partitive noun, where the difference between indefinite and definite partitive noun phrases is addressed (see examples (21) and (22)).

19. Contrary to what might be expected on the basis of the present study, Dekeyser (1975) shows that there was a trend towards more singular concord with collective nouns in nineteenth-century English. However, Dekeyser (1975: 46) also shows that, at least with animate referents, the presence of *of* + plural complement made plural verbal concord with collective nouns more likely; it is thus possible that partitive constructions with singular partitive nouns and plural complements were not subject to the same constraints as collective nouns.

20. d.f. $= 1$; $\chi^2 = 0.300$; p $= 0.584$.

21. Reid's (1991) data were taken from both spoken and written material. The written data came from 'a variety of sources that represented the writer's normal reading patterns'

(Reid 1991: 251). Some spoken data were taken from conversations, but most of the examples 'were drawn from two daily radio news programmes of one and one half and two hours' duration' which 'consisted of both written text read aloud and interview features, the latter comprising a significant portion of the programmes' (Reid 1991: 252). The written and spoken data were pooled, as they displayed similar patterns.

22. See Levin (2001) for an account of agreement with a number of collective nouns in Present-day English.

23. d.f. $= 1$; $\chi^2 = 0.150$; p $= 0.699$.

24. Reid (1991: 172) prefers the term 'Occurrence' to 'verb' for this category, as '[c]onstruing a lexical stem as an Occurrence can happen in so many ways that it is not, we believe, a procedure amenable to characterization in purely formal terms'. However, as he (1991: 171–2) admits that '[w]ords designating Occurrences would normally be said to belong to the syntactic category "verb"' , I will use traditional terminology in the present discussion.

25. For FLOB: d.f. $= 1$; $\chi^2 = 30.787$; p < 0.001. For the total figures: d.f. $= 1$; $\chi^2 = 43.722$; p < 0.001.

26. The witness in (30), the gardener John Burroughs, also uses plural concord in similar clauses, but such variation may be due to inherent variability in Burroughs's dialect (see Trudgill 2000: 34–5).

Appendix

This appendix lists the CONCE corpus source texts, and the text-level codes used in the corpus. The information draws on appendices 1 and 2 in Smitterberg (2005). More detailed information on the source texts will be provided in the forthcoming manual to the CONCE corpus.

In the list of source texts, the entries are sorted first according to period and secondly according to genre (in alphabetical order). All word counts given were obtained using the computer program Hcount.

List of source texts

Period 1 (1800–1830)

Debates

The Parliamentary Debates from the Year 1803 to the Present Time: Forming a Continuation of the Work Entitled 'The Parliamentary History of England from the Earliest Period to the Year 1803.' Vol. XV. Word count: 19,908.

Drama

Holcroft, T. *The Vindictive Man.* Word count: 13,639.

Morton, T. *The School of Reform; or, How to Rule a Husband.* Word count: 8,829.

Poole, J. *Lodgings for Single Gentlemen.* Word count: 8,843.

Fiction

Austen, J. *Emma.* Word count: 9,975.

Hook, T. E. *Maxwell.* Word count: 22,077.

Shelley, M. W. *The Last Man.* Word count: 9,980.

History

Hallam, H. *The Constitutional History of England from the Accession of Henry VII. to the Death of George II.* Word count: 10,142.

Lingard, J. *A History of England from the First Invasion by the Romans to the Accession of Henry VIII*. Word count: 10,373.

Milman, H. H. *The History of the Jews*. Word count: 10,389.

Letters

Austen = *Jane Austen: Selected Letters 1796–1817* (ed. R. W. Chapman). Word count: 10,321.

Blake = *The Letters of William Blake with Related Documents* (ed. G. Keynes). 3rd edn. Word count: 8,101.

Byron = *Byron's Letters and Journals* (ed. L. A. Marchand). Word count: 12,327.

Coleridge = *Letters of Samuel Taylor Coleridge* (ed. E. H. Coleridge). Word count: 9,086.

Hutchinson = *The Letters of Sara Hutchinson from 1800 to 1835* (ed. K. Coburn). Word count: 19,987.

Keats = *The Letters of John Keats: Complete Revised Edition with a Portrait Not Published in Previous Editions and Twenty-four Contemporary Views of Places Visited by Keats* (ed. H. B. Forman). Word count: 9,084.

Shelley = *The Letters of Mary W. Shelley* (ed. F. L. Jones). Word count: 11,725.

Southey = *Letters of Robert Southey: a Selection* (ed. M. H. Fitzgerald). Word count: 13,755.

Wordsworth, Mary (1) = *The Love Letters of William and Mary Wordsworth* (ed. B. Darlington). Word count: 12,203.

Wordsworth, Mary (2) = *The Letters of Mary Wordsworth 1800–1855* (ed. M. E. Burton). Word count: 15,035.

Science

Lyell, C. *Principles of Geology, Being an Attempt to Explain the Former Changes of the Earth's Surface, by Reference to Causes Now in Operation*. Word count: 11,898.

Malthus, T. R. *An Essay on the Principle of Population; or, a View of Its Past and Present Effects on Human Happiness; with an Inquiry into Our Prospects Respecting the Future Removal or Mitigation of the Evils Which It Occasions*. 5th edn. Word count: 10,472.

Ricardo, D. *On the Principles of Political Economy, and Taxation*. Word count: 15,667.

Trials

Angus = *The Trial of Charles Angus, Esq., on an Indictment for the Wilful Murder of Margaret Burns, at the Assizes Held at Lancaster, on Friday, 2d September. 1808*. 2nd edn. Word count: 17,812.

Bowditch = *Abduction of Maria Glenn. The Trial of James Bowditch and Nine Others, at the Suit of the King, and on the Prosecution of George Lowman*

Tuckett, Esq. for Conspiracy, Assault, and False Imprisonment. At the Late Summer Assizes for the County of Dorset, July 25, 1818. Word count: 24,736.
Martin = *Report of the Trial of Jonathan Martin, for Having, on the Night of the First of February, 1829, Set Fire to York Minster. Which Trial Took Place at the Yorkshire Spring Assizes, on Tuesday, March 31st, 1829, Before Mr. Baron Hullock.* Word count: 19,812.

Period 2 (1850–1870)

Debates
Hansard's Parliamentary Debates: Third Series, Commencing with the Accession of William IV. 13° & 14° Victoriæ, 1850. Vol. 112. Word count: 19,385.

Drama
Marston, W. *A Hard Struggle.* Word count: 6,756.
Robertson, T. W. *Society.* Word count: 11,756.
Taylor, T. *The Ticket-of-leave Man.* 2nd edn. Word count: 11,031.

Fiction
Dickens, C. *The Personal History of David Copperfield.* Word count: 11,584.
Gaskell, E. *Cranford.* Word count: 11,166.
Yonge, C. M. *Hopes and Fears; or, Scenes from the Life of a Spinster.* Word count: 16,295.

History
Froude, J. A. *History of England from the Fall of Wolsey to the Death of Elizabeth.* Word count: 10,007.
Grote, G. *History of Greece.* Word count: 10,426.
Macaulay, T. B. *The History of England from the Accession of James the Second.* Word count: 10,071.

Letters
Barrett Browning = *The Letters of Elizabeth Barrett Browning* (ed. F. G. Kenyon). Word count: 13,970.
Browning = *New Letters of Robert Browning* (eds. W. C. DeVane and K. L. Knickerbocker). Word count: 7,841.
Darwin = *The Correspondence of Charles Darwin* (eds. F. Burkhardt and S. Smith). Word count: 19,349.
Dickens = *The Letters of Charles Dickens* (Vol. 6, eds. G. Storey, K. Tillotson and N. Burgis). Word count: 11,577.
Eliot = *The George Eliot Letters* (ed. G. S. Haight). Word count: 10,247.
Gaskell = *The Letters of Mrs Gaskell* (eds. J. A. V. Chapple and A. Pollard). Word count: 10,795.

Jewsbury = *Selections from the Letters of Geraldine Endsor Jewsbury to Jane Welsh Carlyle* (ed. A. Ireland). Word count: 10,896.
Macaulay = *The Letters of Thomas Babington Macaulay* (ed. T. Pinney). Word count: 13,672.
Thackeray = *The Letters and Private Papers of William Makepeace Thackeray* (ed. G. N. Ray). Word count: 16,337.
Wilson = *The Collected Works of Walter Bagehot* (ed. N. St John-Stevas). Word count: 16,432.

Science
Darwin, C. *On the Origin of Species by Means of Natural Selection, or the Preservation of Favoured Races in the Struggle for Life.* Word count: 10,694.
Faraday, M. *Experimental Researches in Chemistry and Physics.* Word count: 10,084.
Goschen, G. J. *The Theory of the Foreign Exchanges.* Word count: 10,901.

Trials
Boyle = *Boyle v. Wiseman. Verbatim Report of the Trial Boyle v. Wiseman. Tried at Kingston, April 3, 1855.* Word count: 15,605.
Hill = *An Account of the Trial of John Singleton Copley Hill, Clerk in the British Mercantile Agency, 13, Old Jewry Chambers, London, (Sole Conductor, Mr. George Caster,) for an Attempt to Obtain Money under False Pretences.* Word count: 11,205.
Palmer = *The Queen v. Palmer. Verbatim Report of the Trial of William Palmer at the Central Criminal Court, Old Bailey, London, May 14, and Following Days, 1856, before Lord Campbell, Mr. Justice Cresswell, and Mr. Baron Alderson.* Word count: 25,258.
Smith = *A Full and Correct Report of the Trial of Mr. Jeremiah Smith for Wilful and Corrupt Perjury, at the Central Criminal Court, March 2nd, 1854.* Word count: 8,502.

Period 3 (1870–1900)

Debates
The Parliamentary Debates: Authorised Edition. Fourth Series: Commencing with the Sixth Session of the Twenty-fourth Parliament of the United Kingdom of Great Britain and Ireland. 55 Victoriæ, 1892. Vol. IV. Word count: 19,947.

Drama
Gilbert, W. S. *Engaged.* Word count: 11,438.
Jones, H. A. *The Case of Rebellious Susan.* Word count: 9,210.
Pinero, A. W. *Dandy Dick.* Word count: 8,442.

Fiction

Besant, W. *All Sorts and Conditions of Men: an Impossible Story*. Word count: 9,698.

Braddon, M. E. *Hostages to Fortune*. Word count: 10,390.

Hardy, T. *Far from the Madding Crowd*. Word count: 10,025.

History

Gardiner, S. R. *History of England from the Accession of James I. to the Outbreak of the Civil War 1603–1642*. Word count: 10,121.

Green, J. R. *History of the English People*. Word count: 10,208.

Walpole, S. *A History of England from the Conclusion of the Great War in 1815*. New and revised edn. Word count: 10,235.

Letters

Arnold = *Letters of Matthew Arnold 1848–1888* (ed. G. W. E. Russell). Word count: 8,641.

Butler, May = *The Correspondence of Samuel Butler with His Sister May* (ed. D. F. Howard). Word count: 8,385.

Butler, Samuel (1) = *The Family Letters of Samuel Butler 1841–1886* (ed. A. Silver). Word count: 11,520.

Butler, Samuel (2) = *The Correspondence of Samuel Butler with His Sister May* (ed. D. F. Howard). Word count: 11,020.

Hardy = *Thomas Hardy: Selected Letters* (ed. M. Millgate). Word count: 4,419.

Holland = *Letters of Mary Sibylla Holland* (ed. B. Holland). Word count: 12,686.

Huxley = *Life and Letters of Thomas Henry Huxley* (ed. L. Huxley). Word count: 5,137.

Rossetti = *The Family Letters of Christina Georgina Rossetti with Some Supplementary Letters and Appendices* (ed. W. M. Rossetti). Word count: 10,303.

Thackeray Ritchie = *Letters of Anne Thackeray Ritchie with Forty-two Additional Letters from Her Father William Makepeace Thackeray* (ed. H. Ritchie). Word count: 18,780.

Science

Bateson, W. *Materials for the Study of Variation Treated with Especial Regard to Discontinuity in the Origin of Species*. Word count: 10,141.

Galton, F. *Natural Inheritance*. Word count: 10,315.

Lockyer, J. N. *The Chemistry of the Sun*. Word count: 10,147.

Trials

Bartlett = *The Trial of Adelaide Bartlett for Murder Held at the Central Criminal Court from Monday, April 12, to Saturday, April 17, 1886* (ed. E. Beal). Word count: 20,926.

Maybrick = *The Necessity for Criminal Appeal As Illustrated by the Maybrick Case and the Jurisprudence of Various Countries* (ed. J. H. Levy). Word count: 24,033.

Tichborne = *Tichborne v. Lushington. Before Lord Chief Justice Bovill and a Special Jury*. Word count: 22,629.

List of text-level codes

The bullet list below explains text-level codes that may occur in corpus examples from CONCE in the present volume. In the list, '_' stands for 'any text'.

- _(^_^)_. Font other than main font: will be used for italics, typeface variation etc. in the final version of the corpus.
- _[\ _ \ ]_. Editor's comment: indicates text inserted by the editor of the work from which the corpus text was taken.
- _[^_^]_. Our comment: gives information about the text or indicates omissions in the text.
- _[$_$]_. Metatextual material: encloses text that is not part of the recorded or constructed speech in speech-related genres, e.g. question/answer indications in Trials, and stage directions in Drama; also used around emendations added by the compilation team.
- _{ \ _ \ }_. Letter heading: encloses information about addressees, addresses, and dates in Letters, whether or not this information was part of the actual letter or an editor's comment.

References

Aarts, Flor and Aarts, Jan. 1982. *English Syntactic Structures*. Oxford: Pergamon Press.

Adams, Eleanor N. 1917. *Old English Scholarship in England from 1566–1800*. (Yale Studies in English 55.) New Haven and London: Yale University Press and Humphrey Milford, Oxford University Press.

Altenberg, Bengt. 1982. *The Genitive v. the of-construction: a Study of Syntactic Variation in Seventeenth-century English*. (Lund Studies in English 62.) Lund: Gleerup.

Altick, Richard D. 1957. *The English Common Reader: a Social History of the Mass Reading Public 1800–1900*. Chicago and London: University of Chicago Press.

Andersson, Herman. 1892. *Some Remarks on the Use of Relative Pronouns in Modern English Prose*. Lund: Gleerup.

Arnaud, René. 1973. *La forme progressive en anglais du XIXᵉ siècle*. Lille. (No publisher.)

Atkinson, Dwight. 1996. 'The Philosophical Transactions of the Royal Society of London, 1675–1975: a Sociohistorical Discourse Analysis'. *Language in Society* 25, 333–71.

Austin, Frances (ed). 1991. *The Clift Family Correspondence 1792–1846*. Sheffield: Centre for English Cultural Tradition and Language.

Bäcklund, Ingegerd. 1984. *Conjunction-headed Abbreviated Clauses in English*. (Studia Anglistica Upsaliensia 50.) Stockholm: Almqvist and Wiksell International.

Bailey, Richard W. 1996. *Nineteenth-century English*. Ann Arbor: University of Michigan Press.

——— 2003. 'The Ideology of English in the Late Eighteenth Century'. In: Dossena, Marina, and Jones, Charles (eds.). *Insights into Late Modern English*, 21–44. (Linguistic Insights 7.) Bern: Peter Lang.

Baker, Carl L. 1995 [1989]. *English Syntax*. 2nd edn. Cambridge, MA: MIT Press.

Barber, Charles. 1964. *Linguistic Change in Present-day English*. Edinburgh: Oliver and Boyd.

——— 1997 [1976]. *Early Modern English*. 2nd edn. Edinburgh: Edinburgh University Press.

Bauer, Laurie. 1994. *Watching English Change. An Introduction to the Study of Linguistic Change in Standard Englishes in the Twentieth Century*. London: Longman.

Beal, Joan C. 2004. *English in Modern Times: 1700–1945*. London: Arnold.

Besnier, Niko. 1989. 'Literacy and Feelings: the Encoding of Affect in Nukulaelae Letters'. *Text* 9(1), 69–92.

Bevan, Favell. 1836. *Reading without Tears, or, a Pleasant Mode of Learning to Read*. London.

Biber, Douglas. 1988. *Variation across Speech and Writing*. Cambridge: Cambridge University Press.

1995. *Dimensions of Register Variation: a Cross-linguistic Comparison*. Cambridge: Cambridge University Press.

Biber, Douglas and Burgess, Jena. 2000. 'Historical Change in Language Use of Women and Men'. *Journal of English Linguistics* 28, 21–37.

Biber, Douglas and Finegan, Edward. 1989. 'Styles of Stance in English: Lexical and Grammatical Marking of Evidentiality and Affect'. *Text* 9(1), 93–124.

1997. 'Diachronic Relations among Speech-based and Written Registers in English'. In: Nevalainen, Terttu and Kahlas-Tarkka, Leena (eds.). *To Explain the Present: Studies in the Changing English Language in Honour of Matti Rissanen*, 253–75. (Mémoires de la Société Néophilologique de Helsinki 52.) Helsinki: Société Néophilologique.

Biber, Douglas, Finegan, Edward, and Atkinson, Dwight. 1994a. 'ARCHER and Its Challenges: Compiling and Exploring A Representative Corpus of Historical English Registers'. In: Fries, Udo, Tottie, Gunnel, and Schneider, Peter (eds.). *Creating and Using English Language Corpora. Papers from the Fourteenth International Conference on English Language Research on Computerized Corpora, Zürich 1993*, 1–13. (Language and Computers: Studies in Practical Linguistics 13.) Amsterdam and Atlanta, GA: Rodopi.

Biber, Douglas, Finegan, Edward, Atkinson, Dwight, Beck, Ann, Burges, Dennis, and Burges, Jena. 1994b. 'The Design and Analysis of the ARCHER Corpus: A Progress Report [A Representative Corpus of Historical English Registers]'. In: Kytö, Merja, Rissanen, Matti, and Wright, Susan (eds.). *Corpora across the Centuries. Proceedings of the First International Colloquium on English Diachronic Corpora, St Catharine's College Cambridge, 25–27 March 1993*, 3–6. (Language and Computers: Studies in Practical Linguistics 11.) Amsterdam and Atlanta, GA: Rodopi.

Biber, Douglas, Johansson, Stig, Leech, Geoffrey, Conrad, Susan, and Finegan, Edward. 1999. *Longman Grammar of Spoken and Written English*. Harlow: Pearson.

Boulton, James T. (ed.). 1964. *Of Dramatick Poesie*. London: Oxford University Press.

Bradshaw, John. 1965. *A Concordance of the Poetical Works of Milton*. London: George Allen and Unwin.

Brittain, Lewis. 1788. *Rudiments of English Grammar*. Louvain.

Brook, George Leslie. 1970. *The Language of Dickens*. London: André Deutsch.

Brorström, Sverker. 1963. *The Increasing Frequency of the Preposition* about *during the Modern English Period: with Special Reference to the Verbs* Say, Tell, Talk, *and* Speak. (Stockholm Studies in English 9.) Stockholm: Almqvist and Wiksell.

Buchanan, James. 1762. *The British Grammar: or an Essay, in Four Parts, towards Speaking and Writing the English Language Grammatically, and Inditing Elegantly*. London.

Burnet, James. 1773–92. *Of the Origin and Progress of Language*. 6 vols. London.

Caffyn, John. 1998. *Sussex Schools in the Eighteenth Century: Schooling Provision, Schoolteachers and Scholars*. Lewes: Sussex Record Society, No. 81.

Cannon, Charles D. 1959. 'A Survey of the Subjunctive Mood in English'. *American Speech* 34, 11–19.

Carpenter, William B. 1875. *The Microscope and Its Revelations*. London: J. A. Churchill.

Cassell's New Latin–English, English–Latin Dictionary. 1975. 5th edn. London: Cassell.

Celce-Murcia, Marianne and Larsen-Freeman, Diane. 1983. *The Grammar Book*. Rowley: Newbury House.

Coates, Jennifer. 1996. *Women Talk. Conversation between Women Friends*. Oxford: Blackwell.

Coates, Jennifer and Cameron, Deborah. 1988. 'Some Problems in the Sociolinguistic Explanation of Sex Differences'. In: Coates, Jennifer and Cameron, Deborah (eds.). *Women in Their Speech Communities: New Perspectives on Language and Sex*, 13–26. London: Longman.

Colquhoun, Patrick. 1806. *A Treatise on Indigence*. London.

Comrie, Bernard. 1989. *Language Universals and Linguistic Typology*. 2nd edn. Oxford: Blackwell.

CONCE = A Corpus of Nineteenth-century English, compiled by Merja Kytö (Uppsala University) and Juhani Rudanko (University of Tampere).

Cook, Chris and Stevenson, John 1996. *The Longman Handbook of Modern British History 1714–1995*. 3rd edn. London and New York: Longman.

Corson, David. 1985. *The Lexical Bar*. Oxford and New York: Pergamon Press.

Cruden, Alexander. 1737. Many editions since then, generally known as: *Cruden's Concordance*.

Curme, George O. 1931. *A Grammar of the English Language*. Volume II: *Syntax*. Boston: D.C. Heath and Company [reprint 1977. Verbatim Printing. Essex, CT].

Dekeyser, Xavier. 1975. *Number and Case Relations in 19th Century British English: a Comparative Study of Grammar and Usage*. Antwerp and Amsterdam: Uitgeverij De Nederlandsche Boekhandel.

Denison, David. 1993. *English Historical Syntax: Verbal Constructions*. London and New York: Longman.

1998. 'Syntax'. In: Romaine, Suzanne (ed.). *The Cambridge History of the English Language*. Vol. IV: *1776–1997*, 92–329. Cambridge: Cambridge University Press.

Dewe, Michael (ed.). 2002. *Local Studies Collection Management*. Aldershot: Ashgate.

Dilworth, Thomas. 1751. *A New Guide to the English Tongue*.

Dryden, John. 1668. *Of Dramatick Poesie*. See Boulton (1964).

1679. *Troilus and Cressida*. London: Jacob Tonson and Abel Swall.

Edwards, Viv. 1990. *A Directory of English Dialect Resources: the English Counties*. Swindon: Economic and Social Research Council.

Eglesham, Wells. 1780. *A Short Sketch of English Grammar*. London.

Elliott, Ralph Warren Victor. 1984. *Thomas Hardy's English*. Oxford: Blackwell.

Encyclopædia Britannica. See 'Woman Suffrage'.

Fairman, Tony. 1996. 'Dick and Sal: or, Jack and Joanses Fair'. *Antiquarian Book Monthly* 23(3), 10–15.

1999. 'English Pauper Letters 1800–1834, and the English Language'. In: Barton, David and Hall, Nigel (eds). *Letter Writing as a Social Practice*, 63–82. Amsterdam and Philadelphia: John Benjamins.

2002a. 'Mainstream English'. *English Today* 18(1), 57–62.

2002b. '*riting these fu lines:* English Overseers' Correspondence, 1800–1835'. *Verslagen en Mededelingen van de Koninklijke Academie voor Nederlandse Taal- en Letterkunde* 112(3), 557–73.

2003. 'Letters of the English Labouring Classes and the English Language, 1800–1835'. In: Dossena, Marina and Jones, Charles (eds.). *Insights into Late Modern English*, 265–82. (Linguistic Insights 7.) Bern: Peter Lang.

2005. 'Schooling the Poor in Horsmonden, 1797–1816'. *The Local Historian* 35(2), 12–131.

Fanego, Teresa. 1996. 'On the Historical Development of English Retrospective Verbs'. *Neuphilologische Mitteilungen* 97, 71–9.

Fell, John. 1784. *An Essay towards an English Grammar*. London.

Fischer, Olga. 1992. 'Syntax'. In: Blake, Norman (ed.). *The Cambridge History of the English Language*. Vol. II: *1066–1476*, 207–408. Cambridge: Cambridge University Press.

Fowler, Henry Watson. 1926. *A Dictionary of Modern English Usage*. Oxford: Clarendon.

Fowler, Henry Watson and Fowler, Francis George. 1908. *The King's English*. 2nd edn. Oxford: Clarendon.

Fox, Barbara and Thompson, Sandra. 1990. 'A Discourse Explanation of Relative Clauses in Conversation'. *Language* 66, 297–316.

Francis, Gill, Hunston, Susan, and Manning, Elizabeth (eds.). 1996. *Collins Cobuild Grammar Patterns 1: Verbs*. London: HarperCollins.

Fries, Charles C. 1940. *American English Grammar*. New York: Appleton-Century-Crofts.

Geisler, Christer. 2002. 'Investigating Register Variation in Nineteenth-century English: a Multi-dimensional Comparison'. In: Reppen, Randi, Fitzmaurice, Susan M., and Biber, Douglas (eds.). *Using Corpora to Explore Linguistic Variation*, 249–71. (Studies in Corpus Linguistics 9.) Amsterdam and Philadelphia: John Benjamins.

2003. 'Gender-based Variation in Nineteenth-century English Letter Writing'. In: Leistyna, Pepi and Meyer, Charles F. (eds.). *Corpus Analysis: Language Structure and Language Use*, 87–106. (Language and Computers: Studies in Practical Linguistics 46.) Amsterdam and New York: Rodopi.

Geisler, Christer and Johansson, Christine. 2002. 'Relativization in Formal Spoken American English'. In: Modiano, Marko (ed.). *Studies in Mid-Atlantic English*, 87–109. Gävle: Gävle University Press.

Gerson, Stanley. 1967. *Sound and Symbol in the Dialogue of the Works of Charles Dickens*. (Stockholm Studies in English 19.) Stockholm: Almqvist and Wiksell.

Givón, Talmy. 1993. *English Grammar: a Function-based Introduction*. 2 vols. Amsterdam and Philadelphia: John Benjamins.

Görlach, Manfred. 1998. *An Annotated Bibliography of Nineteenth-century Grammars of English*. Amsterdam and Philadelphia: John Benjamins.

1999. *English in Nineteenth-century England: an Introduction*. Cambridge: Cambridge University Press.

2001. *Eighteenth-century English*. Heidelberg: Winter.

Graham, Timothy (ed.). 2000. *The Recovery of Old English: Anglo-Saxon Studies in the Sixteenth and Seventeenth Centuries*. Kalamazoo, MI: Medieval Institute Publications.

Griggs, Earl Leslie (ed.). 1956–9. *Collected Letters of Samuel Taylor Coleridge*. 6 vols. Oxford: Clarendon Press.

Halliday, M. A. K. 1988. 'On the Language of Physical Science'. In: Ghadessy, Mohsen (ed.). *Registers of Written English: Situational Factors and Linguistic Features*, 162–78. London and New York: Pinter Publishers.

Harsh, Wayne. 1968. *The Subjunctive in English*. Alabama: University of Alabama Press.

Harvie, Christopher. 2001. 'Revolution and the Rule of Law (1789–1851)'. In: Morgan, Kenneth O. (ed.). *The Oxford History of Britain*, 470–517. Revised edn. Oxford and New York: Oxford University Press.

Helsinki Corpus = The Helsinki Corpus of English Texts (1991). Helsinki: Department of English, University of Helsinki.

Hene, Birgitta. 1984. *'Den dyrkade Lasse och stackars lilla Lotta'*. (Umeå Studies in the Humanities 64.) Stockholm: Almqvist and Wiksell.

Hickey, Raymond (ed.). 2004. *Legacies of Colonial English: Studies in Transported Dialects.* Cambridge: Cambridge University Press.

Hoffmann, Sebastian. 2004. 'Using the OED Quotations Database as a Corpus – a Linguistic Appraisal'. *ICAME Journal* 28, 17–30.

Houston, Rab A. 1985. *Scottish Literacy and the Scottish Identity.* Cambridge: Cambridge University Press.

Huddleston, Rodney and Pullum, Geoffrey K. 2002. *The Cambridge Grammar of the English Language.* Cambridge: Cambridge University Press.

Hundt, Marianne. 1998. 'It Is Important That This Study (*Should*) Be Based on the Analysis of Parallel Corpora: on the Use of the Mandative Subjunctive in Four Major Varieties of English'. In: Lindquist, Hans, Klintborg, Staffan, Levin, Magnus, and Estling, Maria (eds.). *The Major Varieties of English*, 159–75. (Acta Wexionensia. Humanities 1.) Växjö: Växjö University.

Jacobson, Sven. 1980. 'Issues in the Study of Syntactic Variation'. In: Jacobson, Sven (ed.). *Papers from the Scandinavian Symposium on Syntactic Variation, Stockholm, May 18–19, 1979*, 23–36. (Stockholm Studies in English 52.) Stockholm: Almqvist and Wiksell International.

Jacobsson, Bengt. 1963. 'On the Use of *That* in Nonrestrictive Relative Clauses'. *Moderna språk* 57, 406–16.

  1975. 'How Dead Is the English Subjunctive?' *Moderna språk* 69, 218–31.

  1994. 'Nonrestrictive Relative *That*-clauses Revisited'. *Studia Neophilologica* 66(2), 181–95.

Jespersen, Otto. 1914. *A Modern English Grammar on Historical Principles.* Part II: Syntax (Vol. I). Heidelberg: Winter.

  1961 [1940]. *A Modern English Grammar on Historical Principles.* Part V: Syntax (Vol. IV). London and Copenhagen: George Allen and Unwin and Ejnar Munksgaard.

  1949. *A Modern English Grammar on Historical Principles.* Part VII: Syntax. Copenhagen: Ejnar Munksgaard.

Johansson, Christine. 1995. *The Possessive Relativizers* WHOSE *and* OF WHICH *in Present-day English. Description and Theory.* (Studia Anglistica Upsaliensia 90.) Uppsala: Acta Universitatis Upsaliensis.

  1997. 'The Positional Variation of the Possessive Relativizer *of Which*'. In: Fries, Udo, Müller, Viviane, and Schneider, Peter (eds.). *From Ælfric to the New York Times: Studies in English Corpus Linguistics*, 51–64. (Language and Computers: Studies in Practical Linguistics 19.) Amsterdam and Atlanta, GA: Rodopi.

  2002. 'Pied Piping and Stranding from a Diachronic Perspective'. In: Peters, Pam, Collins, Peter, and Smith, Adam (eds.). *New Frontiers of Corpus Research*, 147–62. (Language and Computers: Studies in Practical Linguistics 36.) Amsterdam and New York, NY: Rodopi.

Johansson, Christine and Geisler, Christer. 1998. 'Pied Piping in Spoken English'. In: Renouf, Antoinette (ed.). *Explorations in Corpus Linguistics*, 82–91. (Language and Computers: Studies in Practical Linguistics 23.) Amsterdam and Atlanta, GA: Rodopi.

Johnson, Samuel. 1755. *A Dictionary of the English Language: in Which the Words Are Deduced from Their Originals, and Illustrated in Their Different Significations by Examples from the Best Writers. To Which Are Prefixed, a History of the Language, and an English Grammar.* 2 vols. London: W. Strahan.

Jørgensen, Erik. 1990. '*Remember* and *Forget* with Gerund and Infinitive Objects'. *English Studies* 71, 147–51.

Karlsson, Fred, Voutilainen, Atro, Heikkilä, Juha, and Anttila, Arto (eds.). 1995. *Constraint Grammar: a Language-independent System for Parsing Unrestricted Text.* (Natural Language Processing 4.) Berlin and New York: Mouton de Gruyter.

Kay-Shuttleworth, James. 1970 [1832]. *The Moral and Physical Condition of the Working Classes Employed in the Cotton Manufacture in Manchester.* Reprint. London: Frank Cass & Co.

      1973 [1841]. *Four Periods of Public Education as Reviewed in 1832, 1839, 1846, 1862.* Brighton: Harvester Press.

Keenan, Edward and Comrie, Bernard. 1977. 'Noun Phrase Accessibility and Universal Grammar'. *Linguistic Inquiry* 8, 63–99.

Kingsley Kent, Susan. 1999. *Gender and Power in Britain, 1640–1990.* London and New York: Routledge.

Kjellmer, Göran. 2002. 'On Relative *Which* with Personal Reference'. *Studia Anglica Posnaniensia* 37, 17–38.

Knüpfer, Hans. 1922. 'Die Anfänge der periphrastischen Komparation im Englischen'. Diss. Heidelberg. Also in *Englische Studien* 55 (1921), 321–89.

Koch, C. Friedrich. 1863–9. *Historische Grammatik der englischen Sprache.* Vols. I–III. Weimar: Hermann Böhlau.

Kortmann, Bernd. 2004. A Fresh Look at Late Modern English Dialect Syntax. Paper presented at the Second International Conference on the English Language in the Late Modern Period 1700–1900 (LMEC2), University of Vigo (Spain), 25–27 November 2004.

Kytö, Merja. 1996a. '"The Best and Most Excellentest Way": the Rivalling Forms of Adjective Comparison in Late Middle and Early Modern English'. In: Svartvik, Jan (ed.). *Words. Proceedings of an International Symposium, Lund, 25–26 August 1995,* 123–44. (Konferenser 36.) Stockholm: Kungl. Vitterhets Historie och Antikvitets Akademien.

      1996b. *Manual to the Diachronic Part of the Helsinki Corpus of English Texts: Coding Conventions and Lists of Source Texts.* 3rd edn. Helsinki: Department of English, University of Helsinki.

Kytö, Merja, and Romaine, Suzanne. 1997. 'Competing Forms of Adjective Comparison in Modern English: What Could Be *More Quicker* and *Easier* and *More Effective?*' In: Nevalainen, Terttu and Kahlas-Tarkka, Leena (eds.). *To Explain the Present: Studies in the Changing English Language in Honour of Matti Rissanen,* 329–52. (Mémoires de la Société Néophilologique de Helsinki 52.) Helsinki: Société Néophilologique.

      2000. 'Adjective Comparison and Standardisation Processes in American and British English from 1620 to the Present'. In: Wright, Laura (ed.). *The Development of Standard English, 1300–1800: Theories, Descriptions, Conflicts,* 171–94. Cambridge: Cambridge University Press.

Kytö, Merja, Rudanko, Juhani, and Smitterberg, Erik. 2000. 'Building a Bridge between the Present and the Past: a Corpus of 19th-century English'. *ICAME Journal* 24, 85–97. Available online at http://gandalf.aksis.uib.no/journal.html.

Labov, William. 2001. *Principles of Linguistic Change*. Vol. II: *Social Factors*. (Language in Society 29.) Malden, MA and Oxford: Blackwell.

Lakoff, Robin. 1975. *Language and Woman's Place*. New York: Harper and Row.

Lass, Roger. 1987. *The Shape of English: Structure and History*. London: J. M. Dent and Sons.

Leech, Geoffrey and Culpeper, Jonathan. 1997. 'The Comparison of Adjectives in Recent British English'. In: Nevalainen, Terttu and Kahlas-Tarkka, Leena (eds.). *To Explain the Present: Studies in the Changing English Language in Honour of Matti Rissanen*, 353–73. (Mémoires de la Société Néophilologique de Helsinki 52.) Helsinki: Société Néophilologique.

Leech, Geoffrey and Svartvik, Jan. 2002. *A Communicative Grammar of English*. 3rd edn. Harlow: Longman.

Leith, Dick. 1997. *A Social History of English*. 2nd edn. London and New York: Routledge.

Leneman, Leah. 1998. 'A Truly National Movement: the View from outside London'. In: Joannou, Maroula and Purvis, June (eds.). *The Women's Suffrage Movement. New Feminist Perspectives*, 37–49. Manchester and New York: Manchester University Press.

Levin, Magnus. 2001. *Agreement with Collective Nouns in English*. (Lund Studies in English 103.) Stockholm: Almqvist and Wiksell.

Lewis, Jane. 1991. *Women and Social Action in Victorian and Edwardian England*. Aldershot: Edward Elgar.

Liardet, Frederick. 1838. *Riot in Kent: Report Made to the Central Society of Education on the State of the Peasantry at Boughton, Herne-hill, and the Ville of Dunkirk near Canterbury*. London.

Lindkvist, Karl-Gunnar. 1950. *Studies on the Local Sense of the Prepositions* in, at, on, *and* to, *in Modern English*. (Lund Studies in English 20.) Lund: Gleerup.

Ljunggren, Wilhelm Philip Ferdinand. 1893–4. *On the Auxiliaries* Shall *and* Will *in the English Language, Especially with Regard to Modern English*. Vols. I–II. Diss. Lund. Carlskrona: Printed at Länsboktryckeriet.

Macaulay, Thomas Babington. 1907. *Critical and Historical Essays*. 2 vols. London: J. M. Dent.

McCloskey, James. 1988. 'Syntactic Theory'. In: Newmeyer, Frederick J. (ed.). *Linguistics: the Cambridge Survey*, 18–59. Cambridge: Cambridge University Press.

Mair, Christian. 2002a. 'Three Changing Patterns of Verb Complementation in Late Modern English: a Real-time Study Based on Matching Text Corpora'. *English Language and Linguistics* 6, 105–31.

    2002b. 'Gerundial Complements after *Begin* and *Start*: Grammatical and Sociolinguistic Factors, and How They Work against Each Other'. In: Rohdenburg, Günter and Mondorf, Britta (eds.). *Determinants of Grammatical Variation in English*, 329–45. (Topics in English Linguistics 43.) Berlin: Mouton de Gruyter.

    2006. *Twentieth-century English*. Cambridge: Cambridge University Press.

Matthew, H. C. G. 2001. 'The Liberal Age (1851–1914)'. In: Morgan, Kenneth O. (ed.). *The Oxford History of Britain*, 518–81. Revised edn. Oxford and New York: Oxford University Press.

Mätzner, Eduard. 1860–5. *Englische Grammatik*. Vols. I–II. Berlin: Weidmann.

Michael, Ian. 1987. *The Teaching of English: from the Sixteenth Century to 1870*. Cambridge: Cambridge University Press.

Mitchell, Bruce. 1985. *Old English Syntax, I.* Oxford: Clarendon Press.

Moessner, Lilo. 2000. What Happened to the Subjunctive in Early Modern English? Paper presented at the Eleventh International Conference on English Historical Linguistics, Santiago de Compostela (Spain), 7–11 September 2000.

Mondorf, Britta. 2002. 'The Effect of Prepositional Complements on the Choice of Synthetic or Analytic Comparatives'. In: Cuyckens, Hubert and Radden, Günter (eds.). *Perspectives on Prepositions*, 65–78. Tübingen: Niemeyer.

2003. 'Support for *More*-support'. In: Rohdenburg, Günter and Mondorf, Britta (eds.). *Determinants of Grammatical Variation in English*, 251–304. (Topics in English Linguistics 43.) Berlin: Mouton de Gruyter.

Murray, Lindley. 1795. *English Grammar, Adapted to the Different Classes of Learners.* York.

1797. *English Exercises.* York.

1804. *An English Spelling-book; with Reading Lessons.* York.

Mustanoja, Tauno F. 1960. *A Middle English Syntax.* Part I: *Parts of Speech.* (Mémoires de la Société Néophilologique de Helsinki 23.) Helsinki: Société Néophilologique.

OED = The Oxford English Dictionary. 1989. 2nd edn. J. A. Simpson and E. S. C. Weiner, eds. Oxford: Clarendon Press.

OED = The Oxford English Dictionary. http://dictionary.oed.com. (As accessed 2001.) (As cited in Grund and Walker, this volume.)

Övergaard, Gerd. 1995. *The Mandative Subjunctive in American and British English in the Twentieth Century.* (Studia Anglistica Upsaliensia 94.) Uppsala: Acta Universitatis Upsaliensis.

Page, Norman. 1972. *The Language of Jane Austen.* Oxford: Blackwell.

Palmgren, Fredr. 1896. *An Essay on the Use in Present English Prose of When, After, Since, As Introducing Temporal Clauses.* Diss. Uppsala. Stockholm: Central Press.

Persson, Gunnar. 1990. *Meanings, Models and Metaphors. A Study in Lexical Semantics in English.* (Umeå Studies in the Humanities 92.) Stockholm: Almqvist and Wiksell.

Perttunen, Jean Margaret. 1986. *The Words Between.* 2nd edn. Helsinki: Duodecim.

Peters, Pam. 1998. 'The Survival of the Subjunctive: Evidence of Its Use in Australia and Elsewhere'. *English World-wide* 19(1), 87–103.

Phillipps, Kenneth Charles. 1970. *Jane Austen's English.* London: André Deutsch.

1978. *The Language of Thackeray.* London: André Deutsch.

1984. *Language and Class in Victorian England.* Oxford: Basil Blackwell.

Plank, Frans. 1984. 'The Modals Story Retold'. *Studies in Language* 8, 305–64.

Polifke, Monika. 1999. *Richard Mulcasters 'Elementarie': Eine kultur- und sprachhistorische Untersuchung.* (Anglistische Forschungen 274.) Heidelberg: Winter.

Potter, Simeon. 1969. *Changing English.* London: André Deutsch.

Pound, Louise. 1901. *The Comparison of Adjectives in English in the XV and the XVI Century.* (Anglistische Forschungen 7.) Heidelberg: Carl Winter.

Poutsma, H. 1914–29. *A Grammar of Late Modern English.* 2nd edn. (Part I), 1st edn. (Part II). Groningen: P. Noordhoff.

1914. *A Grammar of Late Modern English.* Part II: *The Parts of Speech;* Section I, A: Nouns, Adjectives and Articles. Groningen: P. Noordhoff.

1926. *A Grammar of Late Modern English.* Part II: *The Parts of Speech;* Section II: *The Verb and the Particles.* Groningen: P. Noordhoff.

1926–9. *A Grammar of Late Modern English.* Groningen: Noordhoff.

1929 [1905]. *A Grammar of Late Modern English*. Part I: *The Sentence*. 2nd edn. Groningen: P. Noordhoff.

MS. Dictionary of Constructions of Verbs, Adjectives, and Nouns. Unpublished. Copyright: Oxford University Press.

Quirk, Randolph. 1961a. *The Study of the Mother Tongue: an Inaugural Lecture Delivered at University College London, 21 February 1961*. London: H. K. Lewis and Co. Ltd.

1961b. 'Some Observations on the Language of Dickens'. *A Review of English Literature* 2, 19–28.

1974. *The Linguist and the English Language*. London: Edward Arnold.

Quirk, Randolph, Greenbaum, Sidney, Leech, Geoffrey, and Svartvik, Jan. 1972. *A Grammar of Contemporary English*. London: Longman.

1985. *A Comprehensive Grammar of the English Language*. London and New York: Longman.

Raumolin-Brunberg, Helena. 2002. 'Stable Variation and Historical Linguistics'. In: Raumolin-Brunberg, Helena, Nevala, Minna, Nurmi, Arja, and Rissanen, Matti (eds.). *Variation Past and Present. VARIENG Studies on English for Terttu Nevalainen*, 101–16. (Mémoires de la Société Néophilologique de Helsinki 61.) Helsinki: Société Néophilologique.

Reay, Barry. 1996. *Microhistories: Demography, Society and Culture in Rural England, 1800–1930*. Cambridge: Cambridge University Press.

Redford, Bruce (ed.). 1992. *The Letters of Samuel Johnson*. Oxford: Clarendon Press.

Reid, Wallis. 1991. *Verb and Noun Number in English: a Functional Explanation*. London and New York: Longman.

Richards, Jack C. (ed.). 1974. *Error Analysis: Perspectives on Second Language Acquisition*. London: Longman.

Rissanen, Matti. 1984. 'The Choice of Relative Pronouns in Seventeenth-century American English'. In: Fisiak, Jacek (ed.). *Historical Syntax*, 419–35. (Trends in Linguistics. Studies and Monographs 23.) Berlin: Mouton.

1986. 'Variation and the Study of English Historical Syntax'. In: Sankoff, David (ed.). *Diversity and Diachrony*, 97–109. (Current Issues in Linguistic Theory 53.) Amsterdam and Philadelphia: John Benjamins.

1999. 'Syntax'. In: Lass, Roger (ed.). *The Cambridge History of the English Language*. Vol. III: *1476–1776*, 187–331. Cambridge: Cambridge University Press.

Robinson, Eric (ed.). 1985. *The Parish*. London: Viking.

Rohdenburg, Günter. 2004. The Role of Functional Constraints in the Evolution of the English Complementation System. Paper for the International Conference on English Historical Linguistics, Vienna.

Rohdenburg, Günter and Schlüter, Julia. 2000. 'Determinanten grammatischer Variation im Früh- und Spätneuenglischen'. *Sprachwissenschaft* 25, 443–96.

Romaine, Suzanne. 1982. *Socio-historical Linguistics: Its Status and Methodology*. Cambridge: Cambridge University Press.

1984. 'On the Problem of Syntactic Variation and Pragmatic Meaning in Sociolinguistic Theory'. *Folia Linguistica* XVIII(3–4), 409–37.

1998a. 'Introduction'. In: Romaine, Suzanne (ed.). *The Cambridge History of the English Language*. Vol. IV: *1776–1997*, 1–56. Cambridge: Cambridge University Press.

(ed.). 1998b. *The Cambridge History of the English Language*. Vol. IV: *1776–1997*. Cambridge: Cambridge University Press.

1999. *Communicating Gender*. Mahwah, NJ: Lawrence Erlbaum.

Rudanko, Juhani. 1991. 'On Verbs Governing *in -ing* in Present-day English'. *English Studies* 72, 55–72.

1996. *Prepositions and Complement Clauses: a Syntactic and Semantic Study of Verbs Governing Prepositions and Complement Clauses in Present-day English.* Albany, NY: State University of New York Press.

1999. *Diachronic Studies of English Complementation Patterns: Eighteenth Century Evidence in Tracing the Development of Verbs and Adjectives Selecting Prepositions and Complement Clauses.* Lanham, MD: University Press of America.

Rydén, Mats. 1966. *Relative Constructions in Early Sixteenth Century English. With Special Reference to Sir Thomas Elyot.* (Studia Anglistica Upsaliensia 3.) Uppsala: Acta Universitatis Upsaliensis.

1970. 'Determiners and Relative Clauses'. *English Studies* 51, 47–52.

1974. 'On Notional Relations in the Relative Clause Complex'. *English Studies* 55, 542–5.

1979. *An Introduction to the Historical Study of English Syntax.* (Stockholm Studies in English 51.) Stockholm: Almqvist and Wiksell.

1983. 'The Emergence of *Who* as Relativizer'. *Studia Linguistica* 37, 126–30.

1984. 'När är en relativsats nödvändig?' *Moderna språk* 78, 19–22.

Rydén, Mats and Brorström, Sverker. 1987. *The Be/Have Variation with Intransitives in English: with Special Reference to the Late Modern Period.* (Stockholm Studies in English 70.) Stockholm: Almqvist and Wiksell.

Schibsbye, Knut. 1970 [1965]. *A Modern English Grammar.* 2nd edn. London: Oxford University Press.

Schneider, Edgar W. 1996a. 'Constraints on the Loss of Case-marking in English *Wh*-pronouns. Four Hundred Years of Real-time Evidence'. In: Arnold, Jennifer, Blake, Renée, Davidston, Brad, Schwenter, Scott, and Solomon, Julie (eds.). *Sociolinguistic Variation. Data, Theory and Analysis. Selected Papers from NWAV 23 at Stanford,* 429–93. Stanford: CSLI Publications.

1996b. 'Towards Syntactic Isomorphism and Semantic Dissimilation: the Semantics and Syntax of Prospective Verbs in Early Modern English'. In: Britton, Derek (ed.). *English Historical Linguistics 1994,* 199–220. (Current Issues in Linguistic Theory 135.) Amsterdam: John Benjamins.

Serner, Gunnar. 1910. *On the Language of Swinburne's Lyrics and Epics: A Study.* Diss. Lund. Lund and Cambridge: Hjalmar Möller and W. Heffer and Sons.

Smith, Carlotta. 1964. 'Determiners and Relative Clauses in a Generative Grammar of English'. *Language* 40, 37–52.

Smitterberg, Erik. 2003. Multal Quantifiers in Nineteenth-century English. Paper presented at the 24th ICAME Conference, 23–27 April 2003, Guernsey.

2005. *The Progressive in 19th-century English: a Process of Integration.* (Language and Computers: Studies in Practical Linguistics 54.) Amsterdam and New York: Rodopi.

Sopher, Haveem. 1974. 'Prepositional Relative Clauses'. *Linguistics* 133, 63–83.

Sørensen, Knud. 1985. *Charles Dickens: Linguistic Innovator.* Aarhus: Arkona.

1989. 'Dickens on the Use of English'. *English Studies* 70, 551–9.

'Statistical Inquiries of the Central Society of Education into the Social Condition of the Working Classes'. 1837. *Central Society of Education Papers* 1, 338–59.

Stein, Gabrielle. 1997. *John Palsgrave as Renaissance Linguist: a Pioneer in Vernacular Language Description.* Oxford: Clarendon Press.

Stephens, William B. 1987. *Education, Literacy and Society, 1830–1870: the Geography of Diversity in Provincial England*. Manchester: Manchester University Press.

Stitt, Megan Perigoe. 1998. *Metaphors of Change in the Language of Nineteenth-century Fiction: Scott, Gaskell, and Kingsley*. Oxford: Clarendon Press.

Stokes, Myra. 1991. *The Language of Jane Austen: a Study of Some Aspects of Her Vocabulary*. London: Macmillan.

Storey, Mark (ed.). 1985. *The Letters of John Clare*. Oxford: Clarendon Press.

Strang, Barbara M. H. 1970. *A History of English*. London: Methuen.

Sundby, Bertil, Bjørge, Anne Kari, and Haugland, Kari E. 1991. *A Dictionary of English Normative Grammar 1700–1900*. Amsterdam and Philadelphia: John Benjamins.

Super, R. H. (ed.). 1962. *The Complete Prose Works of Matthew Arnold*. Ann Arbor, MI: University of Michigan Press.

Sutherland, Robert D. 1970. *Language and Lewis Carroll*. The Hague: Mouton.

Svensson, Patrik. 1998. *Number and Countability in English Nouns: an Embodied Model*. (Umeå Studies in the Humanities 142.) Uppsala: Swedish Science Press.

Swan, Michael. 1995. *Practical English Usage*. 2nd edn. Oxford, New York and Athens: Oxford University Press.

Sweet, Henry. 1891–8. *A New English Grammar: Logical and Historical*. Oxford: Clarendon Press.

Taavitsainen, Irma. 1994. 'On the Evolution of Scientific Writings from 1375 to 1675: Repertoire of Emotive Features'. In: Fernández, Francisco, Fuster, Miguel, and Calvo, Juan José (eds.). *English Historical Linguistics 1992*, 329–42. (Current Issues in Linguistic Theory 113.) Amsterdam and Philadelphia: John Benjamins.

Tao, Hongyin. 2001. 'Discovering the Usual with Corpora: the Case of *Remember*'. In: Simpson, Rita C. and Swales, John M. (eds.). *Corpus Linguistics in North America*, 116–44. Ann Arbor, MI: University of Michigan Press.

Trudgill, Peter. 2000. *Sociolinguistics: an Introduction to Language and Society*. 4th edn. London: Penguin.

2001. 'Third-person Singular Zero: African-American English, East Anglian Dialects and Spanish Persecution in the Low Countries'. In: Fisiak, Jacek and Trudgill, Peter (eds.). *East Anglian English*, 179–86. Cambridge: D. S. Brewer.

Visser, F. Th. 1963–73. *An Historical Syntax of the English Language*. 3 vols. Leiden: Brill.

1966. *An Historical Syntax of the English Language*. Part 2: *Syntactical Units with One Verb (Continued)*. Leiden: Brill.

Vosberg, Uwe. 2003. 'The Role of Extractions and *Horror Aequi* in the Evolution of *–ing* Complements in Modern English'. In: Rohdenburg, Günter and Mondorf, Britta (eds.). *Determinants of Grammatical Variation in English*, 305–27. (Topics in English Linguistics 43.) Berlin: Mouton de Gruyter.

Vyse, Charles. 1791. *The New London Spelling-book*. (In print in several editions from 1776–1850.)

Walker, John. 1791. *A Critical Pronouncing Dictionary*. London.

Walker, Terry. 2005. 'Second Person Singular Pronouns in Early Modern English Dialogues 1560–1760'. PhD thesis, Uppsala University.

Wallin-Ashcroft, Anna-Lena. 2000. 'Great Men and Charming Creatures'. PhD thesis, Umeå University.

Warren, Beatrice. 1984. *Classifying Adjectives*. (Gothenburg Studies in English 56.) Gothenburg: Acta Universitatis Gothoburgensis.

Watts, Richard J. 1999. 'The Social Construction of Standard English: Grammar Writers as a "Discourse Community"'. In: Bex, Tony and Watts, Richard J. (eds.). *Standard English: The Widening Debate*, 40–68. London and New York: Routledge.

Webster's Dictionary of English Usage. 1989. E. Ward Gilman, ed. Springfield, MA: Merriam Webster.

Western, August. 1897. *Om brugen af* can, may *og* must*: en sproghistorisk undersøgelse*. (Videnskabsselskabets Skrifter (II), Historisk-filosofisk Klasse, 1897:1.) Kristiania: Jacob Dybwad.

Westin, Ingrid. 2002. *Language Change in English Newspaper Editorials*. (Language and Computers: Studies in Practical Linguistics 44.) Amsterdam and New York: Rodopi.

'Woman Suffrage'. *Encyclopædia Britannica* from Encyclopædia Britannica Online. <http://search.eb.com/eb/article?tocId=9077370> [Accessed 29 January 2005].

Wyld, H. C. 1936 [1920]. *A History of Modern Colloquial English*. 3rd edn. Oxford: Blackwell.

Yeo, Richard. 1981. 'Scientific Method and the Image of Science 1831–1890'. In: MacLeod, Roy and Collins, Peter (eds.). *The Parliament of Science*, 65–88. Northwood: Science Reviews.

Zandvoort, R. W. 1948. *A Handbook of English Grammar*. 3rd edn. Groningen: J. B. Wolters.

Name index

Aarts, Flor 183
Aarts, Jan 183
Adams, Eleanor N. 15
Altenberg, Bengt 183
Altick, Richard D. 7, 64
Andersson, Herman 2
Arnaud, René 1
Arnold, Matthew 82
Atkinson, Dwight 111
Austen, Jane 16
Austin, Frances 60

Bäcklund, Ingegerd 8, 11, 108
Bailey, Richard 2, 82, 110, 217
Baker, Carl L. 146
Barber, Charles 136, 137, 179, 197
Bauer, Laurie 197
Beal, Joan C. 1, 15
Besnier, Niko 206
Bevan, Favell 64, 67, 83
Biber, Douglas 4, 6, 90, 94, 110, 112, 118,
    119, 125, 133–5, 138, 154, 157, 172, 180,
    183–5, 187–8, 192–5, 204–6, 212–13, 243,
    246, 249–51, 267–8, 270
Bickham, George 86
Boulton, James 81
Bradshaw, John 87
Brittain, Lewis 140
Brook, George Leslie 16
Brorström, Sverker 1, 15, 172
Buchanan, James 140
Bunyan, John 81
Burgess, Jena 172
Burnet, James 81–2

Caffyn, John 63, 67
Cameron, Deborah 172, 177

Cannon, Charles 108
Carpenter, William B. 81
Carroll, Lewis 16
Celce-Murcia, Marianne 264
Clare, John 65, 81, 84
Coates, Jennifer 172, 177, 206
Colquhoun, Patrick 62
Comrie, Bernard 142, 180–1
Cook, Chris 62
Corson, David 82
Culpeper, Jonathan 194, 198, 205,
    210–11
Curme, George O. 204

Darwin, Charles 10, 30, 114, 120, 191
Dekeyser, Xavier 1, 7, 261–2, 270
Denison, David 1, 7, 90, 92, 103, 108, 118, 217,
    243, 260–1, 268
Dewe, Michael 56
Dickens, Charles 16
Dilworth, Thomas 74
Dryden, John 80–2, 87

Edwards, Viv 87
Eglesham, Wells 140
Elliott, Ralph Warren Victor 16
Elyot, Thomas 78

Fairman, Tony 3–4, 9, 14–15, 68, 85
Fanego, Teresa 218
Fell, John 140
Finegan, Edward 4, 6, 112, 206, 243,
    249–50
Fischer, Olga 136
Fowler, Francis George 228
Fowler, Henry Watson 228
Fox, Barbara 153, 181

Subject index

adjectives
> comparison of 12–13, 194–212
>> absolute superlatives 199–200
>> double comparison 194–6
>> frequency of variants 198
>> in Early Modern English 195–6, 205
>> in Middle English 195–6, 205
>> in Old English 195
>> in Present-day English 195–6, 199–200, 204, 210–12
>> in twentieth-century English 197
>> in eighteenth-century English 50–2
>> modifying nouns 17–54
>>> *see also* modifiers
>> semantic classification of 21–4, 26–31, 35–51

clauses
> adverbial 5, 89–104
> in connection with passive verb phrases 121–4, 130–1
> relative 7
>> *see also* pronouns, relativizers
>> restrictive vs. non-restrictive 145–8
conjunctions 98–100
corpora
> *see* sources of primary data

Early Modern English 89–90, 136–7, 183–4, 195–6, 205, 215, 218
eighteenth-century English 50–2, 218
EngCG–2 26, 134, 244
extralinguistic factors 3, 6
> gender 3, 6–9, 15, 17–54, 97–8, 171–9, 259

gender roles 17–18, 48–9
gender style 206–8
gender-linked terms 19–20
genre 6–7, 14–15, 94–7, 253–9
> *see also* medium, written vs spoken/speech-related language
> *see also* style
> genre development 4
> genre diversification 4, 6, 112
> idiolectal difference 128–33
> intra-genre variation 201, 249–50
genre and gender combined 8–9
speaker roles 166–72
time 4–7
> *see also* linguistic change
time and gender combined 97–8, 205–10
time and genre combined 95–7, 201–5

grammarians 141, 157
> *see also* prescriptivism

idiolects 8, 174–9, 190–1
> Darwin's idiolect 30, 114, 120, 128–33, 191
inflectional comparison
> *see* adjectives, comparison of

linguistic change 4, 9–15, 25–7, 35, 39, 47–50, 52–3, 93–4, 100, 102–3, 174, 198, 201, 212, 221, 226, 236–7, 241, 250, 260–1, 268
> short-term 3, 5
> women as leaders 7, 172
linguistic stability 1, 9–15, 112–16, 124, 126, 133–4, 138, 180, 193, 249–50, 253, 263
linguistic variation 4, 194–212

For EU product safety concerns, contact us at Calle de José Abascal, 56–1°, 28003 Madrid, Spain or eugpsr@cambridge.org.

www.ingramcontent.com/pod-product-compliance
Ingram Content Group UK Ltd.
Pitfield, Milton Keynes, MK11 3LW, UK
UKHW042152130625
459647UK00011B/1302